REGULATING PRIMARY MARKETS IN THE CAPITAL MARKETS UNION

Stay ahead of the curve with this essential book, offering a comprehensive and up-to-date analysis of the Prospectus Regulation (including its recent amendment by the Listing Act) and the pathbreaking Regulation on European Crowdfunding Service Providers (ECSPR).

Placing the discussion in the context of the Capital Markets Union (CMU), this book provides a fresh and insightful perspective on the ever-evolving regulatory landscape of EU primary capital markets, setting out a practical roadmap for achieving effective and inclusive regulation.

With a keen focus on the dynamic relationship between legal uniformity and differentiation, the book addresses 2 pivotal questions: how can the imperative of investor protection be balanced with the goal of providing businesses with improved and cost-effective access to EU primary securities markets? How can the pursuit for greater unification be practically reconciled with the growing demand for regional solutions in a post-Brexit era?

Unveiling a unique normative framework, the book provides a holistic perspective; it explores the underlying objectives and intricate complexities of the CMU, critically evaluates the transformative potential of regulatory actions, sheds light on potential inconsistencies, and offers insightful suggestions for future reforms.

A must-read for policymakers, scholars, legal practitioners and anyone seeking to comprehend the current and emerging challenges in the regulation of EU primary capital markets.

Hart Studies in Commercial and Financial Law: Volume 15

Hart Studies in Commercial and Financial Law

Series Editors: John Linarelli and Teresa Rodríguez de las Heras Ballell

This series offers a venue for publishing works on commercial law as well as on the regulation of banking and finance and the law on insolvency and bankruptcy. It publishes works on the law on secured credit, the regulatory and transactional aspects of banking and finance, the transactional and regulatory institutions for financial markets, legal and policy aspects associated with access to commercial and consumer credit, new generation subjects having to do with the institutional architecture associated with innovation and the digital economy including works on blockchain technology, work on the relationship of law to economic growth, the harmonisation or unification of commercial law, transnational commercial law, and the global financial order. The series promotes interdisciplinary work. It publishes research on the law using the methods of empirical legal studies, behavioural economics, political economy, normative welfare economics, law and society inquiry, socio-legal studies, political theory, and historical methods. Its coverage includes international and comparative investigations of areas of law within its remit.

Volume 1: The Financialisation of the Citizen: Social and Financial Inclusion through European Private Law
Guido Comparato

Volume 2: MiFID II and Private Law: Enforcing EU Conduct of Business Rules
Federico Della Negra

Volume 3: Reforming Corporate Retail Investor Protection: Regulating to Avert Mis-Selling
Diane Bugeja

Volume 4: The Future of Commercial Law: Ways Forward for Change and Reform
Edited by Orkun Akseli and John Linarelli

Volume 5: The Cape Town Convention: A Documentary History
Anton Didenko

Volume 6: Regulating the Crypto Economy: Business Transformations and Financialisation
Iris H-Y Chiu

Volume 7: The Future of High-Cost Credit: Rethinking Payday Lending
Jodi Gardner

Volume 8: The Enforcement of EU Financial Law
Edited by Jan Crijns, Matthias Haentjens and Rijnhard Haentjens

Volume 9: International Bank Crisis Management: A Transatlantic Perspective
Marco Bodellini

Volume 10: Creditor Priority in European Bank Insolvency Law: Financial Stability and the Hierarchy of Claims
Sjur Swensen Ellingsæter

Volume 11: Chinese and Global Financial Integration through Stock Connect: A Legal Analysis
Flora Huang

Volume 12: The Governance of Macroprudential Policy: How to Build Regulatory Legitimacy Through a Social Justice Approach
Tracy C Maguze

Volume 13: A Socio-Legal Theory of Money for the Digital Commercial Society: A New Analytical Framework to Understand Cryptoassets
Israel Cedillo Lazcano

Volume 14: Venture Capital Investment and Government Incentives: Law, Regulation and Policy Design
Tamara Wilkinson

Volume 15: Regulating Primary Markets in the Capital Markets Union: Between Uniformity and Differentiation
Konstantinos Serdaris

Regulating Primary Markets in the Capital Markets Union

Between Uniformity and Differentiation

Konstantinos Serdaris

• HART •
OXFORD • LONDON • NEW YORK • NEW DELHI • SYDNEY

HART PUBLISHING
Bloomsbury Publishing Plc
Kemp House, Chawley Park, Cumnor Hill, Oxford, OX2 9PH, UK
1385 Broadway, New York, NY 10018, USA
29 Earlsfort Terrace, Dublin 2, Ireland

HART PUBLISHING, the Hart/Stag logo, BLOOMSBURY and the Diana logo are trademarks of Bloomsbury Publishing Plc

First published in Great Britain 2025

A catalogue record for this book is available from the British Library.

Library of Congress Cataloging-in-Publication data

Names: Serdaris, Konstantinos, author.

Title: Regulating primary markets in the capital markets union : between uniformity and differentiation / Konstantinos Serdaris.

Description: Oxford ; New York : Hart Publishing, 2025. | Series: Hart studies in commercial and financial law ; volume 15 | Includes bibliographical references and index. | Summary: "Stay ahead of the curve with this essential book, offering a concise, comprehensive and up-to-date analysis of the Prospectus Regulation (including its recent amendment by the EU Listing Act) and the pathbreaking Regulation on European Crowdfunding Service Providers (ECSPR). Placing the discussion in the context of the Capital Markets Union, this book provides a fresh and insightful perspective on the ever-evolving regulatory landscape, setting out a practical roadmap for achieving effective and inclusive regulation. A must-read for policymakers, scholars, legal practitioners and anyone seeking to comprehend the current and emerging challenges in the regulation of EU primary capital markets"—Provided by publisher.

Identifiers: LCCN 2024043019 (print) | LCCN 2024043020 (ebook) | ISBN 9781509974986 (hardback) | ISBN 9781509975020 (paperback) | ISBN 9781509974993 (Epub) | ISBN 9781509975006 (ebook)

Subjects: LCSH: Capital market—Law and legislation—European Union countries. | Financial institutions—Law and legislation—European Union countries.

Classification: LCC KJE2245 .S47 2025 (print) | LCC KJE2245 (ebook) | DDC 346.24/08—dc23/eng/20240913

LC record available at https://lccn.loc.gov/2024043019

LC ebook record available at https://lccn.loc.gov/2024043020

ISBN: HB: 978-1-50997-498-6
ePDF: 978-1-50997-500-6
ePub: 978-1-50997-499-3

Typeset by Compuscript Ltd, Shannon

This book is gratefully dedicated
to my parents, Georgios and Vasiliki,
for their unwavering support and love.

FOREWORD

There are many legal areas which consist of regulation for the public good. Looking at the overall development, however, two would seem to have reached – successively and in different moments in time – the status of *primus inter pares*. They can be seen as lead disciplines for the overall development in several respects. In them, a theoretical foundation transcending disciplines – such as information theory – has primarily evolved or a whole regulation philosophy – such as the ordo-liberal school – has developed. In them, the key question has been more disputed and developed than in any other field: whether the regulation aimed primarily at the public good should also be enforced by the private advocate general, ie whether there should be private law claims. Additionally, they may also constitute those areas which apply to the business world more generally (and not only to one segment, for instance to credit institutions), where the European side is most dominant. I speak of competition law, which gained this status already in the Treaty of Rome in 1958, engendered the *Courage* case as the case decided by the CJEU which really paved the way for the idea of a private advocate general in Europe and was at the centre of attention for the ordo-liberal school.

Capital markets law in Europe is of a more recent date. Information theory, and more specifically the information efficiency paradigm of capital markets and its exact mechanism, rest on the seminal articles by George Akerlof and Eugene Fama of 1970. Regulation itself in the area of information – reaching well beyond capital markets law, for instance into areas as huge as consumer (contract) law – took two decades longer to develop in Europe. The consumer has been developed into a powerful private advocate general, recently with the *Dieselgate* case decided by the CJEU in spring 2023; the investor less so. However, a European Capital Markets Union was the key project for a whole EU Commission's term (and remains high on the agenda). Almost all major pieces of legislation (except for MiFID I+II) have developed from EU Directives into EU Regulations, directly applicable in the whole of Europe, genuinely European. Moreover, if the mega-task of climate neutrality is approached nowadays, the main thrust in the European Union would seem to adopt as its key instruments company and capital markets law.

With this background, one foundational endeavour would seem to be what is desperately needed and what this book proposes. It proposes to bring together those threads which from a theoretical perspective are paramount, indispensable for a solid foundation, and for assessing how the democratic EU legislature has made its choices for EU capital markets law. There are three levels. The first level is that of foundational research, of the development of theory in the main questions of how information is perceived to have an impact on choices, how well equipped the addressees are to profit from it, and what are the flanking rules for optimising the impact. The theoretical background consists primarily, but by no means exclusively, of economic information theory and its development since the founding fathers named it; behavioural theory with such concepts as rationality, bounded rationality, cognitive biases, apathy and the rest; and additionally communication theory, with such phenomena as herding and information cascades. Researching these interdisciplinary foundations leads, of course, to a whole ocean of concepts, with a certain order emerging, but multi-faceted, partly contradictory, with a good degree of heterogeneity. This explains and informs the second level. The European legislature, in EU capital markets law, had to make choices, democratic choices. Seen from the pure air of foundational interdisciplinary theory, these choices may not always meet the expectations of certain scholars or certain disciplines, but they rest on democratic decision-making and consent reached in society. Hence, the second level must consist in unearthing, meticulously and covering the vast terrain of overall EU capital markets law, the set of goals, aims and underlying rationales which the EU legislature put the strongest emphasis on; in other words, the choices the EU legislature made – or seems to have made – based on such foundational interdisciplinary insight. For instance, for the ban on insider trading, resting such a ban on increased costs for issuers or resting it on the fear for overall trust in the fairness capital markets are certainly two pairs of shoes – even though both are prominent as 'theories' in foundational interdisciplinary research. Finally, the third level consists of questions of coherence. The question can be asked about the coherence between goals, aims and underlying rationales in different legal acts – how consistently they have been chosen. The question can also be asked about the legal acts themselves and the rules contained in them, namely how well they flow from the goals, aims and underlying rationales invoked for justifying them.

It is the great challenge – and indeed the great achievement – of the book presented here to have gone this way. In this depth and width, the very foundations of European Capital Markets Law have seldom been presented – from the interdisciplinary foundations, via the policy decisions which the European legislature then indeed took, right down to the single rules. It thus truly lays foundations.

Stefan Grundmann
Chair of German and European Private & Business Law, Humboldt-University, Berlin, and Chair of Transnational Law and Theory, European University Institute, Florence (alumnus)

ACKNOWLEDGEMENTS

This book is the culmination of a long academic journey that began in 2017 when I started my doctoral studies. It would not have become a reality without the support of many people who guided and accompanied me along the way.

First and foremost, I would like to express my sincere gratitude to my 'Doktorvater', Professor Dr Dr Stefan Grundmann, for giving me the unique opportunity to pursue my research at two outstanding institutions: the European University Institute (EUI) in Florence and Humboldt University in Berlin. This experience has significantly broadened my horizons and contributed to my professional and personal growth. I extend my warmest thanks to him for his encouragement, knowledge, patience, and, most importantly, his immense compassion, which supported me through my toughest hours and helped me discover my true capabilities.

This book has greatly benefitted from the input of many esteemed scholars. I am forever indebted to Professor Alexandra Mikroulea and Associate Professor Nikolaos Vervesos from the University of Athens Law School, who endorsed my research project from its inception. Their support and insightful guidance opened a whole new world of opportunities and knowledge for me. I am also especially grateful to Professor Niamh Moloney from the London School of Economics, who served as the Chair of my PhD Examining Board. Her work has been a great source of inspiration, and I feel honoured to have had the opportunity to receive valuable feedback from her. I also want to thank Professor Christos Gortsos, Professor Danny Busch, Professor Paraskevi Paparseniou and Assistant Professor Eugenia Macchiavello for providing me with valuable insights into EU financial markets law and for helping me to clarify some important issues related to my research.

I gratefully acknowledge the scholarships provided by the Hellenic State Scholarship Foundation (IKY) and the EUI, which supported my doctoral studies and enabled the research that underpins this book. Furthermore, I wish to acknowledge the support I received from my colleagues at Southampton Law School and Utrecht University Law School, where I began and completed the writing of this book. Many thanks are due to the publishing team at Hart Studies in Commercial and Financial Law for their guidance and support throughout the book publication process.

This book would never have been completed without the unconditional love and support of my family and loved ones. My greatest debt of gratitude is, therefore, owed to my beloved parents, Georgios and Vasiliki, as well as my sister, Sofia, and my partner, Dafni. Thank you is a very small phrase to convey my appreciation for all the sacrifices you have made for me. I am extremely fortunate and blessed to have you in my life.

Utrecht,
9 July 2024

TABLE OF CONTENTS

TABLE OF ABBREVIATIONS

AFME	Association for Financial Markets in Europe
AIFM	Alternative Investment Fund Manager
AIFMD	2011 Alternative Investment Fund Managers Directive
BaFin	Bundesanstalt Für Finanzdienstleistungsaufsich
BGH	Der Bundesgerichtshof
BIS	Bank for International Settlements
BU	Banking Union
BV	Besloten Vennootschap
BW	Burgerlijk Wetboek
CCD	Consumer Credit Directive
CEPS	Centre for European Policy Studies
CESR	Committee of European Securities Regulators
CIS	Collective Investment Scheme
CJEU	Court of Justice of the European Union
CME	Coordinated Market Economy
CML Rev	Common Market Law Review
CMU	Capital Markets Union
COD	Ordinary legislative procedure
COM	Communication from the Commission
CONSOB	Commissione Nazionale per le Società e la Borsa
CRD IV	2013 Capital Requirements Directive IV
CRD V	2019 Capital Requirements Directive V
CRR	2013 Capital Requirements Regulation

CRR II	2019 Capital Requirements Regulation II
CSP	Crowdfunding Service Provider
CUP	Cambridge University Press
DG FISMA	Directorate-General for Financial Stability, Financial Services & Capital Markets Union
DGS	Deposit Guarantee Schemes
EBA	European Banking Authority
EBI	European Banking Institute
EC	European Community
ECB	European Central Bank
ECMH	Efficient Capital Markets Hypothesis
ECMI	European Capital Markets Institute
ECSPR	European Crowdfunding Service Providers Regulation
EEA	European Economic Area
EIB	European Investment Bank
EIF	European Investment Fund
EIOPA	European Insurance and Occupational Pensions Authority
EMD	E-Money Directive
EMIR	European Market Infrastructure Regulation
EMU	European Monetary Union
ESAs	European Supervisory Authorities
ESBG	European Savings and Retail Banking Group
ESFS	European System of Financial Supervision
ESM	European Stability Mechanism
ESMA	European Securities and Markets Authority
ESME	European Securities Markets Expert Group
ESRB	European Systemic Risk Board
EU	European Union
FESE	Federation of European Securities Exchanges
FinTech	Financial Technology

FSAP	Financial Services Action Plan
GDP	Gross Domestic Product
GDPR	General Data Protection Regulation
GewO	Gewerbeordnung
GmbH	Gesellschaft mit beschränkter Haftung.
HLF	High-level Forum
ICMA	International Capital Markets Association
ICO(s)	Initial Coin Offering(s)
IMF	International Monetary Fund
IODS	INSEAD OEE Data Services
IOSCO	International Organization of Securities Commissions
IPO	Initial Public Offering
ISD	Investment Services Directive
KID	Key Information Document
KIIS	Key Investment Information Sheet
LME	Liberal Market Economy
MAD	2003 Market Abuse Directive
MAR	2014 Market Abuse Regulation
MCD	Mortgage Credit Directive
MiFID I	2004 Markets in Financial Instruments Directive I
MiFID II	2014 Markets in Financial Instruments Directive II
MiFIR	2014 Markets in Financial Instruments Regulation
MTF	Multilateral Trading Facility
NBER	National Bureau of Economic Research
NCA	National Competent Authority
NFC(s)	Non-financial corporation(s)
NPV	Net Present Value
OECD	Organisation for Economic Co-operation and Development
OEE	Observatoire de l'Epargne Européenne

OJ	Official Journal of the European Union
OTC	Over-the-counter
OTF	Organized Trading Facility
OUP	Oxford University Press
P2P	Peer-to-peer
PDS	Product Disclosure Statement
PEPP	Portable pan-European Personal Pension Products
PRIPs	Packaged Retail Investment Products
PSD II	2015 Payment Services Directive II
Q&A	Questions and Answers
SAFE	Survey on the Access to Finance of Enterprises
SBA	Small Business Act
SEC	Securities and Exchange Commission
SME(s)	Small and medium-sized enterprise(s)
SPV	Special Purpose Vehicle
SRM	Single Resolution Mechanism
SSD	Schuldscheindarlehen
SSM	Single Supervisory Mechanism
STO(s)	Security Token Offering(s)
SWD	Commission Staff Working Document
TESG	Technical Expert Stakeholder Group
TEU	Treaty on European Union
TFEU	Treaty on the Functioning of the European Union
UCITS	Undertaking for Collective Investment in Transferable Securities
URD	Universal Registration Document
VermAnIG	Gesetz über Vermögensanlagen
VoC	Varieties of Capitalism
WKSI(s)	Well-known seasoned issuer(s)
WpHG	Wertpapierhandelsgesetz
WpPG	Wertpapierprospektgesetz

TABLE OF CASES

TABLE OF LEGISLATION

EU LEGISLATION

Treaties

Commission Recommendations

Directives

NATIONAL LEGISLATION

France

Germany

Italy

Netherlands

United Kingdom

United States

Introduction

I. Background and Context of the Study

The idea of unifying European capital markets and the legal framework governing their operation is nearly as old as the Treaty of Rome itself.[1] The underlying assumption dates back to 1966 with the publication of the seminal Segré Report.[2] The report posited that a single financial market, supported by a well-functioning and harmonised regulatory system allowing market actors easy access to the capital markets of Member States, would broaden capital pools for businesses, offer investors wider and better diversification opportunities, and contribute to economic growth and job creation.[3] While the EU's commitment to reducing barriers to cross-border capital market activity has been a consistent feature of the harmonisation programme,[4] it was not until the 1999 Financial Services Action Plan (FSAP)[5] that the integration agenda began to focus on the relative merits of market finance. This development was primarily driven by a wide array of empirical studies that found a positive correlation between financial market development and growth.[6] Consequently, by the end of the FSAP era, it was widely recognised that, alongside a robust banking sector, an integrated, deep, and economically efficient EU financial market is essential for enhancing capital allocation and supporting long-term economic performance.[7]

[1] Treaty establishing the European Economic Community 1957.

[2] European Economic Community, 'The Development of a European Capital Market', Report of a Group of Experts appointed by the EEC Commission, November 1966.

[3] London Economics, 'Quantification of the Macro-Economic Impact of Integration of EU Financial Markets', Final Report to the European Commission, November 2002. See also E Ferran, *Building and EU Securities Market* (CUP, 2004) 12; N Moloney, *EU Securities and Financial Markets Regulation*, 4th edn (OUP, 2023) 7.

[4] See eg Commission, 'Completing the Internal Market' White Paper from the Commission to the European Council', COM (85) 310 final, 14 September 1985, which set forth an agenda of 279 legislative measures to be implemented by 1992 and proposed the core elements of the single market as it is known today.

[5] Commission, 'Implementing the framework for financial markets: action plan', COM (1999) 232 final, 11 May 1999.

[6] See eg J Jayaratne and P Strahan, 'The Finance-Growth Nexus: Evidence from Bank Branch Deregulation' (1996) 111 *Quarterly Journal of Economics* 639; R Levine, 'Financial Development and Economic Growth: Views and Agenda' (1997) 35 *Journal of Economic Literature* 688; A Demirgüg-Kunt and V Maksimovic, 'Law, Finance, and Firm Growth' (1998) 53 *Journal of Finance* 2107; R Levine and S Zervos, 'Stock Markets, Banks, and Economic Growth' (1998) 88 *American Economic Review* 537.

[7] Commission, White Paper on Financial Services Policy, COM (2005) 629 final, 1 December 2005, 6.

The global financial crisis, however, made it painfully clear that the structure and level of integration of the EU financial system fell well short of policymakers' goals and aspirations. Despite efforts made over the years, corporations in most Member States were excessively dependent on banks for external funding, and Europe's capital markets remained highly fragmented and organised along national lines.[8] As a result, when the crisis began affecting the real economy, the European financial sector was not sufficiently diversified or integrated enough to mitigate the severity of the shock. Against this backdrop, in 2015, the Juncker administration presented a long-term and ambitious action plan to create a European Capital Markets Union (CMU).[9] The strategic objective behind this initiative was to establish a more diversified and integrated financial system by strengthening the capital markets in all Member States and deepening their level of integration.[10] In turn, this was expected to improve access to finance for businesses, provide more opportunities for risk diversification for investors and contribute to the EU's overarching goals of enhancing economic growth and financial stability.[11]

Now, nearly a decade after the introduction of the initial building blocks for establishing a fully-fledged CMU, the discussion about the necessity of a well-functioning, single market for capital is more relevant than ever. Indeed, overcoming the lasting effects of the COVID-19 crisis and financing the EU's digital transformation and sustainable transition require the mobilisation of substantial investments, which cannot be solely covered by traditional sources like public funds and bank loans. At the same time, the United Kingdom's departure from the European single market ('Brexit') underscores the importance of ensuring that EU capital markets continue to be an integral and competitive component of the global financial system by reducing the legal and administrative barriers to cross-border operations. In this context, it comes as no surprise that the von der Leyen Commission reaffirmed the EU's commitment to advancing the CMU,[12] unveiling a new action plan tailored to address the aforementioned challenges more effectively.[13]

The strong political backing received by the CMU project since its inception has deeply influenced legal research, leading to extensive policy and scholarly contributions addressing various issues related to the institutional and regulatory framework of the reform programme.[14] However, given the multitude of legislative

[8] Commission Staff Working Document, 'Economic Analysis Accompanying the Action Plan on Building a Capital Markets Union', SWD (2015) 183 final, 30 September 2015, 10–12.

[9] Commission, 'Action Plan on Building a Capital Markets Union', COM (2015) 468 final, 30 September 2015.

[10] ibid 3.

[11] SWD (2015) 183 final (n 8) 8.

[12] U von der Leyen, 'A Union that strives for more: My agenda for Europe' (16 July 2019), available at: commission.europa.eu/system/files/2020-04/political-guidelines-next-commission_en_0.pdf.

[13] Commission, 'A Capital Markets Union for People and Businesses – New Action Plan', COM (2020) 590 final, 24 September 2020.

[14] From the extensive literature see K Hopt, 'Die Schaffung einer Kapitalmarktunion in Europa – langwierig und schwierig, aber notwendig' (2015) 26 *Europäische Zeitschrift für Wirtschaftsrecht* 289; W-G Ringe, 'Capital Markets Union for Europe: A Commitment to the Single Market of 28' (2015) 9

measures proposed for implementation within the CMU framework,[15] similar attention should also be devoted to assessing their alignment with the pursued objectives. This is particularly crucial as EU capital market law is undergoing a dynamic process of change, stressing the need for legal scholars to play a more active role in identifying potential inconsistencies and offering recommendations for future improvements. In this vein, the book at hand aims to contribute to this endeavour by delving deeper into the coherence between policy ambitions and regulatory actions within the CMU framework.

II. Scope and Focus

Unlike the Banking Union (BU), the other major single market initiative of the post-crisis reform period,[16] the CMU is not a top-down project. It does not introduce any sweeping legislation or create new EU-level institutions. Instead, it comprises various legislative and non-legislative measures designed to collectively remove barriers to the efficient functioning and integration of EU capital markets.[17] Among these measures, this book focuses on legal interventions aimed at modernising the rules governing European primary markets and the activities taking place within them. The rationale for this choice is quite straightforward: an effective EU primary market law system has significant potential to achieve the overarching objectives of the CMU.

Indeed, the primary market can broadly be defined as the segment of the financial market where new transferable securities, such equity (shares) or debt (bonds), are issued and sold to investors for the first time.[18] In this market, therefore, companies, governments and other entities can raise capital directly from

Law and Financial Markets Review 5; N Moloney, 'Capital Markets Union: "Ever Closer Union" for the EU Financial System?' (2016) 41 *European Law Review* 307; N Véron and G Wolff, 'Capital Markets Union: A Vision for the Long Term' (2016) 2 *Journal of Financial Regulation* 130; P Schammo, 'Market Building and the Capital Markets Union: Addressing Information Barriers in the SME Funding Market' (2017) 14 *European Company and Financial Law Review* 271; D Busch, 'A Capital Markets Union for a Divided Europe' (2017) 3 *Journal of Financial Regulation* 262; L Quaglia and D Howarth, 'The Policy Narratives of European Capital Markets Union' (2018) 25 *Journal of European Public Policy* 990; D Busch, E Avgouleas and G Ferrarini (eds), *Capital Markets Union in Europe* (OUP, 2018); F Allen et al (eds), *Capital Markets Union and Beyond* (MIT Press, 2019).

[15] For an overview of these interventions see D Busch, 'Capital Markets Union' in F Fabbrini and M Ventoruzzo (eds), *Research Handbook on EU Economic Law* (Edward Elgar, 2019).

[16] From the vast literature see N Moloney, 'European Banking Union: Assessing its Risks and Resilience' (2014) 51 *Common Market Law Review* 1609; L Quaglia and D Howarth, *The Political Economy of European Banking Union* (OUP, 2016); J-H Binder and C Gortsos, *The European Banking Union: a compendium* (C.H. Beck, 2016); D Busch and G Ferrarini (eds), *European Banking Union*, 2nd edn (OUP, 2020); J-H Binder et al, *European Banking Union: Brussels Commentary* (Nomos/Hart Publishing, 2023).

[17] COM (2015) 468 final (n 9) 4; COM (2020) 590 final (n 13) 2.

[18] F Fabozzi and P Peterson-Drake, *Finance: Capital Markets, Financial Management, and Investment Management* (Wiley, 2009) 127.

investors through the issuance of these new financial instruments.[19] This process typically involves the intermediation of a third party (eg, an investment bank) that distributes the securities to the public or places them with institutional investors, often providing additional services, such as underwriting and price setting.[20]

Thus defined, the primary market serves two principal economic functions. First, it allows corporates to accumulate capital, which can then be used to fund new activities, increase production and, consequently, support growth. Second, it offers investors the opportunity to diversify their portfolio across various investment assets, thus fostering greater risk-sharing and ultimately contributing to financial stability.[21] In this regard, a well-functioning, deep, and integrated primary market is crucial for enhancing both the ability of EU businesses to access finance and that of investors to find suitable investment opportunities aligned with their risk profile. Therefore, legal interventions that advance in this direction can play a crucial role in successfully delivering the CMU, warranting closer scrutiny.

Two such initiatives are deemed particularly significant and are further discussed here. The first encompasses the Prospectus Regulation,[22] including its recent amendment by the Listing Act Regulation.[23] This piece of legislation lays down uniform requirements for the drawing up, approval and distribution of the disclosure document which must be published when securities are publicly offered or admitted to trading on a regulated market. The second initiative involves the Regulation on European Crowdfunding Service Providers for business (ECSPR),[24] which prescribes a common framework governing the provision of crowdfunding services in the EU. In particular, it addresses the authorisation, organisation and supervision of crowdfunding platforms, along with the conditions for offering securities through them. These measures not only form the cornerstone of efforts to achieve the CMU's objectives within the primary markets sphere, but they are also closely interconnected and mutually reinforcing, regulating capital-raising activity across various stages of a company's lifecycle. However, they also differ in terms of the regulatory approach adopted. For instance, the ECSPR replaces the complex and expensive prospectus publication duty with the obligation for project owners to prepare a less burdensome Key Investment Information Sheet (KIIS). This discrepancy primarily stems from the distinct characteristics of participants

[19] K Pilbeam, *Finance and Financial Markets*, 2nd edn (Palgrave Macmillan, 2005) 30.

[20] See eg S Grundmann, *Bankvertragsrecht. Investment Banking II* (De Gruyter, 2016) 20 ff.

[21] Commission Staff Working Document, 'Initial Reflections on the Obstacles to the Development of Deep and Integrated EU Capital Markets', SWD (2015) 13 final, 18 February 2015, 7 and 9.

[22] Regulation (EU) 2017/1129 of the European Parliament and of the Council on the prospectus to be published when securities are offered to the public or admitted to trading on a regulated market [2017] OJ L168/12.

[23] Regulation (EU) 2024/2809 of the European Parliament and of the Council amending Regulations (EU) 2017/1129, (EU) No 596/2014 and (EU) No 600/2014 to make public capital markets in the Union more attractive for companies and to facilitate access to capital for small and medium-sized enterprises OJ L, 2024/2809.

[24] Regulation (EU) 2020/1503 of the European Parliament and of the Council on European crowdfunding service providers (ECSP) for business [2020] OJ L347/1.

in the crowdfunding market, mainly consisting of start-ups and retail investors. Besides, the critical role played by platform intermediaries in the crowdfunding context adds further complexity to the regulatory landscape. In this regard, the comparison of these regulatory interventions can offer valuable insights that may lead to more robust conclusions regarding the impact of primary market legislation in achieving the objectives of the CMU.

On the contrary, the recently enacted Markets in Crypto-assets Regulation (MiCAR),[25] despite its relevance to primary market law, does not fall within the scope of this analysis. More specifically, MiCAR establishes disclosure requirements for the issuance, public offering and admission to trading of crypto-assets in the Union, and sets out conditions for the provision of crypto-asset related services. These provisions are typical of the regulation of primary market activities, as better exemplified in the Prospectus Regulation and the ECSPR. However, the types of crypto-assets covered by MiCAR include e-money tokens, asset-referenced tokens, and other crypto-assets that do not fall under the previous categories,[26] such as non-pegged payment tokens, like Bitcoin, or utility tokens. By contrast, crypto-assets that qualify as financial instruments, as defined in MiFID II,[27] are explicitly excluded from the scope of MiCAR.[28] Accordingly, the issuance of crypto-assets that qualify as securities ('security tokens') will continue to be governed by the Prospectus Regulation (and potentially the ECSPR) regardless of the underlying technology, based on the principle of 'same activities, same risks, same rules'.[29] In this context, the analysis of MiCAR appears redundant for the purposes of this book as it does not directly pertain to the definition of primary capital markets followed here. This notwithstanding, it is worth noting that MiCAR encompasses a range of innovative provisions that can be relevant to the overall discussion.

III. Research Questions and Objectives

Considering the importance of strong, liquid and integrated European primary markets in mobilising investment flows and helping companies diversify their funding sources, it is no surprise that the regulatory initiatives discussed here are central to completing the CMU.[30] Indeed, harmonising the prospectus regime with a view to removing obstacles to the smooth and efficient functioning of the

[25] Regulation (EU) 2023/1114 of the European Parliament and of the Council on markets in crypto-assets [2023] OJ L150/40.

[26] ibid Art 1(1).

[27] Art 4(1)(15) Directive 2014/65/EU of the European Parliament and of the Council on markets in financial instruments [2014] OJ L173/349.

[28] Art 2(4)(a) MiCAR.

[29] ibid recital 3. See also D Busch and M Lehmann, 'Uniform Prospectus Liability Rules for Europe' (2023) 14 *Journal of European Tort Law* 113, 119.

[30] Recital 1 Prospectus Regulation and recital 3 ECSPR.

internal market for securities while ensuring a high level of investor protection was a flagship initiative of the 2015 CMU Action Plan.[31] Similarly, establishing a common framework for the provision of crowdfunding services in the EU was a key component of the mid-term review of the CMU Action Plan, aimed at improving access to finance for businesses.[32] In this respect, it is essential to examine whether these initiatives are well-positioned to successfully achieve their intended objectives.

However, providing a definitive answer to this inquiry presents considerable challenges, as it greatly depends on the capacity of the regulatory framework to effectively accommodate the inherent diversity within the CMU. More specifically, while the term 'Union' may suggest a shift toward legal uniformity and convergence, paradoxically, the concept of differentiation, often overlooked in the literature,[33] plays a prominent role in the CMU project. This primarily relates to the varied and occasionally conflicting interests and needs of the diverse range of actors addressed by the reform agenda, spanning from SMEs to established multinationals, and from households to institutional investors.[34] But apart from that, the divergent national perspectives that became apparent during the negotiating process concerning the structure[35] and governance[36] of the EU financial system also highlight the significance of differentiation. Therefore, any attempt to construct an EU legal framework that fosters the development and integration of primary markets must consider not only the unique preferences and priorities of Member States but also the varying impact that the respective measures may have on market participants, considering their size, capacity, and requirements.

In light of the above, in addressing the main research question, two sub-questions arise that necessitate careful examination and recur through the entire book: first, how can greater unification and enhanced flexibility for regional

[31] COM (2015) 468 final (n 9) 12.

[32] Commission, 'Mid-Term Review of the Capital Markets Union Action Plan', COM (2017) 292 final, 8 June 2017, 13.

[33] From an early stage, however, certain authors articulated concerns regarding the diversity among political and market stakeholders involved in the CMU, foreseeing significant challenges for both the institutional and regulatory design of EU capital markets, see eg N Moloney, 'Institutional Governance and Capital Markets Union: Incrementalism or a "Big Bang"?' (2016) 13 *European Company and Financial Law Review* 376; L Quaglia, D Howarth and M Liebe, 'The Political Economy of European Capital Markets Union' (2016) 54 (s1) *Journal of Common Market Studies* 185; C Kumpan, 'Die Europäische Kapitalmarktunion und ihr Fokus auf kleinere und mittlere Unternehmen' (2016) 45 *Zeitschrift für Unternehmens- und Gesellschaftsrecht* 2.

[34] COM (2015) 468 final (n 9); COM (2020) 590 final (n 13).

[35] The CMU garnered enthusiastic support from Member States with substantial and diversified financial sectors, such as the UK, Luxembourg, Sweden, and the Netherlands. In contrast, the German and French governments initially showed less enthusiasm, partly due to the significance of bank credit in their countries and partly due to a perceived limited need to enhance alternative finance, see Quaglia, Howarth and Liebe (n 33) 192 ff.

[36] In line with the assumption of intergovernmentalism, most Member States aimed to shape the CMU integration process according to their preferences, seeking to prevent conferring competitive advantages on other States. This becomes particularly evident in the delayed discussion on strengthening the powers of ESMA, which was only raised after the Brexit referendum, as the UK was resolute in vetoing any attempts toward centralising supervision, see UK Government, 'Building a Strong Capital Markets Union' (Response to the Commission Green Paper on Capital Markets Union), 2015.

solutions be reconciled; and second, how should legal rules be structured to ensure improved and cost-effective access for businesses to European primary markets while maintaining adequate investor protection. By examining these issues, the analysis aims to elucidate the challenges of establishing a harmonised, yet adaptable, regulatory framework for EU primary capital markets within the CMU context; assess the effectiveness of the legislative actions taken so far in addressing these challenges, identifying any inconsistencies and areas for improvement; and, where applicable, suggest refinements, amendments and solutions for potential future application that could improve regulatory interventions in this segment of EU capital markets.

IV. Structure and Contribution

To provide the reader with a clear and organised view of the presented ideas and arguments, this book is structured into four chapters. In particular, the first two chapters are foundational, setting the scene of the analysis. Chapter one lays the groundwork for the main part of the study by offering a systematic exploration of the underlying concept and assumptions of the CMU. Additionally, it presents a distinct and comprehensive taxonomy of the objectives pursued, thereby contributing to the deeper understanding of this project. Chapter two seeks to define a normative framework that serves as a guiding compass for the EU's regulatory endeavours within the realm of primary capital markets. This framework places significant emphasis on addressing the divergent national conditions and the diverse requirements of the market participants involved. Accordingly, it draws the relevant normative criteria from various welfare economic theories, including information economics, behavioural law and economics, and transaction cost economics, as well as from the economic theories of federalism and regulatory competition. By doing so, it provides a benchmark against which the success of legislative actions in the area of primary markets can be assessed. At the same time, it promotes a comprehensive and systematic approach to regulatory decision-making, which can foster consistency and coherence in the EU's regulatory interventions in this area.

The last two chapters delve into the details of the individual legislative acts. In chapter three, the main reforms introduced by the Prospectus Regulation are discussed, along with its recent amendments through the Listing Act Regulation, while chapter four offers a detailed yet concise overview of the ECSPR. In both cases, the analysis is accompanied by a thorough evaluation of the effectiveness of these reforms in actively progressing the completion of the CMU. Moreover, targeted reform proposals are formulated to enhance the ability of the discussed measures to achieve the overarching objectives of the CMU initiative. That way, the study seeks to assist readers in gaining a more profound understanding of primary market legislation while actively contributing to shaping the CMU agenda in this domain.

1

Unfolding the European Capital Markets Union: Concept and Objectives

I. Introduction

The initial idea of constructing a Capital Markets Union (CMU) can be traced back to President Juncker's opening statement in the European Parliament Plenary session in July 2014. Presenting his political guidelines for the next European Commission he would state: 'Over time, I believe we should complement the new European rules for banks with a Capital Markets Union. To improve the financing of our economy, we should further develop and integrate capital markets. This would cut the cost of raising capital, notably for SMEs, and help reduce our very high dependence on bank funding. This would also increase the attractiveness of Europe as a place to invest'.[1] At the time, the CMU project was in the making and, hence, the interpretation attributed to its future development tended to differ according to the diverging interests and role of its commentators.[2]

But things have changed greatly since then. Indeed, the withdrawal of the UK, Europe's most important financial hub, from the EU; the unprecedented economic crisis caused by the COVID-19 pandemic; and Europe's efforts to transition towards a digital and sustainable economy have been instrumental in turning the CMU into a fully-fledged single market initiative, which has become part of the EU's 'nomenclature' in the financial and banking fields.[3] It is no surprise, therefore,

[1] Jean-Claude Juncker, 'A new start for Europe: my agenda for jobs, growth, fairness and democratic change', (Strasbourg, 15 July 2014) commission.europa.eu/publications/president-junckers-political-guidelines_en.

[2] Characteristic in this regard is a quote from Verena Ross, the Executive Director of ESMA, when providing evidence before the House of Lords in October 2014: 'If you ask 10 people, they will give you 10 different answers as to what capital markets union means', House of Lords, EU Economic and Financial Affairs Sub-Committee, 'Review of the EU financial regulatory framework (written and oral evidence)' (2014) 421.

[3] Along with the Lamfalussy four-level process, the European System of Financial Supervision (ESFS), the Single Supervisory and Resolution Mechanisms (SSM and SRM) and, of course, the Banking Union (BU).

that a vast amount of legal literature has been devoted to this subject,[4] thereby contributing significantly to a better understanding of its most important legal aspects. Yet, as the impacts of most legal interventions are only now beginning to unfold, new and challenging tasks emerge for financial law scholars who need to explore, both normatively and empirically, their alignment with the objectives defined in the CMU. In doing so, however, it is important to carefully unfold the underlying concept of this policy initiative and by extension, identify the aims it seeks to achieve. This chapter delves into this laborious task, seeking to lay the foundations for the core aim of this book: assessing the coherence between these objectives and the regulatory measures introduced within a specific segment of the CMU, namely the primary capital markets.

II. The History and Development of the CMU

A. Financial and Economic Background

To comprehend the concept and objectives underpinning the CMU, it is essential to carefully consider the financial and economic context within which this policy initiative was developed. More specifically, a quick glance at the initial reactions of institutional stakeholders to President Juncker's declarations reveals that, even at an early stage, there existed a widespread consensus advocating the necessity to realise the CMU vision.[5] Ever since, completing the CMU remained a top priority during the Juncker Presidency and continued without challenge under the von der Leyen Commission.[6] This strong political support is rooted in the undisputed need to address the significant shortcomings in the EU financial system which, as revealed during recent financial and economic crises, can significantly impact economic growth and financial stability: first, the overreliance of EU businesses on bank financing, and secondly, the fragmentation of EU capital markets.[7]

[4] See generally, D Busch, E Avgouleas and G Ferrarini (eds), *Capital Markets Union in Europe* (OUP, 2018); F Allen et al (eds), *Capital Markets Union and Beyond* (MIT Press, 2019); R Veil (ed), *Regulating EU Capital Markets Union – Volume I: Fundamentals of a European Code* (OUP, 2024).

[5] See eg Y Mersch, 'Capital markets union – the "why" and the "how"' (Dinner speech at the Joint EIB-IMF High Level Workshop, 22 October 2014) www.bis.org/review/r141023g.htm; S Maijoor, 'Capital Markets Union: building competitive, efficient capital markets trusted by investors', 6 November 2014, ESMA/2014/1339.

[6] U von der Leyen, 'A Union that strives for more: My agenda for Europe' (16 July 2019) commission.europa.eu/system/files/2020-04/political-guidelines-next-commission_en_0.pdf.

[7] Commission Staff Working Document, 'Economic Analysis Accompanying the document Action Plan on Building a Capital Markets Union', SWD (2015) 183 final, 30 September 2015, 8; High-Level Forum on the Capital Markets Union, 'A new Vision for Europe's capital markets', Final Report, June 2020, 5.

i. Over-reliance on the Banking Sector and Underdeveloped Capital Markets

When the CMU was launched, a persistent feature of the European financial system had been the relatively limited development of both private and public equity and debt markets, particularly when juxtaposed with their US counterparts.[8] Generally, direct finance has always played a smaller role in the EU economy as European businesses have primarily relied on intermediated finance from banks. At that time, however, Europe boasted the world's largest banking system,[9] with loans serving as the principal instrument for financing Europe's non-financial corporations (NFCs),[10] while the extent of penetration of capital markets within the economies of EU Member States varied significantly.

More specifically, there are two chief methods used to gauge the development of financial systems, ie the size, efficiency and sophistication of their financial sector.[11] The first one emphasises the main categories of financial assets as a percentage of all financial assets and gross domestic product (GDP). Applying this method, significant disparities in financial system development were observed among EU countries during the inception of the CMU.[12] Non-bank financial intermediation accounted for over 50 per cent of GDP in merely nine Member States, with this figure surpassing 100 per cent solely in Luxembourg, Ireland, and Sweden.[13] Similar variations were also evident in the relative scale of stock market capitalisation compared to national GDP. In larger economies (ie, those with GDP above the EU national average), domestic stock market capitalisation was robust mainly in the UK (121 per cent), Sweden (112 per cent) and the Netherlands (98 per cent). Conversely, it remained notably lower in Germany (51 per cent), hitting its lowest point in Italy (35 per cent). In smaller economies (nominal GDP below the EU national average), domestic stock market capitalisation exceeded 125 per cent of GDP in Luxembourg, 84 per cent in Finland, and 75 per cent in Ireland, while

[8] Although the EU and American economies are comparable, Europe's public equity and debt markets are half the size of the US' ones (as a percentage of GDP). More specifically, by end 2013, total EU stock market capitalisation, amounted to €8.4 trillion (around 65% of GDP) and the total value of outstanding debt securities exceeded €22.3 trillion (171% of GDP). On the other hand, stock market capitalisation and outstanding debt securities in the US during the same period exceeded 130% and 220% of GDP respectively (Source: ECMI statistical package, 2014). The situation is similar between private equity and debt markets in the US and in Europe. In particular, the number of private equity transactions is almost double that of the EU, whilst private placement markets for bonds are up to three times bigger in the US.

[9] The total assets of the euro area domestic banks stood at €24.2 trillion on a consolidated basis at the end of 2016, see European Central Bank, 'Report on financial structures' (October 2017) 24.

[10] In 2016, the loans provided by the overall financial sector accounted to about 52% of euro area GDP with few changes over time. In the same year, listed shares accounted for about 13% and debt securities represented about 9% of GDP, ibid 11.

[11] F Allen and D Gale, *Comparing Financial Systems* (MIT Press, 2000) 4–6.

[12] European Capital Markets Institute (ECMI), Statistical Package 2015.

[13] L Quaglia, D Howarth and M Liebe, 'The Political Economy of European Capital Markets Union' (2016) 54 (s1) *Journal of Common Market Studies* 185, 187–88 (Figure 1).

remaining below 10 per cent in Cyprus, Slovakia, Latvia, and Lithuania.[14] The second method focuses on analysing the sources of external funding for NFCs. Here again, substantial variations were noticeable among Member States. For instance, in countries like Cyprus, Greece, and Portugal, which faced substantial economic challenges during the crisis, securities markets played a minor role in NFCs' funding. Consequently, companies there remained heavily dependent on bank loans which accounted for more than 40 per cent of their total liabilities. In contrast, countries like France, Germany, and the Netherlands, saw a more substantial contribution of capital markets in corporate financing, with equity and investment fund shares averaging over 55 per cent of NFCs' total liabilities. Nordic companies also leaned more on equity and debt securities, constituting over 50 per cent of their balance sheet capitalisation. Finally, in the relatively smaller and less developed markets of Central and Eastern Europe, firms exhibited less reliance on external financing, preferring to resort to own funds instead.[15]

Different factors could explain the disposition, or even the partiality, of the financial system in most European countries towards banks. First, an economy's financial structure, namely whether it leans more towards intermediated or market-based finance, aligns with its level of economic development. This connection emerges from the observation that wealthier nations generally feature a more robust capital markets sector, as evidenced by the previous analysis on the varied roles of capital markets in different Member States. Thus, the overall tendency towards banking finance could partly stem from divergences in the levels of economic development among EU nations, particularly between those in the centre and those in the periphery.[16] Moreover, the financial structure is intricately linked to the composition of the corporate sector. As will be explained later, the EU economy is dominated by small and medium-sized enterprises (SMEs). Typically, these firms encounter challenges in obtaining capital directly through the public market, primarily due to information asymmetries, their risk profile,[17] and the expenses associated with a public offering.[18] Hence, they tend to resort to banks for financing, which, among other things, have a comparative edge in gathering information about these enterprises. However, it is true that bank-centredness could also impact the structure of the European corporate sector. Simply put, if companies have limited access to financing options beyond bank loans, their ability to secure the required capital for further growth would also be constrained.

[14] ibid 188 (Table 1). See also ECMI (n 12).

[15] See generally Eurostat, 'Non-financial corporations – statistics on financial assets and liabilities' (2016) Figure 11: Financial liabilities of non-financial corporations by financial instrument.

[16] For the distinction between centre and periphery in the EU, see eg D Kukovec, 'Law and the Periphery' (2015) 21 *European Law Journal* 406.

[17] This is because their business prospects are more difficult for investors to evaluate, they are less diversified, and they are often not in the possession of collateral.

[18] The costs related to going public can amount to 10 to 15% of proceeds for IPOs valued at less than EUR 6 million, see European IPO Task Force, 'European IPO Report 2020' (6 March 2020) 12.

Legal factors have also had a significant influence on Europe's financial systems. According to the law and finance scholarship, for example, the strong orientation of European continental countries towards banking finance can be linked to their Civil Code legal tradition, which often favours robust and influential banks over decentralised and atomistic capital markets.[19] Additionally, unlike the US, which separated investment and retail banking activities until at least 1999, most EU countries have favoured the universal banking model, contributing to the strengthening of banks. Aside from legal influences, political factors have also significantly shaped the formation of financial systems. For instance, France has historically promoted big banks by fostering a policy of national champions within the banking sector.[20] Consequently, large credit institutions have prevailed over other entities within the country's financial sector. Similarly, Germany has fostered the growth of smaller, cooperative, and regional banks, elucidating the significance of bank credit in this country.[21]

From a practical standpoint, the scattered distribution of trading venues across Europe has not facilitated the development of capital markets either. Indeed, contrary to the US, where market activity is centralised,[22] multiple venues operate within the EU. This situation prevents the essential networking and scalability from occurring, concurrently creating information advantages for participants in each separate market.[23] Finally, the bank-centric structure of most EU economies has also been influenced by savers' behaviour. Especially in Member States with lower GDP per capita[24] (eg, Croatia, Greece, Slovakia, Cyprus), households tend to retain the majority of their disposable financial assets in currency and bank deposits. Consequently, the portion of domestic capital available for businesses in these countries is restricted.

ii. *Incomplete and Limited Capital Market Integration*

Another concerning aspect of the EU's financial system, particularly pronounced at the time of the CMU's inception, was that despite various measures and policies aimed at fostering a single market, cross-border financial integration, especially in the capital markets domain, remained rather limited,[25] as was evident primarily

[19] R La Porta et al, 'Legal Determinants of External Finance' (1997) 52 *Journal of Finance* 1131.

[20] D Howarth, 'France and the International Financial Crisis: The Legacy of State-led Finance' (2013) 26 *Governance* 369.

[21] Quaglia, Howarth and Liebe (n 13) 193.

[22] M Johnston, 'How New York Became the Center of American Finance' (27 September 2018), www.investopedia.com/articles/investing/022516/how-new-york-became-center-american-finance.asp.

[23] T Beck, 'Does Europe Need a Capital Market Union? And How Would We Get There?' in F Allen, E Carletti and J Gray (eds), *The New Financial Architecture in the Eurozone* (EUI, 2015) 118.

[24] For the calculation see IMF, World Economic Outlook Database, January 2018.

[25] N Véron and G Wolff, 'Capital Markets Union: A Vision for the Long Term' (2016) 2 *Journal of Financial Regulation* 130, 135; European Court of Auditors, 'Capital Markets Union – Slow Start Towards an Ambitious Goal', Special Report (November 2020) 79.

in quantity but also in price indicators.[26] More specifically, following the slump caused by the financial and sovereign crises, EU capital markets remained overwhelmingly fragmented along national lines.[27] Concerning private equity markets, the share of funding that European private equity firms attracted from investors outside of their country of establishment barely exceeded one fifth of their overall funding.[28] The picture was similar when it came to public equity and corporate bond markets, where investors tended to prefer domestic instruments over cross-border holdings. In fact, although intra-EU home bias decreased since the crisis, it remained quite high until recently (77 per cent) indicating investors' hesitance in most Member States to invest in the rest of the EU.[29]

The limited integration of European capital markets could be attributed to various barriers to cross-border activities. To begin with, studies have indicated that cultural differences (including ethnicity, language, and religion),[30] along with other factors hindering transnational communications (such as telephone costs, trading times, etc),[31] significantly correlate with the lack of trust in cross-border market activity, thus negatively affecting market integration. Furthermore, infrastructure obstacles, notably impediments to securities trading across national borders, further inhibit capital market integration.[32] Most importantly, however, given that financial market integration in the EU is predominantly reliant on regulatory interventions,[33] the failure to establish a conducive environment for cross-border capital market activity is primarily attributed to the EU's inability to eliminate legislative or regulatory barriers in critical legal domains. Indeed, despite substantial harmonisation in EU securities law, Europe has consistently faced a lack of convergence in implementing, supervising and enforcing these frameworks, resulting in legal uncertainty for market actors. Meanwhile, in non-harmonised areas, particularly within the private realm of capital markets, national measures and the absence of standardisation have erected additional barriers to capital

[26] While price indicators capture discrepancies in prices or returns caused by the geographic origin of the assets, quantity indicators try to quantify the effects of market frictions faced by the demand for and supply of investment opportunities, see L Baele et al, 'Measuring Financial Integration in the Euro Area', European Central Bank Occasional Paper Series No. 14 (April 2004) 11.

[27] Between 2009 and 2013, the total capital inflows directed to EU economies from abroad decreased from approximately 15% of GDP in the period 2004–2009 to an average of 5%, indicating the fragmentation of EU financial markets as a whole.

[28] See generally I Gonçalves Raposo and A Lehmann, 'Equity finance and capital market integration in Europe', Bruegel Policy Contribution, Issue No 3, January 2019, 10 and the studies cited there.

[29] Commission Staff Working Document, 'European Financial Stability and Integration Review (EFSIR), SWD (2020) 40 final, 3 March 2020, 17–18.

[30] See especially L Guiso, P Sapienza and L Zingales, 'Does Culture Affect Economic Outcomes?' (2006) 20 *Journal of Economic Perspectives* 23.

[31] See eg R Portes and H Rey, 'The determinants of cross-border equity flows' (2005) 65 *Journal of International Economics* 269.

[32] S Kalemli-Ozcan et al, 'Financial Integration and Risk Sharing: The Role of the Monetary Union' in B Mackowiak et al (eds), *The Euro at Ten: Lessons and Challenges*, (European Central Bank, 2009).

[33] N Moloney, *EU Securities and Financial Markets Regulation*, 4th edn (OUP, 2023) 8.

movement, thereby limiting market actors from fully leveraging the potential of these markets. Moreover, EU company law has traditionally focused on harmonising specific essential provisions for safeguarding shareholders and creditors of EU companies. On the contrary, substantive company law and models of corporate governance vary significantly among Member States, thus hampering the integration process. Besides, considerable disparities in insolvency and tax laws across Member States have heightened uncertainty and costs for both issuers and investors, further hindering the emergence of a pan-European market.[34]

The fragmentation of EU capital markets became even more pronounced in financially weaker economies that were disproportionately reliant on bank finance, primarily due to the absence of 'real' cross-border banking integration. Between 1999 and 2007, the period following the establishment of the euro area and preceding the financial crisis, banking integration relied excessively on cross-border interbank lending.[35] However, these interbank claims were unevenly distributed, with inflows largely concentrated in peripheral countries, which fuelled local credit bubbles and increased vulnerability to sudden capital reversals.[36] These results became apparent in 2008, amidst the dual impact of the global financial crisis and the euro area sovereign debt crisis. This adverse economic setting not only halted any progress of credit market integration but also triggered a process of financial fragmentation,[37] with banking activities, assets, and risks relocating back to home jurisdictions in an attempt to mitigate risk exposure.[38] As a consequence, cross-border capital flows to banks in the euro area and the EU decreased both in absolute and relative terms,[39] making access to bank lending extremely challenging and costly, especially in those Member States that experienced acute sovereign funding stress. Even today, despite the unprecedented policy interventions that stabilised the financial fragmentation process, pre-crisis levels have not been attained.[40]

[34] Commission Staff Working Document, 'Initial Reflections on the Obstacles to the Development of Deep and Integrated EU Capital Markets', accompanying the document Green Paper Building a Capital Markets Union, SWD (2015) 13 final, 18 February 2015, 14–21.

[35] M Hoffmann et al, 'Banking integration in the EMU: Let's get real!' (*VOX CEPR Policy Portal*, 10 January 2019) cepr.org/voxeu/columns/banking-integration-emu-lets-get-real; P Hartmann, A Maddaloni and S Manganelli, 'The Euro-Area Financial System: Structure, Integration and Policy Initiatives' (2003) 19 *Oxford Review of Economic Policy* 180; PR Lane, 'EMU and Financial Integration', Institute for International Integration Studies Discussion Papers, No 272, December 2008; A Sapir and G Wolff, 'The neglected side of banking union: reshaping Europe's financial system' Bruegel Policy Contributions Issue No 792, September 2013.

[36] SWD (2015) 183 final (n 7) 11.

[37] N Battistini, M Pagano and S Simonelli, 'Systemic Risk and Home Bias in the Euro Area', European Economy, Economic Papers 494, April 2013.

[38] D Schoenmaker, 'Post-Crisis Reversal in Banking and Insurance Integration: An Empirical Survey', European Economy, Economic Papers 496, April 2013.

[39] S Merler and J Pisani-Ferry, 'Sudden stops in the Euro area', Bruegel Policy Contribution Issue No 06, March 2012; Lane (n 35).

[40] See especially ECB, 'Financial Integration and Structure in the Euro Area', April 2022.

B. An Evolving Project in a Dynamic Environment

The outlined deficiencies in the EU financial system illuminate the specific context that prompted the formation of the CMU initiative. Yet, translating this ambition into a concrete reform agenda has proven challenging, given the highly volatile economic and political environment that characterises the evolution of the CMU project. The 2016 decision of the UK to withdraw from the EU, the dramatic impact of the COVID-19 pandemic and the ascent of the sustainable finance agenda keep reshaping the identity of the CMU which, nearly a decade after its introduction, grapples with defining its place within the EU financial policy spectrum. This stands in stark contrast to the other major post-crisis reform in the European financial sector, namely the Banking Union, the main aspects of which were clear from the outset, focusing on establishing a comprehensive and harmonised regulatory framework in the banking sector, encompassing both substantive and primarily institutional aspects.[41]

i. The CMU Green Paper

In February 2015, amid ongoing struggles faced by several EU countries due to the crisis, the Commission initiated a three-month consultation via a Green Paper with the aim 'to develop an action plan to put in place the building blocks for a fully functioning CMU by 2019'.[42] Starting from the Commission's top priority to foster a 'sustainable return to growth and job creation', and the necessity to make Europe 'more resilient to future shocks', the Green Paper emphasised the increased role that capital markets should play in channelling funds to the economy. Accordingly, the CMU vision was specified, that would be the creation of a 'true single market for capital' which should strengthen the flow of capital from investors to European investment projects, ultimately improving the allocation of risk and financial assets across the EU.[43] However, apart from setting the perimeter of the CMU project, the Green Paper provided limited specificity regarding its implementation agenda. Instead, it focused on broadly delineating key policy priorities, describing areas of regulatory intervention that already garnered widespread support (eg, reviewing the Prospectus Directive or reforming the securitisation regime), and suggesting potential areas for future action. The degree of 'constructive ambiguity' evident at this early stage of the initiative's development was clearly an attempt

[41] For a comprehensive analysis of the BU and its measures, see D Busch and G Ferrarini (eds), *European Banking Union* (OUP, 2015); J-H Binder and C Gortsos, *The European Banking Union: a compendium* (Beck/Hart Publishing, 2016); J-H Binder et al (eds), *European Banking Union: Brussels Commentary* (Nomos/Hart Publishing, 2023).

[42] Commission, 'Green Paper on Building a Capital Markets Union', COM (2015) 63 final, 18 February 2015, 3.

[43] ibid 3, 4.

to secure the widest possible support from Member States,[44] particularly the UK, whose relations with Brussels were already strained.[45] And the Commission largely succeeded in this endeavour, as the CMU proposal received considerable support from local stakeholders right from the outset, including notably the City of London and major political actors.[46]

ii. The 2015 CMU Action Plan

The foundational building blocks for establishing a fully-fledged CMU would be illustrated shortly after the conclusion of the relevant consultations. In September 2015, the Commission unveiled its 'Action Plan on Building a Capital Markets Union'.[47] Consistent with the Green Paper, the Action Plan provided a comprehensive depiction of the state of play in European capital markets. It reiterated that the aspiration of the CMU would be to transform this situation by pursuing both to strengthen capital markets in all Member States, thereby complementing Europe's strong tradition on banking finance, and to further deepen the level of integration of these markets.[48] At the same time, it presented the initial areas of intervention along with the accompanying short and mid-term regulatory reforms and market-led initiatives which should cumulatively create a coherent framework for putting a single market for capital into place.[49] In the meantime, the Commission committed to ongoing efforts in identifying additional barriers that hinder more robust and integrated capital markets in Europe, also pledging to introduce additional measures by 2017, after evaluating the progress achieved by that period.[50]

iii. The 2017 Mid-term Review and Brexit

In early 2017, the European Commission launched a consultation on the mid-term review of the CMU.[51] It sought to gather insights into how the proposed measures

[44] For the role of ambiguity as a strategy in enabling broad coalitions during contentious projects in the history of European integration, see S Hoffmann, *The European Sisyphus: Essays on Europe, 1964–1994* (Westview Press, 1995).

[45] For some commentators, the CMU represented a political gesture which aimed at keeping the UK an active part of the EU, by prioritising an area of the single market where the former possessed a clear competitive advantage, W-G Ringe, 'Capital Markets Union for Europe: A Commitment to the Single Market of 28' (2015) 9 *Law and Financial Markets Review* 5.

[46] For example, the House of Lords viewed the CMU as a 'golden opportunity to promote capital markets as an alternative to bank funding and, therefore, enhance the role of the City of London in the functioning of the EU economy', European Union Committee, *The post-crisis EU financial regulatory framework: do the pieces fit?* (HL 2014–15, 103) 94.

[47] Commission, 'Action Plan on Building a Capital Markets Union', COM (2015) 468 final, 30 September 2015.

[48] ibid 3.

[49] Chief among the proposed regulatory reforms were those leading to the 2017 EU Securitisation Regulation, the 2017 Prospectus Regulation and the 2019 SME Growth Market Reform Regulation.

[50] COM (2015) 468 final (n 47) 28.

[51] Commission, 'Consultation Document on Capital Markets Union Mid-Term Review 2017', 20 January 2017.

outlined in the 2015 CMU Action Plan could be adjusted and concluded in light of political changes and evolving market conditions, which were transforming the structure and operation of EU capital markets. At that time, the UK's referendum vote in favour of exiting the Single Market; the significant opportunities, along with the risks, associated with the application of technology-enabled innovation in the financial sector (FinTech); as well as the pressing need to mobilise additional resources for socially, economically, and environmentally sustainable investments were posing substantial new challenges to the goal of achieving a truly integrated and efficient EU capital market. Consequently, it was deemed necessary to reassess the CMU and its reform agenda.[52]

Considering the UK's central role in the development of the CMU project, some commentators expressed scepticism about the future of this initiative, suggesting that Brexit would, at the very least, negatively impact its completion.[53] However, EU policy makers saw an opportunity to accelerate the implementation of initial measures and intensify the reform efforts.[54] As a result, in the Mid-term review published in June 2017,[55] the Commission not only reaffirmed its commitment to further deepening and integrating the EU capital market framework but also aspired to revamp the CMU agenda in response to the changing dynamics of EU policymaking.[56] This involved placing greater emphasis on centralised supervision with corresponding enhancement of ESMA's role,[57] alongside a stronger focus on increasing the capacity of Europe's regional markets in an attempt to offset the City's departure.[58]

iv. The New CMU Action Plan and the COVID-19 Crisis

By the end of its term, the Juncker administration had largely fulfilled its key promise to submit the legislative proposals laid out in the 2015 CMU Action Plan and the Mid-term review.[59] Nevertheless, it remained uncertain whether or when these initiatives would steer the EU towards a more balanced financial system,

[52] See especially D Busch, 'A Capital Markets Union for a Divided Europe' (2017) 3 *Journal of Financial Regulation* 262, 263; W-G Ringe, 'The Politics of Capital Markets Union: From Brexit to Eurozone' in Allen et al (eds) (n 4) 341.

[53] D Howarth and L Quaglia, 'Brexit and the Single European Financial Market' (2017) 55 (s1) *Journal of Common Market Studies* 149, 152–53.

[54] Commission, 'Capital Markets Union – Accelerating Reform', COM (2016) 601 final (14 September 2016); European Council meeting conclusions, 28 June 2016.

[55] Commission, 'Mid-Term Review of the Capital Markets Union Action Plan', COM (2017) 292 final, 8 June 2017.

[56] Ringe (n 52) 345–46.

[57] On the enhanced role of ESMA following Brexit and the Commission's 2017 proposals, see generally N Moloney, *The Age of ESMA: Governing EU Financial Markets* (Hart Publishing, 2018).

[58] Commission Staff Working Document, 'Economic analysis accompanying the Mid-Term Review of the Capital Markets Union Action Plan' SWD (2017) 224 final, 8 June 2017, 14, 20–21.

[59] European Commission, 'Capital Markets Union: progress on building a single market for capital for a strong Economic and Monetary Union', COM (2019) 136 final, 15 March 2019, 3–4.

where deeper and more integrated capital markets would reduce Europe's heavy dependence on banks. Indeed, achieving a fully-fledged CMU is a long-term endeavour which requires not only time, effort, and resources but also, crucially, a steadfast political commitment and active involvement from all Member States and relevant stakeholders. In this context, in late 2019, the Commission launched a High-Level Forum (HLF), with the mandate to feed into its work on future CMU policies. Drawing on the HLF's final recommendations,[60] the von der Leyen Commission presented a new action plan in September 2020,[61] comprising 16 actions, which cumulatively aimed at finally completing the ambitious and overdue project of building a CMU that serves European citizens and businesses.

The overarching themes addressed in the new CMU Action Plan are broadly aligned with the Commission's key priorities for the 2019–2024 term.[62] These encompass, in particular, supporting the green transition and digital transformation, fostering a more inclusive and robust economy, enhancing the international role of the euro, and boosting the competitiveness and financial autonomy of the EU.[63] What is particularly notable, though, is the acknowledgement of the vital role that an effective CMU could play in alleviating the detrimental effects of the COVID-19 pandemic on the EU economy.[64] Initial responses to the COVID-19 crisis involved massive financial aid injected into affected businesses and households by the EU,[65] Member State governments,[66] and central banks.[67] Nonetheless, considering the scale and anticipated duration of the crisis, a substantial amount of capital will be required to revive the economy, which, based on recent history, cannot be derived solely through bank loans and public funds. It therefore comes as no surprise that the removal of barriers impeding the development and integration of EU capital markets forms a pivotal element of the Commission's post-COVID-19 recovery strategy.[68]

[60] High-Level Forum on the Capital Markets Union (n 7).

[61] Commission, 'A Capital Markets Union for People and Businesses-New Action Plan', COM (2020) 590 final, 24 September 2020.

[62] von der Leyen (n 6). See also the European Commission's Priorities for 2019–2024, commission.europa.eu/strategy-and-policy/priorities-2019-2024_en.

[63] COM (2020) 590 final (n 61) 4–6.

[64] ibid 1; High-Level Forum on the Capital Markets Union (n 7) 4.

[65] Commission, 'Europe's moment: Repair and Prepare for the Next Generation', COM (2020) 456 final, 27 May 2020.

[66] For the measures taken by EU countries to weather the crisis, see OECD COVID 19 Policy Tracker, oecd.github.io/OECD-covid-action-map/.

[67] P Cavallino and F De Fiore, 'Central banks' response to Covid-19 in advanced economies' BIS Bulletin No 21, 5 June 2020, bis.org/publ/bisbull21.htm.

[68] This became even more apparent in July 2020 when the Commission adopted the Capital Markets Recovery Package, incorporating targeted adjustments to key EU capital market rules which are at the core of the CMU, Commission, 'Coronavirus response: Making capital markets work for Europe's recovery', 24 July 2020, Press Release, ec.europa.eu/commission/presscorner/detail/en/ip_20_1382.

III. The Objectives of the CMU

A. Strategic Objective

The preceding analysis of the historical context and evolution of the CMU project over the past decade should shed light on the strategic objective guiding this policy initiative. In broad terms, this entails establishing a more resilient and diversified financial system by advancing the development of EU capital markets and increasing their level of integration.[69] Deciphering the specifics of this objective has been quite challenging, however. Hence, this section seeks to clarify how the vision of more developed and integrated capital markets translates into practice.

i. Fostering the Development of EU Capital Markets

Capital markets development is shaped by two key factors: first, the size of these markets, measured by the aggregate value of non-bank financial institutions' activity relative to GDP; and second, market liquidity which essentially reflects the number of participants (both buyers and sellers) involved in capital markets and the resulting transaction volumes they generate. While the overall size of capital markets has increased significantly since the CMU was launched,[70] there persists a perceptible discrepancy across Member States.[71] Capital markets across the EU not only lag behind their US counterparts, as mentioned earlier, but they also remain relatively smaller in terms of GDP output compared to pre-crisis levels.[72] In this regard, the CMU's strategic objective of fostering the development of capital markets in all Member States reflects the need to increase the size of market-based financing mechanisms in the EU and the liquidity of their supporting infrastructures (eg, stock exchanges).

However, this is not a straightforward task. For one thing, it requires deep pools of long-term capital, such as pension and insurance assets, as well as direct investments, given that no market can thrive without the influx of savings or funds into market instruments.[73] In other words, the development of capital markets

[69] SWD (2015) 183 final (n 7) 8. See also Ringe (n 45) 5; P Schammo, 'Capital Markets Union and Small and Medium-Sized Enterprises (SMEs): A Preliminary Assessment' in Allen, Carletti and Gray (eds) (n 23) 146.

[70] However, it is debatable whether the rise in market activity can be attributed to the CMU or if it instead the result of the natural process of recovery from the financial crisis.

[71] In 2019, for example, capital markets in Central and Eastern Europe significantly lagged behind those in Northern European countries like the Netherlands and Sweden. Even among more developed countries, there was significant variation in market size, with Spanish markets being less than half the size of those in Germany, European Court of Auditors (n 25) 8 (Figure 1).

[72] P Asimakopoulos and W Wright, 'Unlocking the Growth Potential in European Capital Markets Analysis of the Size, Depth & Growth Potential of Capital Markets in the EU' (*New Financial*, June 2019) 10–12.

[73] COM (2015) 63 final (n 42) 16.

hinges on sizeable investment demand from diverse investors with distinct risk-return profiles and financial capacities, who are willing to allocate their investable resources. This implies, in turn, that on the supply side a wide range of financial instruments exists, offering diverse choices of issuers, credit risks, etc., to cater to the investment needs of all categories of asset demand. In order for this to occur, more companies need to be willing to turn to capital markets to finance their operations. This largely depends on the availability of additional and more attractive financing options, allowing them to better match their funding needs with available investment capital.

But apart from expanding their size and depth, more developed capital markets also reflect the need for better functioning market-based funding channels. The primary function of these markets, which renders them indispensable for the entire financial system, lies in providing a venue where corporations in search of long-term equity and debt capital can connect with investors interested in offering such capital.[74] Put differently, capital markets fulfil the critical financial intermediation role of redistributing resources from economic agents with surplus funds to entities in need of those funds.[75] In that sense, the aim of further developing capital markets in the EU, as provided for in the CMU initiative, reflects the endeavour to improve their efficiency as intermediaries between the supply and demand of investment capital. In this context, therefore, the development of capital markets is also tied to their efficient functioning.

The extent, now, to which a capital market can be considered efficient is basically determined by three factors. First, available investment capital should be allocated to its most productive uses, ie where it is most urgently needed and can be most promisingly employed ('allocational efficiency').[76] The efficient allocation of resources is primarily associated with the ability of prices to accurately and swiftly reflect all available information, thereby indicating the true value of the underlying financial instrument ('informational efficiency').[77] According to the semi-strong form of the Efficient Capital Market Hypothesis (ECMH),[78] stock prices will readily, though not always immediately,[79] adjust to the release

[74] For an analysis of the main functions of financial systems, see J Armour et al, *Principles of Financial Regulation* (OUP, 2016) 24 ff.

[75] J Madura, *Financial Markets and Institutions*, 11th edn (Cengage Learning, 2015) 15; K Pilbeam, *Finance and Financial Markets*, 2nd edn (Palgrave Macmillan, 2005) 22.

[76] S Tadesse, 'The Allocation and Monitoring Role of Capital Markets: Theory and International Evidence' (2004) 39 *Journal of Financial and Quantitative Analysis* 701, 705.

[77] For the allocational function of capital markets via the price mechanism, see eg SJ Grossman and JE Stiglitz, 'On the Impossibility of Informationally Efficient Markets' (1980) 70 *The American Economic Review* 393; SJ Grossman, 'Further results on the informational efficiency of competitive stock markets' (1978) 18 *Journal of Economic Theory* 81.

[78] EF Fama, 'Efficient Capital Markets: A Review of Theory and Empirical Work' (1970) 25 *The Journal of Finance* 383.

[79] The rapidity of prices' response to available information is 'relative', meaning that markets are more or less efficient depending on how quickly they yield efficient equilibrium prices, see especially RJ Gilson and RH Kraakman, 'The Mechanisms of Market Efficiency' (1984) 70 *Virginia Law Review* 549, 560.

of all commercially exploitable and relevant information about an issuer's business or transactions, thus serving as 'accurate signals for resource allocation'.[80] Under such conditions, investors will be able to thoroughly assess the quality of the instruments offered and the associated risks, thus reducing the likelihood of making 'wrong' investment decisions.[81] Second, investors should have confidence in the integrity of the market mechanism,[82] which, in turn, stimulates their active participation in the market and prevents them from withdrawing their money from it ('institutional efficiency').[83] A consistent regulatory system regarding market transparency, combined with an effective and independent supervisory and enforcement mechanism, are the most important preconditions towards this direction.[84] Finally, non-income producing expenses (ie, transaction costs) that market participants, especially borrowers and investors, encounter when accessing and transacting in the market should be reduced,[85] ensuring they are reasonable and fair[86] for all parties involved ('operational efficiency').[87] This is achieved, on the one hand, by decreasing issuers' costs linked to raising capital in the market and the subsequent expenses of remaining in the market. On the other hand, it entails reducing the costs incurred by investors while searching for and assessing the attributes of financial instruments.

ii. Deepening Capital Market Integration in the EU

The establishment of a fully integrated single market for capital stands as the second major pillar of the CMU's strategic objective. Capital market integration generally involves the financial interconnection of markets across various countries, seeking to enhance private risk sharing through cross-regional asset holdings and achieve price and return convergence for financial assets and services within

[80] Fama (n 78) 383.

[81] L Enriques and S Gilotta, 'Disclosure and Financial Market Regulation' in E Ferran, N Moloney and J Payne (eds), *Oxford Handbook on Financial Regulation* (OUP, 2014) 514–15.

[82] M Oulds, in S Kümpel and A Wittig (eds), *Bank- und Kapitalmarktrecht*, 2nd edn (Beck, 2011) 1833; N Vokuhl, *Kapitalmarktrechtlicher Anlegerschutz und Kapitalerhaltung in der Aktiengesellschaft* (Nomos, 2007) 180.

[83] H Brinckmann, in R Veil (ed), *European Capital Markets Law*, 2nd edn (Hart Publishing, 2017) 268–69.

[84] BS Black, 'The Legal and Institutional Preconditions for Strong Securities Markets' (2001) 48 *UCLA Law Review* 781, 790 ff. Especially concerning the significance of price accuracy in fostering investor trust in the market and consequently improving its liquidity, see M Kahan, 'Securities Laws and the social costs of "inaccurate" stock prices' (1992) 41 *Duke Law Journal* 979, 1017–25.

[85] S Grundmann, *Bankvertragsrecht. Investment Banking II* (De Gruyter 2016) 16; FJ Fabozzi and P Peterson Drake, *Finance: Capital Markets, Financial Management, and Investment Management* (Wiley, 2009) 114.

[86] This is mainly achieved by placing the burden of transaction costs bearing on those who can better afford or diminish them, in line with the concept of the cheapest cost avoider, see RH Coase, 'The Problem of Social Cost', (1960) 3 *The Journal of Law & Economics* 1.

[87] R Veil, 'Concept and Aims of Capital Markets Regulation' in Veil (ed) (n 83) 25.

the same risk category.[88] For capital markets in different countries to be considered fully integrated, the following three conditions should cumulatively apply to all potential market participants sharing the same characteristics: a) a unified set of legal rules for offering or dealing with specific financial instruments or services, b) equal access to market-based activities (such as capital-raising, investing, and financial intermediation) in the interconnected national markets, and c) fair treatment while active in these markets.[89] Based on this definition, capital markets integration exhibits three key features. First, it remains independent of distinct financial structures and varying levels of financial development among countries. This suggests that market integration does not inherently lead to a convergence in financial structures or ensure uniform availability and depth of funding tools. Consequently, a country's preference for a bank-based or market-based financial structure may persist despite the integration process.[90] Second, even upon completing market integration, frictions in accessing or investing capital may persist. This implies that the yardstick for deeming national capital markets as integrated is not the complete absence of impediments to optimal capital allocation, but rather whether any remaining frictions affect these markets symmetrically.[91] Finally, full integration mandates ensuring equal access to market activities and financial services for all participants, regardless of their location, along with fair treatment once market access is granted. Hence, any systematic discrimination against foreign market participants within a financial area indicates that the relevant markets are not fully integrated.[92]

The ambition to integrate EU capital markets is not new, dating back to the Treaty of Rome in 1957 and its goal to create a single market enabling the free movement of capital and services among its Member States. However, it has evolved considerably over the years, influenced by a complex interplay of economic, social, and political factors. The groundwork for a European capital market was laid in 1966 with the release of the influential Segré Report,[93] which shaped numerous market integration themes that remain pertinent in

[88] G de Brouwer, 'Monetary and Financial Integration in Asia: Empirical Evidence and Issues' in Asian Development Bank (ed), *Asian Economic Cooperation and Integration: Progress, Prospects, and Challenges* (Asian Development Bank, 2005) 269–98; D Valiante, *Europe's Untapped Capital Market: Rethinking financial integration after the crisis* (CEPS, 2016) 45.

[89] Baele et al (n 26) 6.

[90] It has been observed, for example, that the significance of currency deposits and loans across euro area countries has become more diverse over time, even following the introduction of the euro, which was a significant stride towards financial integration, see Hartmann, Maddaloni and Manganelli (n 35).

[91] For instance, if all financial contracts in Germany and France are written in English, it represents a friction that symmetrically impacts the citizens of both countries. Thus, it does not constitute a barrier to financial integration between the two countries, see Baele et al (n 26) 6.

[92] However, a market can also be partially integrated. This situation may occur if, for example, a country or a region does not favour domestic investors over foreign ones but imposes restrictions on the listings of foreign firms on the domestic exchange, ibid 7.

[93] European Economic Community, 'The Development of a European Capital Market', Report of a Group of Experts appointed by the EEC Commission, November 1966.

today's regulatory landscape. Taking stock of the fragmentation of capital market at that time, attributed to Member States imposing divergent and duplicative rules on market participants, it highlighted the benefits of market integration and suggested remedies that resulted in the first set of issuer disclosure Directives from 1979 to 1982.[94] These measures sought to construct a single securities market, making it easier for issuers to raise capital by eradicating disparities among Member States' laws through comprehensive harmonisation of national rules and regulations.[95] The second phase ensued in 1985 with the Commission publishing its Internal Market White Paper.[96] Building on the European Court of Justice's landmark ruling on *Cassis de Dijon*,[97] the White Paper outlined a series of actions aimed at achieving a single market by 1992. It also emphasised the Commission's intention to expedite the integration process by combining a minimum harmonisation approach, allowing flexibility and innovation at the national level, with the concept of mutual recognition. Particularly concerning capital markets, it perceived the 'liberalization of financial services, linked to capital movements, as representing a major step towards financial integration in the Community and the widening of the Internal Market'.[98] Accordingly, it expanded the regulatory scope of the harmonisation programme to encompass, besides disclosure-oriented issuer-related reforms,[99] the first investment services regime in the securities sector.[100]

The introduction of the single currency in 1999 marked the beginning of the third phase in the evolution of EU capital markets law. In this changing monetary and economic environment, the mutual recognition model was deemed insufficient on its own to drive the integration of EU financial markets.[101] In response, the Commission actively pursued the development of appropriate legal reforms to strengthen financial market integration. The work programme for implementing

[94] These included Council Directive 79/279/EEC coordinating the conditions for the admission of securities to official stock exchange listing [1979] OJ L 66/21; Council Directive 80/390/EEC coordinating the requirements for the drawing up, scrutiny and distribution of the listing particulars to be published for the admission of securities to official stock exchange listing [1980] OJ L100/1; and Council Directive 82/121/EEC on information to be published on a regular basis by companies the shares of which have been admitted to official stock-exchange listing [1982] OJ L48/26.

[95] Moloney (n 33) 83.

[96] Commission, 'Completing the Internal Market: White Paper from the Commission to the Council', COM (85) 310 final, 14 September 1985.

[97] Case 120/78 *Rewe-Zentral AG v Bundesmonopolverwaltung für Branntwein* ECLI:EU:C:1979:42, [1979] ECR 649.

[98] Commission, *White Paper*, COM (85) 310 final (n 96) 27.

[99] Namely Council Directive 88/627/EEC on the information to be published when a major holding in a listed company is acquired or is disposed of [1988] OJ L348/62; Council Directive 89/298/EEC coordinating the requirements for the drawing-up, scrutiny and distribution of the prospectus to be published when transferable securities are offered to the public [1989] OJ L124/8; and Directive 89/592/EEC coordinating regulations on insider dealing [1989] OJ L334/30.

[100] Directive 93/22/EEC on investment services in the securities field [1993] OJ L141/27.

[101] Commission, 'Financial Services: Building a Framework for Action', COM (1998) 625 final, 28 October 1998.

these reforms was delineated in the Financial Services Action Plan (FSAP).[102] The FSAP signalled a significant shift in the harmonisation approach, by centralising regulation within the EU marketplace. This aimed to limit national control over financial market rules, thus preventing 'gold plating' and ensuring effective implementation. Further impetus to this approach was given from the Lamfalussy Report[103] which introduced the seminal four-level regulatory process in financial services.[104] At the end of the FSAP era, the EU had in place a comprehensive regulatory framework for financial markets, consisting mainly of the 2003 Prospectus Directive, the 2004 Transparency Directive, the 2004 Markets in Financial Instruments Directive ('MiFID I'), and the 2003 Market Abuse Directive ('MAD').[105]

However, the financial and sovereign debt crises revealed that, despite numerous horizontal regulatory measures implemented over the years, substantial divergences persisted among the regulatory approaches of Member States. Simultaneously, they unveiled the mismatch between the Pan-EU operation of market actors and the national boundaries of supervision regimes.[106] In this post-crisis framework, a fourth phase of EU capital markets law emerged, focusing on completing the 'single rulebook' and the supervisory architecture.[107] It also sought to bridge regulatory gaps among Member States by increasing the use of directly applicable regulations. Aligned with this expansive regulatory context, the CMU surpasses previous policy initiatives in this field, by encompassing a series of actions aimed at advancing European capital markets from mere mutual recognition toward achieving supervisory and regulatory convergence, ultimately benefiting the entire EU economy. In this regard, the CMU's strategic objective of further integrating EU capital markets highlights the necessity for a more sustainable process of market integration. This should facilitate heightened cross-border market activity and risk-sharing among Member States, thus also adding further value to post-crisis reforms, notably the BU, in the pursuit of establishing a truly single financial system in the EU.[108]

B. Overarching Objectives

In the previous section, it was explained that the core of the CMU initiative revolves around establishing a more complete and diversified financial system,

[102] Commission, 'Implementing the Framework for Financial Markets: Action Plan', COM (1999) 232 final, 11 May 1999.

[103] Committee of Wise Men on the Regulation of European Securities Markets, Final Report, 15 February 2001.

[104] See generally Moloney (n 33) 864.

[105] See Directive 2003/71/EC [2003] OJ L345/64; Directive 2004/109/EC [2004] OJ L390/38; Directive 2004/39/EC [2004] OJ L145/1; and Directive 2003/6/EC [2003] OJ L96/16 respectively.

[106] See generally N Moloney, 'EU Financial Market Regulation after the Global Financial Crisis: "More Europe" or more Risks?' (2010) 47 *CML Rev* 1317.

[107] Report of the High-Level Group in Financial Supervision in the EU, 25 February 2009.

[108] The Five Presidents Report, 'Completing Europe's Economic and Monetary Union', 22 June 2015, 12.

by placing greater emphasis on the development of well-functioning, deep and integrated capital markets. However, this strategic objective is not an end in itself but rather an essential means for advancing the overarching objectives set by the EU[109] concerning both the end-users of capital markets, namely companies and investors,[110] and the economy as a whole. With regard to the former, an efficient single market for capital is crucial for improving businesses' access to funds and providing investors with additional opportunities to put their money to work.[111] From a broader macroeconomic perspective, stronger and more integrated capital markets are considered vital for securing a more sustainable growth path and safeguarding financial stability in the EU.[112]

i. *Improving Access to Finance for Businesses*

a. Financing Needs and Options Across the Corporate Lifecycle

A business can finance its operations and investments in productive capacity either through internally generated funds or by sourcing funds externally.[113] In the former case, funds principally comprise profits retained within the company instead of being distributed to shareholders. External funding, on the other hand, primarily consists of proceeds derived from equity and debt issuances,[114] as well as bank loans. Generally, EU companies tend to prefer internal financing over external funding sources, given especially the potential impact on corporate governance and control that the latter may entail.[115]

However, the need for external financing features prominently in every stage of a firm's lifecycle, whether for basic maintenance or for further expansion and growth. The particular funding requirements of a business vary depending on several factors, including its stage of development, growth objectives, innovativeness, operational sector, and risk tolerance.[116] More specifically, during the

[109] COM (2020) 590 final (n 61) 2.

[110] For the focus of the CMU on the end-users of capital markets, see eg Parliament, 'Resolution of 19 January 2016 on stocktaking and challenges of the EU Financial Services Regulation: impact and the way forward towards a more efficient and effective EU framework for Financial Regulation and a Capital Markets Union', para 2.

[111] SWD (2015) 183 final (n 7) 13.

[112] COM (2015) 63 final (n 42) 4. See also N Anderson et al, 'A European Capital Markets Union: implications for growth and stability', Bank of England, Financial Stability Paper No. 33, February 2015.

[113] For a more comprehensive analysis of these primary forms of business financing and other intermediate options, see E Ferran, *Company Law and Corporate Finance* (OUP, 1999) 457 ff.; IG McNeil, *An Introduction to the Law on Financial Investment*, 2nd edn (Hart Publishing, 2005) 208 ff.

[114] In certain cases, companies issue hybrid financial instruments which incorporate both equity and debt characteristics and include, among others, preference shares, convertible bonds and bonds with warrants attached.

[115] For an analysis of the factors influencing corporate finance structures, see E Ferran and L-C Ho, *Principles of Corporate Finance Law* (OUP, 2008) 54–56.

[116] N Churchill and V Lewis, 'The Five Stages of Small Business Growth' *Harvard Business Review*, May 1983.

start-up phase, a company needs funding for researching, evaluating, and/or developing an initial idea or project. Given the typical absence of retained earnings during this phase, the firm typically secures funding from external sources, mostly from 'family, friends, and fools'.[117] When a company succeeds in establishing its project or idea, it enters the growth stage, generating a steady income and attracting new consumers. Despite increased retained earnings, the demand for external financing remains high at this stage, primarily sourced from bank loans, peer-to-business lending, and private equity.[118] As a firm expands and strengthens its position in the market, its financing structures tend to adjust to its profits, retained earnings, and available collateral. During this expansion phase, businesses often seek to leverage their stability by issuing shares or bonds to the public. In the final stage of a firm's lifecycle, its ability to sustain growth declines. If all retained earnings have been utilised, the company may need to exit the market unless external financing can be secured.[119]

b. The Financing Constraints of EU Companies

Despite the progress made since the introduction of the 2015 CMU Action Plan, the realisation of an ideal scenario where companies at different developmental stages can meet their diverse funding needs remains elusive. On the contrary, European companies, particularly smaller ones, encounter numerous constraints in accessing external funding.[120] Several factors have contributed to this situation. Most notably, EU capital markets, which could significantly broaden the external financing options for firms, not only remain fragmented but often lack the desired size and depth.[121] This becomes apparent when comparing the financing structures of EU companies with those of other advanced economies. For example, the size of equity markets in Europe, measured as the total market capitalisation of listed firms relative to GDP, is significantly smaller compared to the US and Japan.[122] Similarly, the level of venture capital investments is nearly ten times lower in EU countries (relative to their GDP) than in the US.[123] Furthermore, structural challenges, especially the high costs associated with financing through EU public equity

[117] DJ Cumming and SA Johan, *Venture Capital and Private Equity Contracting: An International Perspective*, 2nd edn (Elsevier, 2014) 6–7.

[118] SWD (2015) 183 final (n 7) 31.

[119] ibid 32.

[120] COM (2020) 590 final (n 61) 7. Especially on the limited impact of the CMU in broadening the financing opportunities of SMEs, see European Court of Auditors (n 25) 14 ff.

[121] Commission Staff Working Document, 'Impact Assessment Report accompanying the Proposal for a Regulation amending Regulations (EU) 2017/1129, (EU) No 596/2014 and (EU) No 600/2014 to make public capital markets in the Union more attractive for companies and to facilitate access to capital for small and medium-sized enterprises' SWD (2022) 762 final, 7 December 2022, 14.

[122] M Demertzis, M Domínguez-Jiménez and L Guetta-Jeanrenaud, 'Europe Should not Neglect its Capital Markets Union', Bruegel Policy Contribution Issue No 13, June 2021, 4–5.

[123] ibid 6–7.

markets – largely due to extensive disclosure and reporting requirements[124] – are not only deterring businesses from entering and raising funds in these markets,[125] but have also led to a surge of companies' delisting.[126] Besides high costs, EU businesses, particularly SMEs, face information limitations and a restricted investor base, since they are often unaware of available market-based funding options. At the same time, due to market fragmentation, they might not always be visible to potential investors outside their country of registration.[127] Finally, certain firm-specific factors, including poor credit standing, insufficient profitability, absence of viable business plans, and engagement in industries requiring restructuring, also adversely impact the accessibility of external funding for EU enterprises.[128]

c. The CMU as a Tool for Supporting the 'Real' Economy

The preceding analysis suggests that EU capital markets are not effectively fulfilling their role in providing the necessary growth capital to businesses across the Union. Even among listed firms, reliance on bank financing is significantly higher compared to other developed regions, as highlighted by the distribution of debt-to-equity ratios.[129] In this context, the development of deeper and more integrated capital markets, as envisioned in the CMU, plays a crucial role in complementing Europe's strong tradition of banking finance and can further contribute to supporting the real economy.[130] More specifically, by expanding and diversifying funding avenues for businesses, eliminating cross-border capital raising barriers, lowering capital costs and bridging the information gap between borrowers and investors, the CMU is expected to provide substantial advantages to EU companies seeking funds for scaling up or restructuring. For instance, SMEs at the beginning of the funding escalator will find it easier to secure seed and early-stage funding from alternative market sources like venture capital funds. Meanwhile, larger and established medium-sized businesses will have improved access to public markets, both domestically and cross-border. This situation should particularly benefit firms and investment projects in Member States with less developed financial sectors, as it will facilitate their ability to attract foreign capital.[131] Additionally, all firms could benefit from more affordable access to credit, as capital markets will probably

[124] For a detailed analysis of initial and ongoing listing costs, see Oxera, 'Primary and Secondary Equity Markets in the EU', Final Report, November 2020, 61 ff.

[125] In 2021, for example, only 11% of global IPOs took place in the EU, more than three times less compared to the US, see PwC, 'Global IPO Watch 2021' pwc.com/gx/en/audit-services/ipo-centre/assets/pwc-global-ipo-watch-2021.pdf.

[126] Since 2012, the number of delistings in EU capital markets has more than doubled, SWD (2022) 762 final, 15–16 (Figure 2).

[127] COM (2015) 468 final (n 47) 9.

[128] IMF, *Uneven Growth: Short- and Long-Term Factors*, World Economic Outlook, April 2015.

[129] Demertzis, Domínguez-Jiménez and Guetta-Jeanrenaud (n 122) 5–6.

[130] COM(2015) 468 final (n 47) 3; SWD (2015) 183 final (n 7) 13.

[131] E Labaye et al, 'A New Dawn: Reigniting Growth in Central and Eastern Europe', McKinsey Global Institute, December 2013; COM (2020) 590 final (n 61) 5.

foster competition in the financial system and alleviate borrowing constraints imposed by banks.[132]

But rather than just complementing bank financing, more developed and integrated capital markets can enable investments in projects and areas characterised by high credit risks, which banks might be hesitant to fund. This is especially true for early-stage, innovative ventures in the technology sector where the problems of uncertainty, information asymmetry and agency costs (also known as the 'trio of problems') are particularly pronounced.[133] This is attributed not only to their startup status but also to the technological or scientific risks linked to these activities, making it very challenging to assess their value in advance.[134] Moreover, given that most innovative companies often lack sufficient collateral and banks must adhere to risk-based capital requirements, it becomes apparent that the latter can only allocate a limited portion of credit to riskier projects, resulting in numerous promising ventures remaining unfunded. Capital markets, in contrast, are better placed to cover the financing needs of such enterprises. While banks serve as intermediaries between depositors and borrowers, also sharing a portion of the risk,[135] capital markets directly connect those in need of capital with potential investors. Among the latter, there exists an inherent diversity of views and risk preferences, making it possible for even the riskiest ventures to secure funding. Furthermore, certain non-bank financial intermediaries, such as investment funds, have developed specific mechanisms to address the 'trio of problems' inherent in early-stage innovative projects.[136] More generally, capital markets' ability to bundle together multiple investors, each contributing a portion of the necessary funds, enables the financing of projects that would be challenging for a single bank to fund from a microeconomic perspective. Therefore, the inclusive nature of capital markets implies that completing the CMU can help improve access to finance not only for incumbent firms but also, even more crucially, for young, risky and innovative entrepreneurial ventures.[137] This becomes increasingly significant considering that a thriving community of high-tech, pioneering companies is pivotal for Europe's digital and sustainable transition.[138]

[132] L Laeven, 'The Development of Local Capital Markets: Rationale and Challenges', IMF Working Paper 14/234, December 2014.

[133] RJ Gilson, 'Engineering a Venture Capital Market: Lessons from the American Experience' (2003) 55 *Stanford Law Review* 1067, 1070.

[134] ibid 1077. This applies to all 'credence goods', whose quality must be trusted or taken in faith, see generally U Dulleck, R Kerschbamer and M Sutter, 'The Economics of Credence Goods: An Experiment on the Role of Liability, Verifiability, Reputation, and Competition' (2011) 101 *American Economic Review* 526.

[135] For an analysis of the vital role of banks as intermediaries in the financial system and their risk transformation function, see S Grundmann, *Bankvertragsrecht. 'Organisation und Kreditwesen Bank-Kunden-Verhältnis* (De Gruyter, 2016) 6 ff.

[136] See generally Gilson (n 133) 1078 ff.

[137] SWD (2015) 183 final (n 7) 13.

[138] Commission 'An SME Strategy for a Sustainable and Digital Europe', COM (2020) 103 final, 10 March 2020, 3.

ii. Fostering Participation in EU Capital Markets

a. Understanding the Investor Base

Businesses seeking funding are key participants in capital markets. These entities facilitate the fundamental functions of capital markets by providing investors with the opportunity to obtain a share of their future revenues or other financial returns. Nevertheless, market-based finance is not a unilateral activity. As discussed in the preceding section, for companies to have access to market funding, investors should be willing to allocate their financial resources to business projects, despite the inherent risks associated with such decisions. Consequently, investors represent the other essential component of capital markets and constitute the second focal point of the CMU initiative.[139]

In general, investors can be classified into two groups: retail and institutional. The retail category encompasses individuals, households, as well as other entities, mainly NFCs, that do not invest in a professional capacity.[140] Retail investors typically make long-term asset allocation decisions and are characterised by a relatively lower level of sophistication and risk tolerance within the market. Institutional investors comprise legal entities such as banks, insurance companies, investment firms, pension and collective investment funds, governments, large corporations, and individuals engaged in professional investment activities. As a rule, they tend to be more financially sophisticated and risk-tolerant compared to retail investors, allocating substantial amounts of money, usually across a diverse range of investments.[141]

Retail investors represent the largest ultimate suppliers of funds in the EU economy, holding financial assets totalling 221 per cent of GDP.[142] However, their funds are usually channelled to fund seekers through financial intermediaries. Indeed, the majority of their assets (nearly 70 per cent) are held in bank deposits and currency (31.1 per cent), or in pension entitlements and claims against life-insurance companies (38.7 per cent).[143] Conversely, only a small portion is invested directly in the public market, including listed shares and debt securities.[144] Moreover, many households hold a substantial stake (around 20 per cent) of equity in their own family businesses.[145] Besides, when assessing the potential overall supply of funds that individuals can contribute to the economy, real estate property should also be taken into account, as it forms the most significant (approximately 40 per cent)

[139] COM (2015) 468 final (n 47) 18; COM (2017) 292 final (n 55) 57; COM (2020) 590 final (n 61) 10 f.

[140] SWD (2015) 13 final (n 34) 7; SWD (2015) 183 final (n 7) 59.

[141] SWD (2015) 183 final (n 7) 59–60.

[142] Eurostat, 'Households – Statistics on Financial Assets and Liabilities' (2018).

[143] ibid.

[144] The direct ownership of shares by European households decreased from 28% in 1975 to 10–11% since 2007, see OEE and IODS, 'Who Owns the European Economy? Evolution of the Ownership of EU Listed Companies Between 1970 and 2012', August 2013.

[145] SWD (2015) 183 final (n 7) 58.

nonfinancial asset held among households in the EU-27.[146] Nevertheless, households across the EU display considerable variations in both the quantity and types of financial assets held. For instance, in the Netherlands and Denmark, households' total financial assets represent 323.2 per cent and 297.7 per cent of GDP, respectively, while in Latvia and Romania, these figures stand at only 89.4 per cent and 60.3 per cent of GDP, respectively. At the same time, Dutch and Danish households allocate a large portion (66.4 per cent and 52 per cent respectively) of their financial assets to insurance, pensions, and standardised guarantees. In contrast, Greek and Cypriot households favour currency, accounting for approximately 66 per cent and 60 per cent of GDP, respectively.[147]

b. The Impediments to Investors' Participation in Capital Markets

The previous analysis suggests that, despite holding significant financial assets, retail investors in the EU demonstrate limited interest in capital market investments, such as listed shares, bonds or investment funds. Meanwhile, although non-bank financial intermediaries in the euro area, including pension funds and insurance companies, maintain a substantial asset base (around EUR 50 trillion),[148] their portfolio exposure to asset classes directly funding the real economy within the EU remains limited.[149] Several reasons could explain this scepticism toward participating in capital markets.

As regards retail investors, their portfolio structure seems to reflect their limited ability to assess the default risk and business prospects of borrowers. Consequently, the limited interest in investing can be largely attributed to information asymmetries, high transaction costs, and agency problems. In addition, while transferable securities offer higher returns and enhanced protection against inflation, their susceptibility to business cycle fluctuations heightens the risk of losses and illiquidity. At the same time, unlike bank deposits, they lack comparable legal protection, rendering them less secure.[150] Therefore, the significant portion of households' investments in bank deposits or long-term saving products underscores their preference for assets offering liquidity, stable nominal value and the assurance of trusted financial institutions. Furthermore, a diversified investment portfolio that includes direct holdings in riskier financial assets, such as securities and investment products, demands a higher level of wealth and financial sophistication – attributes that are less prevalent among retail investors.[151] For example,

[146] Commission Staff Working Document, 'European Financial Stability and Integration', SWD (2015) 98, 27 April 2015, Chapter 2, Box A.

[147] Eurostat (n 142).

[148] ECB (n 40) 28.

[149] ibid 37.

[150] See eg Directive 2014/49/EU of the European Parliament and of the Council on deposit guarantee schemes [2014] OJ L173/149.

[151] For an overview of financial literacy levels in different Member States, see G Nicolini, *Financial Literacy in Europe – Assessment Methodologies and Evidence from European Countries* (Routledge, 2019) 141.

equity holdings not only provide limited diversification gains, particularly when households' non-financial income correlates closely with the business cycle,[152] but also entail high risks that can be challenging and costly for the average investor to manage. Moreover, retail investors place a high value on safety and predictability, making their confidence in the integrity and proper functioning of the market mechanism decisive for their participation.[153] Nevertheless, corporate scandals in the early 2000s[154] prompted numerous households to withdraw their funds from the market, with subsequent financial crises, including the one induced by COVID-19,[155] and ensuing market volatility, further exacerbating investor mistrust in the market mechanism. Finally, market fragmentation hinders the participation of retail investors from Member States with less developed capital markets by constraining their access to available investments beyond their country of residence.[156]

Similar to their retail counterparts, institutional investors' participation in capital markets is strongly influenced by risk-return considerations. As a consequence, information asymmetry, transaction costs, illiquidity, and market uncertainty significantly impact their portfolio management decisions. While institutional investors are better positioned than retail ones to handle information problems, acquiring such capacity involves significant transaction costs associated with gathering sufficiently comprehensive and precise information necessary for a thorough assessment of the benefits and risks of their investment decisions.[157] Hence, the share of assets held by institutional investors in deposits or fixed-income financial instruments primarily reflects a cost-benefit analysis. Put differently, investing in these assets allows institutional investors to attain indirect or reduced exposure to investment risks, without incurring the high information costs linked to developing the capacity to manage such risks. But apart from the aforementioned considerations, legal factors could also affect the interest or capability of institutional investors to invest in specific assets. For instance, sovereign exposures receive preferential treatment in the current EU prudential regulatory framework for banks and insurance undertakings,[158]

[152] A Vissing-Jorgensen, 'Towards an Explanation of Household Portfolio Choice Heterogeneity: Nonfinancial Income and Participation Cost Structures', NBER Working Paper 8884, April 2002.

[153] SWD (2015) 183 final (n 7) 62.

[154] Characteristic in this regard are the Enron scandal and other financial scandals that emerged following the market downturn in 2000, see generally JW Markham, *A Financial History of Modern U.S. Corporate Scandals: From Enron to Reform* (Routledge, 2005).

[155] COM (2020) 590 final (n 61) 10.

[156] SWD (2015) 183 final (n 7) 64–65.

[157] These costs are both direct and indirect, the latter stemming from the public good nature of information which results in imperfectly appropriable benefits from its production, see eg FH Easterbrook and DR Fischel, 'Mandatory Disclosure and the Protection of Investors' (1984) 70 *Virginia Law Review* 669, 681.

[158] See generally Basel Committee on Banking Supervision, 'The regulatory treatment of sovereign exposures', BIS Discussion Paper, December 2017.

unlike other financial instruments which are subject to more stringent capital requirements. Besides, national restrictions may also limit certain categories of institutional investors, particularly pension funds, from investing in riskier asset classes, such as illiquid private (non-listed) equity securities of SMEs and unsecured debt.

c. The CMU as a Tool for Promoting Capital Market Investments

The reluctance of retail and institutional investors to reallocate their portfolios towards more market-based instruments has far-reaching effects on capital markets' ability to effectively fulfil their functions. For one thing, it negatively impacts the size and depth of the markets, leading to a scarcity of essential investment capital for businesses. At the same time, it curtails investors' opportunities for more efficient resource allocation and risk diversification, thereby affecting their potential returns and their resilience against economic shocks. This is because capital markets exemplify a characteristic 'chicken-and-egg' problem. When they lack sufficient depth and liquidity, issuers confront a limited investor base in primary markets. Consequently, investors encounter challenges when attempting to exit their investments through secondary markets, and traders in secondary markets have a limited array of instruments and counterparties to engage with.[159] In other words, each group would be more willing to participate in capital markets if the other groups were equally more active. Against this background, the CMU seeks to boost the flow of funds directed into capital markets by establishing a safer, more dynamic and competitive investment environment.

More specifically, deeper and more integrated capital markets can provide investors with a wider range of investment products from across the Union, better catering to their individual needs, constraints and characteristics, particularly their financial standing, experience and risk tolerance.[160] In addition, increased competition among EU non-bank financial intermediaries, coupled with enhanced legal certainty, can facilitate easier and more cost-effective market entry for investors. This, in turn, could encourage broader market engagement and contribute to attracting a more diverse pool of capital providers.[161] Finally, through ensuring the timely disclosure of an ample amount of accurate information, efficient capital markets can empower investors to make more informed decisions, thereby also increasing their trust in the market.[162]

[159] SWD (2015) 183 final (n 7) 57.
[160] ibid 102.
[161] See generally SWD (2017) 224 final (n 58) 79 ff.
[162] The promotion of investor confidence through disclosure has been a key driver of the EU's regulatory approach in capital markets, Veil (n 87) 24–25. However, the correlation between mandatory disclosure rules and public confidence in the market has faced strong criticism from scholars like Easterbrook and Fischel (n 157) 692–93.

iii. Supporting Economic Growth

a. Financial Structure and Economic Growth

Modern financial systems integrate both bank-based and market-based finance channels, each with distinct features that present both advantages and drawbacks for economic growth. These characteristics have sparked intense theoretical debates among economists and policymakers regarding the optimal financial structure for fostering economic growth. More specifically, proponents of bank-based financial systems emphasise the positive impact of strong banks on growth, highlighting their ability to: (i) address agency problems and information asymmetries inherent in the relationship between creditors and borrowers by actively monitoring the latter, thereby improving capital allocation and mitigating moral hazard;[163] (ii) effectively manage intertemporal and liquidity risks;[164] (iii) mobilise capital to exploit economies of scale;[165] and (iv) secure debt repayment through intricate collateral arrangements and enforcement proceedings that individual investors typically cannot implement.[166] By contrast, proponents of market-based financial systems stress the advantages of well-functioning capital markets in bolstering growth due to their capacity to: (i) incorporate publicly available information into securities prices, enabling efficient investment decisions;[167] (ii) improve corporate governance through performance-based senior management compensation, varied voting structures, and potential takeovers should the stock price fall below a fair value;[168] and (iii) facilitate better cross-sectional risk diversification.[169] Moreover, some commentators focus on the constraints

[163] D Diamond, 'Financial Intermediation and Delegated Monitoring' (1984) 51 *The Review of Economic Studies* 393; J Stiglitz, 'Credit Markets and the Control of Capital' (1985) 17 *Journal of Money, Credit and Banking* 133; A Boot and A Thakor, 'Financial System Architecture' (1997) 10 *The Review of Financial Studies* 693, 696. In contrast, investors in liquid markets can easily sell their shares, reducing their incentives to monitor corporate activities, see A Bhide, 'The hidden costs of stock market liquidity' (1993) 34 *Journal of Financial Economics* 1.

[164] Allen and Gale (n 11); V Bencivenga and B Smith, 'Financial Intermediation and Endogenous Growth' (1991) 58 *The Review of Economic Studies* 195.

[165] E Sirri and P Tufano, 'The Economics of Pooling' in D Crane et al (eds), *The Global Financial System: A Functional Approach* (Harvard Business Law Press, 1995).

[166] This holds especially true in relationship-based economic systems that lack institutional safeguards to protect investors, see generally R Rajan and L Zingales, 'Which capitalism? Lessons from the East Asian crisis' (1998) 11 *Journal of Applied Corporate Finance* 40.

[167] Grundmann (n 85) 23 ff. However, the efficiency of the price formation process has encountered increased scrutiny since the financial crisis, which revealed widespread biases that distort rational investor decision-making, see eg E Avougleas, 'The Global Financial Crisis, Behavioural Finance and Financial Regulation in Search of a New Orthodoxy' (2009) 9 *Journal of Corporate Law Studies* 23.

[168] M Jensen and K Murphy, 'Performance Pay and Top-Management Incentives' (1990) 98 *Journal of Political Economy* 225; T Lambert, *How to Regulate: A Guide for Policymakers* (CUP, 2017) 119 ff. On the contrary, banks may collude with firm management against other investors, obstructing the removal of underperforming managers, see E Wenger and C Kaserer, 'The German System of Corporate Governance: A Model Which Should Not Be Imitated' in S Black and M Moersch (eds), *Competition and Convergence in 42 Financial Markets: The German and Anglo-American Models* (Elsevier Science, 1998).

[169] R Levine, 'Stock Markets, Growth and Tax Policy' (1991) 46 *Journal of Finance* 1445; M Obstfeld, 'Risk-taking, Global Diversification and Growth' (1994) 84 *American Economic Review* 1310.

of bank-based systems in fostering economic growth compared to market-based ones. For example, banks are seen as hindering innovation not only by favouring conservative, non-risky entrepreneurial ventures,[170] but also by extracting informational rents that shield established firms with close bank ties from competition.[171] At the same time, it is suggested that firms relying on banking finance, might be dissuaded from pursuing profitable projects, as banks wield bargaining power over a project's profits, potentially reducing expected returns.[172]

However robust they may be, the aforementioned theories do not offer a conclusive answer regarding the ideal structure of the financial system. Pre-crisis empirical economic research was also unhelpful as it failed to provide sufficient evidence indicating whether economies, industries, or firms grow faster in countries where the financial system leans more on banks or capital markets. Indeed, relevant evidence suggested that variations in economic growth across countries are primarily linked to the overall level of development in the financial sector[173] rather than the specific structure of the financial system.[174] These findings are consistent with the financial services view, which asserts that economic growth is mainly influenced by the effectiveness of the financial sector in channelling funds into the economy, regardless of whether such financing is provided through banks or markets.[175] They also resonate with the law and finance perspective, which posits that the distinction between growth-facilitating and growth-impeding financial systems relies more on the integrity and efficiency of the regulatory framework for providing financial services than on their market or bank orientation.[176]

Post-crisis empirical research, however, indicates that depending on specific criteria and circumstances, particularly the level of economic development and the overall macroeconomic environment, a market-based or a bank-based system might be better placed to support growth. More specifically, recent studies illustrate that as economies mature, the optimal financial structure shifts towards

[170] D Weinstein and Y Yafeh, 'On the Costs of a Bank-centered Financial System: Evidence from the Changing Main Bank Relations in Japan' (1998) 53 *Journal of Finance* 635.

[171] M Hellwig, 'Banking, Financial Intermediation and Corporate Finance' in A Giovannini and C Mayer (eds), *European Financial Integration* (CUP, 1991).

[172] R Rajan, 'Insiders and Outsiders: The Choice between Informed and Arm's-Length Debt' (1992) 47 *Journal of Finance* 1367.

[173] J Boyd and B Smith, 'The Evolution of Debt and Equity Markets in Economic Development' (1998) 12 *Economic Theory* 519; R Levine and S Zervos, 'Stock Markets, Banks, and Economic Growth' (1998) 88 *American Economic Review* 537.

[174] R Levine, 'Bank-based or market-based financial systems: which is better?' (2002) 11 *Journal of Financial Intermediation* 398, 402.

[175] R Merton and Z Bodie, 'A Conceptual Framework for Analyzing the Financial Environment' in Crane et al (n 165); R Levine, 'Financial Development and Economic Growth: Views and agenda' (1997) 35 *Journal of Economic Literature* 688; A Demirgüç-Kunt and R Levine, *Financial Structures and Economic Growth: A Cross-Country Comparison of Banks, Markets, and Development* (MIT Press, 2001); T Beck and R Levine, 'Industry Growth and Capital Accumulation: Does having a Market- or Bank-Based System Matter?' (2002) 64 *Journal of Financial Economics* 147.

[176] R La Porta et al, 'Law and Finance' (1998) 106 *Journal of Political Economy* 1113.

capital markets, driven largely by the growing demand for a wider range of risk management and capital-raising tools that exceed traditional banks' capacities.[177] As a result, in more advanced economies, an expansion in the size of the banking sector may lead to a decline in the production of economic goods and services.[178] This phenomenon is known as the 'vanishing effect' of financial depth on economic growth,[179] suggesting that once private credit surpasses a certain threshold (approximately 80 per cent–100 per cent of the GDP), its impact on economic activity becomes negligible or even negative.[180] On the contrary, further capital market development seems to yield a positive incremental impact on economic activity.[181] Other studies also reveal that financial systems geared towards market-based intermediation are more effective in moderating severe fluctuations within the business cycle. Indeed, in periods of mild economic downturns, healthy banks serve as the primary channel for financing growth, mainly by extending credit to firms.[182] Yet, when recessions coincide with financial crises, capital markets appear more adept at supporting growth.[183] Under such circumstances, banks often undergo restructuring and deleveraging, which curtails their lending capacity and hampers their ability to finance business activities. In contrast, deep and liquid markets provide access to a broader array of funding options and a larger pool of potential investors, alleviating the growth constraints caused by banks' limited credit capacities during financial shocks.[184]

b. The CMU as a Tool for Enhancing and Sustaining Growth

In view of the empirical findings outlined above, two arguments emerge regarding the potential adverse effect of an overly bank-dependent financial system on economic growth. First, in times of economic expansion, if bank loans to

[177] See eg A Demirguc-Kunt, E Feyen and R Levine, 'The Evolving Importance of Banks and Securities Markets' (2013) 27 *The World Bank Economic Review* 476, 479; C Kaserer and MS Rapp, 'Capital Markets and Economic Growth: Long-Term Trends and Policy Challenges', Research Report, March 2014, 1.

[178] Demirguc-Kunt, Feyen and Levine (n 177) 478.

[179] See eg P Rousseau and P Wachtel, 'What Is Happening to the Impact of Financial Deepening on Economic Growth?' (2011) 49 *Economic Inquiry* 276.

[180] K Gründler, 'The Vanishing Effect of Finance on Economic Development' (2021) 25 *Macroeconomic Dynamics* 536, 537; JL Arcand, E Berkes and U Panizza, 'Too much Finance?' (2015) 20 *Journal of Economic Growth* 106, 109; S Cecchetti and E Kharroubi, 'Reassessing the impact of finance on growth', BIS Working Paper No 381, July 2012, 1; European System Risk Board, 'Is Europe Overbanked?', Reports of the Advisory Scientific Committee No 4, June 2014, 12 ff.

[181] Demirguc-Kunt, Feyen and Levine (n 177) 478–79.

[182] P Bolton et al, 'Relationship and Transaction Lending in a Crisis' (2016) 29 *Review of Financial Studies* 2643.

[183] J Allard and R Blavy, 'Market Phoenixes and Banking Ducks: Are Recoveries Faster in Market-Based Financial Systems?' IMF Working Papers No 213, September 2011; L Gambacorta, J Yang and K Tsatsaronis, 'Financial structure and growth' (2014) *March BIS Quarterly Review* 21; J Grjebine, U Szczerbowicz and F Tripier, 'Corporate Debt Structure and Economic Recoveries' (2018) 101 *European Economic Review* 77.

[184] SWD (2015) 183 final (n 7) 10, 18.

households and firms outpace GDP growth, as observed in Europe in the years preceding financial crisis,[185] it could impede overall growth. Second, heavy reliance on banks implies that during long recessions when bank credit tightens, businesses encounter difficulties accessing alternative finance sources, posing significant challenges for recovery and growth. In this regard, the CMU's ambition to establish a more diversified financial system, by increasing the depth and efficiency of EU capital markets, can be viewed as a means to direct a larger share of funding into the economy, both during periods of financial upswings and downturns. This should steer Europe towards an elevated and long-term growth trajectory, also by helping mobilise the significant amount of investment capital which is required to finance the sustainable and digital transition of the economy.[186]

In addition, strengthening the integration of EU capital markets, the other key aspect of the CMU initiative, can further stimulate growth, by broadening cross-border capital-raising and investment opportunities. More specifically, as previously explained, removing barriers in trading financial assets and facilitating the free flow of capital can be advantageous for both investors and businesses. Investors will gain access to a greater variety of investment products, while businesses will benefit from a more diverse selection of financing options, particularly across borders.[187] This enhanced interconnection between borrowers and capital providers in the EU is, in turn, expected to facilitate a more efficient allocation of available funds,[188] thereby contributing to its economic growth.[189] Indeed, in the standard model, the opening of cross-regional investments leads to heightened capital flows from countries with higher savings to those facing capital scarcity, thus accelerating short-term growth in the latter and generating higher returns on savings in the former.[190] From a more nuanced perspective, cross-border capital flows could also alleviate the economy's credit constraints, enabling agents to engage in more productive activities.[191] Furthermore, financial integration can boost growth by intensifying competition between domestic and foreign financial institutions, whilst facilitating access to foreign financial services.[192] Finally, it has been suggested that through the promotion of better risk-sharing, capital market

[185] ibid 10.

[186] The Commission estimates an extra €350 billion in annual energy-related investments compared to the previous decade to achieve the 55% reduction target in greenhouse gas emissions by 2030, COM (2020) 590 final (n 61) 4.

[187] See also R Levine, 'International financial liberalization and economic growth' (2001) 9 *Review of International Economics* 688.

[188] Kalemli-Ozcan et al (n 32).

[189] M Obstfeld and A Taylor, *Globalization and capital markets: Integration, Crisis and Growth* (CUP, 2004) 241.

[190] Y Demyanyk, C Ostergaard and B Sørensen, 'Risk sharing and portfolio allocation in EMU', European Economy – Economic Papers No 334, July 2008, 1.

[191] A Bonfiglioli, 'Financial Integration, Productivity and Capital Accumulation' (2008) 76 *Journal of International Economics* 337.

[192] Levine (n 187); M Giannetti et al, 'Financial Market Integration, Corporate Financing and Economic Growth', European Economy – Economic Papers No 179, November 2002.

integration can incentivise greater domestic risk-taking in innovative projects, further fostering growth.[193]

iv. Strengthening Financial Stability in the EU

a. Financial Structure and Integration as Determinants of Financial Stability

Financial stability broadly refers to the financial system's ability to perform its core functions, namely efficiently allocating economic resources and managing, diversifying, pricing, and distributing risks, in an effective and coherent way, thereby facilitating economic performance even amidst endogenous or external financial imbalances.[194] As such, it is suggested that both the structure of the financial system and the depth of financial integration are important determinants of financial stability in the EU, a prerequisite for promoting sustainable growth and job creation.[195]

Regarding the link between financial structure and stability, empirical studies imply that financial crises have more pronounced effects on financial systems that lean heavily towards banks.[196] Conversely, in economies where equity and debt markets play a more decisive role in financing NFCs, there is a tendency for faster and more robust economic recoveries.[197] Several factors contribute to this, among which the following two appear particularly relevant. First, as already explained, during financial crises, banks strive to manage their balance sheet risk by tightening their lending policies, which impacts their capacity to fulfil their principal function of allocating capital to the economy. Capital markets, on the other hand, exhibit a higher shock-absorbing capacity. Unlike banks, they offer a broad range of investment options tailored to meet diverse investor preferences and needs. This enables effective capital and risk allocation, thereby bridging the gap resulting from banks' lending constraints.[198] Second, large banking systems display higher levels of systemic risk compared to market-based systems, especially during periods of declining asset prices.[199] As has been observed, banks tend to expand their balance sheets and assume more risk when asset prices rise, influenced by the increased values of collateral and bank equity. Nevertheless, as bank operations expand, the pool of creditworthy borrowers diminishes, increasing

[193] G Saint-Paul, 'Fiscal Policy in an Endogenous Growth Model' (1992) 107 *The Quarterly Journal of Economics* 1242; Obstfeld (n 169).

[194] G Schinasi, 'Defining Financial Stability', IMF Working Paper No 187, October 2004, 8 ff.

[195] SWD (2015) 183 final (n 7) 27–8.

[196] In bank-oriented financial systems, recessions are three times more severe (12.5% of GDP) compared to countries with market-oriented financial structures (4.2% of GDP), Gambacorta et al (n 183) 32.

[197] This conclusion is valid even after accounting for other factors, such as the nature of the crisis, policy responses and the level of economic flexibility, Allard and Blavy (n 183) 23.

[198] SWD (2015) 183 final (n 7) 21.

[199] S Langfield and M Pagano, 'Bank Bias in Europe: Effects on Systemic Risk and Growth', ECB Working Paper Series No 1797, May 2015, 10.

the probability of mispricing credit risk and funding projects with negative net present value (NPV).[200] Hence, given that bank-centric financial structures tend to be more leveraged, the risk-taking behaviour observed during credit expansions can pose a threat not only to the stability of individual banks but also to the entire financial system due to contagion effects,[201] as illustrated by the subprime mortgage crisis.[202]

When it comes to the relationship between financial integration and stability, there is broad consensus that more integrated financial markets can improve cross-border private risk sharing, thus contributing significantly to the stability of the financial system.[203] More specifically, private risk sharing can occur both horizontally over space ('cross-sectional') and vertically across time ('intertemporal').[204] Cross-sectional risk sharing happens mainly through capital markets which facilitate the distribution of risk among various agents that operate in a market setting at a specific point in time.[205] This is the case, for example, with equity ownership that is spread among various businesses, providing easier access and liquidation (exit option), while also reducing the volatility of asset returns, particularly in times of persistent downturns.[206] Intertemporal risk sharing primarily involves credit institutions offering liquidity and maturity transformation services. By accumulating 'safe assets' over time, these entities can adjust their lending behaviour to support households and firms in maintaining consumption and production levels in the face of economic shocks.[207] In light of the above, greater capital market integration can further support cross-sectional risk sharing by facilitating the diversification of investment portfolios across different geographic regions and sectors. This reduces the correlation between asset returns and specific country or regional economic fluctuations, contributing to income and consumption smoothing during economic downturns.[208] At the same time, more integrated capital markets can complement intertemporal risk sharing, as the latter is mostly effective against temporary disruptions caused by the drop in value of a specific entity or sector.[209]

[200] Pagano et al (n 180) 17.

[201] Langfield and Pagano (n 199) 10.

[202] See generally Y Demyanyk and O Van Hemert, 'Understanding the Subprime Mortgage Crisis' (2011) 24 *Review of Financial Studies* 1848.

[203] A Kose, E Prasad and M Terrones, 'How Does Financial Globalization Affect Risk-Sharing? Patterns and Channels', IMF Working Paper No 238, October 2007; T Jappelli and M Pagano 'Financial Market Integration under EMU', European Economy – Economic Papers No 312, March 2008.

[204] For this distinction see D Valiante, 'CMU and the Deepening of Financial Integration' in Busch, Avgouleas and Ferrarini, *Capital Markets Union in Europe* (n 4) 14.

[205] F Allen and D Gale, 'A Welfare Comparison of Intermediaries and Financial Markets in Germany and the US' (1995) 39 *European Economic Review* 179, 189 ff.

[206] Valiante (n 204) 14.

[207] See generally F Allen and D Gale, 'Financial Markets, Intermediaries, and Intertemporal Smoothing' (1997) 105 *Journal of Political Economy* 523.

[208] J Cimadomo et al, 'Private and Public Risk Sharing in the Euro Area' (2020) 121 *European Economic Review* 1, 3.

[209] Valiante (n 88) 49.

b. The CMU as a Catalyst for Financial Stability

The previous analysis suggests that a diversified financial system with well-functioning capital markets is crucial for ensuring financial stability. This became particularly evident in the aftermath of the 2008 financial crisis. While the economic shock was global, its repercussions were keenly felt in the EU, especially in eurozone countries grappling with debt, culminating in the onset of the European sovereign debt crisis. Indeed, the strong reliance of EU economies on banks rendered them more vulnerable during the crisis when the combined impact of rising default rates and interbank contagion led to a severe contraction in credit provision. In this regard, by seeking to enhance the depth, liquidity and efficiency of capital markets in the EU, the CMU can broaden diversification in the funding of the economy, consequently bolstering the shock-absorbing capacity of the financial system.[210]

But beyond the need for stronger capital markets, making the EU economy more resilient to economic shocks also requires a more sustainable financial integration process. As the financial crisis emphatically showed, the level of cross-border credit and capital markets risk sharing among EU Member States had remained notably low, especially when compared to the US and Canada.[211] Regarding credit markets, reliance on the model of cross-border interbank debt flows to drive intertemporal consumption smoothing proved particularly weak, since such flows were very limited during the crisis due to banks retracting behind national boundaries.[212] Consequently, a vital cross-border risk sharing channel was unavailable when most needed, leaving companies and households in vulnerable Member States dependent on domestic banks facing severe restructuring or exposed to a weak sovereign unable to offer credit lines.[213] Concerning capital markets, cross-border activities such as equity ownership and direct foreign investments, which could contribute to risk sharing, were not sufficiently developed to effectively mitigate the effects of the crisis.[214] The first decisive move toward enhancing cross-border risk sharing was the establishment of the European Stability Mechanism (ESM).[215] This intergovernmental organisation can grant direct or indirect financial aid for the recapitalisation of euro area financial institutions, provided that financial stability is at risk, and no alternative solutions exist to address the capital shortfall.[216] Hence, it can help relieve their balance sheets and remove the risk

[210] SWD (2015) 183 final (n 7) 10.

[211] V Milano and P Reichlin, 'Risk Sharing Across the US and EMU: The Role of Public Institutions', LUISS SEPE Policy Brief, January 2017; F Balli, S A Basher and J L Rosmy, 'Channels of risk-sharing among Canadian provinces: 1961–2006' (2012) 43 *Empirical Economics* 763.

[212] G-M Milesi-Ferretti et al, 'The Great Retrenchment: International Capital Flows During the Global Financial Crisis' (2011) 26 *Economic Policy* 287.

[213] M Fratzscher and M Rieth, 'Monetary Policy, Bank Bailouts and the Sovereign-Bank Risk Nexus in the Euro Area' (2019) 23 *Review of Finance* 745.

[214] Cimadomo et al (n 208) 10 (Figure 2).

[215] Treaty Establishing the European Stability Mechanism, D/12/3, 2 February 2012.

[216] For the eligibility criteria see ESM, 'Guideline on Financial Assistance for the Recapitalisation of Financial Institutions,' Art 3; ibid, 'Guideline on Financial Assistance for the Direct Recapitalisation of Institutions', Art 3.

of contagion from the financial sector to the sovereign.[217] Completing the CMU is the second pivotal step towards fostering financial stability in the EU. Fully integrated capital markets are expected to boost cross-border investment flows, reinforcing private risk sharing across EU countries and providing an additional buffer against systemic shocks.[218]

IV. The Role of Differentiation in the CMU

A. Differentiation as a Balance between the Divergent Views of Member States

The main rationale for introducing the CMU is that a less fragmented EU financial system, featuring well-developed capital markets across all Member States, could considerably benefit businesses and investors while fostering economic growth and resilience within the region.[219] Nevertheless, the integration of capital markets in the EU and, by extension, the embedding of market finance into the economy is not a straightforward process. The range of institutional factors influencing a Member State's prevailing financial structure is so intricate that endorsing a specific model or approach is fraught with risks. This is clearly illustrated by the Varieties of Capitalism (VoC) analysis, which distinguishes between two main types of market economies: coordinated and liberal. Broadly speaking, within coordinated market economies (CMEs), firms primarily acquire the necessary capital through bank loans and rely extensively on collaborative, non-market relationships to coordinate their activities with other actors and build their competencies.[220] In liberal market economies (LMEs), by contrast, funding is mainly secured though competitive financial markets which are more sensitive to price signals, thus also serving as mechanisms for coordinating firm behaviour with other economic actors.[221] These divergences among market economies are amplified by institutional arrangements, notably national legal frameworks, which tend to be more interventionist in CMEs and more enabling in LMEs.[222] Accordingly, Member

[217] R Goyal et al, 'A Banking Union for the Euro Area' in P Koeva Brooks and M Pradhan (eds), *The Mechanics of a Strong Euro Area* (IMF 2015) 173; COM (2015) 63 final (n 42) 5.

[218] The Five Presidents Report (n 108) 12.

[219] See eg F Allen and L Pástor, 'The Capital Markets Union: Key Challenges' in Allen et al (n 4) 1; Véron and Wolff (n 25) 130.

[220] PA Hall and D Sockice, 'An Introduction to Varieties of Capitalism' in PA Hall and D Sockice (eds), *Varieties of Capitalism. The Institutional Foundations of Comparative Advantage* (OUP, 2001) 8.

[221] ibid.

[222] More recently, though, intergovernmentalism has moved away from the CME versus LME dichotomy towards a broader perspective that delineates the 'market-making' coalition (led by the UK, the Netherlands and Nordic countries), characterised by market-led, more liberal regulation, from the 'market-shaping' coalition (led by France, Italy and Spain), associated with more intrusive regulation.

States are expected to resist policy efforts that jeopardise their economic model and the associated institutional foundations in order to protect their comparative advantage.[223]

The VoC analysis holds significant explanatory power in the CMU context. To begin with, it elucidates why the most supportive Member States from the CMU's inception were the UK, along with Ireland, Luxembourg, Sweden, and the Netherlands. These nations had the most well-developed and diversified financial sectors, consequently anticipating significant gains from the financial liberalisation and diversification promised by this project.[224] At the same time, it showcases how the resistance from such liberal economies, particularly the UK, to embrace further policy centralisation led to the absence of institutional measures, at least in the Green Paper and the Action Plan.[225] But most importantly, it sheds light on why the German and French governments, although generally supportive of the Commission's efforts to improve financing for the 'real' economy, initially approached the CMU with greater caution.[226] More specifically, while both countries boast developed local capital markets, their financial systems have historically been bank-dominated.[227] Especially in the case of Germany there has been a strong presence of small retail and cooperative banks.[228] These smaller institutions perceived the prospect of more robust and integrated capital markets as a clear mid-term threat, prompting them to be very critical of the CMU initiative.[229] Hence, contrary to more liberal market economies, the financial structures in Germany and France implied that their financial sectors would not reap important benefits from the market liberalisation goals of the CMU.[230]

This analysis sees Germany shifting between coalitions, L Quaglia, 'Completing the Single Market in Financial Services: The Politics of Competing Advocacy Coalitions' (2010) 17 *Journal of European Public Policy* 1007.

[223] See generally J Snell, 'Varieties of Capitalism and the Limits of European Economic Integration' (2011) 13 *Cambridge Yearbook of European Legal Studies* 415.

[224] Quaglia, Howarth and Liebe (n 13) 192–93.

[225] As already explained, the need to improve the efficiency and consistency of supervision to achieve the CMU goals only emerged after the UK's withdrawal from the EU, COM (2017) 292 final (n 55) 10–11.

[226] Federal Government of Germany, represented by the German Federal Ministry of Finance, 'German comments to the European Commission's Green Paper on building a Capital Markets Union', 2015; Réponse française au livre vert de la Commission européenne «Construire l'union des marchés de capitaux», 'Priorités et objectifs de la France pour l'Union des marchés de capitaux', 2015.

[227] Howarth, *France and the International Financial Crisis* (n 20) 371.

[228] K-P Schackmann-Fallis and S Scheffler, 'Aligning Financial Systems to Meet the Needs of Citizens and Enterprises' (2017) 86 *Vierteljahrshefte zur Wirtschaftsforschung* 69, 73.

[229] European Association of Cooperative Banks (EACB), 'Response to the Commission's Consultation on the Green Paper on CMU', 2015; European Savings and Retail Banking Group (ESBG), 'Response to the European Commission's Green Paper on "Building a Capital Markets Union"', 2015.

[230] Besides, both countries have historically taken a critical stance against foreign private equity firms and hedge funds, and exhibited a general resistance towards full liberalisation of capital markets, J Buckley and D Howarth, 'Regulating the So-Called "Vultures of Capitalism"' (2011) 49(s1) *Journal of Common Market Studies* 123; H Zimmerman, 'Varieties of Global Financial Governance? British and

This prompted the former finance ministers of both nations to jointly address a letter to the then Commissioner of DG FISMA, conveying their scepticism about adopting the US financial model and emphasising the importance of maintaining the central role of banks, particularly local ones, in all policy initiatives aimed at improving financing conditions within the EU.[231] It was not until Brexit that these two countries began to exhibit a tangible interest in the CMU, perceiving it as an opportunity to attract segments of London's financial industry into their respective financial centres.[232]

From the above analysis, it becomes apparent that, like prior integration initiatives in the financial field, the CMU is the product of a delicate balance between the diverse, and often conflicting, preferences, aspirations and perspectives of the Member States. This is particularly true for those influencing the direction of EU financial policy, specifically with regard to the necessity to foster the development and integration of capital markets.[233] This balance finds its practical application primarily in the variety of measures and actions taken towards completing the CMU, which range from conventional market themes, like reducing fixed costs for access to finance, to enhancing banks' lending capacity. Surprisingly, however, it is also manifested through the discretion occasionally granted to national regulators regarding the implementation of these measures, as will be seen later.[234]

B. Differentiation in the Policy Design

As previously discussed, improving access to finance for businesses and encouraging investor engagement in capital markets lies at the core of the CMU initiative. Nevertheless, the vast disparities among targeted market participants imply that adopting a one-size-fits-all approach is unlikely to be effective. In view of this, special attention is paid to designing policies that accommodate the distinctive requirements and characteristics of market actors. This means, more specifically, that alongside actions of a broader scope, the CMU introduces measures particularly aimed at SMEs and retail investors.

German Approaches to Financial Market Regulation' in E Helleiner, S Pagliari and H Zimmerman (eds), *Global Finance in Crisis* (Routledge, 2010).

[231] W Schäuble and M Sapin, 'Letter to Lord Jonathan Hill', 6 July 2015. The two ministers would even go as far as to refer to the 'proportionality principle', thus implying that they were ready to challenge the Commission's efforts to promote the CMU if that meant that national policy preferences would be undermined.

[232] Ringe (n 52) 346.

[233] For other (semi)peripheral countries, backing the CMU was mainly driven by pragmatic motives, especially the need to secure alternative sources of finance for local businesses, rather than reflecting their distinct financial structures, which remained heavily reliant on banks, Quaglia, Howarth and Liebe (n 13) 194.

[234] See generally ch 3 s IV and ch 4 s III.

i. *The Focus on the Support of SMEs*

Despite their central role, the CMU project lacks a clear definition of SMEs. At the EU level, a standardised definition is laid down in Recommendation 2003/361/EC,[235] encompassing those enterprises with fewer than 250 employees and an annual turnover or balance sheet total not exceeding EUR 50 million and/or EUR 43 million, respectively.[236] Within the context of capital markets law, another criterion that is used to distinguish SMEs from other businesses is market capitalisation, referring to the total monetary market value of their outstanding shares. According to Article 4(13) MiFID II,[237] for example, a company qualifies as an SME if, based on the end-year quotes for the previous three calendar years, its market capitalisation does not exceed an average of EUR 200 million. Regardless of the chosen definition, though, it remains true that SMEs form the backbone of the EU's economy. In 2022, they represented over 99 per cent of all enterprises that operate in the EU-27 non-financial business sector (NFBS), employing approximately 84 million people and generating 51.8 per cent of the total value added.[238] At the same time, they contribute significantly to innovation, with 30 per cent of SMEs in the EU operating in knowledge-intensive or high-tech industries.[239] Therefore, they play a critical role in driving long-term productivity and economic growth in the region.[240] Notwithstanding this, as already briefly discussed, SMEs encounter several challenges in securing external funding throughout their lifecycle, especially when compared to larger undertakings.

Various factors have culminated in this adverse situation. First, smaller firms exhibit greater sectoral and geographical specialisation than larger ones, rendering them more susceptible to business cycle fluctuations and economic shocks.[241] This was clearly demonstrated during the European debt crisis, when accessing finance became very arduous for SMEs.[242] Furthermore, the recent COVID-19

[235] Commission Recommendation 2003/361/EC concerning the definition of micro, small and medium-sized enterprises [2003] OJ L124/36.

[236] ibid Art 2(1).

[237] Directive 2014/65/EU of the European Parliament and of the Council on markets in financial instruments [2014] OJ L173/349.

[238] Commission, 'SME Performance Review – Annual Report on European SMEs 2022/2023', June 2023, 6.

[239] ibid 8.

[240] See eg PM Romer, 'Endogenous Technological Change' (1990) 98 *The Journal of Political Economy* S71; CI Jones, 'R&D-Based Models of Economic Growth' (1995) 103 *The Journal of Political Economy* 759; P Aghion, U Akcigit and P Howitt, 'What Do We Learn from Schumpeterian Growth Theory?' NBER Working Paper No. 18824, 2013.

[241] R Iyer et al, 'Interbank Liquidity Crunch and the Firm Credit Crunch: Evidence from the 2007–2009 Crisis' (2014) 27 *Review of Financial Studies* 347.

[242] For instance, in 2010, the net percentage of large euro firms reporting an increase in their turnover was 36%, in contrast to only a 1% increase for SMEs, see ECB, 'Survey on the Access to Finance (SAFE) of SMEs in the Euro Area – March to September 2010', 22 October 2010.

pandemic and the economic repercussions stemming from ongoing war conflicts have disproportionately impacted their performance.[243] Indeed, European SMEs have historically been overly reliant on bank financing.[244] However, the overall macroeconomic environment not only leads to higher credit risk and lower profitability but also exacerbates liquidity problems and risk aversion in the banking sector. Consequently, this situation can have a negative impact on these businesses, since their often uncertain prospects and lack of collateral may result in significant credit constraints.[245]

Second, SMEs have greater difficulty in meeting their funding needs in public capital markets when compared to large enterprises.[246] On one hand, multiple policy reports confirm that the direct and indirect costs of listing have become excessively burdensome for these companies,[247] particularly when taking into account their actual financing requirements.[248] On the other hand, many SMEs, mainly startups, exhibit high levels of uncertainty and information asymmetry.[249] This affects the ability of most investors to evaluate the prospects and the risks of allocating resources in these businesses, thereby influencing their willingness to invest. Finally, despite the efforts made in recent years, the European alternative finance market has not been particularly successful in offsetting the effects of credit illiquidity in these companies. By way of example, the lack of adequate scale[250] and geographical reach[251] has hindered the development of sufficiently large pools of venture capital for European businesses.[252] Similarly, equity-based crowdfunding, with its considerable potential to support the growth of young

[243] Commission, 'SME Performance Review 2022/2023' (n 238) 16 ff. Adding to that, SMEs are burdened with an excess of debt as a result of the COVID-19 pandemic, see Commission Staff Working Document, 'Monitoring Progress Towards a Capital Markets Union: A Toolkit of Indicators' SWD (2021) 544 final/2, 14 July 2021, 27.

[244] At the time of the CMU Action Plan, bank loans accounted for nearly 75% of the external financing for these businesses, see COM (2015) 468 final (n 47) 7.

[245] See eg ECB, 'Survey on the access to finance of SMEs in the Euro area – October 2011 to March 2012', April 2012; OECD, '*Financing SMEs and Entrepreneurs 2012: An OECD Scoreboard*' (OECD Publishing, 2012).

[246] SWD (2015) 183 final (n 7) 44.

[247] See generally Technical Expert Stakeholder Group (TESG) on SMEs, 'Empowering EU Capital Markets for SMEs – Making Listing Cool Again', Final Report, May 2021, 6.

[248] For instance, while the majority of SMEs require less than EUR 1 million annually to finance their growth ambitions, their average cost solely for preparing a standard prospectus amounts to EUR 65,000, SWD (2022) 762 final (n 121), 121–122 (Table 6).

[249] Gilson (n 133) 1070.

[250] Investments by European venture capital funds amounted to only 0,090% of European GDP in 2022, see Invest Europe, 'Private Equity Activity 2022', May 2023, 50.

[251] Indicatively, over 50% of the total venture capital investments in 2022 were directed towards seven countries (Austria, Belgium, France, Germany, Luxembourg, the Netherlands and Switzerland), ibid 46.

[252] In 2022, venture capital investments in European companies barely exceeded EUR 18 billion, whereas the value of venture capital deals in the US during that year surpassed USD 190 billion, see OECD Data Explorer, stats.oecd.org/Index.aspx?QueryId=87103.

SMEs, has not yet reached the required depth in the EU,[253] while cross-border activity is still limited.[254]

Considering the above, it is not surprising that improving and broadening funding options for SMEs by leveraging the potential of capital markets is at the forefront of the CMU agenda.[255] Unlike larger companies, SMEs face substantial limitations in their funding options and, hence, require greater support in accessing market financing. This becomes even more apparent during times of economic uncertainty and turmoil, as banks show little appetite to extend credit to these companies.[256] In this context, the concept of differentiation underscores the need for capital market interventions that are better tailored to the specific circumstances of smaller businesses.

ii. The Focus on Retail Investors

Similar to the differentiated treatment between SMEs and large companies, the CMU follows a comparable approach on the supply side of capital. This means, more specifically, that while it seeks to promote capital market investments from both retail and institutional investors, it places particular emphasis on addressing the barriers that hinder the participation of the former. This comes as no surprise, given that protecting retail investors and, more recently, fostering long-term household savings through the market, are two fundamental objectives in European capital markets regulation.[257] More specifically, retail investors are confronted with severe informational deficits concerning the quality and other crucial aspects of issuers' investment offers, largely attributed to their frequently limited financial literacy and exposure to serious behavioural risks.[258] As a result, they are more vulnerable to decision-making weaknesses and biases, requiring greater market protection than institutional investors who are better positioned to

[253] The EU equity crowdfunding market totalled USD 1.128 billion in 2020, while in the US it amounted to USD 1.827 billion, T Ziegler et al, 'The 2nd Global Alternative Finance Market Benchmarking Report', June 2021, 46.

[254] D Zetzsche and C Preiner, 'Cross-Border Crowdfunding: Towards a Single Crowdlending and Crowdinvesting Market for Europe' (2018) 19 *European Business Organization Law Review* 217, 227–28.

[255] COM (2015) 63 final (n 42) 13 ff; COM (2015) 468 final (n 47) 7 ff; COM (2020) 590 final (n 61) 3.

[256] After the 2008 financial crisis, while large firms opted for bond issuances, SMEs responded to the reduced availability of bank financing by relying on internally generated funds, SWD (2017) 224 final (n 58) 41.

[257] Moloney (n 33) 772.

[258] See generally M S Barr, S Mullainathan and E Shafir, 'Behaviourally Informed Regulation' in E Shafir (ed), *Behavioural Foundations of Public Policy* (Princeton University Press, 2012); E Avgouleas, 'Reforming Investor Protection Regulation: The Impact of Cognitive Biases' in M Faure and F Stephen (eds), *Essays in the Law and Economics of Regulation: In Honour of Anthony Ogus* (Intersentia, 2008); LA Stout, 'The Mechanisms of Market Inefficiency: An introduction to the new Finance' (2003) 28 *Journal of Corporation Law* 636; RJ Gilson and RH Kraakman, 'The Mechanisms of Market Efficiency Twenty Years Later: The Hindsight Bias' (2003) 28 *Journal of Corporation Law* 715.

make informed and, hence, wealth-maximising investment decisions. Moreover, safety and predictability are major concerns for households, reducing their willingness to direct their savings towards capital market instruments which are inherently riskier than bank deposits.[259] Besides, households' heavy dependence on securities intermediaries, which have often failed to provide adequate protection,[260] adds to the challenge of building the necessary trust in capital markets and convincing them that better returns on their savings can be achieved.

In view of the above, the CMU acknowledges that in formulating appropriate policies to mobilise more investments in the market, it is essential to consider the distinct characteristics, needs and limitations of each investor category. Thus, enhancing retail investors' confidence in capital markets, a prerequisite for ensuring their active participation, stands out prominently in this policy initiative.[261] To that end, alongside the implementation and enforcement of defensive, consumer-oriented rules, the CMU highlights the significance of empowering such investors through initiatives aimed at improving transparency, choice and financial literacy.

[259] SWD (2015) 183 final (n 7) 62.

[260] For a taxonomy of the reasons why these institutions may fail to protect investors, see SJ Choi, 'A Framework for the Regulation of Securities Market Intermediaries' (2004) 45 *Berkeley Business Law Journal* 45, 48 ff.

[261] COM (2015) 63 final (n 42) 9; SWD (2015) 183 final (n 7) 62; COM (2020) 590 final (n 61) 10.

2

Primary Markets Regulation and the Capital Markets Union

I. Introduction

In the previous chapter, it was explained that the CMU constitutes a crisis-inspired, long-term policy initiative focused on fundamentally reshaping financial intermediation within the EU. However, unlike the BU, the other major post-crisis reform in the European financial sector, the CMU does not follow a top-down approach. Right from the outset, there was no intention to introduce any 'big bang' legislation or establish new institutions at the EU level, such as a single supervisory body or a pan-European listing authority.[1] Rather, it embraces a bottom-up approach, seeking to identify and eliminate the barriers that hinder the development of deeper, more efficient, and more integrated EU capital markets. By doing so, it is expected to assist businesses in accessing diversified funding sources from across the EU, offer investors and savers additional investment opportunities, and thereby contribute to fostering growth and financial stability in the region.[2]

It becomes evident, therefore, that completing the CMU requires several actions which shall collectively contribute to constructing the new financial ecosystem.[3] Among these measures, particularly worthy of more detailed examination are those legal interventions aimed at further developing and integrating the primary markets across all Member States. These initiatives are critical as they hold the potential to support EU businesses, investors, and the broader economy, thus significantly advancing the success of CMU. Nonetheless, reform in this sphere is not without complexities. Indeed, while the establishment of a well-functioning single market for capital has been a principal objective guiding regulatory actions undertaken by the European legislature in the financial domain over the past four

[1] F Allen and L Pástor, 'The Capital Markets Union: Key Challenges' in Franklin Allen et al (eds), *Capital Markets Union and Beyond* (MIT Press, 2019) 2.

[2] Commission, 'Action Plan on Building a Capital Markets Union', COM (2015) 468 final, 30 September 2015, 6; ibid, 'A Capital Markets Union for People and Businesses-New Action Plan', COM (2020) 590 final, 24 September 2020, 2.

[3] For an overview of these actions, with focus on legal interventions, see D Busch, 'Capital Markets Union' in F Fabbrini and M Ventoruzzo (eds), *Research Handbook on EU Economic Law* (Edward Elgar, 2019).

decades,[4] the selection of the most suitable policy mixes to achieve this goal is under constant review. This is attributed to the effort to accommodate new ideas and objectives, such as those currently emerging from the CMU. More specifically, whilst the relationship between market efficiency and full, mandatory disclosure requirements has traditionally remained unchallenged in regulatory practice, demands for greater support for SME market finance and the growing importance of the retail investor constituency pose significant challenges to the prevailing disclosure paradigm. Moreover, the interplay between centralised and decentralised rule-setting functions is under reconsideration due to the differing perspectives among Member States regarding the extent to which market finance should be embedded into their economies and the level of legal harmonisation.

That said, it is crucial to define a normative framework for regulating primary markets in the CMU. This forms the core theme of this chapter which, through this theoretical analysis, seeks to lay down the appropriate benchmarks for evaluating the adequacy and efficacy of the implemented legal interventions in achieving the outlined objectives of this policy initiative.

II. The Role of Primary Markets Law in the CMU

In developing its visionary project to create a fully-fledged CMU, the Commission emphasised, from the beginning, the importance of addressing challenges, especially in three critical areas: (a) improving access to market finance for all businesses throughout Europe, particularly SMEs; (b) broadening and diversifying funding sources by further engaging institutional and, predominantly, retail investors; and (c) enhancing market functionality, linking borrowers and investors more efficiently, both within Member States and across borders.[5] In this regard, at the heart of the CMU agenda lies the establishment of a regulatory framework that increases the appeal of capital markets for businesses and investors, simultaneously removing barriers to cross-border funding and investment activities. Among the various legislative initiatives that move in this direction, those pertaining to the primary markets are of paramount importance. To understand why this is the case, it is necessary to delineate the scope and functions of these markets, particularly within the framework of the internal market.

A. Defining the Scope of Primary Markets

As discussed in the first chapter, businesses can finance their operations and investments either internally, primarily through retained profits, or externally, utilising

[4] R Veil, 'Concept and Aims of Capital Markets Regulation' in R Veil (ed), *EU Capital Markets Law*, 2nd edn (Hart Publishing, 2017) 24–25.

[5] Commission, 'Green Paper Building a Capital Markets Union', COM (2015) 63 final, 18 February 2015, 13.

proceeds from equity and debt financial instruments, as well as bank loans. When a company opts to raise external financing by issuing new financial instruments to investors, it operates in the primary market. Accordingly, the primary market refers to the segment of the capital market where companies, but also government entities and other public sector institutions, can raise funds by directly selling new equity or debt issues to investors.[6] Thus defined, the primary market denotes the initial placement of financial instruments. This occurs either through their introduction into actual trading, often starting with the application for admission to a trading venue,[7] or through an offer to potential investors where the issuer does not anticipate or desire widespread trading of the instruments. The instruments can be placed with a single or a select group of investors who engage in transactions with covenants and pricing tailored to suit their requirements (eg, private debt placements and private equity deals).[8] They can also be made available to the general public through a public offer for sale or subscription, which, as a result of technology-enabled innovations in the financial sector, can now also be solicited via an internet platform (eg, investment-based crowdfunding).

The primary market is distinct from the secondary market, where previously issued financial instruments are bought and sold (traded) by investors, typically through the intermediation of an investment firm, with little or no involvement from the issuing company.[9] Therefore, in contrast to the primary market, no capital raising activities take place in the secondary market. This is because the proceeds of the transactions are directed to the investors selling the financial instruments, not to the entity that initially issued these instruments. The secondary market is further divided into the auction market and the dealer or over-the-counter (OTC) market. In the former, trading occurs in a centralised location, usually a stock exchange, where buyers and sellers are matched based on predetermined rules, according to prices set through competitive bids and offers. In the dealer market, trading is facilitated by dealers, often referred to as 'market makers', who maintain an inventory of securities and execute buying and selling orders for these securities on their own account via electronic networks at a quoted price.[10]

From the above, it becomes apparent that the distinction between primary and secondary markets does not separate different trading venues or market types, but rather delineates distinct phases in which capital markets are utilised. However, strong interconnections exist between these markets and the corresponding legal rules governing them.[11] Indeed, a well-functioning, liquid secondary market is

[6] K Pilbeam, *Finance and Financial Markets*, 2nd edn (Palgrave Macmillan, 2005) 30.
[7] S Grundmann, *Bankvertragsrecht. Investment Banking II* (De Gruyter, 2016) 53.
[8] FA Schäfer, 'Emission und Vertrieb von Wertpapieren nach dem Wertpapierverkaufsprospektgesetz' (1991) 23–24 *Zeitschrift für Wirtschaftsrecht* 1557, 1559.
[9] P Collins, *Regulation of Securities, Markets and Transactions: A Guide to the New Environment* (Wiley, 2011) 348.
[10] See M Pagano and A Röell, 'Auction and Dealership Markets: What is the Difference?' (1992) 36 *European Economic Review* 613, 615–16.
[11] Grundmann (n 7) 54–55.

crucial for the smooth operation of the primary market, as investors' ability to swiftly cash out their investments enhances confidence, thus facilitating issuers in raising capital.[12] Similarly, an active primary market can provide diverse trading opportunities in the secondary market that cater to the preferences and needs of various investors.[13]

B. Key Functions and Characteristics of Primary Markets

As explained elsewhere,[14] perhaps the most essential function of capital markets, rendering them indispensable to the financial system, is their role in providing an alternative means – besides banks – for allocating capital within the economy.[15] This refers to the ability of capital markets to pool resources from individual investors and direct them to agents requiring capital for investments in productive capacity.[16] In doing so, they enhance liquidity,[17] while offering businesses and investors an effective risk management strategy.[18] These functions become particularly evident when examining primary equity and debt markets as defined earlier. By allowing corporations to directly raise funds from investors through the issuance of new securities, these markets facilitate the generation of new capital which can be used to finance new activities, while distributing the relevant risks. At the same time, by enabling investors to diversify their portfolios across various investment assets, primary markets can help generate returns on idle funds and accrue capital to sustain consumption during economic downturns.[19]

Considering the crucial role that primary markets can play in supporting businesses and investors, and, consequently, in fostering growth and financial stability in the EU, it becomes clear why establishing a supportive legal framework to ensure their development and integration can significantly contribute to the successful completion of the CMU. From a functional perspective, this legal framework should primarily encompass rules addressing the relationship between issuers and the investing public during the initial placement of financial

[12] Commission Staff Working Document, 'Initial Reflections on the Obstacles to the Development of Deep and Integrated EU Capital Markets', SWD (2015) 13 final, 18 February 2015, 7.

[13] AFME, 'Capital Markets Union – Measuring Progress and Planning for Success', September 2018, 11.

[14] See ch 1 s III A.

[15] E Avgouleas, *Governance of Global Financial Markets: the Law, the Economics, the Politics* (CUP, 2012) 6, 24; J Armour et al, *Principles of Financial Regulation* (OUP, 2016) 24 ff.

[16] S Tadesse, 'The Allocation and Monitoring Role of Capital Markets: Theory and International Evidence' (2004) 39 *Journal of Financial and Quantitative Analysis* 701, 705.

[17] F Allen et al, 'Financial Intermediation, Markets, and Alternative Financial Sectors' in G Constantinides, M Harris and R Stulz (eds), *Handbook of the Economics of Finance*, Vol. 2A (North Holland, 2012) 768; F Mishkin, K Matthews and M Giuliodori, *The Economics of Money, Banking and Financial Markets: European edition* (Pearson, 2013) 23 ff.

[18] P Diamond, 'The Role of a Stock Market in a General Equilibrium Model with Technological Uncertainty' (1967) 57 *The American Economic Review* 759; F Allen, 'Stock Markets and Resource Allocation' in C Mayer and X Vives (eds), *Capital Markets and Financial Intermediation* (CUP, 1993) 87 ff.

[19] SWD (2015) 13 final (n 12) 7.

instruments, including their admission to trading on a stock exchange.[20] These include, above all, the obligation to publish a prospectus and the liability arising thereof.[21] However, securities are typically placed by the issuer through financial intermediaries, mainly investment banks, either independently or more frequently as part of an underwriting syndicate.[22] Therefore, the regulation of the intermediaries' activities in this context should also fall under primary market law, given that their involvement is fundamental to the market's existence.[23]

III. A Framework for the Regulation of Primary Markets in the CMU

While the development of more robust and integrated European primary markets depends on various factors, such as the overall economic environment, taxation and financial literacy, which may not be immediately amenable to regulatory intervention, law remains a powerful tool in this endeavour. It is in fact the main mechanism at the EU's disposal.[24] Indeed, since the capital market is a product of rules rather than a natural system, alterations in these rules will likely prompt a restructuring of the market. Yet, the relationship between law, financial market development, and cross-border activity is an intricate and delicate one. Hence, in order to comprehend how law can facilitate the desired transformations, it is essential to delve into specifics. This necessitates the creation of a normative framework to identify the most suitable regulatory options for achieving the CMU objectives.

In this context, two challenging issues stand out and should be highlighted from the outset: first, the direction and, second, the scope of regulatory interventions at the EU level. Regarding the first issue, any legislative measure should, in principle, stem from a fair assessment and the reconciliation of the often conflicting interests among the involved parties. For the purposes of this analysis, these encompass both issuers and investors, characterised by varying sizes and diverse needs. Concerning the scope of interventions, it is important to distinguish between pursuing 'more Union', which involves the removal of cross-border barriers, and fostering 'more developed capital markets' at the Member State level. Although top-down interventions at the EU level are certainly beneficial in driving capital market integration and strengthening national markets, substantial change requires bottom-up initiatives at the domestic level. In this respect, allowing for some diversity might be more suitable than implementing a 'one-size-fits-all'

[20] S Grundmann, 'Europäisches Kapitalmarktrecht' (1996) 115 *Zeitschrift für Schweizerisches Recht* 103, 121; S Weber, *Kapitalmarktrecht – Eine Untersuchung des österreichischen Rechts und des Europäischen Gemeinschaftsrechts* (Springer, 1999) 7.

[21] Grundmann (n 7) 53. For a comprehensive analysis of the relevant rules in the EU context, see D Busch, G Ferrarini and JP Franx (eds), Prospectus Regulation and Prospectus Liability (OUP, 2020).

[22] Pilbeam (n 6) 30.

[23] S Heinze, *Europäisches Kapitalmarktrecht: Recht des Primärmarktes* (C.H. Beck, 1999) 4–5.

[24] N Moloney, *EU Securities and Financial Markets Regulation*, 4th edn (OUP, 2023) 8.

solution. That being the case, the main challenge in regulating primary markets within the CMU lies in balancing two seemingly opposing sets of objectives. First, improving access to market finance for businesses, while still ensuring adequate investor protection. And, second, striving for greater uniformity and standardisation in the legal framework, while affording national regulators some discretion to accommodate local structures and preferences.

A. Developing Primary Markets – The Importance and Limits of Disclosure

In the domain of public primary markets, where securities are publicly offered or admitted to trading for the first time, conduct regulation, mainly in the form of mandatory disclosure requirements for issuers, has been the dominant regulatory mechanism deployed worldwide.[25] Its principal objective is to guarantee the efficiency of these markets in allocating capital to firms offering securities. This is generally accomplished by enabling issuers of high-quality securities to signal their value, thereby reducing the cost of capital raising, while concurrently safeguarding investors against fraudulent issuers.[26] Therefore, creating an effective disclosure regime is an essential prerequisite for increasing the appeal of primary markets for both issuers and investors, thus ensuring their development.

i. The Functions of Issuer Disclosure Obligations in Primary Markets

From the policymakers' perspective, there are several reasons justifying the widespread use of issuer-disclosure rules on primary markets.[27] To begin with, disclosure is a relatively cheap regulatory tool. By prescribing a specific duty, it does not entail any direct government expenditures,[28] except potentially those associated with the establishment and operation of an enforcement agency. Furthermore, it is a policy choice with a high likelihood of garnering multilateral support. It addresses political pressure and meets investors' demand for increased regulation, which is particularly pronounced in the aftermath of financial scandals and crises.[29] At the same time, it faces less resistance from affected groups, who

[25] B Black, 'The Legal and Institutional Preconditions for Strong Securities Markets' (2001) 48 *UCLA Law Review* 781, 782.

[26] Moloney (n 24) 75–76.

[27] Activities on secondary markets come with additional disclosure obligations, occurring periodically and on an ad-hoc basis, see H Brinckmann, in Veil (ed) (n 4) 278.

[28] O Ben-Shahar and C E Schneider, 'The Failure of Mandated Disclosure' (2011) 159 *University of Pennsylvania Law Review* 647, 682.

[29] But see E Ferran, 'Crisis-driven Regulatory Reform: Where in the World is the EU Going?' in E Ferran et al (eds), *The Regulatory Aftermath of the Global Financial Crisis* (CUP, 2012) 3–4, stressing the public choice concerns linked to crisis-driven regulatory reforms.

generally favour heightened levels of disclosure over more invasive measures that restrict or prohibit specific behaviours.[30] Finally, mandatory disclosure resonates well with two fundamental principles of private law,[31] namely those of the free market and private autonomy.[32]

But apart from the relative merits of disclosure as a regulatory technique, its prevalence is primarily linked to the crucial functions it performs for market participants and, by extension, the entire economy. More specifically, when securities are offered to the public or admitted to trading for the first time, there exists an inherent information asymmetry between the issuer (and its underwriters) and potential investors. This is because the former possess significantly more information about the quality, prospects and true value of the securities offered compared to the latter. Indeed, potential investors will probably own limited information about the past performance of a new issuer, as well as the capabilities and inclinations of its management. The issue of information asymmetry is exacerbated by the fact that at this stage, at least when entirely new securities are issued,[33] there is no existing secondary market, and consequently, no market price has been established yet. According to the semi-strong form of the efficient capital market hypothesis (ECMH),[34] this would serve as an accurate signal of the actual value of the offered securities by rapidly incorporating all publicly available information.[35]

One of the main consequences of information asymmetry is that it exposes investors to the risk of fraud by unscrupulous issuers. These issuers might exploit their informational advantage to sell overvalued securities that do not possess the claimed quality or are not as suitable for individual investors compared to other securities available on the market. In neoclassical economic theory, this constitutes a major potential source of market failure, as it may result in suboptimal investment decisions, thereby affecting the allocational efficiency of the market.[36] Moreover, if investors consistently incurred losses in securities transactions,

[30] L Enriques and S Gilotta, 'Disclosure and Financial Market Regulation' in E Ferran, N Moloney and J Payne (eds), *Oxford Handbook on Financial Regulation* (OUP, 2015) 512.

[31] See generally F Böhm, 'Rule of Law in a Market Economy' in A Peacock and H Willgerodt (eds), *Germany's Social Market Economy: Origins and Evolution* (Springer, 1989).

[32] Ben-Shahar and Schneider (n 28) 681. For an enlightening treatise on the relation between information and private autonomy, see S Grundmann, W Kerber and S Weatherhill (eds), *Party Autonomy and the Role of Information in the Internal Market* (De Gruyter, 2001).

[33] By contrast, in an offering by an established issuer, whose identical securities are already traded on a liquid secondary market, investors can trust that the price they pay is fair and unbiased if it closely aligns with the price in the secondary market, see M Fox, 'Initial Public Offerings in the CMU: A US Perspective' in D Busch, E Avgouleas and G Ferrarini (eds), *Capital Markets Union in Europe* (OUP, 2018) 274.

[34] E Fama, 'Efficient Capital Markets: A Review of Theory and Empirical Work' (1970) 25 *The Journal of Finance* 383.

[35] On the mechanisms that operate in the direction of incorporating new information into prices, see RJ Gilson and RH Kraakman, 'The Mechanisms of Market Efficiency' (1984) 70 *Virginia Law Review* 549, 565 ff.

[36] See, generally, BC Greenwald and JE Stiglitz, 'Externalities in Economies with Imperfect Information and Incomplete Markets' (1986) 101 *The Quarterly Journal of Economics* 229.

their confidence in the market would be undermined, leading to reluctance or unwillingness to invest, potentially jeopardising the functioning, if not the very existence, of the market.[37] In this regard, the main function of disclosure is to protect investors against dishonest issuers. This protection does not shield them from potential losses; rather, it aims to provide them with all necessary information about the issuing entity and its securities, enabling informed and efficient investment choices.[38]

In addition to risks for investors, information asymmetry also poses risks for issuers. In the jargon of economics, the primary capital market is a characteristic example of a 'market for lemons'.[39] Using the market for used cars as an example, Akerlof coined this phrase to illustrate a problem where, due to the inability of the demand side, caused by asymmetric information, to ascertain the quality of the products offered, sellers of high-quality products are gradually driven out of the market. This occurs because purchasers are only willing to offer the expected price for a product of lower quality, often referred to as a 'lemon'. In the primary market, the lemon's problem is much more pronounced compared to the used cars' market.[40] The buyer of a used car can take a test drive, perform a mechanical inspection, and inquire about others' experience with the same car. In contrast, investments in newly issued securities are characterised by a much higher degree of information asymmetry. Due to their nature as 'credence goods', the quality of these investments cannot be assessed ex-ante, and an ex-post assessment might occur long after their acquisition or be very difficult to observe.[41] This implies that, absent a workable response, investors cannot differentiate high-quality securities from those offered by firms with less promising projects. As a result, they discount the prices they are willing to pay to reflect the average expected return for the total pool. This compels issuers to issue more securities and at lower prices than if investors had full information to value the offer.

Nevertheless, issuing more securities increases the cost of capital as the firm is bound to pay more in future dividends or interest. This implies that, even when a project is more promising than others, it may not yield sufficient revenues to justify these higher expected obligations, discouraging the highest-quality issuers from entering the market. On the contrary, discounted prices will not dissuade issuers of unworthy securities, who will persist in the market, thereby displacing

[37] As aptly pointed out, the functioning of the market and investor protection are two 'communicating vessels' that support each other, see K Hopt, *Der Kapitalanlegerschutz im Recht der Banken* (Beck, 1975) 52.

[38] L Gullifer and J Payne, *Corporate Finance Law: Principles and Policy*, 1st edn (Hart Publishing, 2011) 416.

[39] G Akerlof, 'The Market for "Lemons": Quality Uncertainty and the Market Mechanism' (1970) 84 *The Quarterly Journal of Economics* 488.

[40] For the application of the 'lemons problem' in securities markets, see S Myers and N Majluf, 'Corporate Financing and Investment Decisions When Firms Have Information that Investors Do Not Have' (1984) 13 *Journal of Financial Economics* 187.

[41] R Gilson, 'Engineering a Venture Capital Market: Lessons from the American Experience' (2003) 55 *Stanford Law Review* 1067, 1076 ff.

the next-highest-quality issuers and so forth. This consequence becomes even more dramatic as, in addition to harming good-quality issuers, it also adversely affects markets overall.[42] This is not only because efficient allocation no longer takes place, as the selection of securities is not based on their quality, and capital flows are directed towards undeserving offerings ('adverse selection'). Even worse, it might be the case that offers are not made at all. Indeed, when the expected quality of a security is such that the demand side is only willing to pay a price that is not even worth the paper it is printed on, the market is not only characterised by adverse selection but unravels completely.[43] In this context, the initial disclosure obligations imposed on issuers serve as a tool to counteract the lemons problem and the resulting losses to economic welfare, insofar as they enable the more accurate pricing of the offered securities, facilitating a more efficient allocation of investment capital.

ii. The Rationale of Mandatory Initial Disclosure

Although the beneficial functions of disclosure during a public offer or listing are widely acknowledged, this does not self-evidently imply that a mandatory initial disclosure regime is necessary or desirable. Indeed, ever since disclosure has been deemed a vital prerequisite for ensuring the efficiency of allocation within capital markets, the million-dollar question has been whether the provision of information should be regulated, or if market forces would naturally compel firms to provide it in optimal amounts.[44] This matter has sparked extensive debate in the literature.[45]

The main argument put forth by proponents of voluntary disclosure is that issuers possessing private information about the high quality of their securities will deliberately disclose it to the public in order to signal their superiority over other firms.[46] In other words, it is assumed that issuers of the highest-quality securities

[42] S Grundmann, 'Wissen und Information' in S Grundmann, H-W Micklitz and M Renner (eds), *Privatrechtstheorie* (Mohr Siebeck, 2015) 979–80.

[43] Akerlof (n 39) 495–96.

[44] A Ferrell, 'The Case for Mandatory Disclosure in Securities Regulation Around the World' (2007) 2 *Brooklyn Journal of Corporate, Financial & Commercial Law* 81, 81; S Grundmann, *European Company Law*, 2nd edn (Intersentia, 2012) 485.

[45] On the merits of mandatory disclosure, see generally J Seligman, 'The Historical Need for a Mandatory Corporate Disclosure System' (1983) 9 *The Journal of Corporation Law* 1; J Coffee Jr., 'Market Failure and the Economic Case for a Mandatory Disclosure System' (1984) 70 *Virginia Law Review*, 717; MB Fox, 'Retaining Mandatory Securities Disclosure: Why Issuer Choice Is Not Investor Empowerment' (1999) 85 *Virginia Law Review* 1335. Against mandatory disclosure, see H Kripke, *The SEC and Corporate Disclosure: Regulation in Search of a Purpose* (Law & Business, 1979); R Romano, 'Empowering Investors: A Market Approach to Securities Regulation' (1998) 107 *The Yale Law Journal* 2359; JR Macey, 'A Pox on Both Your Houses: Enron, Sarbanes-Oxley and the Debate Concerning the Relative Efficacy of Mandatory Versus Enabling Rules' (2003) 81 *Washington University Law Review* 329.

[46] S Ross and H Kripke, 'Disclosure Regulation in Financial Markets: Implications of Modern Finance Theory and Signaling Theory' in F Edwards (ed), *Issues in Financial Regulation* (McGraw-Hill, 1979) 177–202; S Grossman and O Hart, 'Disclosure Laws and Takeover Bids' (1980) 35 *The Journal of Finance* 323, 323–24.

will voluntarily adhere to a regime of full public disclosure to prevent investors from erroneously assuming that they withhold information indicative of poor firm quality, potentially resulting in a lower valuation of their securities.[47] Issuers with slightly lower-quality securities will adopt the same disclosure regime to avoid confusion with less reputable issuers. This pattern continues until issuers remaining silent are perceived by the market as offering the lowest-quality securities.

However, the application of the signalling theory as the foundation for opposing mandatory disclosure in public primary markets has various shortcomings. The concept of signalling as a comprehensive safeguard against adverse selection begins from the assumption that those overseeing the firm's policy (ie, managers and controlling shareholders) genuinely wish to commit themselves to a public disclosure system that maximises the current market valuation of the firm's securities. However elegant or appealing, though, this assumption is quite unrealistic. Considering the agency problem inherent in the relationship between company insiders and potential investors, there are compelling reasons to believe that managers would be very hesitant to disclose 'bad news' without a duty to do so.[48] Therefore, in the absence of mandatory initial disclosure, a system relying solely on voluntary disclosure would likely result in the underproduction of information. This, in turn, could prompt investors to discount the value of the securities offered to reflect the average quality expected from the overall pool.[49]

Honest managers, seeking to prevent this negative scenario, would then need to disclose all information, both positive and negative, related to their business. However, the issue with such a solution is that, contrary to what the signalling model assumes,[50] disclosure involves high private costs for issuers. These costs are not only linked to the fixed expenses and the diversion of management and staff time that stem from the production and provision of information ('operational' or 'direct' costs). They also pertain to the benefits that the dissemination of proprietary information might provide to other firms, including competitors and stakeholders ('interfirm' or 'indirect' costs).[51] More specifically, information exhibits many features of a typical public good.[52] First, it is non-rivalrous, meaning that the use of a certain piece of information by someone does not preclude others from using it as well. Second, it is imperfectly appropriable, as it is very challenging

[47] R Romano, 'The Need for Competition in International Securities Regulation' (2001) 2 *Theoretical Inquiries in Law* 387, 544 and 562.

[48] In fact, it is suggested that the more unfavourable the news, the greater the negative consequences for managers, increasing the temptation to withhold information, RH Kraakman, 'Disclosure and Corporate Governance: An Overview Essay' in G Ferrarini et al (eds), *Reforming Company and Takeover Law in Europe* (OUP, 2004) 100.

[49] Gullifer and Payne (n 38) 422.

[50] The signalling theory builds on the assumption that disclosure is costless, see Grossman and Hart (n 46) 323.

[51] For a distinction between these two types of costs and the relevant terminology, see Fox (n 33) 285; FH Easterbrook and DR Fischel, 'Mandatory Disclosure and the Protection of Investors' (1984) 70 *Virginia Law Review* 669, 707–709.

[52] Coffee Jr. (n 45) 725.

to exclude someone from using it, even if they have not paid the relevant price.[53] Hence, information disclosed by an individual issuer is also useful for investors in gaining a better appreciation of the value of securities offered by other firms, indirectly benefiting them.[54] Moreover, disclosure may unveil valuable information to a firm's competitors, thus improving their position at the expense of the disclosing firm.[55] This means that the private costs of an issuer willing to disclose, without other issuers being obliged to do the same, would probably exceed the relevant gains by an amount equal to these indirect costs. Therefore, without a mandatory disclosure framework, the amount of information provided by issuers in the primary market would be less than socially optimal.[56]

Against these shortcomings, proponents of voluntary disclosure argue that the problem of underproduction of information and the associated social costs could be addressed through the discovery efforts of information intermediaries and investors, along with other mechanisms that issuers could employ to signal their quality, such as hiring a reputable investment bank to market the offering or requiring directors to hold substantial quantities of securities.[57] Nevertheless, these proposals do not offer a compelling justification for abolishing mandatory disclosure. Regarding intermediaries, despite their crucial role in acquiring, processing, and disseminating information, enabling investors to piggyback on their efforts,[58] considerations related to the public-good character of information also apply in their case, deterring them from fulfilling these functions, when the benefits do not outweigh the costs.[59] Besides, if information gathering were entrusted to intermediaries, information asymmetry would most likely worsen, as their research efforts would focus on fewer companies, primarily the largest ones.[60] With respect to investors, unlike in private companies where they can negotiate the information needed for decision-making, in the context of a public offer, it would not only be impractical but also economically inefficient to require them to individually bargain for such information.[61] This is because the management of the issuer already possesses or can easily discover that information, thus being in a better position to bear the cost of its production and distribution.[62]

[53] Enriques and Gilotta (n 30) 521.

[54] Easterbrook and Fischel (n 51) 685.

[55] ibid 686.

[56] See M Fox, 'Securities Disclosure in a Globalizing Market: Who Should Regulate Whom' (1997) 95 *Michigan Law Review* 2498, 2532 ff.

[57] For an analysis of available market solutions, see Gullifer and Payne (n 38) 422–23; Fox (n 33) 277 ff.

[58] Easterbrook and Fischel (n 51) 687–89; S Grundmann and W Kerber, 'Information Intermediaries and Party Autonomy – The Example of Securities and Insurance Markets' in Grundmann, Kerber and Weatherhill (n 32) 269 ff.

[59] G Hadfield, R Howse and M Trebilcock, 'Information-Based Principles for Rethinking Consumer Protection Policy' (1998) 21 *Journal of Consumer Policy* 131, 144; Grundmann and Kerber (n 58) 275–76.

[60] Gullifer and Payne (n 38) 422.

[61] Heinze (n 23) 358.

[62] See D Zetzsche, *Aktionärsinformation in der börsennotierten Aktiengesellschaft* (Carl Heymanns, 2006) 37.

Finally, as regards reputational means and other market mechanisms utilised by issuers to distinguish their securities as high-quality, while generally beneficial, they can only serve as subsidies and not as substitutes for disclosure requirements.

On a final note, a frequently cited argument in favour of mandatory disclosure pertains to its capacity to improve the standardisation of information provided to investors.[63] More specifically, uniformity in the amount, format, and timing of disclosure is valuable for investors as it enhances the comprehensibility and comparability of firm-specific information, enabling a better assessment of the value of their securities. Moreover, it makes it easier to establish wrongdoing in the absence of a certain piece of information than if investors had to prove that the missing information was material and its omission was fraudulent.[64] However, considering the various and often conflicting interests of different issuers, establishing and promoting a common disclosure format through private ordering would undoubtedly be challenging and time-consuming. Therefore, even assuming optimal private incentives towards disclosure, the information provided by issuers in a voluntary system would be idiosyncratic, thus diminishing its value to potential investors.[65] Mandatory disclosure addresses this problem, providing a common framework for initial disclosure duties in a more rapid and cost-effective manner.

iii. Behavioural and Cost Considerations in the Disclosure System

a. Cognitive Limitations and Biases: Addressing Suboptimal Use of Information

The arguments in favour of voluntary disclosure must not be disregarded. Nevertheless, the imperfections of a disclosure system based solely on market forces and the relative merits of mandatory disclosure as a tool for ensuring the efficient allocation of investment capital within the market have led most regulators to accept mandatory disclosure rules as an essential feature of primary market regulation. That being the case, the question arises as to how to determine the correct amount and form of the information to be disclosed.

The primary condition would be that the disclosed information is beneficial for investors. In meeting this requirement, policymakers, both in the EU and internationally, have been guided by the traditional economic theory on human decision-making, commonly known as the 'Rational Choice Theory'.[66] Despite some disagreements about the details of this theory,[67] in its most prevalent

[63] See eg Kraakman (n 48) 101; E Rock, 'Securities Regulation as a Lobster Trap: A Credible Commitment Theory of Mandatory Disclosure' (2002) 23 *Cardozo Law Review* 675, 686.

[64] Armour et al (n 15) 163.

[65] Enriques and Gilotta (n 30) 524.

[66] T Ulen, 'Information and the Market Economy – Cognitive Errors and Legal Correctives' in Grundmann, Kerber and Weatherhill (n 32) 106.

[67] For an overview of the different views, see R Korobkin and T Ulen, 'Law and Behavioral Science: Removing the Rationality Assumption from Law and Economics' (2000) 88 *California Law Review* 1051, 1060 ff.

version, namely the 'expected utility theory',[68] it posits that humans have transitive preferences and their behaviour is constantly oriented towards maximising the utility they derive from those preferences, subject to external constraints (eg, income, time, cognitive resources, legal rules etc).[69] Within the context of capital markets, this implies that rational investors, having perceived and processed all available information, along with the advantages and disadvantages of any alternatives, will opt for the optimal course of action to maximise their expected benefits while minimising expected costs.[70] In this regard, mandatory and extensive initial disclosure requirements have been considered crucial in assisting investors in their cost-benefit analysis of competing options, thus facilitating more efficient fund allocation.

However, the rationality model, while undeniably useful for forming hypotheses about market behaviour,[71] has been contested by well-documented empirical evidence in psychology and other behavioural sciences, stressing the limits of its regulatory expansion, particularly the view that more information is always better.[72] Among these findings, two are of special interest to primary markets law: cognitive capacity limits and bounded rationality. According to the former, there is a limit to the amount of information that the average human brain's working memory can simultaneously process.[73] As a result, when all channels of information processing are fully utilised, any additional information triggers information overload, resulting in stress, confusion and a deterioration in the quality of decisions made.[74] This has far-reaching effects on the regulation of disclosure obligations in primary markets.[75] If too many items are disclosed simultaneously, as is often the case, they may not reach the working memory, especially when the content is technical and complex.[76] This suggests that, at least in certain cases,

[68] Originally introduced by Daniel Bernoulli in 1738 and later enriched by the von Neumann–Morgenstern utility theorem, see J von Neumann and O Morgenstern, *Theory of Games and Economic Behavior*, 60th Anniversary edn (Princeton University Press, 2004).

[69] M Friedman and LJ Savage, 'The Utility Analysis of Choices Involving Risk' (1948) 56 *Journal of Political Economy* 279, 287–88 and 303–304; K Mathis and AD Steffen, 'From Rational Choice to Behavioural Economics' in K Mathis (ed), *European Perspectives in Behavioural Law and Economics* (Springer, 2015) 32 ff.

[70] E Avgouleas, 'The Global Financial Crisis and the Disclosure Paradigm in European Financial Regulation: The Case for Reform' (2009) 6 *European Company and Financial Law Review* 440, 442–43.

[71] T Ulen, 'Rational Choice and the Economic Analysis of Law' (1994) 19 *Law and Social Inquiry* 487, 488–89.

[72] As better summarised by L Loss, *Securities Regulation*, 2nd edn, Vol. 1 (Wolters Kluwer, 1961) 21 ('Disclosure, again disclosure, and still more disclosure').

[73] See G Miller, 'The Magical Number Seven, Plus or Minus Two: Some Limits on our Capacity for Processing Information' (1956) 63 *Psychological Review* 81; A Baddeley, 'Working Memory: Theories, Models, and Controversies'(2012) 63 Annual Review of Psychology 1.

[74] See J Buchanan and N Kock, 'Information Overload: A Decision Making Perspective' in M Köksalan and S Zionts (eds), *Multiple Criteria Decision Making in the New Millennium* (Spring, 2001).

[75] See generally T Paredes, 'Blinded by the Light: Information Overload and Its Consequences for Securities Regulation' (2003) 81 *Washington University Law Quarterly* 417.

[76] Securities and Exchange Commission, *Disclosure to Investors: A Reappraisal of Federal Administrative Policies Under the '33 and '34 Acts. The Wheat Report* (Commerce Clearing House, 1969) 62–63.

better investment choices may result from focusing on the quality and framing of disclosed information, rather than its quantity.[77]

The concept of bounded rationality, now, was initially introduced by Herbert Simon to describe the inherent limitations of human knowledge and computational skills.[78] In particular, it postulates that when faced with complex issues beyond their cognitive abilities, individuals will aim for an adequate or satisfactory result ('satisficing'), instead of pursuing an unattainable optimal solution ('optimising'). In addition, they tend to unconsciously rely on mental shortcuts ('heuristics') when making probability judgements and solving problems, which, in certain circumstances, may lead to cognitive biases, that is systematic errors in the thinking process, preventing accurate decision-making.[79] Some of these biases are especially relevant to the regulation of initial disclosure requirements. For example, optimism bias may cause investors to disregard or downplay the probability of incurring losses, based on the false belief that they are less likely to experience such a negative event.[80] Moreover, due to availability bias, investors might not always adhere to an objective cost-benefit analysis but, instead, focus on events that are readily available to them.[81] Accordingly, they might over- or underestimate an investment risk based on the ease of recalling similar events, potentially resulting in inaccurate and suboptimal investment decisions.[82] Finally, due to the certainty effect,[83] they might become risk-averse even when the probabilities of monetary losses are not particularly high, leading them to refrain from investing in potentially profitable projects.

The previous analysis suggests that problems of bounded rationality and information overload influence investors' choices. Therefore, when regulating disclosure obligations on primary markets, these behavioural insights should be considered. However, it is crucial to note that while these problems are widespread, they are not universal, as investors operate along a continuum ranging from full to bounded rationality.[84] In this respect, the regulatory response to cognitive errors should carefully consider the consequences for all investors, as well as for actors

[77] On the role of framing in decision making, see A Tversky and D Kahneman, 'The Framing of Decisions and the Psychology of Choice' (1981) 211 *Science* 4.

[78] H A Simon, 'Rational Choice and the Structure of the Environment' (1956) 63 *Psychological Review* 129.

[79] A Tversky and D Kahneman, 'Judgment under Uncertainty: Heuristics and Biases' (1974) 185 *Science* 1124.

[80] HK Baker and J Nofsinger, 'Psychological Biases of Investors' (2002) 11 *Financial Services Review* 97, 103.

[81] A Tversky and D Kahneman, 'Availability: A Heuristic for Judging Frequency and Probability' (1973) 5 *Cognitive Psychology* 207, 221.

[82] See generally P Slovic, *The Perception of Risk* (Routledge, 2000) 37–38.

[83] D Kahneman and A Tversky, 'Prospect Theory: An Analysis of Decision under Risk' (1979) 47 *Econometrica*, 263, 268–69; P Fishburn and G Kochenberger, 'Two-Piece Von Neumann-Morgenstern Utility Functions' (1979) 10 *Decision Sciences* 503.

[84] S Grundmann and P Hacker, 'Conflicts of Interests' in D Busch and G Ferarrini (eds), *Regulation of the EU Financial System: MiFID II and MiFIR* (OUP, 2017) 178.

on the opposite side of the market. This means, more specifically, that if regulation aimed at removing or counteracting distortions ('debiasing' and 'pro-biasing') takes opportunities from market players capable of rational decision-making based on the careful processing of extensive information, then renouncing the 'informed investor' standard should not be pursued. Doing so might jeopardise the efficiency of allocation within the market.[85] In such cases, therefore, only supplements to full primary market disclosure can be justified, and only to the extent necessary to ensure an informed decision from those susceptible to cognitive failures.

The situation is, nevertheless, different in cases of extensive cognitive limitations and biases among investors, which might lead to a market failure. The starting point for any regulatory intervention in these instances should be the distinction between 'day-to-day economic losses' on the one hand and 'existential losses' on the other.[86] Outside the sphere of existential losses, the guiding principle for regulators should be the empowerment of investors in making their own sufficiently informed and careful – yet autonomous – decisions. Regulatory measures in this regard could involve reducing the information load, while also determining its format and order, starting from the most important and perhaps highlighting the items most valuable for investors in view of their level of education, experience, attentiveness, and so on. If, however, the consequences of cognitive failures threaten the very financial existence of investors (eg, when insolvency risk is highly probable), then more paternalistic measures are also justified.[87] In ascending order of intensity, these could range, indicatively, from risk warnings and other prudential requirements from the side of issuers or, where applicable, the intermediaries, to the introduction of investment limits and restrictions in accessing a certain investment.

b. The Economic Effects of Disclosure: Balancing Costs and Benefits

Apart from satisfying investors' needs, the second criterion for determining the appropriate amount of information to be disclosed by issuers is that the marginal costs associated with the preparation and dissemination of disclosure documents should not exceed the marginal benefits from financing on the capital market. As previously explained, mandatory disclosure imposes both direct and indirect costs on issuers. At the same time, elevated disclosure requirements result in a corresponding increase in liability risks, constituting another significant cost for

[85] Grundmann (n 44) 484.

[86] S Grundmann, 'Targeted Consumer Protection' in D Leczykiewicz and S Weatherhill (eds), *The images of the consumer in EU law legislation, free movement and competition law* (Hart Publishing, 2016) 238.

[87] Grundmann (n 7) 31. An intervention is considered paternalistic when it is selected by a central planner with the aim of influencing the choices of affected parties in a direction that will, at least, prevent them from becoming worse-off, R Thaler and C Sunstein, 'Libertarian Paternalism' (2003) 93 *American Economic Review* 175.

disclosing firms due to potential exposure to litigation.[88] Yet, these costs and, consequently, the optimal level of disclosure, may vary among issuers, depending on distinctive factors such as the firm's size, stage of development, and field of operation. For example, the direct costs linked to the publication of information during a public offering are largely fixed. As a result, owing to economies of scale, they tend to be proportionately higher for smaller issuers, making their recourse to capital market financing more burdensome compared to larger issuers.[89] Furthermore, young, innovative firms, in principle, place greater value on confidentiality compared to incumbents, thus rendering indirect costs higher for them. Besides, litigation costs might impose a heavier burden on small firms that lack the necessary resources or expertise to counteract the risk of liability should a possible lawsuit arise.

Without some form of remedy, therefore, disclosure costs might hinder the promotion of a significant portion of worthy projects. This represents a loss not only for the fund-seeking firms but also for investors, who have a more limited range of instruments to choose from, and for the economy as a whole, as available capital may not necessarily be directed toward projects with the highest profitability. This is not meant to suggest, of course, that an overall reduction of disclosure standards is desirable or needed. Instead, it calls for a careful calibration and, in some instances, exemptions to disclosure requirements so as to alleviate the burden on specific issuers for which full disclosure entails disproportionate transaction and compliance costs. Nonetheless, it is true that any attempt to deregulate initial disclosure requirements based on issuer size and needs is confronted with significant challenges related to finding the right equilibrium with the conflicting interests of other market participants. Indeed, while issuers seek to reduce the regulatory costs arising from disclosure, investors are, generally, interested in as much information as possible. In this respect, an overly easy access to market financing for businesses would be counter-efficient without adequate protective measures for investors. Meanwhile, an overall reduction of disclosure standards might prevent issuers of the highest quality securities from signalling their superiority, thus exacerbating adverse selection.

In light of the above, it could be suggested that the fundamental principle behind any cost-benefit balance of primary market disclosure obligations should be that of Pareto efficiency.[90] This means, in other words, that a reduction of

[88] C Leuz and P Wysocki, 'The Economics of Disclosure and Financial Reporting Regulation: Evidence and Suggestions for Future Research' (2016) 54 *Journal of Accounting Research* 525, 551–53; Enriques and Gilotta (n 30) 531; Heinze (n 23) 383.

[89] W Schön, 'Corporate Disclosure in a Competitive Environment – the Quest for a European Framework on Mandatory Disclosure' (2006) 6 *Journal of Corporate Law Studies* 259, 288; G Ferrarini and A Ottolia, 'Corporate Disclosure as a Transaction Cost: The Case of SMEs' (2013) 9 *European Review of Contract Law* 363, 374.

[90] This refers to an economic state where any reallocation of resources enhances the welfare of at least one individual, without adversely affecting another, given a certain initial allocation of goods, see V Pareto, *Manuale di economia politica con una introduzione alla scienza sociale* (Università Bocconi Editore, 2006) 326 ff.

or exemption from disclosure duties should only be accepted when it not only increases the welfare of the issuer but does so without making investors or other issuers worse-off. In practice, this could be the case, among other scenarios, when the relevant information is already public and easily accessible to investors, when investors can obtain all necessary information directly from the issuer, when the omitted information would not benefit investors (eg, considering their cognitive abilities), or when the invested amounts are so small that any potential losses for investors, and the resulting impact on market confidence, appear insignificant compared to the potential gains for issuers.[91] In the same vein, any segmentation among issuers operating in the same market based on individual characteristics (eg, size) should be avoided.

iv. Limits of Disclosure and Supplementary Measures

a. Supervision and Enforcement of Disclosure Duties

The preceding discussion highlights that, while mandatory disclosure rules are crucial in addressing information asymmetry between issuers and potential investors, they also entail certain drawbacks, associated with investors' limited capacity to absorb complex and lengthy information and the substantial costs that disclosure imposes on issuers. These shortcomings, albeit not necessarily incurable, reveal the limits of relying solely on disclosure duties as a regulatory strategy, stressing the need for additional measures to support market efficiency. Among the available solutions, perhaps the most critical in this direction is the implementation of effective supervisory and enforcement mechanisms.[92]

Indeed, like all legal provisions prescribing positive actions in the market, rules imposing disclosure obligations in primary markets have inherent limits if not accompanied by a robust supervisory and enforcement system that can credibly ensure their compliance in practice.[93] To understand why this is the case, let us consider a scenario where the information held by an issuer could have a negative impact on the valuation of their securities by prospective investors. If this information were disclosed, the market price would adjust to reflect the actual value of the investment. Accordingly, they would only proceed with the offer if the anticipated revenues exceeded the amount required to cover their funding needs. Nevertheless, if the issuer had the opportunity to omit the negative information or provide false statements, they could potentially secure a high enough price to make

[91] See also Grundmann (n 44) 486–87.

[92] TMJ Möllers, 'Efficiency as a Standard in Capital Market Law – The Application of Empirical and Economic Arguments for the Justification of Civil Law' (2009) 20 *European Business Law Review* 243, 245; Armour et al (n 15) 80.

[93] See generally N Moloney, 'Supervision in the Wake of the Financial Crisis: Achieving Effective Law in Action – A Challenge for the EU' in E Wymeersch, K Hopt and G Ferrarini (eds), *Financial Regulation and Supervision. A Post Crisis Analysis* (OUP, 2012) 71–72.

the otherwise inauspicious offering appear worthwhile. This implies that without a reliable framework ensuring the prompt detection and, if necessary, punishment of any material omissions or misstatements, issuers might be tempted to breach their disclosure duties. In that respect, supervision and enforcement should be essentially regarded as complementary elements in achieving the public policy goals underlying disclosure obligations in primary markets. More specifically, they contribute to the accurate formation of prices for the offered securities, thus ensuring that investable capital is directed to those projects that are most beneficial to the parties involved.[94] At the same time, they enhance investors' confidence and trust in the markets, thereby increasing their willingness to invest,[95] which also carries positive implications for primary market development.[96]

Considering the above, the next decisive question is what form should supervision and enforcement take. One solution could be to delegate these functions exclusively to public authorities. These entities typically hold a comprehensive set of monitoring, investigatory, and sanctioning powers, enabling them to guarantee issuer's adherence to their disclosure duties. Specifically, they can intervene both preventively, by conducting ex-ante verification of the completeness and accuracy of information provided to investors, and reactively, through the initiation of repressive actions, mainly of an administrative nature, in case of infringements.[97] However, a system relying solely on public supervision and enforcement would have limited deterring and compliance effects. Even if competent authorities are appropriately empowered, they may not always possess the necessary resources or motivation to prevent or punish all possible violations.[98] For this reason, regulators must also establish private enforcement rules in the event of a breach of disclosure obligations or material misstatements to the market.[99] This approach is further supported by the idea that issuers would be more inclined to comply

[94] P Davies, 'Damages Actions by Investors on the Back of Market Disclosure Requirements' in Busch, Avgouleas and Ferrarini (n 33) 321.

[95] L Zingales, 'The Future of Securities Regulation' (2009) 47 *Journal of Accounting Research* 391, 397; N Moloney, *How to Protect Investors: Lessons from the EC and the UK* (CUP, 2010) 426; E Vandendriessche, *Investor Losses: A Comparative Legal Analysis of Causation and Assessment of Damages in Investor Litigation* (Intersentia, 2015) 45–46.

[96] See generally R La Porta, F Lopez-de-Silanes and A Shleifer, 'What Works in Securities Laws' (2006) 61 *The Journal of Finance* 1; H Jackson and J Zhang, 'Private and Public Enforcement of Securities Regulation' in J Gordon and W-G Ringe (eds), *The Oxford Handbook of Corporate Law and Governance* (OUP, 2018).

[97] I McNeil, 'Enforcement and Sanctioning' in Ferran, Moloney and Payne (n 30) 292 ff; L Enriques et al, 'Corporate Law and Securities Markets' in R Kraakman et al (eds), *The Anatomy of Corporate Law: A Comparative and Functional Approach* (OUP, 2017) 259.

[98] Black (n 25) 800; L Klöhn, 'Private Versus Public Enforcement of Laws – A Law and Economics Perspective' in R Schulze (ed), *Compensation of Private Losses: The Evolution of Torts in European Business Law* (De Gruyter, 2011) 189–90; H Jackson and M Roe, 'Public and Private Enforcement of Securities Laws: Resource-based Evidence' (2009) 93 *Journal of Financial Economics* 207, 208.

[99] G Ferrarini and P Guidici, 'Liability for Misstatements to the Market: The Post-Parmalat Years' in R Huang and N Howson (eds), *Enforcement of Corporate and Securities Law: China and the World* (CUP, 2017) 400. For the deterring and compensatory role of private enforcement, highlighting its importance as an enforcement mechanism, see Vandendriessche, *Investor losses* (n 95) 48 ff.

with their disclosure duties out of concern for potential damages claimed by investors, rather than facing administrative or even criminal sanctions.[100] This is due to the fact that individuals entitled to compensation have a much greater incentive than public agencies to come forward and enforce the law.[101] Besides, a system of civil liability for omitted or misleading information appears justified also from a fairness perspective, as it prevents issuers from retaining profits they should not have obtained.[102] However, a caveat must be added here: the intensity of both private and public enforcement should be balanced with the disclosure obligations of issuers. The imposition of extensive disclosure requirements, combined with a rigorous enforcement system, would exponentially increase liability risks without necessarily improving the quality of information shared in the market, given that issuers would probably adopt a more formalistic approach to disclosure in response to these heightened risks.[103]

If private enforcement is deemed necessary, two final issues shall be addressed: the range of those liable to investors and the standard of their liability. Concerning the first issue, as a general rule, all natural and legal persons with direct control over the information provided to investors shall be held liable. These should encompass not only the issuer, its management, and third parties (such as accountants, lawyers, and other experts) responsible for preparing the disclosed information, but also underwriters and other entities involved in its distribution. Especially with regard to underwriters, they participate actively in the promotion of the issuer's securities, mainly through book building and other marketing activities.[104] Hence, holding them accountable for the information given by issuers, incentivises them to perform their monitoring duties diligently and impartially, thus also mitigating the risk of omissions or misstatements.[105] Regarding the standard of liability, consistent with the classic law and economics approach,[106] it should be sufficiently high to discourage potential wrongdoers from violating their duties, though not excessively high, as overdeterrence is counter-efficient.[107] This implies, more specifically, that a scienter-based liability regime should be avoided. In such a scenario, the issuer or intermediary would escape liability unless the investor could affirmatively prove that they were aware or highly reckless in not being aware of the incorrect or omitted information.[108] A strict liability regime is also not preferable. Extending liability to inaccuracies that could not be reasonably

[100] See Fox (n 33) 288.

[101] S Shavell, *Foundations of Economic Analysis of Law* (Belknap Press, 2004) 579.

[102] The problem, of course, is that the principle of restitution is interpreted in various ways across jurisdictions, each carrying different implications from a deterrence standpoint.

[103] Enriques and Gilotta (n 30) 531–32.

[104] M Fleuriet, *Investment Banking Explained: An Insider's Guide to the Industry*, 2nd edn (McGraw-Hill Education, 2019) 157.

[105] Davies (n 94) 328.

[106] RA Posner, *Economic Analysis of Law*, 7th edn (Aspen Publishers, 2007) 662 ff.

[107] Shavell (n 101) 571 ff; GJ Stigler, 'The Optimum Enforcement of Law' (1970) 78 *Journal of Political Economy* 526.

[108] Fox (n 33) 288.

detected by those responsible for the content of the disclosures transforms issuers and underwriters into insurers, thereby raising the costs of securities offerings and, potentially, deterring them from entering the market.[109] For these reasons, adopting a negligence standard wherein the defendant must demonstrate engagement in adequate due diligence (shifting the burden of proof) appears more effective. This approach ensures an adequate level of deterrence while relieving liability at the point where the cost of undertaking additional discovery efforts surpasses the potential gains for investors resulting from greater precision.[110]

b. The Critical Role of Financial Intermediaries

To improve companies' access to market financing, as envisioned in the CMU, there is a need for the mobilisation (or 'pooling') of funds from various sources. Without access to a diverse pool of investors, many promising projects would be limited to economically inefficient scales, hindering the flow of capital to its most profitable uses.[111] However, aggregating the resources of numerous diverse investors poses a significant challenge. It involves not only considerable transaction costs but also overcoming the informational asymmetries associated with instilling confidence in savers as they relinquish control of their savings. Given these frictions, financial intermediaries play an indispensable role in facilitating pooling.[112] These economic agents act as middlemen between suppliers and borrowers of funds within a specific market setting, either by receiving capital from the former and channelling it to the latter ('market-making'), or by helping the two sides to meet and transact ('matchmaking').[113]

Especially within the context of primary markets, the intermediation functions provided by certain entities, most notably investment banks, are considered essential for addressing the challenges that information and transaction costs pose to the efficient allocation of resources.[114] This is primarily attributed to their ability to create more favourable transaction conditions than if investors and issuers were interacting directly. More specifically, intermediaries fulfil three key functions during the placement of new securities.[115] First, they serve as a bridge between

[109] M Fox, 'Regulating Public Offerings of Truly New Securities: First Principles' (2016) 66 *Duke Law Journal* 673, 714.

[110] See also Davies (n 94) 328–29.

[111] See generally E Sirri and P Tufano, 'The Economics of Pooling' in D Crane et al (eds), *The Global Financial System: A Functional Approach* (Harvard Business Law Press, 1995).

[112] Avgouleas (n 15) 24.

[113] See generally A Rubinstein and A Wolinsky, 'Middlemen' (1987) 102 *Quarterly Journal of Economics* 581; A Yavas, 'Marketmakers versus Matchmakers' (1992) 1 *Journal of Financial Intermediation* 33; G Biglaiser, 'Middlemen as Experts' (1993) 24 *RAND Journal of Economics* 212; D Spulber, 'Market Microstructure and Intermediation' (1996) 10 *Journal of Economic Perspectives* 135.

[114] See eg R Levine, 'Financial Development and Economic Growth: Views and Agenda' (1997) 35 *Journal of Economic Literature* 688, 690–91.

[115] A-K Achleitner, *Handbuch Investment Banking*, 3rd edn (Gabler, 2002) 24ff; R Merton and Z Bodie, 'A Conceptual Framework for Analyzing the Financial Environment' in Crane et al (eds) (n 111) 12–16.

fund seekers and investors, providing the former with the required network and facilities to sell their securities.[116] Second, by undertaking activities like underwriting, particularly when performed on a 'firm-commitment' basis,[117] they participate in risk-sharing, thereby alleviating issuers of some of the risks associated with the placement of securities. But, most importantly, through actively engaging in the acquisition, processing, and verification of information, they help economise on transaction costs and strengthen investors' trust in the market.[118]

Indeed, individual investors, especially retail ones, often lack the time, capacity, or means to collect and evaluate information on the risk and return attributes of available investment options, hindering their ability to make informed decisions about whether and where to invest. At the same time, issuers offering securities for the first time, may lack the necessary resources or time to invest in reputation building before the contemplated offer, preventing them from signalling ex-ante the quality of the information provided to the market.[119] In this setting, the pivotal role of intermediaries becomes particularly evident. By leveraging the expertise of their professional staff and capitalising on economies of scale, these entities can acquire and process information about the issuer and the offered securities more rapidly and at lower cost compared to individual investors.[120] Additionally, as 'repeat players' in the market, intermediaries can credibly vouch for an issuer, given their reputational capital is at stake.[121] Allowing a company to falsify or exaggerate its prospects would lead to a reputational loss exceeding any one-time gain they might receive.[122] At the same time, they face the risk of liability to investors if they endorse faulty disclosure and may incur administrative sanctions for failing to act according to their duties.[123] Considering these attributes, therefore, financial intermediaries can significantly influence the efficiency of the market's response to a new issue.

However, the reliance of investors and issuers on reputational intermediaries presents its own set of problems. First, agency problems may arise between intermediating firms (agents) and their clients (principals) when their interests diverge, and monitoring is challenging.[124] These, in turn, may give rise to agency costs,

[116] Moloney (n 24) 347.

[117] Underwriting agreements fall into two main categories: (a) best efforts agreements, where underwriters promise to do their best to sell as many securities as possible without, however, committing to buy in case of undersubscription; and (b) firm commitment agreements, where underwriters guarantee to purchase the newly issued securities regardless of whether they can place them with investors, see K Weiss Hanley, 'The economics of primary markets' (9 July 2017) 5, papers.ssrn.com/sol3/papers.cfm?abstract_id=3046256.

[118] See also Gilson and Kraakman (n 35) 618 ff; Grundmann (n 7) 22–24.

[119] Gilson and Kraakman (n 35) 619–20.

[120] Grundmann and Kerber (n 58) 269–70; Levine (n 114) 695.

[121] See also Moloney (n 24) 638.

[122] J Coffee Jr., 'Gatekeeper Failure and Reform: The Challenge of Fashioning Relevant Reforms' in Ferrarini et al (n 52) 461.

[123] Black (n 25) 787.

[124] See generally P Mahoney, 'Manager-Investor Conflicts in Mutual Funds' (2004) 18 *Journal of Economic Perspectives* 161; Coffee Jr. (n 122) 461.

which can be particularly high in primary markets, due to the strong incentives for mis-selling arising from intermediaries' frequent exposure to funded projects or the remuneration structures agreed with issuers.[125] Second, within a market where most intermediaries safeguard their reputation, new entrants have the chance to freeride on their reputational spill-overs of established firms, making profits by pretending that their recommendations of an issuer's securities are impartial and sound.[126] The presence of 'bogus' intermediaries, though, erodes the reputational capital of the entire industry, fostering a general sentiment of mistrust, especially among investors.[127]

Against this background, the primary challenge for regulatory intervention is addressing the risks to effective intermediation without imposing undue regulatory burdens. In dealing with the free-rider problem, regulators have typically imposed some form of statutory authorisation. This is granted either by the state or other self-regulatory, state-supervised organisations (eg, stock exchanges)[128] to prevent deceitful, unreliable, or otherwise incompetent intermediaries from entering the market.[129] To mitigate client-facing agency costs, intermediaries are typically required to adhere to default and standardised conduct standards, encompassing disclosure, fair treatment, quality of advice, and order handling rules. Additionally, operational requirements, such as managing conflicts of interests, performing internal controls and safeguarding clients' assets are usually mandated.[130] The described regulatory system should enable high-quality intermediaries to signal their competence to clients, preventing unsound intermediaries from dominating the market and, thus, protecting investors from poor capital allocation decisions. Of course, the solutions described above are by no means exclusive. Instead, establishing well-functioning intermediation channels is a complex procedure that usually requires regulators to consider the specificities of different market conditions, segments, and participants.[131]

B. Integrating Primary Markets – Harmonisation or Regulatory Competition?

The preceding analysis reveals that creating a facilitative legal framework for the development of primary capital markets in the EU is a complex procedure,

[125] See also S Choi, 'A Framework for the Regulation of Investment Intermediaries' (2004) 1 *Berkley Business Law Journal* 45, 50 ff; Moloney (n 24) 348–49.

[126] Black (n 25) 788.

[127] L Enriques, 'Conflicts of Interest in Investment Services: The Price and Uncertain Impact of MiFID's Regulatory Framework' in G Ferrarini and E Wymeersch (eds), *Investor Protection in Europe: Corporate Law Making, the MiFID and Beyond* (OUP, 2006) 324.

[128] See eg P Mahoney, 'The Exchange as Regulator' (1997) 83 *Virginia Law Review* 1453.

[129] Moloney (n 24) 349.

[130] See generally A Page and R Ferguson, *Investor Protection* (Weidenfeld and Nicolson, 1992) 59 ff.

[131] Moloney (n 24) 350.

requiring the synthesis of different regulatory tools and a careful balance between multiple conflicting interests. The most decisive factor in the regulatory design, however, is the imperative need for integrating primary markets. Indeed, the regulation of EU primary markets is grounded in the Treaty objective of building a single market,[132] comprising 'an area without internal frontiers in which the free movement of [...] services and capital is ensured'.[133] Accordingly, the EU regulator has focused on removing barriers and reducing costs arising from divergences in national legal systems, seeking to construct a truly integrated European financial market and facilitate cross-border activities.

A major challenge in integrating primary markets through the law is determining the proper institutional level to allocate the authority for establishing legal rules.[134] Within the unique and complex governance system that characterises the EU,[135] two competing view have emerged: harmonisation ('centralisation') and competition among legal rules ('decentralisation').[136] Both approaches have their respective advantages and shortcomings. Moreover, they can be viewed either as alternatives,[137] wherein the law is exclusively provided by either the EU or the Member States, or as complementary,[138] in which case the EU sets some minimum core standards for state law or legal rules are offered by both the EU and national regulators.

[132] Consolidated version of the Treaty on European Union [2012] OJ C326/13, Art 3(3).

[133] Consolidated version of the Treaty on the Functioning of the European Union [2012] OJ C 326/47, Art 26(2).

[134] See generally O Beaud, 'The Allocation of Competences in a Federation – A General Introduction' in L Azoulai (ed), *The Question of Competence in the European Union* (OUP, 2014).

[135] By most contemporary definitions, the EU exhibits characteristics of both a confederation and a federation. However, it resists formal classification as either, constituting an alliance of sovereign states with a hybrid ('dual') system of supranational and intergovernmental decision-making based on the principles of proportionality, see eg D Karmis and W Norman, 'The Revival of Federalism in Normative Political Theory' in D Karmis and W Norman (eds), *Theories of Federalism: A Reader* (Palgrave Macmillan, 2005) 6; P Genschel and M Jachtenfuchs, 'Beyond Market Regulation: Analysing the European Integration of Core State Powers' in P Genschel and M Jachtenfuchs (eds), *Beyond the Regulatory Polity(?): The European Integration of Core State Powers* (OUP, 2014) 2–4; N Walker, 'Constitutional Pluralism Revisited' (2016) 22 *European Law Journal* 333, 352 (advocating the idea of constitutional pluralism, where the 'overlap of the heterarchically related constitutional authorities [...] becomes a condition of legitimacy of the combined whole').

[136] See generally H Hauser and M Hosli, 'Harmonization or Regulatory Competition in the EC (and the EEA)?' (1991) 4 *Aussenwirtschaft* 265; H Siebert and M Koop, 'Institutional Competition versus Centralization: Quo vadis Europe?' (1993) 9 *Oxford Review of Economic Policy* 15. Especially within EU securities regulation, see E Ferran, *Building an EU Securities Market* (CUP, 2004) 50 ff.; I Chiu, *Regulatory Convergence in EU Securities Regulation* (Kluwer Law International, 2008) 3 ff.

[137] S Woolcock, *The Single European Market – Centralization or Competition Among National Rules?* (Royal Institute of International Affairs, 1994) 5 ff.

[138] J-M Sun and J Pelkmans, 'Regulatory Competition in the Single Market' (1995) 33 *Journal of Common Market Studies* 67; S Grundmann and W Kerber, 'European System of Contract Laws – a Map for Combining the Advantages of Centralized and Decentralized Rule-making' in S Grundmann and J Stuyck (eds), *An Academic Greenpaper on European Contract Law* (Kluwer Law International, 2002).

i. Integration Through Harmonisation of Legal Rules

Harmonisation originates from the ancient Greek word *ἁρμονία* (harmonía), which means congruence, accord, or joint.[139] At that time, it was mostly used in music to denote the blending of two contrasting elements: a higher and lower note.[140] Nowadays, harmonisation implies minimising alterations and reducing significant divergences to achieve greater approximation and conformity between systems. Within the legal sphere, this involves coordinating various legal provisions or systems to establish common requirements or standards.[141] In the regulation of primary markets, therefore, it necessitates creating a uniform set of substantive and conflict-of-law rules for the initial issuance of securities.[142] A prerequisite for this is the presence of a 'monopoly' regulator that can introduce and consistently implement the harmonised rules.[143] In this respect, an essential element of harmonisation is centralised rulemaking, which provides greater consistency, certainty and more effective control. Nevertheless, it would be a mistake to assume that harmonisation is simply a function of regulation or 'law on the books'. Convergence of institutional and market structures, especially regarding the enforcement and administration of legal rules, plays an equally important role.[144]

The harmonisation of EU primary markets law can yield several advantages. First, if issuers and investors adhere to a single set of rules, they can save on transaction costs, such as expenses related to information acquisition or hiring local experts.[145] These savings are expected to boost the scale of cross-border transactions, as access to foreign markets is not impeded by variations in applicable laws, thus fostering economic growth and enhancing risk-sharing. Furthermore, regulatory uniformity can enhance legal certainty, thus strengthening the confidence of issuers and investors in the integrity of financial markets and encouraging their active participation.[146] Finally, centralised rule-setting can reduce cross-border externalities that may arise from the regulation (or lack thereof) of a certain activity at the Member State level.[147]

But despite the benefits a harmonised regulatory regime for EU primary markets may bring to market participants and the economy as a whole, it is also

[139] A Hornby and S Wehmeier, *Oxford Advanced Learner's Dictionary*, 7th edn (Cornelsen, 2005).

[140] See Richard Cohn et al, *Harmony* (Grove Music Online, 2001).

[141] S Andreadakis, 'Regulatory Competition or Harmonization: The Dilemma, the Alternatives and the Prospect of Reflexive Harmonization' in M Andenas and C Baasch Andersen (eds), *Theory and Practice of Harmonization* (Edward Elgar, 2012) 102.

[142] H Scott, 'Internationalization of Primary Public Securities Markets' (2000) 63 *Law and Contemporary Problems* 71, 78.

[143] S Deakin, 'Is Regulatory Competition the Future for European Integration?' (2006) 13 *Swedish Economic Policy Review* 71, 75.

[144] See eg A Shleifer, 'Understanding Regulation' (2005) 11 *European Financial Management* 439.

[145] S Grundmann, 'Costs and Benefits of an Optional European Sales Law' (2013) 50 *Common Market Law Review* 225, 228.

[146] E Avgouleas, 'The Harmonisation of Rules of Conduct in EU Financial Markets: Economic Analysis, Subsidiarity and Investor Protection' (2000) 6 *European Law Journal* 72, 89.

[147] N Moloney, *EU Securities and Financial Markets Regulation*, 3rd edn (OUP 2014) 19.

associated with certain drawbacks. To begin with, harmonisation is not responsive to the diverse preferences and problems among Member States. Indeed, the centralisation of regulatory powers limits the ability of national regulators to tailor their laws to the needs of local market participants,[148] which can prove rather problematic given the varying sizes of capital markets across the Union.[149] For example, if Member States have differing views on the suitable level of investor protection (eg, due to diverse financing needs of domestic businesses), a uniform regulatory response may represent a suboptimal average solution. Moreover, the lengthy, slow, and cumbersome decision-making process at the EU level, often requiring wide and uneasy compromises, suggests that regulatory responses may take time and could eventually become obsolete.[150] In addition, harmonisation has inherent limitations since knowledge on the most appropriate rules for accommodating the needs of EU issuers and investors is widely dispersed among a vast number of people, regions, and institutions. According to Hayek, the solution to any societal problem results from the collective efforts and actions of actors, each possessing fragments of the existing knowledge.[151] This means that in a system of centralised rulemaking, where laws are enacted by a monopoly regulator, the available knowledge on a specific issue may not be fully captured, potentially leading to suboptimal solutions. Finally, similar to any other form of law-making, regulation at the EU level is susceptible to capture by interest groups.[152] Yet, this problem becomes even more pronounced in a system of harmonised primary market rules, as issuers and investors are unable to circumvent the effects of lobbying activities by opting for a different regime.[153]

A word of caution is nonetheless important here. While critics of harmonisation often equate it with legal unification,[154] emphasising concerns related to the lack of diversity and flexibility, it does not necessarily entail the imposition of fully identical rules,[155] nor does it preclude variations among the legal systems being harmonised.[156] Rather, the goal of harmonisation is to create a framework

[148] W Kerber and S Grundmann, 'An Optional European Contract Law Code: Advantages and Disadvantages' (2006) 21 *European Journal of Law and Economics* 215, 231.

[149] Ferran (n 136) 53.

[150] Moloney (n 147) 19.

[151] F von Hayek, 'The Use of Knowledge in Society' (1945) 35 *The American Economic Review* 519, 530.

[152] See generally G Stigler, 'The Theory of Economic Regulation' (1971) 2 *The Bell Journal of Economics and Managements Science* 3.

[153] See also Grundmann and Kerber (n 138) 304.

[154] Unification typically refers to the process in which two or more distinct legal provisions or systems are replaced with a single provision or a unified body of substantial norms, see eg WJ Kamba, 'Comparative Law: A Theoretical Framework' (1974) 23 *The International and Comparative Law Quarterly* 485, 501; MG Warren III, 'Global Harmonization of Securities Laws: The Achievements of the European Communities' (1990) 31 *Harvard International Law Journal* 185, 191.

[155] B Zeller, *CISG and the Unification of International Trade Law* (Routledge, 2007) 12; M Bogdan, *Comparative Law*, 1st edn (Springer, 1994) 30.

[156] M Boodman, 'The Myth of Harmonization of Laws' (1991) 39 *The American Journal of Comparative Law* 699, 701.

within which laws come closer and operate efficiently without creating imbalances and inconsistencies. As the EU experience shows,[157] such a framework can also be established by introducing minimum requirements or standards (a 'bottom-up approach'),[158] the details of which can be agreed upon at the national level, thus allowing for the consideration of local preferences. This brings us to the next focal point of our analysis, that is the role of regulatory competition in fostering primary market integration.

ii. *Integration Through Competition Among National Rules*

The analytical foundation for developing the concept of regulatory competition as a mechanism for the approximation of public policy and regulation was initially laid out by Charles Tiebout. In a seminal article published in 1956,[159] Tiebout employed the general equilibrium theory[160] to formulate a model for markets for local public goods analogous to those for private goods.[161] According to this model, local government units within a sovereign state deliberately compete to attract residents by offering packages of public goods, such as infrastructure, education, and health, in exchange for collecting taxes at varying rates.[162] The locality that most closely aligns with public preferences for these goods, would naturally attract the highest number of residents, thereby generating the highest tax revenues. In their effort to attract these constituents to their regions, other local governments would gravitate towards the 'winning' package of public goods, ultimately leading to the discovery of optimal public expenditure policies.

Subsequent work by development economists, especially Hirschman,[163] further contributed to the understanding of competition among legal rules. Hirschman's central thesis posits that members of any organisation, whether it be a nation, a municipality or an enterprise, essentially have two main ways to express their dissatisfaction with a particular decision or action of the organisation. The first is 'voice', which involves an attempt to repair or improve the affected relationship through the communication of an objection, complaint, or proposal for reform. The second option is 'exit', indicating the decision to withdraw from

[157] See generally, MG Warren III, 'The Harmonization of European Securities Law' (2003) 37 *The International Lawyer* 211.

[158] E Lohse, 'The Meaning of Harmonisation in the Context of EU Law – A Process in Need of Definition' in Andenas and Andersen (n 141) 282.

[159] C Tiebout, 'A Pure Theory of Local Expenditure' (1956) 64 *Journal of Political Economy* 416.

[160] See generally K Arrow and G Debreu, 'The Existence of an Equilibrium for a Competitive Economy' (1954) 22 *Econometrica* 265; G Debreu, *Theory of Value* (Yale University Press, 1959) 98 ff; L McKenzie, 'On the Existence of General Equilibrium for a Competitive Economy' (1959) 27 *Econometrica* 54.

[161] Woolcock (n 137) 5.

[162] See also S Deakin, 'Legal Diversity and Regulatory Competition: Which Model for Europe?' (2006) 12 *European Law Journal* 440, 442.

[163] See A Hirschman, *Exit, Voice and Loyalty: Responses to Decline in Firms, Organizations and States* (Harvard University Press, 1970).

the relationship. In this regard, citizens of a country may express their frustration with government policies by emigrating, protesting or voting for another party. Similarly, dissatisfied employees may opt to leave their unpleasant job or negotiate for better working conditions, and so on.

The aforementioned theories had a significant impact on the regulatory and policy sphere at large and the European legal integration process in particular.[164] From a functional perspective, by assimilating laws to public goods supplied by jurisdictions in response to the preferences of tax payers, they suggested that, given an effective threat of exit, competition among national rules could discipline legislators, thus preventing the enactment of suboptimal regulations.[165] From a functional standpoint, they introduced the benchmarks for defining the institutional conditions necessary for the process of regulatory competition to function in the real world. These encompass diversity of eligible regimes, entity mobility and government responsiveness. More specifically, regulated entities should, initially, have the option to choose the legal regime governing their activities.[166] If such choice is not available, regulated entities cannot seek a different regime, and national regulators lack motivation to improve their laws.[167] In addition, regulated entities should be able to shift between regimes without incurring excessive costs or facing unnecessary obstacles.[168] In the case of the EU, this translates to a genuine single market where individuals and legal entities can freely move between Member States, combined with a system of mutual recognition.[169] Finally, governments should be willing to reconfigure and adjust their regulations as a reaction to regulated entities choosing other regimes.[170] A static model of regulatory competition, where governments do not modify their laws based on the choices of constituents, contradicts the essence of competition as a disciplining mechanism that compels regulators to produce efficient rules.

Based on the above, within the context of European primary markets, regulatory competition describes a scenario where Member States strive to attract market participants by providing the most efficient regulatory environment for

[164] See eg M Cappelletti, M Seccombe and J Weiler, 'Integration Through Law: Europe and the American Federal Experience', in M Cappelletti, M Seccombe and J Weiler (eds), *Integration Through Law: Methods, Tools and Institutions, Book 1: A Political, Legal and Economic Overview* (European University Institute, 1986) 44 (arguing that 'integration rests in the interplay between a genuine concern to preserve that which is different while eliminating that which divides').

[165] See also J Cox, 'Regulatory Competition in Securities Markets: An Approach for Reconciling Japanese and United States Disclosure Philosophies' (1993) 16 *Hastings International and Comparative Law Review* 149, 157.

[166] H Jackson and E Pan, 'Regulatory Competition in International Securities Markets: Evidence from Europe in 1999 – Part I' (2001) 56 *Business Lawyer* 653, 658.

[167] E Pan, 'Harmonization of U.S.-EU Securities Regulation: The Case for a Single European Securities Regulator' (2003) 34 *Law and Policy in International Business* 499, 507.

[168] H Jackson, 'Centralization, Competition, and Privatization in Financial Regulation' (2001) 2 *Theoretical Inquiries in Law* 649, 660.

[169] Pan (n 167) 507.

[170] Jackson and Pan (n 166) 659.

their operations.[171] Assuming issuers seek to attain the highest profit with the least regulatory costs, and investors aim to minimise exposure to fraudulent issuers while maximising investment returns, competition among rules is expected to drive the market towards equilibrium and foster regulatory convergence. More specifically, under perfect market conditions, issuers can anticipate higher securities prices in legal regimes with more stringent rules, comprising a comprehensive disclosure and liability system.[172] This is because investors are better protected against fraud risks, having access to all the information needed to assess the quality of the securities offered, and being able to readily address any damage sustained from material misstatements or omissions of information. On the contrary, investors would be reluctant to invest in a market with less stringent rules, unless they can pay less for the securities to offset the additional risk and information costs. Therefore, issuers of high-quality securities will opt to operate under a legal regime that maximises both their own welfare and that of investors.[173] Where this is not the case, the prospect of exit prompted by interjurisdictional competition should drive regulation toward a Pareto-optimal outcome.[174] Indeed, Member States interested in maintaining or increasing market activity in their territory would modify their laws so that the marginal benefits for market participants would exceed the marginal costs.[175] In turn, the remaining Member States would be compelled to improve their regulatory and supervisory mechanisms to align with the success of their counterparties.[176]

Competition among primary market rules in the EU provides several advantages. First, it allows Member States to tailor their regulations to the specific needs of their economies, avoiding the obligation to adopt a uniform norm that might be unsuitable for local conditions.[177] Second, it enables the establishment of a single market without necessitating Member States to surrender their sovereignty, facilitating interventions in areas where they might be reluctant to cede control over their national laws.[178] Besides, by deliberately avoiding the reliance on a singular solution for any given issue, competition can foster a continuous process of innovation and experimentation, affording regulators the chance to learn from each

[171] See U Geiger, 'The Case for the Harmonization of Securities Disclosure Rules in the Global Market' (1997) *Columbia Business Law Review* 241, 269.

[172] Cox (n 165) 159.

[173] Romano (n 46) 2366–67.

[174] J Coffee Jr., 'Competition Versus Consolidation: The Significance of Organizational Structure in Financial and Securities Regulation' (1995) 50 *The Business Lawyer* 447, 453.

[175] M Perry, 'A Challenge Postponed: Market 2000 Complacency in Response to Regulatory Competition for International Equity Market' (1994) 34 *Virginia Journal of International Law* 701, 705–707; N Demmo, 'U.S. Securities Regulation: The Need for Modification to Keep Pace with Globalization' (1996) 17 *University of Pennsylvania Journal of International Law* 691, 707; S Choi and A Guzman, 'Portable Reciprocity: Rethinking the International Reach of Securities Regulation' (1998) 71 *Southern California Law Review* 903, 923.

[176] Ferran (n 136) 52.

[177] Woolcock (n 137) 16.

[178] For an early contribution on this issue in the area of securities markets, see B Steil, *Competition, Integration and Regulation in EC Capital Markets*, (Royal Institute of International Affairs, 1993) 16–17.

other. This approach promotes the development of a flexible and dynamic regulatory framework, a crucial factor in ensuring that EU countries remain competitive and aligned with market advancements.[179]

Nevertheless, regulatory competition also has its drawbacks and limitations. Initially, doubts arise regarding issuers' incentives to opt for legal regimes that mandate high standards of investor protection.[180] At the same time, it is questionable whether investors have the capacity to meaningfully assess the variations in the level of protection offered by different regimes.[181] These concerns resonate strongly within the EU context.[182] The persistent home bias among issuers and the concentration of institutional investors in specific financial hubs suggest that, even with adjustments to the legal environment to support regulatory competition, the practical preconditions for its effective operation may still be far from satisfied.[183] Moreover, even when competition enables the identification of market preferences, it is uncertain whether Member States would respond by amending their national laws accordingly.[184] An alternative scenario could involve the emergence of national protectionism or ringfencing within the EU, leading to substandard laws ('race to the bottom') or rules favouring local players and national interests, instead of good rules spreading by imitation ('race to the top').[185] Besides, while competition grants policymakers flexibility to experiment and innovate, frequent legislative changes may elevate transaction costs and uncertainty among market participants.[186] Finally, like other forms of regulation, it does not preclude the risk of rule-makers being lured into serving the interests of a small powerful group instead of the general public.[187]

iii. Choosing the Right Model for EU Primary Markets

a. The Case for Harmonisation

Unlike the United States, where federal securities law was created in a legislative vacuum, the integration of capital markets in the EU requires bringing together

[179] J Grundfest, 'Internationalization of the World's Securities Markets: Economic Causes and Regulatory Consequences' (1990) 4 *Journal of Financial Services Research* 349, 372–73.

[180] J Coffee Jr., 'Law and Regulatory Competition: Can They Co-exist?' (2002) 80 *Texas Law Review* 1729, 1730–31.

[181] J Cox, 'Regulatory Duopoly in US Securities Markets' (1999) 99 *Columbia Law Review* 1200, 1234.

[182] S Woolcock, 'Competition Among Rules in the Single European Market' in W Bratton et al (eds), *International Regulatory Competition and Coordination: Perspectives on Economic Regulation in Europe and the United States* (OUP, 1996) 315–16.

[183] G Ferrarini, 'Pan-European Securities Markets: Policy Issues and Regulatory Responses' (2002) 3 *European Business Organization Law Review* 249, 253.

[184] J Cox, 'Rethinking US Securities Regulation in the Shadow of International Regulatory Competition' (1992) 55 *Law and Contemporary Problems* 157, 163–64.

[185] K Heine and W Kerber, 'European Corporate Laws, Regulatory Competition and Path Dependence' (2002) 13 *European Journal of Law and Economics* 47, 52–53; Sun and Pelkmans (n 138) 84–85.

[186] Coffee Jr. (n 174) 473.

[187] For some, the risk of capture is higher where regulators compete with each other, see Woolcock (n 137) 19.

27 sovereign nations, each with its own financial rules and regulations. While, in theory, maximum harmonisation appears to be the most straightforward approach, in practice, it is not only challenging to garner political support but may also prove suboptimal in addressing the specificities of different legal systems. For the latter are often so entrenched in local preferences and market conditions that they cannot be simply removed at the stroke of Brussels' pen without adversely affecting at least some Member States. In this context, it is crucial to formulate some normative criteria to guide EU policymakers in determining the necessity for top-down interventions in primary markets within the CMU framework. Given the strong focus of this initiative on efficiency, the guiding principles for devising these criteria could be drawn from the economic theory of federalism.[188] From that perspective, harmonisation is justified when a legal or economic barrier results in harmful effects on cross-border capital movement that cannot be rectified through actions taken at the Member State level,[189] as long as the harmonised rules increase overall welfare, taking into consideration the costs associated with them.[190]

With this in mind, EU intervention in the field of primary markets is warranted when the following three criteria are cumulatively fulfilled. First, there must be a barrier to capital flow, encompassing any legal rule, market practice, or process that hinders data comparability, compromises procedural integrity, and affects legal certainty during the contracting, execution and enforcement phases of primary market transactions, respectively.[191] This barrier can be either strategic or structural,[192] depending on whether it is shaped by forces external to the financial transaction or emerges naturally during its negotiation, execution or enforcement. In that sense, a strategic barrier may take the form, for example, of a domestic legal provision, an enforcement action by the local judicial or competent supervisory authority, or even a market practice imposed by a dominant player, such as underwriting syndicate. A structural barrier, on the other hand, is typically linked to idiosyncratic conditions, such as language constraints or challenges encountered by new market entrants, like start-up businesses, in attracting investors. Second, the barrier must negatively impact cross-border capital movement, impeding the interaction between national liquidity pools and, hence,

[188] See eg R Inman and D Rubinfield, 'The Economics of Federalism' in F Parisi (ed), *The Oxford Handbook of Law and Economics: Volume 3: Public Law and Legal Institutions* (OUP, 2017).

[189] L White, 'International Regulation of Securities Markets: Competition or Harmonization?' in A Lo (ed), *The Industrial Organization and Regulation of the Securities Industry* (University of Chicago Press, 1996) 222.

[190] L Enriques and M Gatti, 'The Uneasy Case for Top-Down Corporate Law Harmonization in the European Union' (2006) 27 *University of Pennsylvania Journal of International Law* 939, 953.

[191] See also D Valiante, *Europe's Untapped Capital Market: Rethinking Financial Integration After the Crisis* (CEPS Paperback, 2016), 183.

[192] This distinction is borrowed from the theory of entry barriers for businesses, see generally G Stigler, *The Organization of Industry* (University of Chicago Press, 1968) 67; CC von Weizsacker, 'A Welfare Analysis of Barriers to Entry' (1980) 11 *Bell Journal of Economics* 399, 400; M Porter, *Competitive Strategy: Techniques for Analyzing Industries and Competitors* (Free Press, 1980) 9–13.

a more efficient capital allocation.[193] In essence, this occurs when the relevant rule, practice or process leads to a market failure that extends beyond national boundaries. Within the framework of primary markets, examples of such market failures include protectionist barriers to market access and the free movement of capital;[194] transaction costs, uncertainties and inefficiencies arising from multiple applicable regimes;[195] as well as cross-border externalities resulting from the interaction of intermediaries, issuers, and investors within the internal market, such as fraud[196] and financial stability risks.[197] Finally, it should be assessed whether Member States can independently eliminate a potential barrier to cross-border activity and whether the benefits of centralisation outweigh those gained from each country's ability to tailor legal rules to its specific needs. Harmonisation should be the preferred approach only when individual Member States are unable or unwilling to address a market failure with cross-border implications, and top-down EU intervention is better positioned to do so, ultimately enhancing overall welfare.[198] This approach is consistent with the Treaty principle of subsidiarity,[199] which permits Union-level action only if the pursued objectives cannot be more effectively achieved by national regulators alone.[200]

b. Some Space for Regulatory Competition

While regulatory competition has numerous limitations, in the context of EU primary markets, there are instances where allowing some room for differentiation is justified, if not necessary. This becomes particularly evident when someone considers the heterogeneity of preferences and problems within the EU.[201]

[193] Valiante (n 191) 184.

[194] Grundmann and Kerber (n 138) 301; Enriques and Gatti (n 190) 956.

[195] R van den Bergh, 'Regulatory Competition or Harmonization of Laws? Guidelines for the European Regulator' in A Marciano and J-M Josselin (eds), *The Economics of Harmonizing European Law* (Edward Elgar, 2002) 34.

[196] G Benston, 'Regulation of Stock Trading: Private Exchanges vs. Government Agencies – Commentary' (1997) 83 *Virginia Law Review* 1501, 1506.

[197] P Davis, 'Problems of Banking Regulation – An EC Perspective' in C Goodhart (ed), *The Emerging Framework of Financial Regulation* (Central Banking Publications, 1998) 535–36.

[198] See also J Trachtman, 'International Regulatory Competition, Externalization, and Jurisdiction' (1993) 34 *Harvard International Law Journal* 47, 50; LA Bebchuk, 'Federalism and the Corporation: The Desirable Limits on State Competition in Corporate Law' (1992) 105 *Harvard Law Review* 1435, 1457.

[199] Art 5(3) TEU.

[200] See generally K Lenaerts, 'The Principle of Subsidiarity and the Environment in the European Union: Keeping the Balance of Federalism' (1993) 17 *Fordham International Law Journal* 846, 851–52; G De Búrca, 'The Principle of Subsidiarity and the Court of Justice as an Institutional Actor' (1998) 36 *Journal of Common Market Studies* 217, 218–20. For a discussion on the role of subsidiarity within the context of economic integration, see J Trachtman, 'L'Etat, C'est Nous: Sovereignty, Economic Integration and Subsidiarity' (1992) 33 *Harvard International Law Journal* 459.

[201] See eg J Trachtman, 'Regulatory Competition and Regulatory Jurisdiction' (2000) 3 *Journal of International Economic Law* 331, 343; C Gerner-Beuerle, 'United in Diversity: Maximum versus Minimum Harmonization in EU Securities Regulation' (2012) 7 *Capital Markets Law Journal* 317, 318–19.

Indeed, given the diverse levels of capital markets development across the Union, Member States may have different preferences, especially with regard to the trade-off between supporting businesses and ensuring investor protection. Hence, the optimal level of regulation may vary among them. The same holds true when the transactional issues that primary law rules seek to address differ among Member States, either in type or frequency. In those cases, competition might offer a more efficient solution, circumventing the challenge of formulating uniform rules suitable for all EU countries. In addition, competition can also be upheld in case that an innovative or novel market practice arises. In this scenario, determining the most suitable regulatory solution requires prior experimentation and the accumulation of knowledge and experience from the users of the law.[202] Accordingly, a decentralised regulatory system seems preferable to centralised rule-making, given its greater capacity to adapt to new findings and support mutual learning through the sharing of best practices.[203] This cannot only promote the discovery of superior outcomes but also potentially serve as a useful acclimating precursor to centralisation.[204] Finally, an argument in favour of competition can be made when Member States have long-established, high-quality national legal rules in place regarding a certain issue (historical status quo situation).[205] Considering the familiarity of local market participants with these rules and the accumulated experience in the judicial system through their implementation, abolishing them in favour of a purely centralised system would appear economically inefficient.[206] In such circumstances, therefore, the significant investments made in national laws would favour solutions that allow for their future utilisation.

Nevertheless, even in cases like those described above, where a general presumption in favour of allowing rules to emerge through a competitive process exists, there is still room for harmonisation to ensure the smooth functioning of the internal market and safeguard regulatory standards against a 'race to the bottom'. As Deakin aptly points out, only the most optimistic or wilfully ignorant would deny the existence of this problem.[207] That said, the main challenge lies in defining the required degree of centralisation to address it. Drawing from the theory of cooperative federalism,[208] the approach suggested here involves a combination of central-level intervention and local-level experimentation. From this perspective, a potential solution in the context of EU primary markets regulation could be

[202] Van den Bergh (n 195) 29–30 and 42.
[203] Grundmann and Kerber (n 138) 303.
[204] Ferran (n 136) 53.
[205] See also Kerber and Grundmann (n 148) 222.
[206] This could be the case even when domestic rules were less effective than a common set of rules, see A Ogus, 'Legal Cultures as (Natural?) Monopoly' in Marciano and Josselin (eds) (n 195) 80.
[207] Deakin (n 162) 443.
[208] See generally R Schütze, *From Dual to Cooperative Federalism: The Changing Structure of European Law* (OUP, 2009); J Zimmerman,' National-State Relations: Cooperative Federalism in the Twentieth Century' (2001) 31 *Publius* 15.

'reflexive harmonisation'.[209] This concept was largely shaped by the 'new approach' to harmonisation and standardisation initiated by the Commission in 1985, in an effort to eliminate technical barriers to trade in the Community.[210] According to this approach, instead of promulgating rigidly prescriptive rules, European law should focus on articulating general principles and standards. Beyond this baseline, mutual recognition will foster competition between national rules.[211] In this regard, the aim of reflexive harmonisation is not to replace state-level regulation. Quite the contrary, it seeks to enhance flexibility and autonomy in meeting regulatory goals by providing a platform for domestic solutions to emerge, while steering national rules away from spontaneous moves that could lead to sub-optimal outcomes.[212]

An alternative solution could be 'vertical (or external) competition', an idea developed in regulatory theory[213] and practice[214] during the discourse of the project for an optional European contract law code. Under this model, a uniform set of rules enacted at the EU level competes with national rules, allowing legal entities the freedom to choose the applicable law for their transactions. Contrary to harmonisation, therefore, the law established at the central level is not mandatory but optional. This co-existence or overlapping of national and EU provisions without any hierarchical order would be a pioneering approach in capital markets regulation, combining the advantages of both centralised rulemaking and regulatory competition.[215] Indeed, creating a harmonised EU legal regime that market participants could choose to adopt would enhance legal certainty, thereby reducing transaction costs and minimising negative externalities in other jurisdictions. Additionally, the presence of diverse regulatory solutions could foster innovation, particularly crucial in times of dynamic change, and better help unveil errors that need correction, while allowing for local preferences to be considered. In that sense, a two-level system of primary market laws could offer a balanced mix of unity and diversity in cases where the imposition of uniform rules for the entire EU does not seem justified based on the criteria mentioned earlier.

[209] S Deakin, 'Two Types of Regulatory Competition: Competitive Federalism Versus Reflexive Harmonisation. A Law and Economics Perspective on Centros' (1999) 2 *Cambridge Yearbook of European Legal Studies* 231; C Barnard and S Deakin, 'Market Access and Regulatory Competition' in C Barnard and J Scott (eds), *The Law of the Single Market: Unpacking the Premises* (Hart Publishing, 2002).

[210] See also J Pelkmans, 'The New Approach to Technical Harmonization and Standardization' (1987) 25 *Journal of Common Market Studies* 249.

[211] Woolcock (n 137) 9.

[212] Deakin (n 162) 444–45.

[213] See especially, Grundmann and Kerber (n 138); S Grundmann, 'Kosten und Nutzen eines optionalen Europäischen Kaufrechts' (2012) 212 *Archiv für die civilistische Praxis* 502; Kerber and Grundmann (n 148).

[214] Commission, 'Proposal for a Regulation on a Common European Sales Law' COM (2011) 635 final, 11 October 2011.

[215] See also E Ryan, 'Federalism as Legal Pluralism' in P Schiff-Berman (ed), *The Oxford Handbook of Global Legal Pluralism* (OUP, 2020) 500–501.

3

The EU Prospectus Regulation – Overview and Assessment

I. Introduction

The requirement to issue and publish a prospectus forms a cornerstone duty for firms aiming to enter and raise funding on public primary markets. By providing detailed information about the issuer's condition and the securities offered, its principal objective is to alleviate the severe information asymmetry between the issuer (and its advisers) and potential investors. This, in turn, yields positive effects for both the parties involved and the market as a whole. More specifically, regarding issuers, mandatory disclosure in the form of a prospectus enables them to signal their quality, allowing them to demand a fair price for their securities.[1] As for investors, it reduces the risk of fraudulent sales of over-valued securities, exposes sharp practices and, hence, shields them from making poor resource allocation decisions.[2] From that perspective, prospectus obligation (and liability) serves as an effective mechanism for enhancing investor confidence in primary markets, thereby contributing to their proper functioning and development.[3] However, besides efficiency considerations, within EU capital markets law, mandatory prospectus disclosure has also been significantly influenced by the specific goal of internal market integration.[4] In this framework, the harmonisation and standardisation of prospectus requirements aim to reduce the uncertainty and costs arising from diverging regimes, enable comparability and accessibility for

[1] N Moloney, *EU Securities and Financial Markets Regulation*, 4th edn (OUP, 2023) 76; L Gullifer and J Payne, *Corporate Finance Law: Principles and Policy*, 1st edn (Hart Publishing, 2011) 416.

[2] H Scott, 'Internationalization of Primary Public Securities Markets' (2000) 63 *Law and Contemporary Problems* 71, 75; V Wiegel, *Die Prospektrichtlinie und Prospektverordnung – Eine Dogmatische, Ökonomische und Rechtsvergleichende Analyse* (De Gruyter, 2008) 44 ff; D Einsele, 'Kapitalmarktrecht und Privatrecht' (2014) 69 *JuristenZeitung* 703, 711.

[3] L Enriques and S Gilotta, 'Disclosure and Financial Market Regulation' in E Ferran, N Moloney and J Payne (eds), *Oxford Handbook on Financial Regulation* (OUP, 2014) 513–14; D van Gerven, 'General Provisions of Community Law Relating to the Prospectus to be Published when Securities are Offered to the Public or Admitted to Trading' in D van Gerven (ed), *Prospectus for the Public Offering of Securities in Europe: European and National Legislation in the Member States of the European Economic Area*, Vol. I (CUP, 2008) 5–6. But see E Ferran, *Building an EU Securities Market* (CUP, 2004) 34 ff, questioning the role of mandatory prospectus requirements to the development of EU capital markets.

[4] Moloney (n 1) 80; S Grundmann, *European Company Law*, 2nd edn (Intersentia, 2012) 455.

the investor community,[5] and thereby facilitate cross-border capital raising and investment activity.

Since 2003, the requirements governing the preparation, approval and distribution of a prospectus in the EU were stipulated in the Prospectus Directive.[6] Nevertheless, despite the overall positive impact of this piece of legislation in fostering market efficiency and investor protection, the general impression among stakeholders was that it had failed to achieve many of its intended objectives. This was affirmed in the formal evaluation of the Directive, conducted by the Commission in 2015, which identified several weaknesses that hindered the development of strong and truly integrated EU primary markets.[7] These included mainly the high costs related to the drafting and publication of the prospectus, the often inadequate level of protection provided to investors, especially retail ones, and the inconsistencies among Member States regarding the interpretation and application of certain aspects of the Directive. Against this background, the reform of the EU prospectus regime to address these issues was envisioned as one of the first and most crucial legislative actions for completing the CMU.[8]

However, completing this task was anything but straightforward, as it involved addressing the diverse and often conflicting needs, views, and preferences of both market participants and Member States. Thus, the primary concern for EU regulators in revamping the regulatory framework has been to strike a balance between two seemingly opposing pairs of objectives: first limiting administrative burden for issuers while still ensuring an adequate level of investor protection; and, second, achieving greater convergence in the application of the prospectus regime whilst preserving sufficient flexibility for national markets.[9] This chapter examines how this balance is reflected within the Prospectus Regulation,[10] particularly after its recent reform by the EU Listing Act.[11] Additionally, the Regulation's ability to foster the development and integration of EU primary markets is assessed, highlighting any identified shortcomings and, where applicable, suggesting potential improvements.

[5] M Pellegrini, 'Critical Analysis of the Prospectus Directive' (2006) 17 *European Business Law Review* 1679, 1681.

[6] Directive 2003/ 71/ EC of the European Parliament and of the Council on the prospectus to be published when securities are offered to the public or admitted to trading [2003] OJ L345/64.

[7] Commission Staff Working Document, 'Impact assessment accompanying the Proposal for a Regulation of the European Parliament and of the Council on the prospectus to be published when securities are offered to the public or admitted to trading', SWD (2015) 255 final, 30 November 2015, Annex 5, 10 ff.

[8] Commission, 'Action Plan on Building a Capital Markets Union', COM (2015) 468 final, 30 September 2015, 12.

[9] SWD (2015) 255 final (n 7) 16.

[10] Regulation (EU) 2017/1129 of the European Parliament and of the Council on the prospectus to be published when securities are offered to the public or admitted to trading on a regulated market [2017] OJ L168/12.

[11] The Listing Act is a package of measures consisting of a Regulation amending the Prospectus Regulation, MAR and MiFIR; a Directive amending MiFID II; and a new Directive on multiple-vote share structures.

II. The Evolution of the EU Prospectus Regime

As a key component of the EU financial integration process, the evolution of the prospectus regime has been significant, progressing from the initial patchwork disclosure measures in the 1980s, to the 2003 Prospectus Directive and, eventually, the 2017 Prospectus Regulation. Similarly, its institutional framework has also undergone a significant transformation, shifting from a loose system of minimum harmonisation and mutual recognition to the highly detailed rules of the FSAP era, supported by a sophisticated passporting mechanism, and currently, to the crisis-stimulated single rulebook, supported by the administrative expertise of ESMA. Finally, equally impressive has been the reform of the capital markets environment which, in contrast to the standard model of the past, is now marked by a multitude of disparate market actors, disruptive technological developments and a growing trend towards disintermediation. Therefore, to gain a more comprehensive understanding of the essence and intricacies of the Prospectus Regulation, a closer examination of its historical trajectory is necessary.

A. Initial Efforts: Minimum Harmonisation and Mutual Recognition

The first steps toward creating a 'European Prospectus'[12] would focus on positive integration, involving the adoption of minimum disclosure standards for listed issuers.[13] The reasoning behind this strategy was that these issuers, mostly blue-chip companies, were more likely to leverage the right to the free movement of capital, seeking financing in other Member States to meet their funding requirements.[14] Accordingly, coordinating the disclosure requirements related to the admission of securities to official listing ('listing particulars'),[15] was considered sufficient to meet the market needs for Pan-European access. Nevertheless, the emphasis on easing access to stock exchange listing overlooked the reality that a significant portion of the capital raising activity, particularly by smaller enterprises, occurred on unregulated markets. As a result of this approach, EU primary markets remained largely fragmented, given that most issuers, confronted with varying disclosure duties imposed by national regulators for unlisted offers, opted to place their securities at the domestic level.[16]

In 1989, an early attempt to address this gap in the disclosure system was made with the introduction of a common prospectus regime governing the offer of

[12] S Suckow, 'The European Prospectus' (1975) 23 *The American Journal of Comparative Law* 50.

[13] I Chiu, *Regulatory Convergence in EU Securities Regulation* (Kluwer Law International, 2008) 4.

[14] ibid 4, 19.

[15] Council Directive 80/390/EEC coordinating the requirements for the drawing up, scrutiny and distribution of the listing particulars to be published for the admission of securities to official stock exchange listing (Listing Particulars Directive) [1980] OJ L100/1.

[16] Chiu (n 13) 19.

transferable securities to the public, irrespective of any subsequent listing (Public Offers Directive).[17] Similar to the Listing Particulars Directive, it embraced a minimum harmonisation approach, mandating only a general standard of disclosure and allowing Member States the freedom to establish more stringent prospectus requirements for public offers within their territory. This basic disclosure framework was later complemented by a complex scheme of 'mutual recognition', allowing issuers to draft and distribute a single disclosure document. In particular, following approval by the national competent authority (NCA) of a Member State (home country), this document could, once translated, be used for public offers and admission applications of the same securities in all other Member States (host countries), without the need for further approval or any modifications, except for those necessary to meet certain country-specific disclosure standards, mainly related to taxation, paying agents, and notification procedures.[18]

B. The FSAP Era and the Shift Toward Regulatory Convergence

By the end of the 1990s, there was general consensus that the model of minimum harmonisation and mutual recognition had fallen short in establishing truly integrated EU primary markets. The open-textured nature and the array of exceptions and options in the prospectus regime not only led to national discrepancies in its application and interpretation, but also provided Member States significant leeway for 'gold-plating', thereby impeding cross-border activity. At the same time, it became apparent that the disclosure mandated by the relevant Directives exhibited several deficiencies, particularly when compared to international best practices.[19] Indeed, the costs associated with preparing the disclosure documents were prohibitively high for most issuers, and the approval process proved slow and unwieldy, making it insensitive to the needs of frequent issuers.[20] In this context, the reform of the regulatory framework on prospectus disclosure was highlighted as a top priority in the Financial Services Action Plan (FSAP) of 1999,[21] aiming to facilitate capital-raising and investments on an EU-wide basis.

[17] Council Directive 89/298/EEC coordinating the requirements for the drawing-up, scrutiny and distribution of the prospectus to be published when transferable securities are offered to the public [1989] OJ L124/8.

[18] Art 21(1) Public Offers Directive. See also C Gerner-Breuele, 'United in Diversity: Maximum versus Minimum Harmonization in EU Securities Regulation' (2012) 7 *Capital Markets Law Journal* 317, 323.

[19] M Becht, 'European Disclosure for the New Millennium' in K Hopt and E Wymeersch (eds), *Capital Markets and Company Law* (OUP, 2003) 87.

[20] Moloney (n 1) 92.

[21] Commission 'Communication on Implementing the Framework for Financial Markets: Action Plan', COM (1999) 232 final, 11 May 1999.

The adoption of the Prospectus Directive in 2003, following protracted negotiations,[22] marked a radical departure from the previous regime. This is because it exemplified a more sophisticated approach to capital market regulation, placing stronger emphasis on regulatory convergence. This was primarily achieved by limiting Member States' control over financial market rules and harnessing the technocratic capacity of EU bodies, especially the Committee of European Securities Regulators (CESR), in the legislative and supervisory procedure.[23] More specifically, under the Directive, the previous division between a stock exchange listing and issuing a prospectus came to an end. This resulted in a uniform prospectus regime with a single set of disclosure requirements applicable to all issuers across the EU, ensuring that investors could benefit from the same level of information. At the same time, building on the Lamfalussy process,[24] these requirements were further detailed in an implementing act,[25] ensuring consistent application across Member States and alleviating the risk of gold-plating. Furthermore, the earlier mutual recognition system was replaced by the 'single passport' mechanism, increasing the control of the home Member State.[26] Based on that mechanism, once a prospectus has been approved by the home NCA, it is valid for a public offer or an admission to trading throughout the EU, without the host NCA having the authority to undertake any approval or other administrative procedure related to the prospectus.[27]

The Prospectus Directive proved dynamic. At the substantive level, the financial crisis and associated concerns regarding the efficiency of the EU's public equity markets and their impact on growth provided critical impetus for reform.[28] During this period, the review of the Directive's implementation identified a wide array of potential improvements, mainly centred on cutting red tape for issuers and enhancing transparency and investor protection levels.[29] Accordingly, the 2010 Amending Prospectus Directive[30] and its accompanying

[22] The Commission's original proposal in 2001 was largely discarded by the European Parliament, leading to a revised proposal being presented in 2003.

[23] See also Moloney (n 1) 84.

[24] Committee of Wise Men, 'Final Report on the Regulation of European Securities Markets', 15 February 2001 (Lamfalussy Report).

[25] Commission Regulation (EC) 809/2004 implementing Directive 2003/71/EC as regards information contained in prospectuses as well as the format, incorporation by reference and publication of such prospectuses and dissemination of advertisements [2004] OJ L149/1.

[26] See generally P Schammo, *EU Prospectus Law – New Perspectives in Regulatory Competition in Securities Markets* (CUP, 2011) 137 ff.

[27] The host NCA could only request the translation of the summary, see Art 17 Prospectus Directive.

[28] At the procedural level, the Prospectus Directive was first amended by Directive 2010/78/EU [2010] OJ L 331/120 (Omnibus I), which aligned the original delegations to administrative rulemaking with the establishment of the European Supervisory Authorities (ESAs).

[29] Commission, 'Staff Working Document accompanying the proposal for a Directive amending Directive 2003/71/EC on the prospectus to be published when securities are offered to the public or admitted to trading', SEC (2009) 1223, 23 September 2009, 3–4.

[30] Directive 2010/73/EU of the European Parliament and of the Council amending Directive 2003/71/EC on the prospectus to be published when securities are offered to the public or admitted to trading [2010] OJ L327/1.

administrative rules[31] grappled with two key issues. First, they sought to reduce the cost of capital raising on EU capital markets by introducing a 'proportionate disclosure regime'[32] for specific types of offerings (eg, by SMEs), and by expanding or clarifying the scope of exemptions for others, notably private placements, wholesale issues and bond distributions through 'retail cascades'. Second, they aimed to refine the content and format of the summary prospectus to increase its relevance as a source of information for retail investors. Thus, in contrast to the crisis-era regulatory zeitgeist, the reforms of the prospectus regime were predominantly deregulatory in nature, a shift that can be attributed to the EU's steadfast commitment to market finance as a tool for supporting growth and stability, as later explicitly articulated in the CMU.

C. The CMU and the 2017 Prospectus Regulation

i. Contextual Problems and Drivers for Reform

The evaluation of the amended Prospectus Directive, initially scheduled for January 2016,[33] commenced in February 2015 as an essential component of the CMU initiative and its efforts to strengthen and further integrate EU capital markets.[34] After an online public consultation, discussions with national supervisors and ESMA, and meetings with stakeholders and expert groups, the review process ultimately culminated in a proposal for a Prospectus Regulation.[35] This was accompanied by an Impact Assessment,[36] which outlined the driving forces behind the suggested reforms. In this document, the Commission noted that, despite the positive accomplishments of the Community acquis, especially as regards the harmonisation of standards for prospectus disclosure and approval across the Union,[37] the prospectus regime still suffered from considerable shortcomings, which also had an impact on the functioning and integration of European primary markets.

To begin with, the process of drafting and obtaining approval for prospectuses under the Directive remained costly, burdensome and time-consuming.[38] This was particularly evident for equity prospectuses, which, due to their extensive length

[31] See mainly Commission Delegated Regulation (EU) No 486/2012 amending Regulation (EC) No 809/2004 as regards the format and the content of the prospectus, the base prospectus, the summary and the final terms and as regards the disclosure requirements [2012] OJ L150/1.

[32] Recital 18 Directive 2010/73/EU.

[33] ibid Art 4.

[34] Commission, 'Green Paper on Building a Capital Markets Union', COM (2015) 63 final, 18 February 2015, 10.

[35] Commission, 'Proposal for a Regulation on the Prospectus to be published when securities are offered to the public or admitted to trading', COM (2015) 583 final, 30 November 2015.

[36] SWD (2015) 255 final (n 7).

[37] ibid 6.

[38] ibid 8–9.

and detailed content,[39] typically incurred an average cost of EUR 1 million, with legal fees accounting for approximately 40 per cent of the total compliance expenses.[40] Besides, by definition, becoming listed entails substantial fixed costs, which are also relatively higher for smaller issuers due to economies of scale.[41] Consequently, the absence of sufficient differentiation and flexibility in the content of the prospectus under the Prospectus Directive, especially concerning SMEs,[42] deterred many promising projects from seeking finance on the public market, as the costs often outweighed the relevant benefits.[43] Meanwhile, the lack of a proportionate disclosure regime for secondary issuances meant that already public companies faced challenges in raising additional capital,[44] which adversely affected growth and stability. Another major concern was the prospectus' effectiveness in meeting the information needs of investors. For one thing, the length of prospectuses coupled with the fact that they were often drafted more to address potential liability risks rather than to provide appropriate and suitable information, rendered them overly detailed, thus impeding investors' ability to identify the necessary information for their decision-making.[45] At the same time, the summary prospectus was criticised for being too thorough, cumbersome, and difficult to read, making it unsuitable for enabling the average investor to grasp the benefits and relevant risks of an investment.[46] As a result, the effectiveness of prospectus disclosure in fulfilling its central function of protecting investors was impaired, eroding their confidence in the market and hindering its proper functioning and development. Finally, the extent of harmonisation achieved by the Prospectus Directive was deemed insufficient.[47] An illustrative example of this problem was the discrepancies among Member States regarding the threshold that triggered the prospectus publication duty, stemming from the divergent implementation of the discretion to exempt public offers with a nominal value below EUR 5 million from this obligation.[48] Similarly, disparities were observed in the handling of prospectus approvals among NCAs, as well as in the application and enforcement of certain provisions, and in the interpretation of the concept of 'public offer'. These inconsistencies created legal uncertainty among issuers and investors, preventing them from pursuing cross-border activities, and greatly increasing home-bias.[49]

[39] For example, the prospectus published under ABN AMRO's IPO on 10 November 2015 consisted of no less than 729 densely printed pages, see D Busch, 'A Capital Markets Union for a Divided Europe' (2017) 3 *Journal of Financial Regulation* 262, 272.
[40] SWD (2015) 255 final (n 7) 8.
[41] Oxera, 'Primary and Secondary Equity Markets in the EU', Final Report, November 2020, 65–66.
[42] SWD (2015) 255 final (n 7) 8–9.
[43] IOSCO, 'SME Financing through Capital Markets: Final Report', July 2015, 38.
[44] SWD (2015) 255 final (n 7) 23–24.
[45] ibid 9.
[46] ibid Annex 6, s 5.
[47] ibid 10.
[48] Art 1(2)(h) Prospectus Directive.
[49] SWD (2015) 255 final (n 7) 12–13.

ii. Objectives of the New Prospectus Rules

The legislative procedure progressed smoothly, with the Council and the Parliament reaching a political agreement in December 2016.[50] Subsequently, the final text of the Regulation, closely resembling the Commission's initial proposal, was adopted in June 2017 and entered into full force two years later, leading to the repeal of the Prospectus Directive. The new rules sought to address the major shortcomings of the previous regime by focusing on facilitating effective capital raising for all EU companies in financial markets and making the prospectus a more relevant tool for informing potential investors.[51]

In this regard, the fist specific objective of the Prospectus Regulation is to alleviate undue regulatory and administrative burdens for all issuers, with a particular emphasis on SMEs and other entities disproportionately affected by the costs linked to preparing and publishing a full prospectus, by providing disclosure rules that are better tailored to meet their specific needs.[52] The second and equally important objective is to strengthen investor protection, by improving the effectiveness and quality of the information provided in the prospectus and its summary. This should empower investors, especially retail ones, to better compare and assess the quality of different securities and issuers, enabling them to make more informed decisions and increasing their confidence in capital markets.[53] Finally, these two goals are flanked by the overarching objective of market integration, aiming for greater convergence in disclosure regimes and supervisory practices across Member States.[54] This is expected to boost cross-border capital flows, thus promoting economic growth and financial stability in the Union.[55]

iii. Revision to a Regulation

In line with the post-crisis maximum harmonisation approach in EU capital markets law,[56] the revised prospectus rules are presented in the form of a directly applicable Regulation instead of a Directive. This choice aims to address implementation issues associated with the transposition of Directives and ensure greater uniformity in the application and interpretation of the relevant rules across the Union. Indeed, a Regulation is generally more effective in enhancing legal certainty and reducing compliance and search costs resulting from divergent national measures. As such, it is better placed to support cross-border activity for

[50] Council of the EU, 'Council Confirms Deal on Prospectus Rules', Press Release, 20 December 2016, available at www.consilium.europa.eu/en/press/press-releases/2016/12/20/prospectus/.

[51] SWD (2015) 255 final (n 7) 15; COM (2015) 583 final (n 35) 3.

[52] COM (2015) 583 final (n 35) 3; SWD (2015) 255 final (n 7) 15–16.

[53] SWD (2015) 255 final (n 7) 14–15.

[54] Recitals 3 and 7 Prospectus Regulation; SWD (2015) 255 final (n 7) 14–15.

[55] COM (2015) 583 final (n 35) 4.

[56] See eg Regulation (EU) No 596/2014 of the European Parliament and of the Council on market abuse (Market Abuse Regulation) [2014] OJ L173/1.

issuers and investors, also contributing to the CMU's objective of further integrating capital markets.[57] Moreover, the Prospectus Regulation is supplemented by Delegated Regulations, which aim to maintain consistency in the application of essential provisions in the prospectus regime. These Regulations cover various aspects, including the content, format, scrutiny and approval of prospectuses;[58] the marketing of securities;[59] and the information required in a prospectus exemption document related to a takeover, merger or division.[60]

The Regulation does not, however, completely eliminate Member States' control over prospectus rules. For instance, similar to the previous regime, NCAs or exchanges may still impose additional requirements, notably regarding corporate governance, when admitting securities to trading.[61] Competent authorities may also require the inclusion of supplementary information in the prospectus, where necessary for the protection of investors.[62] Moreover, national regulators are granted a certain degree of flexibility in imposing specific disclosure requirements for small public offerings that do not fall within the scope of the Regulation.[63] Finally, while the Regulation places particular emphasis on the coordination and convergence of investigatory, supervisory, and administrative sanctioning powers among Member States,[64] the public enforcement and supervision of the obligations arising from it remain exclusively the responsibility of NCAs.[65] Similarly, civil liability for issuers and other entities responsible for the information provided in the prospectus continues to be governed by national law.[66]

In view of the above, it becomes apparent that despite the maximum harmonisation model adopted by the Prospectus Regulation, some room for regulatory competition among Member States still exists. Overall, however, the level of regulatory approximation envisaged by the prospectus regime is extensive, with mandatory and comprehensive prospectus requirements now forming an integral part of the EU legal framework for primary markets.[67]

D. COVID-19 and EU Listing Act Reforms

Shortly after the Prospectus Regulation took effect, the COVID-19 pandemic erupted, leading Member States to implement precautionary measures to contain

[57] Recital 5 Prospectus Regulation.
[58] Commission Delegated Regulation (EU) 2019/980 [2019] OJ L166/26.
[59] Commission Delegated Regulation (EU) 2019/979 [2019] OJ L166/1.
[60] Commission Delegated Regulation (EU) 2021/528 [2021] OJ L106/32.
[61] Recital 8 Prospectus Regulation.
[62] ibid Art 32(1)(a).
[63] As will be explained in detail below, and following the adoption of the Listing Act Regulation, the current threshold for exempted small offers is EUR 12 million though Member States have the option to reduce this amount to EUR 5 million, ibid Art 3(2)(b) and (2a).
[64] ibid Arts 33, 34 and 37.
[65] ibid Art 31.
[66] ibid Art 11(1).
[67] See already under the Prospectus Directive, L Enriques and T Tröger, 'Issuer Choice in Europe' (2008) 67 *The Cambridge Law Journal* 521, 525; Schammo (n 26) 69 ff.

and control its transmission. These measures, however, had a severe impact on the EU economy, with many firms facing a massive slump in sales and profits. Against this background, in July 2020, the Commission presented a 'Capital Markets Recovery Package',[68] comprising targeted amendments to EU capital market rules aimed at supporting the flow of funding to the real economy, and thereby accelerating the necessary economic recovery.[69] Especially regarding the prospectus regime, the principal consideration was to prevent situations where the cost of preparing a prospectus would discourage financially distressed companies from accessing new equity financing.[70] This concern was amplified by the fact that the short-term loans and liquidity lines provided to several European businesses at the onset of the pandemic, in an attempt to secure their continuity, had substantially increased their debt levels, jeopardising their future recovery.[71] In this context, Regulation (EU) 2021/337[72] introduced a new type of short-form prospectus, known as the 'EU Recovery prospectus', which aimed to facilitate the rapid recapitalisation of EU companies in the immediate aftermath of the pandemic by simplifying the procedure for already listed issuers to raise capital on public markets.[73]

However, due to its main focus on alleviating the direct financial impact of the pandemic on businesses, the EU Recovery prospectus regime only had a limited duration and expired on 31 December 2022.[74] Therefore, while it largely succeeded in providing temporary relief to some corporations,[75] industry stakeholders continued to argue that further regulatory action was required to make public listing in the EU more attractive, particularly for SMEs.[76] Indeed, the review of the Prospectus Regulation revealed that, at least during the first years of its implementation, it did not succeed in reversing the declining trend in prospectus approvals observed over the last 15 years.[77] Market feedback indicated that, in certain cases, the requirements for drafting a prospectus remained burdensome,

[68] Commission, Coronavirus response: Making capital markets work for Europe's recovery, Press Release, 24 July 2020, ec.europa.eu/commission/presscorner/detail/en/IP_20_1382.

[69] Commission, 'Staff Working Document accompanying the EU Capital Markets Recovery Package', SWD (2020) 120 final, 24 July 2020.

[70] ibid 5–6.

[71] ibid 5.

[72] Regulation (EU) 2021/337 of the European Parliament and of the Council amending Regulation (EU) 2017/1129 as regards the EU Recovery prospectus and targeted adjustments for financial intermediaries and Directive 2004/109/EC as regards the use of the single electronic reporting format for annual financial reports, to support the recovery from the COVID-19 crisis [2021] OJ L68/1.

[73] ibid Recital 5. See also C Gortsos and M Terzi, 'The Prospectus Regulation (Regulation (EU) 2017/1129) and the Recent Proposal for an EU Recovery Prospectus: Elements of Continuity and Change with the Past and the Way Forward', EBI Working Paper Series, No. 79, 4 December 2020, ssrn.com/abstract=3742863.

[74] Art 1(9) Regulation (EU) 2021/337.

[75] Commission Staff Working Document, 'Impact Assessment Report accompanying the Proposal for a Regulation amending Regulations (EU) 2017/1129, (EU) No 596/2014 and (EU) No 600/2014 to make public capital markets in the Union more attractive for companies and to facilitate access to capital for small and medium-sized enterprises' SWD (2022) 762 final, 7 December 2022, 10.

[76] ibid 10. See also High-Level Forum on the Capital Markets Union, 'A new Vision for Europe's Capital Markets', Final Report, June 2020, 14.

[77] SWD (2022) 762 final (n 75) Annex 6, 155 ff.

thereby deterring companies from seeking access to public capital markets through either an IPO or secondary issuances.[78] For instance, many stakeholders argued that the Prospectus Regulation at times demanded information that was not justified from an investor protection standpoint (eg, because ample information is already publicly available) or failed to adequately differentiate among issuers according to their specific needs and circumstances, including their size.[79] Moreover, the procedure governing the scrutiny and approval of prospectuses was frequently perceived as complex and time-consuming, especially for companies engaged in cross-border offerings.[80] Specifically, senior managers of firms seeking to list reported spending considerably more time on the process than before.[81] At the same time, issuers criticised the lack of sufficient harmonisation in the supervisory practices of NCAs,[82] resulting in reduced predictability and overly lengthy prospectuses.[83]

To address these drawbacks, in December 2022, the Commission proposed a Regulation[84] which, among other provisions, included targeted amendments to the Prospectus Regulation. This was part of a broader package of legislative measures, known as the 'EU Listing Act', which sought to enhance the attractiveness of EU public markets and streamline access to capital for companies of all sizes, with a special focus on SMEs.[85] Ultimately, after lengthy negotiations, the Council and the Parliament reached a provisional agreement on the Listing Act in February 2024,[86] paving the way for the reform of the prospectus regime a few months later through the enactment of Regulation (EU) 2024/2809 (Listing Act Regulation).[87] The adopted measures aim to further reduce the cost and complexity of going public by eliminating unnecessary regulatory burdens and increasing flexibility for issuers.[88]

[78] ibid 20 and 22. See also Technical Expert Stakeholder Group (TESG) on SMEs, 'Empowering EU Capital Markets for SMEs – Making Listing Cool Again', Final Report, May 2021, 6.

[79] SWD (2022) 762 final (n 75) Annex 2, 85 ff.

[80] ibid 23.

[81] See Oxera (n 41) 68, mentioning that between 30% and 50% of CEO and CFO's time in the six months prior to listing is spent on the listing process.

[82] See generally ESMA, 'Peer Review of the Scrutiny and Approval Procedures of Prospectuses by Competent Authorities', Report, 21 July 2022.

[83] SWD (2022) 762 final (n 75) 24.

[84] Commission, 'Proposal for a Regulation amending Regulations (EU) 2017/1129, (EU) No 596/2014 and (EU) No 600/2014 to make public capital markets in the Union more attractive for companies and to facilitate access to capital for small and medium-sized enterprises', COM (2022) 762 final, 7 December 2022.

[85] Commission, 'Capital Markets Union: New Proposals on Clearing, Corporate Insolvency and Company Listing to Make EU Capital Markets More Attractive', Press Release, 7 December 2022, ec.europa.eu/commission/presscorner/detail/en/ip_22_7348.

[86] Council, 'Listings on European stock exchanges: Council and Parliament agree on new act', Press Release, 1 February 2024, www.consilium.europa.eu/en/press/press-releases/2024/02/01/listings-on-european-stock-exchanges-council-and-parliament-agree-new-act/.

[87] Regulation (EU) 2024/2809 of the European Parliament and the Council amending Regulations (EU) 2017/1129, (EU) No 596/2014 and (EU) No 600/2014 to make public capital markets in the Union more attractive for companies and to facilitate access to capital for small and medium-sized enterprises OJ L, 2024/2809.

[88] SWD (2022) 762 final (n 75) 11.

This is considered a significant step towards completing the CMU, as it is expected to improve access to market financing for European companies, while ensuring that investor protection and market integrity remain intact.[89]

III. A Legal Mapping of the Prospectus Regulation

As previously discussed, consistent with the overarching objectives of the CMU initiative, the Prospectus Regulation, as amended by the Listing Act Regulation, seeks to establish a harmonised and efficient regulatory framework for prospectus requirements which should facilitate more effective capital raising for EU companies in capital markets, while enabling investors to make well-informed decisions based on comprehensible, accessible, and concise disclosure.[90] Accordingly, the reforms introduced by the new prospectus regime can be broadly divided into two groups, depending on whether they are designed to support issuers or investors.

More specifically, the first group comprises measures aimed at better aligning prospectus publication duties with the diverse types of issuers across the Union, considering the classes of securities issued and the targeted investors. These measures focus on two main aspects: first, recalibrating and expanding the exemptions from the obligation to draw up a prospectus, particularly for small public offerings; and, second, introducing special disclosure regimes tailored to specific issuer groups, namely SMEs and other mid-cap companies, listed issuers seeking additional capital through secondary issuances, issuers of wholesale debt securities, and frequent issuers of securities. Additionally, these provisions are complemented by rules directed towards ensuring greater convergence in the criteria and procedures followed by NCAs during the scrutiny and approval of prospectuses.

The measures in the second group seek to enhance the accessibility, effectiveness, and relevance of the prospectus as a disclosure tool for investors, while also achieving greater consistency between the prospectus and other EU disclosure rules. These essentially involve: (a) calibrating and further standardising the content, length, and format of the prospectus and its summary to increase their utility as sources of information, particularly for retail investors; (b) limiting the risk factors included in the prospectus to those that are considered material for an informed decision and specific to the issuer and its securities; (c) introducing more detailed rules on the publication of prospectuses and establishing a storage mechanism operated by ESMA to offer investors timely and free access to all approved prospectuses in the EU; and (d) implementing a more unified and comprehensive approach regarding the administrative sanctions imposed by NCAs in order to deter issuers from breaching their disclosure duties. In the following text, these

[89] ibid 10 f.
[90] SWD (2015) 255 final (n 7) 15; SWD (2022) 762 final (n 75) 6.

reforms will be discussed in greater detail, starting with defining the regulatory perimeter and analysing the exemptions to the prospectus duty.

A. Setting the Regulatory Perimeter

Given the significant compliance and potential liability costs associated with the obligation to publish a prospectus, delineating its subjective and material scope has constantly presented a considerable challenge for policymakers. Similar to its predecessor, the regulatory perimeter of the Prospectus Regulation is shaped by two key factors: the types of financial instruments issued and the market segments employed. Additionally, a series of exceptions are in place, strategically limiting the Regulation's applicability by exempting certain transactions from mandatory prospectus requirements.

i. Securities

The prospectus publication duty under the Regulation is tied to the issuance of 'securities'. These are defined as transferable securities within the meaning of Article 4(1)(44) MiFID II, with the exception of money market instruments having a maturity of less than 12 months.[91] This limitation on the types of instruments covered stems from two main reasons. First, while the prospectus obligation may also be relevant for other financial instruments, its significance from an EU perspective becomes particularly apparent when transferability and negotiability are guaranteed. In such cases, clear implications for the internal market arise, thus justifying the establishment of European standards.[92] Second, for money market instruments, the efforts involved in preparing a prospectus appear excessive compared to the benefits, given both their short maturity and the fact that they are primarily intended for professional investors.[93]

The definition of transferable securities in MiFID II is broad, encompassing equity and non-equity classes of securities which are negotiable on the capital market, including shares, bonds (along with any related depositary receipts), and other securities granting holders the right to acquire or sell any such securities.[94] In this context, equity and non-equity securities are further defined, considering also their differential treatment with regard to certain aspects of the Regulation, particularly the content requirements of the prospectus. The first category, thus, comprises shares and other transferable securities equivalent to shares in companies, as well as convertible securities such as warrants, covered warrants, and

[91] Article 2(a) Prospectus Regulation.
[92] S Grundmann, *Bankvertragsrecht. Investment Banking II* (De Gruyter, 2016) 166–67.
[93] ibid 167.
[94] Art 4(1)(44) MiFID II.

certificates, provided they are issued by the issuer of the underlying shares or an entity within the issuer's group.[95] Non-equity securities, on the other hand, include all those securities that do not qualify as equity securities.[96] This vague definition, however, raises concerns about discrepancies in the classification of complex securities and hybrid instruments, notably depositary receipts and convertible notes, considering that, unlike its predecessor,[97] the Regulation does not provide any guidance on this matter.[98]

Finally, the Regulation delineates several types of securities that fall outside its scope of application.[99] These exemptions closely mirror those outlined in the Prospectus Directive[100] and include units issued by open-ended collective investment undertakings,[101] government and quasi-sovereign debt securities, shares in the capital of Member States' central banks, securities guaranteed by a Member State or one of its local or regional authorities, as well as securities issued by non-profit organisations to obtain capital for funding their objectives.[102] At the same time, attention has been given to excluding special classes of securities unique to certain Member States, namely non-fungible shares of capital in a housing association that confer the right to occupy an apartment or other forms of property, as observed in Finland.[103]

ii. Market Segments

a. Admission to a Regulated Market

During the early phases of EU securities law, only official stock exchange listing necessitated the issuance of a prospectus. However, the enactment of the Prospectus Directive abolished the listing requirement, rendering the obligation to issue a prospectus contingent upon the admission of securities to trading on a regulated market located or operating within the EU.[104] This situation remained unchanged under the Prospectus Regulation,[105] which continues to utilise this

[95] Art 2(b) and recital 10 Prospectus Regulation.
[96] ibid Art 2(c).
[97] Recital 12 Prospectus Directive.
[98] See also S Revell and E Cole, 'Practical Issues Arising from the Implementation of the Prospectus Directive – What Are the Equity Capital Markets Worrying About?' (2006) 1 *Capital Markets Law Journal* 77, 86–87.
[99] Art 1(2) Prospectus Regulation.
[100] Art 1(2)(a)–(e) and (g) Prospectus Directive.
[101] For such open-ended funds, specific disclosure requirements typically apply, see eg Directive 2009/65/EC of the European Parliament and of the Council on the coordination of laws, regulations and administrative provisions relating to undertakings for collective investment in transferable securities (UCITS) [2009] OJ L302/32, Arts 68 ff.
[102] Art 1(2)(a)–(e) Prospectus Regulation.
[103] ibid Art 1(2)(f). See also P Lucantoni, 'Prospectus Directive' in M Lehmann and C Kumpan (eds), *European Financial Services Law – Article-by-Article Commentary* (Nomos, 2019) 954.
[104] Art 3(3) Prospectus Directive.
[105] Art 3(3) Prospectus Regulation.

market segment, as defined in MiFID II,[106] as a proxy for the large and liquid public trading venues that are expected to uphold the strictest regulatory standards for issuers seeking admission of their securities. In contrast, the admission to trading on a multilateral trading facility (MTF) or the publication of bid and offer prices do not, by themselves, trigger the prospectus requirement. Nonetheless, a prospectus should be provided when such actions are accompanied by a communication that constitutes a public offering within the meaning of the Regulation,[107] since a prospectus is required in these cases anyhow.[108]

This perimeter control within the prospectus regime largely reflects the pivotal role that regulated markets, particularly stock exchanges, play in the capital-raising process and in mitigating agency problems. In particular, issuers can market their securities more effectively and raise more capital when a liquid market exists for investors to sell their securities and realise their investments. This is because investors generally view liquid markets favourably, resulting in higher valuations for securities traded within them.[109] Furthermore, enhanced liquidity can serve as a central governance incentive for management. Indeed, managers can benefit in several ways from the positive performance of share prices, including through pay-for-performance schemes, and the prevention of takeover attempts that might lead to their replacement. As a result, they are more inclined to prioritise investors' interests and strive to maximise shareholder value.[110] But the regulated market perimeter also reflects the dynamics of differentiation and competition among trading venues.[111] This implies, more specifically, that EU trading venues opting to operate as regulated markets can distinguish themselves as high-quality market segments, thus contributing to the Regulation's objectives of supporting market finance for issuers and protecting investors.

b. Public Offers – Irrespective of Admission

In practice, however, the selected market segment for listing the securities is often irrelevant. This is because, similar to its predecessor,[112] the Prospectus Regulation stipulates that the prospectus obligation is triggered when securities are offered to the public in the Union,[113] irrespective of whether they are subsequently admitted to trading. The entity subject to this obligation is not necessarily the issuer within the meaning of Article 2(h) of the Regulation. Instead, it is the offeror, comprising

[106] Art 4(1)(21) MiFID II.
[107] Recital 14 Prospectus Regulation.
[108] See also Moloney (n 1) 104.
[109] Gullifer and Payne (n 1) 408.
[110] See eg D Diamond and R Verrecchia, 'Optimal Managerial Contracts and Equilibrium Security Prices' (1982) 37 *The Journal of Finance* 275; E Avgouleas, *Governance of Global Financial Markets: The Law, the Economics, the Politics* (CUP, 2012) 29–30.
[111] Moloney (n 1) 104.
[112] Art 3(1) Prospectus Directive.
[113] Art 3(1) Prospectus Regulation.

any natural or legal person whose actions are directed at offering securities to the public.[114] In this regard, an underwriter who offers securities, either on its own account ('firm commitment') or through a best efforts agreement, shall be considered an offeror under the Regulation.[115] Consequently, they are obliged to make the prospectus available and, if the issuer has not yet fulfilled this duty, to draft and publish it.[116]

The concept of a public offer was initially defined in the Prospectus Directive, marking a major achievement at the time of its adoption.[117] Despite some challenges in interpretation that arose thereafter,[118] the definition remained largely unchanged under the new Regulation. An 'offer of securities to the public' is defined in Article 2(d) based on three key elements: first, there must be a communication, regardless of its form or means, regarding the offer of transferable securities; second, the communication must include sufficient information on the terms of the offer and the securities offered, enabling investors to decide whether to purchase or subscribe for those securities; and, third, it must be directed at a broad group of investors (*incertae personae*),[119] involving at least more than one individual or entity.[120] This definition also applies when the securities are placed through financial intermediaries. With regard to the first two elements, the Regulation does not introduce any novelties. Even before the Prospectus Directive, it was clear that securities could be offered via any marketing activity undertaken by the issuer or the offeror, as long as it provides sufficient information to enable an informed decision.[121] Thus, the means of communication used are irrelevant, provided that the terms of the offer and the features of the securities concerned are adequately described.[122] For example, online promotional messages for bonds presenting information on the minimum investment, interest rate and associated fees would constitute a public offer of securities.[123] Moreover, while the communication must

[114] ibid Art 2(i). See also T Preuße, 'Begriffsbestimmungen' in E Schwark and D Zimmer (eds), *Kapitalmarkrechts-Kommentar*, 5th edn (C.H. Beck, 2020) §2 WpPG (paras 34–36).

[115] Grundmann (n 4) 490; S Heinze, *Europäisches Kapitalmarktrecht: Recht des Primärmarktes* (C.H. Beck, 1999) 191.

[116] See also S Weber, 'Kapitalmarkt- Börsen- und Investmentrecht' in M Dauses (ed), *Handbuch des EU-Wirtschaftsrechts* (C.H. Beck, 1994) F.III., para 65.

[117] The importance of a standardised definition for 'offers of securities to the public' was highlighted in the Lamfalussy report. It stressed that the absence of consensus across Member State led to inconsistencies, with the same activity being considered a private placement in some jurisdictions but not in others. This disparity discouraged firms from pursuing cross-border capital-raising initiatives and hindered access to a large, liquid, and integrated financial market, Committee of Wise Men, *Final Report* (n 24) 85.

[118] See L Enriques and M Gatti, 'Is There a Uniform EU Securities Law After the Financial Services Action Plan?' (2008) 14 *Stanford Journal of Law, Business & Finance* 43, 56.

[119] A Zahid and A McGee, 'A Defective Proposal in Need of a Rethink' (2002) 23 *The Company Lawyer* 250, 251; F Schäfer, 'Emission und Vertrieb von Wertpapieren nach dem Wertpapierverkaufsprospektgesetz' (1991) 23–24 *Zeitschrift für Wirtschaftsrecht* 1557, 1559 ff.

[120] This is already evident from the wording of the text which explicitly refers to 'persons'.

[121] See also Grundmann (n 4) 491.

[122] ibid.

[123] EFTA Court, Case E-10/20, *ADCADA Immobilien AG PCC in Konkurs v Financial Market Authority (Finanzmarktaufsicht)*, 18 June 2021 [para 39].

be made in relation to a specific securities offer,[124] there is no requirement to prove an actual intention to sell.[125] In this regard, an *invitatio ad offerendum*, typical during the book-building process, should be considered an offer to the public,[126] if the price can be deduced, directly or indirectly, from the provided information.[127] With respect to the third element, namely the range of addressees, no major amendments were introduced either. It has long been acknowledged that even if the investors targeted by an offer can be identified by specific characteristics, such as profession or income, the offer is still deemed public.[128] The only limitation is that the recipients must have the option to decide whether they want to purchase or subscribe to the offered securities.[129]

What is noteworthy, however, and has changed since the Regulation came into force, is the significant broadening, if not omnipresence, of the concept of a public offer.[130] More specifically, an important innovation of the Prospectus Directive was the delineation of the perimeter between public offerings, where the obligation to publish a prospectus was required unless specific exemptions applied,[131] and private placements,[132] where prospectus requirements did not apply ('safe harbours'), provided that no admission of the securities to a regulated market was sought.[133] The Prospectus Regulation has eliminated this distinction, assimilating formerly private placements to exempted public offerings.[134] This choice, not attributable to an error,[135] reflects a regulatory approach, particularly evident in the UK,[136] which presumes any offer of securities as public by default. Therefore, any exemptions from prospectus requirements can be granted only through specific legal provisions. While such an approach could be justified as part of an effort to improve consistency in applying the notion of public offers across the Union,

[124] Commission de Surveillance du Secteur Financier, Circular 05/225 regarding the notion 'offer of securities to the public', 16 December 2005, 4, www.cssf.lu/wp-content/uploads/cssf05_225eng.pdf.

[125] Grundmann (n 4) 491.

[126] ibid. See also J Busche in *Münchener Kommentar zum Bürgerlichen Gesetzbuch*, 8th edn (C.H. Beck, 2018) §145 (para 10).

[127] van Gerven (n 3) 17.

[128] K Hopt, *Die Verantwortlichkeit der Banken bei Emissionen: Recht und Praxis in der EG, in Deutschland und in der Schweiz* (C.H. Beck, 1991) 66; Schäfer (n 119) 1560.

[129] Hence, allocations of securities where there is no element of choice on the part of the recipients do not qualify as public offerings, see Recital 22 Prospectus Regulation; and ESMA, 'Q&A on the Prospectus Regulation', ESMA/2019/31-62-1258, 31 February 2023 (version 12) 34.

[130] A Pietrancosta and A Marraud des Grottes, 'La Notion de «Placement Privé» Abolie par le Règlement Prospectus du 14 juin 2017?' (2018) 1 *Bulletin Joly Bourse* 60.

[131] These exemptions were prescribed in Art 4(1) Prospectus Directive.

[132] Art 3(2) Prospectus Directive referred to 'types of offers', thus explicitly differentiating them from the exempted 'offers of securities to the public' outlined in Art 4(1).

[133] ibid 3(3).

[134] Art 1(4) Prospectus Regulation refers to 'types of offers of securities to the public', which also include the private placements mentioned in Art 3(2) Prospectus Directive.

[135] This is evident in recitals 12, 13, 20, and 25 of the Prospectus Regulation, which characterise previously considered private placements as 'offers of securities to the public'.

[136] The types of offers mentioned in section 86 of the Financial Services and Markets Act 2000, which transposed Art 3(2) of the Prospectus Directive in the UK, are termed 'exempt offers to the public'.

it raises significant practical and doctrinal concerns. Indeed, the removal of the distinction between private placements and exempted public offers contradicts regulatory practices deeply rooted in the legal systems of many Member States,[137] creating legal uncertainty among market participants and exacerbating interpretation issues. Additionally, the broad expansion of the public offering concept, to the point of questioning the viability of private placements, undermines its very essence, stripping it of any distinctive characteristics it previously held.

iii. *Exemptions*

While the EU prospectus regime primarily focuses on prospectus requirements, one of its most notable achievements lies in delineating the circumstances under which issuers can raise capital without being subject to these requirements.[138] These exemptions, which were further expanded by the Prospectus Regulation, and subsequently by the EU Listing Act, fall under various categories relevant to instances where a reduced level of disclosure can be justified.

The first category encompasses offers directed at investors who do not fit the traditional retail investor profile, and thus may require less protection. It also covers offers addressed to a select group of individuals or legal entities known to the issuer, who are able to access all relevant information directly from them or their intermediary. These include, in particular, offers addressed solely to qualified investors; offers made to fewer than 150 persons per Member State; and offers of securities with a high denomination per unit or high minimum subscription per investor (equal to at least EUR 100,000).[139]

Another category of exemptions covers certain funding transactions where disclosure is typically already available. As with the previous regime, these exemptions cover the public offering of specific types of securities, including, among others: shares issued in substitution for shares of the same class;[140] equity securities issued in connection with a takeover through an exchange offer, as well as equity securities offered, allotted, or to be allotted in connection with a merger or division, provided that the related transaction is not considered a reverse acquisition and a document containing information describing the transaction and its impact on the issuer is made available;[141] and non-equity securities issued in a

[137] This is particularly evident under the French Monetary and Financial Code (Code Monétaire et Financier), which distinguishes between 'public' and 'non-public' offerings, see Art L 411-2. Similarly, in German Law, a private placement is not considered an offer to the public, see Preuße (n 114) §2 WpPG (para 18). This approach can also be observed in Belgium, Italy, Portugal, and Spain.

[138] These exemptions do not only refer to the publication duty, as the text suggests, but also encompass the drafting and approval of the prospectus, see Schammo (n 26) 126.

[139] Art 1(4)(a)–(d) Prospectus Regulation.

[140] ibid Art 1(4)(e).

[141] ibid Art 1(4)(f) and (g) in conjunction with Arts 1(6a) and (6b), as the latter were inserted by Regulation (EU) 2019/2115 of the European Parliament and of the Council amending Directive 2014/65/EU and Regulations (EU) No 596/2014 and (EU) 2017/1129 as regards the promotion of the use of SME growth markets [2019] OJ L 320/1.

continuous or repeated manner by a credit institution, as long as the securities offered are not subordinated, convertible, or exchangeable, and their total consideration in the Union is less than EUR 150 million per credit institution calculated over a 12-month period.[142] Similar exceptions to the prospectus requirements also apply when the aforementioned types of securities are admitted to trading on a regulated market.[143]

In the same vein, under certain conditions, secondary issuances of securities are also exempted from prospectus requirements. Already under the Prospectus Directive, issuers of shares fungible with shares already admitted to trading on a regulated market were not subject to the duty to draw up a prospectus, provided that the newly admitted shares did not represent, during a 12-month period, more than 10 per cent of the shares admitted on that market.[144] The Prospectus Regulation broadened the scope of this exemption to include all types of securities and initially raised the applicable threshold to 20 per cent, before increasing it to 30 per cent.[145] To balance this, the previous unlimited exemption for the listing of shares resulting from the exchange or conversion of other securities[146] was limited to 30 per cent over a 12-month period.[147] However, when the Regulation was introduced, these exemptions would not apply in case the admission of the new securities to trading was combined with an offer to the public. In order to reduce complexity and limit unnecessary costs and burdens, the Listing Act Regulation extended the prospectus exemption to offers of securities fungible with securities already admitted to trading on a regulated market or an SME growth market for more than 18 months, so long as the offered securities are not issued in connection with a takeover bid, merger, or division.[148] This exemption also applies to offers of securities to be admitted to trading on a regulated or SME growth market, provided they are fungible with securities already listed on the same market and do not represent more than 30 per cent of those securities within a 12-month period.[149] At the same time, given that subscription rights are inherently tied to the issuance of new securities, the exemption further encompasses the right to subscribe for shares fungible with existing ones.[150] To ensure an adequate level of

[142] ibid Art 1(4)(j) as amended by the Listing Act Regulation.

[143] ibid Art 1(5)(d)–(i). However, in accordance with Articles 1(6a)(a) and 1(6b)(a) and (b), the admission of equity securities following an exchange offer, merger, or division cannot benefit from the prospectus exemption unless the offered securities have already been admitted to trading on a regulated market or are fungible with securities admitted to such market prior to the transaction. This prevents unlisted companies from listing their shares on a regulated market without producing a prospectus, see recital 13 Regulation (EU) 2019/2115.

[144] Art 4(2)(a) Prospectus Directive.

[145] Art 1(5)(a) Prospectus Regulation as amended by the Listing Act Regulation.

[146] Art 4(2)(g) Prospectus Directive.

[147] Art 1(5)(b) Prospectus Regulation as amended by the Listing Act Regulation.

[148] ibid Art 1(4)(db) as inserted by the Listing Act Regulation.

[149] ibid Art 1(4)(da) as inserted by the Listing Act Regulation.

[150] Recital 11 Listing Act Regulation.

investor protection, when an offer is made under this exemption, a short document (not exceeding 11 A4-sized pages) containing some key information should be made available to the public and filed with the competent authority of the home Member State, without requiring approval.[151] It should be noted, though, that this exemption does not apply if the issuer is undergoing insolvency proceedings or restructuring, to prevent the proceeds from being used for these purposes.[152]

Finally, a longstanding exemption exists for public offerings where the total consideration is so small that the costs for the issuer resulting from the publication of a prospectus would probably be disproportionate to the expected proceeds.[153] Nevertheless, a major challenge for EU regulators has been to determine the precise threshold below which the prospectus duty should be waived, ensuring that investor protection is not compromised. More specifically, the Prospectus Directive set this threshold at EUR 5 million, calculated over a period of 12 months from the date of the offer.[154] Member States were, nonetheless, free to impose prospectus or other disclosure requirements at the national level for offers below that threshold, provided they exceeded EUR 100,000.[155] Following the introduction of the Prospectus Regulation, the minimum exemption threshold was increased to EUR 1 million.[156] At the same time, given the diverse sizes of capital markets across the EU, national regulators were offered the possibility to raise this threshold for domestic offers up to EUR 8 million.[157] In both cases, Member States retained the authority to impose some disclosure requirements they considered appropriate for the protection of investors at the national level, provided they did not impose an undue or disproportionate burden on issuers.[158] This approach resulted in the introduction of varying exemption thresholds for small public offerings across the EU,[159] as well as diverse disclosure requirements, which created complexity and a lack of clarity for both issuers and investors.[160] Against this background, the EU Listing Act introduces a dual threshold system which seeks to streamline national thresholds while also accommodating the varying sizes of national markets within the Union.[161] Under the new regime, a default threshold of EUR 12 million is established, below which the Regulation does not apply,[162] whilst the minimum

[151] Arts 1(4)(da)(i) and 1(4)(db)(iii) in conjunction with Annex IX Prospectus Regulation as inserted by Listing Act Regulation.

[152] ibid Arts 1(4)(da)(ii) and 1(4)(db)(ii).

[153] ibid recital 12.

[154] Art 1(2)(h) Prospectus Directive.

[155] ibid Art 3(2)(e).

[156] Art 1(3) Prospectus Regulation.

[157] ibid Art 3(2). For a detailed analysis see S Schulz, 'Neue Schwellenwerte für Wertpapierprospekte' (2018) 21 *Neue Zeitschrift für Gesellschaftsrecht* 921, 922 ff.

[158] Recitals 12 and 13 Prospectus Regulation.

[159] ESMA, 'National Thresholds Below which the Obligation to Publish a Prospectus Does not Apply' 3 July 2023, www.esma.europa.eu/document/list-prospectus-thresholds.

[160] Recital 7 Listing Act Regulation.

[161] ibid recital 8.

[162] Art 3(2)(b) Prospectus Regulation as amended by the Listing Act Regulation.

threshold of EUR 1 million is removed. However, Member States may opt for a lower threshold of EUR 5 million instead,[163] if this is considered more appropriate based on their local circumstances.[164] When calculating the relevant threshold, issuers should consider the total value of all exempted public offers of securities, including ongoing ones, made within 12 months preceding the date of a new offer.[165] Even if an offer falls below this threshold, though, Member States may still require the publication of a disclosure document. This document should contain either the information included in the prospectus summary or information specified by national law, provided that in the latter case, the extent of disclosure does not exceed that contained in the summary.[166]

B. Improving Access to Public Markets for EU Companies

Besides the extensive list of prospectus exemptions, the significance of differentiation within the Prospectus Regulation is further highlighted by the introduction of various voluntary prospectus formats, detailed below. This innovative approach, further refined following the Listing Act Regulation, seeks to better align prospectus requirements with the distinct circumstances of issuers, particularly those whose securities are already listed on regulated or SME Growth markets, as well as SMEs and other small-cap companies.

i. The EU Follow-on Prospectus

a. Background, Objectives and Scope

A 'proportionate disclosure regime' for offers of shares by issuers who already had shares of the same class admitted to trading on a regulated market or an MTF was initially introduced by the 2010 Amending Prospectus Directive.[167] However, despite the significant alleviations provided under this regime, it saw limited practical usage,[168] mainly due to its narrow scope, as it was exclusively applicable to rights issues.[169] As a result, much of the information already in the public domain would still need to be disclosed in the prospectuses required for subsequent issuances, leading to unnecessary burdens for listed issuers. In view of this, the

[163] Ibid Art 3(2a).

[164] In this case, Member States should notify both the Commission and ESMA of their decision, ibid Art 3(2b).

[165] ibid Art 3(2c).

[166] ibid Art 3(2d). This provision is expected to reduce the discretion granted to Member States under the previous regime, thus enhancing legal certainty and predictability for market participants.

[167] Art 7(2)(g) Prospectus Directive as inserted by Directive 2010/73/EU.

[168] Only 1.2% of all prospectuses approved in 2013–2014 were drawn up under that regime, SWD (2015) 255 final (n 7) Annex 5 (Figure 10).

[169] Art 26a Commission Regulation (EC) 809/2004. These are issues of statutory pre-emption rights which allow for the subscription of new shares and are addressed only to existing shareholders.

Prospectus Regulation introduced a novel 'simplified disclosure regime' specifically tailored for secondary issuances of securities.[170] The aim was to alleviate the administrative burden on companies pursuing multiple rounds of funding in the capital markets, while ensuring that investors continue to receive comprehensive and coherent information.[171]

Nevertheless, the review of the Prospectus Regulation revealed that most issuers perceived the level of disclosure in the simplified prospectuses for secondary issuances as overly prescriptive, especially when compared to the information found in a standard prospectus.[172] Consequently, the process of drawing up such prospectuses was deemed excessively complex and expensive,[173] providing limited value for secondary issuances of listed companies subject to extensive periodic and ongoing disclosure obligations under the Transparency Directive[174] and the Market Abuse Regulation (MAR),[175] respectively. In this context, the EU Listing Act replaces the simplified prospectus for secondary issuances with a shorter and more streamlined document, the 'EU Follow-on prospectus'.[176] This new prospectus format, accessible to EU issuers as of 5 March 2026,[177] seeks to reduce costs and administrative burdens for listed companies, while making it easier for investors to read and comprehend the information contained therein.[178]

Similar to its predecessor, the EU Follow-on prospectus is available to a wide range of issuers whose securities have been continuously admitted to trading on a regulated market or an SME growth market for at least the preceding 18 months before the public offer or admission of the new securities, as well as to the offerors of such securities.[179] In fact, in an effort to enable as many issuers as possible to benefit from this alleviated prospectus type,[180] the scope of the EU Follow-on prospectus is considerably broader than that of the simplified prospectus for

[170] Art 14 Prospectus Regulation.
[171] ibid recital 48.
[172] SWD (2022) 762 final (n 75) 22 f.
[173] The average cost of producing a simplified prospectus was approximately 25% lower than that of a standard prospectus, ibid Annex 4 (Table 7).
[174] Directive 2004/109/EC of the European Parliament and of the Council on the harmonisation of transparency requirements in relation to information about issuers whose securities are admitted to trading on a regulated market [2004] OJ L390/38.
[175] Regulation (EU) 596/2014 of 16 April 2014 on market abuse [2014] OJ L173/1 (MAR).
[176] Art 14a Prospectus Regulation as amended by the Listing Act Regulation.
[177] Art 4(2) Listing Act Regulation. Until that date, any prospectuses drawn up and approved in accordance with the simplified disclosure regime for secondary issuances shall continue to be governed by that regime until the end of their validity, Art 50(2) Prospectus Regulation as inserted by the Listing Act Regulation.
[178] Recital 27 Listing Act Regulation. See also SWD (2022) 762 final (n 75) 56 f.
[179] Art 14a(1) Prospectus Regulation. The requirement of continuous admission for a minimum of 18 months ensures that issuers have completed, at least once, their duty to publish an annual financial report under the Transparency Directive, or in the case of SME Growth Markets, under Delegated Regulation (EU) 2017/565.
[180] Recital 28 Listing Act Regulation.

secondary issuances. In particular, unlike the previous regime, it covers public offers or admissions to trading on a regulated market of securities, irrespective of whether they are fungible with securities already admitted to trading.[181] Furthermore, issuers listed on an SME growth market are now also eligible to use the Follow-on prospectus if they decide to offer new securities to the public.[182] Finally, to support the growth of successful companies and allow them to access a wider range of investors, the EU Follow-on prospectus is accessible to issuers aiming to transition from an SME growth market to a regulated market.[183] It is worth noting, however, that issuers who only have non-equity securities listed on a regulated market or an SME growth market are prohibited from preparing a Follow-on prospectus for the admission to trading of equity securities on a regulated market.[184] This is because such an action requires the disclosure of a comprehensive prospectus, ensuring investors can make informed investment decisions.[185]

b. Content and Format

In specifying the content of the EU Follow-on prospectus, particular attention was given to avoid the duplication of information that has already been publicly disclosed by issuers.[186] Accordingly, the newly introduced Article 14a(2) clarifies that, in derogation from the 'necessary information' test contemplated in Article 6(1), the EU Follow-on prospectus needs to include only information that is essential for investors to understand: the prospects and financial performance of the issuer, including any significant changes in its financial and business position occurred since the end of the last financial year; the rights attached to the securities issued, along with any limitations on the exercise of those rights; as well as the reason of the issuance, its impact on the issuer, and the use of the proceeds. In case of share issuances, the minimum information meeting this relaxed materiality standard is specified in Annex IV of the Prospectus Regulation, and is modelled after the light-touch EU Recovery Prospectus which was introduced as part of the Capital Markets Recovery Package in an effort to support the rapid recapitalisation of companies following the COVID-19 pandemic.[187] For all other types of securities, the required information is outlined in the amended Annex V.[188]

[181] Art 14a(1)(a) Prospectus Regulation as inserted by the Listing Act Regulation. Under the repealed Art 14(1)(a) of the Regulation, fungibility with previously issued securities was a prerequisite for the application of the simplified prospectus for secondary issuances.
[182] ibid Art 14a(1)(b).
[183] ibid Art 14a(1)(c).
[184] ibid Art 14a(1) second subparagraph.
[185] Recital 28 Listing Act Regulation.
[186] ibid recital 27.
[187] Art 14(a) Prospectus Regulation as inserted by Art 1(5) of Regulation (EU) 2021/337.
[188] According to Art 14a(8) Prospectus Regulation, the Commission is further empowered to adopt a delegated act to further specify the content of the EU Follow-on prospectus.

In addition to its main content, the EU Follow-on prospectus shall also include a summary, intended to be a valuable source of information for retail investors.[189] In this regard, it should be positioned at the beginning of the prospectus and written concisely, not exceeding seven A4-sized pages when printed. It should provide key information on the issuer, the securities, and the issuance, enabling investors to determine which public offers or admissions to trading of securities warrant further examination, before reviewing the EU Follow-on prospectus in its entirety to make informed investment decisions.[190]

In terms of format, the EU Follow-on prospectus shall be presented in a way that is easy to read, using characters of readable size, and shall be written in an easily analysable, concise and comprehensible form.[191] Moreover, to streamline the production process and improve accessibility for investors, a limit of 50 pages is mandated for secondary share issuances.[192] However, this page limit does not extend to issues of securities other than shares, given their often complex nature.[193] At the same time, certain components of the prospectus, such as the summary or information incorporated by reference, are excluded from the calculation of the maximum length.[194] Finally, to ensure consistency and enhance readability for all investors throughout the Union, the layout of the EU Follow-on prospectus should be standardised for both equity and non-equity securities. This means that the information within the prospectus should be presented in a fixed sequence, following the order of disclosure described in either Annex IV or V of the Prospectus Regulation, depending on the type of securities involved.[195] For the same reason, the EU Follow-on prospectus should be drawn up as a single document, though issuers of non-equity securities may opt to prepare separate documents instead.[196]

ii. The EU Growth Issuance Prospectus

a. Rationale and Purpose of the Reform

Improving access to capital market financing for SMEs is a central goal of the CMU agenda. These businesses typically require smaller funding amounts compared to larger issuers, often finding the costs of producing a standard prospectus disproportionate to the gains achieved, which may deter them from

[189] Recital 30 Listing Act Regulation.
[190] Art 7(12a) Prospectus Regulation as amended by the Listing Act Regulation.
[191] ibid Art 14a(3) and (5). Similar requirements also apply to the summary, as stipulated in Art 7(12a). Additionally, the summary should not contain cross-references to other parts of the prospectus and should be written in a style that facilitates understanding by investors, avoiding technical and complex language.
[192] ibid Art 14a(5).
[193] Recital 32 Listing Act Regulation.
[194] Art 14a(6) Prospectus Regulation.
[195] ibid Art 14a(7).
[196] ibid Art 14a(4).

accessing public markets.[197] The 2010 Amending Prospectus Directive marked the initial attempt to address this issue by introducing a proportionate disclosure regime, specifically applicable when securities issued by SMEs and other small-cap companies[198] were offered to the public or admitted to trading on a regulated market.[199] However, this initiative fell short of achieving its objectives as the cost reductions it offered to issuers were deemed so minimal that most would opt to issue a full prospectus rather than risking the potential 'stigma' associated with using the regime.[200] Against this background, the Prospectus Regulation introduced the EU Growth prospectus as a streamlined version of a standard prospectus.[201] Its aim was to reduce the administrative burden on smaller issuers when accessing capital markets while still ensuring a sufficient level of investor protection.[202]

Despite some cost savings that resulted from the regulatory adjustments brought by the EU Growth prospectus,[203] many stakeholders believed that this prospectus type failed to achieve a satisfactory equilibrium between securing effective investor protection and maintaining a proportionate administrative burden for issuers.[204] Accordingly, they highlighted the need for additional measures to further alleviate prospectus requirements for SMEs. In line with this recommendation, as part of the EU Listing Act, a new EU Growth issuance prospectus was introduced to replace the EU Growth prospectus.[205] This document, which can be used as of 5 March 2026, is intended to further simplify and relieve the listing documentation for SMEs, allowing them to achieve even greater savings.[206]

b. Scope of Application

In formulating the scope of the EU Growth issuance prospectus, a primary concern for EU regulators was to prevent the establishment of a two-tier disclosure standard on regulated markets based on the issuer's size.[207] This is mainly because such an approach could not only generate confusion among investors but it could also

[197] See eg G Ferrarini and A Ottolia, 'Corporate Disclosure as a Transaction Cost: The Case of SMEs' (2013) 9 *European Review of Contract Law* 363, 365.

[198] These were defined as listed companies with an average market capitalisation of less than EUR 100 million, based on the end-year quotes from the previous three calendar years, see Art 2(1)(t) Prospectus Directive.

[199] Article 26b Commission Regulation (EC) No 809/2004 as inserted by Commission Delegated Regulation (EU) No 486/2012 [2012] OJ L150/1.

[200] Only a mere 1.8% of the prospectuses approved in the Union between 2013 and 2014 were issued based on this proportionate disclosure regime, SWD (2015) 255 final (n 7) 35.

[201] Art 15 Prospectus Regulation.

[202] ibid recital 51.

[203] Its average cost was 25% less than a standard prospectus, SWD (2022) 722 final (n 75) Annex 4 (Table 7).

[204] ibid 29.

[205] Art 15a Prospectus Regulation as inserted by the Listing Act Regulation.

[206] Recital 33 Listing Act Regulation.

[207] ibid recital 35.

undermine the branding effects and associated investor confidence inherent in these markets.[208] Hence, as with its predecessor, this novel type of prospectus is not available to companies whose securities are already traded or are intended to be admitted to trading on a regulated market.[209] At the same time, though, the reach of the EU Growth issuance prospectus has been expanded to include a wider range of beneficiaries, allowing more entities to utilise this alleviated disclosure document when offering securities to the public.

More specifically, the first category of beneficiaries includes SMEs,[210] defined as companies that meet at least two of the following three criteria based on their last annual or consolidated accounts: having an average number of employees during the financial year of less than 250, a total balance sheet not exceeding EUR 43 million, and an annual net turnover not exceeding EUR 50 million.[211] Alternatively, companies with an average market capitalisation of less than EUR 200 million based on their end-year quotes for the previous three calendar years are also included in this category.[212] To promote the utilisation of SME growth markets, the second category of entities that can benefit from the EU growth issuance prospectus includes issuers, other than SMEs, whose securities are traded or are to be traded on such venues.[213] Unlike the previous regime, no additional restrictions based on the issuers' market capitalisation or outstanding shares apply.[214] A third category comprises issuers, other than those mentioned above, whose total aggregated value of securities offered to the public in any given 12 months is less than EUR 50 million,[215] provided they are not listed on an MTF and they had fewer than 499 employees on average during the preceding financial year.[216] Finally, offerors of securities issued by the first two categories of issuers may also draw up an EU Growth issuance prospectus,[217] a provision that is justified as these entities significantly contribute to the promotion of the issuers' securities and, as such, should also benefit from this alleviated prospectus.

[208] See also Moloney (n 1) 491.

[209] Art 15a(1) first subparagraph Prospectus Regulation.

[210] ibid Art 15a(1)(a).

[211] ibid Art 2(f)(i).

[212] ibid Art 2(f)(ii) in conjunction with Art 4(1)(13) MiFID II. Note that according to Art 77(2) of Commission Delegated Regulation (EU) 2017/565, a non-equity issuer is considered an SME for the purposes of Article 4(1)(13) MiFID II if the nominal value of its debt issuances over the previous calendar year, on all trading venues across the Union, does not exceed EUR 50 million. However, it is unclear if the Prospectus Regulation's reference to the SME definition of MiFID II includes this subsequent amendment.

[213] ibid Art 15a(1)(b).

[214] Art 15(1)(b) and (ca) Prospectus Regulation.

[215] When calculating this amount, issuers should consider the total aggregated consideration of all ongoing offers of securities to the public and offers of securities made within the 12 months preceding the start date of a new offer of securities to the public. However, they should exclude offers for which a prospectus was published or those that were exempted from the obligation to publish a prospectus, Art 15a(1) second subparagraph Prospectus Regulation.

[216] ibid Art 15a(1)(c).

[217] ibid Art 15a(1)(d).

c. Content and Format

The content of the EU Growth issuance prospectus is significantly lighter compared to that of a standard prospectus, ensuring that the disclosed information is proportionate to the size and funding needs of the targeted companies, while still maintaining an adequate level of investor protection.[218] In establishing the relevant disclosure requirements, EU regulators considered the level of disclosure of the EU Recovery prospectus, as well as the simplified admission documents required by some SME growth markets in cases of exemption of issuers from the obligation to publish a prospectus.[219] Accordingly, this prospectus type shall only comprise the reduced disclosure items specified in the amended Annexes VII or VIII of the Prospectus Regulation, depending on the type of securities.[220] These cover information that is essential for investors to understand the financial performance and position of the issuers, along with their growth strategy and organisational structure; the main features of the securities offered, including the rights and any limitations attached to them; and the rationale behind the offer, its impact on the overall capital structure of the issuer, and the intended use of proceeds.[221] Moreover, the EU Growth issuance prospectus should include a simplified summary, mirroring the content and format of the EU Follow-on prospectus summary. This should serve as a reference point for investors, especially retail ones, helping them identify offers they want to study further and make informed decisions.[222]

Regarding its format, the EU Growth issuance prospectus should be a document that is easy for issuers, especially SMEs, to draw up and for investors to read.[223] In this respect, it should consist of a single document for both equity and non-equity securities, and be written and presented in an easily analysable, concise, and comprehensible form.[224] Additionally, its structure should be standardised, with the information included therein following the order of disclosure set out in Annexes VII and VIII of the Prospectus Regulation.[225] Finally, to further enhance readability and ease of navigation for investors, EU Growth issuance prospectuses relating to shares should not exceed 75 pages when printed, and they should be displayed in a simple-to-read form, using characters of readable size.[226] Similar to the EU Follow-on prospectus, however, this page limit should not include the summary, information incorporated by reference or any additional information required for issuers with complex financial history or significant financial commitments, or in case of a major gross change.[227]

[218] Recital 34 Listing Act Regulation.
[219] ibid.
[220] Art 15a(4) Prospectus Regulation.
[221] Ibid Art 15a(2).
[222] Recital 36 Listing Act Regulation.
[223] ibid recital 37.
[224] Art 15a(3) and (4) Prospectus Regulation.
[225] ibid Art 15a(7).
[226] ibid Art 15a(5).
[227] ibid Art 15a(6).

iii. Alleviated Prospectus Regime for Wholesale Debt Issuances

a. Background and Objectives

While EU corporate bond markets have traditionally lagged behind their US counterparts,[228] they exhibited considerable growth following the 2008 financial crisis.[229] This was fuelled by several factors, including the decrease in bank lending after the crisis,[230] the more favourable tax treatment of debt over equity financing ('debt-equity bias'),[231] investors' pursuit of higher yields, as well as the special provisions on debt issuances under the Prospectus Directive.[232] However, despite these positive developments, at the beginning of the CMU project, these markets still faced some serious problems, which prevented issuers and investors from fully leveraging their potential. First, they remained quite fragmented, with significant variations in growth among Member States, as 80 per cent of all issuances were concentrated in just six countries (France, UK, Germany, Italy, the Netherlands and Luxembourg).[233] Second, notwithstanding some national initiatives aimed at facilitating bond issuances by SMEs,[234] these firms often encountered greater difficulties accessing bond financing compared to larger enterprises. Most importantly, the reduced liquidity observed in secondary bond markets posed important challenges for trading non-equity securities.[235] More specifically, unlike equity securities, which trade on stock exchanges accessible to a wide range of investors, corporate bonds often trade in over-the-counter (OTC) markets, where a small number of large dealer banks play a central role in market making, and trading mainly occurs in large lots at irregular intervals.[236] However, post-crisis regulatory reforms, such as higher risk-based capital requirements for bank trading books, substantially increased dealer banks' inventory costs for market making, prompting them to be more selective in their trading activities.[237] This steep decline in

[228] See eg S Çelik, G Demirtaş and M Isaksson, 'Corporate Bond Markets in a Time of Unconventional Monetary Policy', OECD Capital Market Series, 2019, 8 (Figure 2).

[229] See generally O Darmouni and M Papoutsi, 'The Rise of Bond Financing in Europe', ECB Working Paper Series, No 2663, May 2020, ssrn.com/abstract=4115175.

[230] Commission Staff Working Document, 'Economic Analysis Accompanying the Action Plan on Building a Capital Markets Union', SWD (2015) 183 final, 30 September 2015, 85.

[231] ibid 52.

[232] These included both the discretion granted regarding the choice of the NCA for approving prospectuses related to non-equity issues, as well as the relaxed disclosure requirements reserved for issuers of large-denomination debt securities, Arts 2(1)(m)(ii), 3(2)(d), 5(2) and 7(2)(b) Prospectus Directive.

[233] Commission, 'Improving European Corporate Bond Markets', Report of the Expert Group on Corporate Bond Markets, November 2017, 13 (Figure 3).

[234] A notable example is Germany, where reduced bank lending spurred the growth of a vibrant corporate bond market for smaller companies ('Mittelstand') and the establishment of trading facilities for these instruments.

[235] See generally ECB, 'Survey on credit terms and conditions in euro-denominated securities financing and OTC derivatives markets (SESFOD)', March 2019; International Capital Market Association (ICMA), 'Remaking the corporate bond market', Report, July 2016.

[236] Commission, *Drivers of Corporate Bond Market Liquidity in the European Union* (EU, 2017) 21.

[237] ibid.

traditional market making, coupled with a rise in passive 'buy and hold' strategies among institutional investors, adversely affected bond market liquidity and reduced firms' prospects for financing through primary bond markets.[238] Given these issues, the Prospectus Regulation further extended and adjusted the alleviated prospectus regime for wholesale debt issuances aiming to enhance the proper functioning of the corporate bond market and boost liquidity.[239]

b. Scope and Content of the Wholesale Debt Prospectus

As already mentioned, the Prospectus Regulation includes an exemption from the obligation to publish a prospectus for companies offering non-equity securities to the public, provided that the minimum denomination per unit is at least EUR 100,000.[240] Therefore, when such securities are admitted to trading on regulated markets, they do not qualify for this exemption as they are subject to the prospectus requirement due to their listing. Even in these instances, however, the Prospectus Regulation provides for a less onerous prospectus,[241] given that such issuances primarily target qualified investors who do not require the same level of protection as retail ones. Additionally, to accommodate the needs of smaller issuers, the scope of the wholesale prospectus also includes non-equity securities, regardless of their denomination, provided they are traded on a regulated market, or a specific segment thereof, accessible only to qualified investors.[242] As a result, any subsequent resale of such securities to non-qualified investors, for example through 'retail cascades',[243] is not permitted, unless a prospectus that is appropriate for them has been drawn up in accordance with the Regulation.[244]

Considering the expertise and bargaining power of investors targeted by the wholesale prospectus for non-equity securities, it contains less rigorous information compared to what is required when such securities are also marketed to retail investors. This mainly builds on the disclosure requirements of the previous regime,[245] with some minor amendments introduced to further reduce compliance costs for issuers, while enhancing transparency for investors.[246] Moreover,

[238] Commission (n 233) 17.
[239] Recital 21 Prospectus Regulation.
[240] ibid Art 1(4)(c). While this exemption applies to all types of securities, there is no evidence of shares with a denomination above EUR 100,000 being issued anywhere in the EU.
[241] ibid Art 6(1)(d) and recital 21.
[242] ibid.
[243] Under this system, issuers sell bonds to underwriters who then sell them to retail distributors who, depending on market conditions, may further sell the securities to retail investors, relying on the initial prospectus under which the securities were first offered.
[244] Recital 21 Prospectus Regulation.
[245] Annexes IX & XIII Commission Regulation (EC) 809/2004.
[246] These include mainly the removal of the requirement to restate the financial statements in the registration document, as well as the obligation to make some of the information displayed in the prospectus also available electronically, see Arts 8(1) and 16 in conjunction with Annexes 7 and 15 Delegated Regulation (EU) 980/2019.

there is no obligation to provide a summary,[247] while issuers benefit from greater flexibility in the choice of language used.[248] Nevertheless, an issuer may also opt to prepare the wholesale prospectus following the model specified for the prospectus of equity and retail non-equity securities.[249] Finally, prior to the introduction of the Listing Act Regulation, if an issuer was eligible to prepare an EU Growth prospectus, a simplified prospectus for secondary issuances, or a universal registration document, the constituent parts of the wholesale prospectus could include the information provided under these specific disclosure regimes.[250] Although Regulation (EU) 2024/2809 does not provide any guidance on this matter, it is safe to assume that a similar provision will be included for the EU Growth issuance and the EU Follow-on prospectuses.

iv. *The Universal Registration Document*

a. Reasons and Importance of the Provision

The legal interventions discussed above aim to alleviate the administrative burden for companies where the costs of complying with typical prospectus requirements appear disproportionate. A similar need for intervention arises for already listed issuers who must undergo the time-consuming process of preparing and approving a full prospectus whenever they make a public offer or apply for admission to trading, thereby preventing them from seizing beneficial market opportunities.

The first significant effort to accommodate the frequent issuers' need for easier and timely access to capital markets was the introduction of the innovative shelf-registration regime by the Prospectus Directive.[251] Under this regime, the issuer, offeror, or entity seeking admission to trading on a regulated market could choose to prepare a 'tripartite prospectus', comprising a separate registration document, securities note, and summary.[252] Once the initial registration document had been prepared and approved by the NCA, it could be kept 'on the shelf' and supplemented by the securities note and summary only when market conditions allowed the issuer to raise financing.[253] In this way, issuers could benefit from a more flexible and time-saving publication procedure, as the registration document, containing the main information about the issuer, usually constitutes the largest

[247] Art 7(1) Prospectus Regulation.
[248] ibid Art 27(5).
[249] Arts 8 and 16 in conjunction with Annexes 1, 6 and 14 Delegated Regulation (EU) 980/2019. In that case, it should be accepted that securities can be resold to non-qualified investors without preparing a new prospectus.
[250] ibid Art 8(1) and 16.
[251] Moloney (n 1) 118.
[252] Article 5(3) Prospectus Directive.
[253] ibid Art 12(1).

part of the prospectus[254] and generates the most discussion during its scrutiny and approval by the NCA. In practice, however, this fast-track regime was utilised in very few Member States,[255] indicating the need for additional improvements. In this direction, the Prospectus Regulation introduces a new optional 'tripartite' regime available to all issuers, including SMEs, whose securities are admitted to trading on regulated markets or MTFs.[256] This allows them to annually prepare and file a universal registration document (URD) with their NCA, providing the necessary flexibility to swiftly react to market opportunities.[257]

b. Content, Format, Filing and Approval

The minimum content and format of the URD, along with the specific procedure for its filing and approval, are detailed in Article 9 of the Regulation and in Delegated Regulation (EU) 2019/980.[258] More specifically, being the central reference point for investors and analysts regarding the issuer's activity and performance, the URD should include information that is essential to understand the company's business, organisation, financial position, earnings, prospects, governance, and shareholding structure.[259] Accordingly, the content of the URD aligns with the disclosure requirements applicable to the standard registration document for equity securities, and should remain the same regardless of the type of securities subsequently offered by the issuer or admitted to trading.[260] Considering this multipurpose character, however, some flexibility is recognised in the order of presenting the relevant information.[261] In addition, to reduce the administrative burden of multiple filings, the Regulation allows issuers to incorporate the annual and half-yearly financial reports required by Articles 4 and 5 of the Transparency Directive into the URD, provided certain requirements are fulfilled.[262] Should that be the case, the URD must include a cross-reference list indicating where each item prescribed in these reports can be found, as well as a responsibility statement using the terms specified in Articles 4(2)(c) and 5(2)(c) of the Transparency Directive.[263]

[254] The registration document typically makes up 2/3 to 4/5 of the size of a standard prospectus, and it can sometimes weigh almost 4 kilograms, SWD (2015) 255 final (n 7) 25. See also ESME, 'Report on Directive 2003/71/EC', September 2007, 10–11.

[255] Almost 70% of all prospectuses produced in the tripartite format between 2013 and 2014 were approved in France, Luxembourg, and Norway. By contrast, this regime was used much less in other advanced markets, like Germany and the UK, SWD (2015) 255 final (n 7) Annex 5 (Figure 11). See also D Fischer-Appelt, 'Prospectus Formats and Shelf Registration' in D Busch, G Ferrarini and JP Franx (eds), *Prospectus Regulation and Prospectus Liability* (OUP, 2020), 299.

[256] Art 9(1) Prospectus Regulation.

[257] ibid recital 39.

[258] Art 3 and Annex 2.

[259] Art 9(1) Prospectus Regulation.

[260] ibid recital 39.

[261] ESMA, 'Technical advice under the Prospectus Regulation', Final Report, 28 March 2018, 21.

[262] Art 9(12) and (13) Prospectus Regulation. These requirements mainly pertain to the timing of the URD's publication, the NCA responsible for its approval, and the language used, which must align with the provisions of the Transparency Directive.

[263] ibid Art 9(12)(a) and (c).

If an issuer chooses to prepare a URD, they must submit it for approval to the NCA of their home Member State, following the procedure outlined in Article 20(2) and (4) of the Prospectus Regulation.[264] Nevertheless, to encourage more issuers to utilise the new regime, once an issuer has filed and received approval of the URD for one financial year,[265] subsequent URDs may be filed without prior approval and reviewed only on an ex-post basis if deemed necessary by the competent authority.[266] In each case, issuers should include a written statement confirming that all required information under the Transparency Directive and MAR has been disclosed and published according to the procedures stipulated therein, either over the last 18 months or since the obligation to disclose this information commenced, whichever is shorter.[267]

Once approved or filed with the NCA, the URD must be made publicly available without undue delay, in accordance with the requirements laid down in Article 21,[268] and must clearly indicate whether it has been approved by the competent authority or not.[269] If the URD is not part of an approved prospectus, the issuer may voluntarily update it without prior approval by filing an amendment with the competent authority at any time.[270] Alternatively, the NCA may request amendments if, during an ex-post filing review, it is found that the URD does not meet the standards of completeness, comprehensibility, or consistency.[271] The issuer should typically address a request for amendment or supplementary information in the next URD filed for the following financial year, unless they plan to integrate the URD into a prospectus, in which case the amendment must be filed at the latest upon submission of the application for prospectus approval.[272] However, where the competent authority identifies a material omission or inaccuracy that is likely to mislead investors regarding facts and circumstances that are essential for an informed decision, the issuer must amend or supplement the URD without undue delay.[273]

If the requirements outlined above are met, an issuer that has filed or received approval for a URD shall be considered a frequent issuer from the moment they submit this document for approval to the competent authority.[274] This implies that when they decide to offer securities to the public or admit them to trading on a regulated market, they only need to prepare the securities note and the summary.[275] At the same, a major innovation of the new regime is the introduction

[264] ibid Art 9(2) first subparagraph.
[265] Before the Listing Act Regulation, the relevant timeframe was two consecutive financial years.
[266] ibid Art 9(2) second subparagraph and 9(8).
[267] ibid Art 9(11)(a). It should be noted that this action is not required if the relevant information has already been incorporated into the URD.
[268] ibid Art 9(4).
[269] Annex 2 Delegated Regulation (EU) 980/2019.
[270] Art 9(7) Prospectus Regulation.
[271] ibid Art 9(9) first subparagraph.
[272] ibid Art 9(9) second subparagraph.
[273] ibid Art 9(9) third subparagraph.
[274] ibid Art 9(11) and recital 39.
[275] ibid Art 10(3) first subparagraph.

of a fast-track approval process of five working days,[276] instead of the standard 10 working days,[277] enabling quicker access to capital markets for issuers.[278] This accelerated process shall apply to the approval of the entire documentation, including the URD and any amendments thereto, provided they have not been already approved by the relevant NCA.[279] Finally, frequent issuers using the notification procedure outlined in Article 26 can also benefit from this special regime. In such instances, the competent authority of the chosen Member State for the prospectus approval should refrain from reviewing the URD and any amendments thereof that have already been approved by the notifying NCA. Instead, only the securities note and the summary should be subject to approval within five days upon receipt of the notification.[280]

v. Harmonised Rules on Prospectus Scrutiny and Approval

a. Context and Objectives of the New Regime

As explained in the second chapter, mandatory prospectus rules are ineffective unless accompanied by an efficient supervision and enforcement system to ensure their proper implementation. The EU prospectus regime embraces this idea, relying on both ex-post public enforcement, and ex-ante supervision through the prior approval of the prospectus by the competent authority of the issuer's home Member State.[281] Prospectus approval is a two-step process, beginning with the scrutiny of the draft prospectus by the competent authority. This enables the NCA to evaluate if the information provided there meets certain criteria, particularly regarding its completeness, consistency and comprehensibility.[282] In this respect, the scrutiny of the prospectus goes beyond a mechanistic review of each disclosure item, although it does not extend to assessing the accuracy and veracity of the relevant information. The second step of the process involves the NCA's decision to approve or refuse approval of the prospectus. This marks the end of the review phase, and given its positive outcome, the final prospectus is filed and published.[283]

[276] ibid Arts 9(11) and 20(6). To benefit from the shorter approval deadline, frequent issuers must inform the NCA at least five days before applying for approval.

[277] ibid Art 20(2).

[278] This concept of a fast-track approval process is inspired by the 'document de reference' system, which was in operation in France for over 20 years, benefiting more than 350 issuers who voluntarily submitted this document to the French competent authority each year.

[279] Art 10(3) second and third subparagraphs Prospectus Regulation. According to recital 43, this is because the registration document, which is the main component of the prospectus, is available for review by the competent authority, even if not yet approved.

[280] ibid Arts 20(6) and 26(2) and (3).

[281] Moloney (n 1) 151. For an analysis of the prospectus approval process, see P Schammo, 'The Prospectus Approval System' (2006) 7 *European Business Organization Law Review* 501, 505 ff.

[282] Art 2(r) Prospectus Regulation.

[283] Schammo (n 26) 215.

The first significant step towards creating a more comprehensive and coherent approach to the prospectus approval process across Member States was the introduction of the Prospectus Directive. The latter streamlined the scope of prospectus scrutiny[284] and introduced minimum standards and time limits.[285] Despite these efforts, however, the peer review conducted by ESMA regarding the implementation of the relevant rules by NCAs[286] revealed considerable divergences in approaches, particularly concerning the applicable scrutiny standards and the procedures that issuers had to follow to have the prospectus approved. These differences ranged from the criteria used to assess the completeness, consistency, and comprehensibility of the information provided in the prospectus, to the approval timeframes, and the flexibility shown during this process based on the unique characteristics of the issuer and the issuance. Additionally, discrepancies were identified in the interpretation of legislative provisions.[287] As a result, issuers faced higher costs and uncertainty when raising capital, which also had adverse effects on cross-border issuances.

Against this background, the Prospectus Regulation aims to eliminate these differences by harmonising and streamlining the criteria for prospectus scrutiny and the rules governing NCA approval procedures. More specifically, it seeks to ensure a more consistent approach among NCAs in scrutinising the completeness, consistency and comprehensibility of the information contained in the prospectus, and to promote a prompt, efficient and proportionate approval process to facilitate capital raising for all issuers.[288] This becomes even more apparent following the Listing Act Regulation, which introduces targeted amendments to the prospectus regime aiming to foster convergence of supervisory practices among NCAs during the scrutiny and approval of prospectuses.[289]

b. Procedural Requirements and Standards

The common standards and procedures for scrutinising and approving prospectuses in the EU are laid down in Article 20 of the Prospectus Regulation, and complemented by Delegated Regulation (EU) 2019/980.[290] In designing these provisions, special emphasis was placed on achieving greater harmonisation in how NCAs conduct the scrutiny and approval process.[291] In this regard, the delegated act

[284] Art 2(1)(q) Prospectus Directive.
[285] ibid Art 13 and Arts 2–5 Commission Delegated Regulation (EU) 2016/301 [2016] OJ L 58/13.
[286] ESMA, 'Peer Review on Prospectus Approval Process', Report, ESMA/2016/1055, 30 June 2016.
[287] ibid 7–10.
[288] Recital 60 Prospectus Regulation.
[289] Recitals 44 and 45 Listing Act Regulation.
[290] Arts 35–45. Note that Art 20(11) Prospectus Regulation, as amended by the Listing Act Regulation, empowers the Commission to complement these provisions regarding certain aspects of the scrutiny and approval process.
[291] See also ESMA, Draft technical advice on format and content of the prospectus', Consultation Paper, 6 July 2017, 15.

establishes specific criteria for assessing the completeness, comprehensibility, and consistency of the information in a draft prospectus,[292] thus reducing the discretion of competent authorities to unilaterally define their review standards. These criteria should assist NCAs in consistently determining whether the prospectus contains all required information according to the disclosure schedules, is free of material discrepancies that may affect its readability and intelligibility, and if its individual parts do not contradict each other and form a coherent whole.

Another fundamental consideration when determining these rules is that the scrutiny of prospectuses inherently involves a qualitative element, as it is not possible to prescribe an exact formula for NCAs to follow in ensuring that a prospectus is comprehensible, consistent, and complete. Indeed, given the specificities of different issuers and issuances, defining precise scrutiny criteria for all types of prospectuses is challenging without risking investor protection or disproportionately affecting certain issuers. Therefore, NCAs maintain some discretion and flexibility when scrutinising prospectuses. More specifically, competent authorities may apply additional scrutiny criteria and request supplementary information in the prospectus when deemed necessary for investor protection.[293] However, to prevent discrepancies arising from the exercise of this discretion[294] and to offer legal certainty to issuers and confidence to investors, the Commission is authorised to adopt delegated rules clarifying the circumstances under which such additional criteria may be applied, as well as the type of information that may be required in addition to what is included in the various types of prospectuses.[295] Furthermore, NCAs are entitled to adopt a lighter scrutiny approach when the information in the draft prospectus has already been reviewed,[296] as further examination would only consume time without yielding additional benefits. In a similar vein, if the prospectus is intended solely for wholesale investors, some scrutiny criteria aimed at ensuring comprehensibility for a potential retail audience (eg, the use of plain language) shall not be considered.[297]

A final consideration in developing the new harmonised regime was to ensure a timely and efficient approval process. To achieve this, a shift towards electronic document submission was considered necessary. Therefore, each draft prospectus must be submitted in a searchable electronic format,[298] enabling NCAs to search for specific words or terms, thus expediting the scrutiny procedure. Additionally, subsequent versions of the draft prospectus should include a marked-up version highlighting all changes made from the previous submission, along with an explanation of how outstanding issues notified by the competent

[292] Arts 36–38 Delegated Regulation (EU) 2019/980.
[293] ibid Arts 39–40.
[294] ESMA, 'Peer Review of the Scrutiny and Approval Procedures of Prospectuses by Competent Authorities', Peer Review Report, 21 July 2022, 56 ff.
[295] Art 20(11) Prospectus Regulation as amended by the Listing Act Regulation.
[296] Art 41 Delegated Regulation (EU) 2019/980.
[297] ibid Art 37(1) second subparagraph.
[298] ibid Art 42(1).

authority were tackled.[299] Moreover, to minimise delays, NCAs should provide guidance on their website regarding the approval process and contact details of the responsible staff.[300] Finally, some time limits regarding the approval of the prospectus are set.[301] While the failure to comply with the said deadlines does not result in automatic approval, competent authorities should still notify the issuer or the offeror, as well as ESMA, of the reasons for the delay, while Member States should also implement appropriate measures to address these failures.[302]

C. Enhancing Investor Protection and Participation

i. The Modernised Prospectus Summary

a. Reasons and Objectives of the Reform

Despite the attractiveness of disclosure as an investor protection tool, empirical evidence suggests that retail investors are unlikely to read or comprehend the full prospectus,[303] due to its lengthy and technical nature, which spans hundreds of pages with complex information.[304] Against this backdrop, the Prospectus Directive introduced, for the first time, the requirement for issuers to produce a prospectus summary as a self-contained part of the prospectus.[305] This document provided key information about the issuer, any guarantor, and the securities in a concise and non-technical manner, with the purpose of helping investors decide which offers and admissions to trading they wanted to explore further.[306] Nevertheless, the review of the Prospectus Directive revealed that the summary did not sufficiently enhance investors' understanding of potential investment opportunities and risks.[307] More specifically, instead of being concise, clear and readable, prospectus summaries were often lengthy and generic, resembling a 'cut and paste' exercise without focusing on the key aspects of the transaction. In addition, the format requirements lacked flexibility, making it challenging for issuers

[299] ibid Art 43(1) and (2).

[300] Art 20(7) Prospectus Regulation and Art 45(1)(b) Delegated Regulation (EU) 2019/980.

[301] The standard timeframe is 10 working days after submitting the final prospectus draft, including any additional information requested by the competent authority. However, this period can be extended to 20 days for an IPO and shortened to 5 and 7 days, respectively, for a prospectus based on a URD or for an EU Follow-on prospectus for shares, Art 20(2),(3),(4),(6) and (6a) Prospectus Regulation as the latter was replaced by the Listing Act Regulation.

[302] Art 20(2) second subparagraph as amended by the Listing Act Regulation.

[303] For a brief overview of this evidence see N Moloney, *How to Protect Investors – Lessons from the EC and the UK* (CUP, 2010) 292–94.

[304] G Schaeken Willemaers, *The EU Issuer – Disclosure Regime: Objectives and Proposals for Reform* (Kluwer Law International, 2011) 37; E Howell, 'An Analysis of the Prospectus Regime: The EU Reforms and the "Brexit" Factor' (2018) 15 *European Company and Financial Law Review* 69, 82.

[305] Art 5(2) Prospectus Directive.

[306] Recital 15 Amending Prospectus Directive.

[307] SWD (2015) 255 final (n 7), Annex 6, 44 ff.

to exclude non-essential information.[308] As a result, most retail investors refrained from reading the summary, relying instead on marketing material prepared for the offering.[309]

To address these shortcomings, the Prospectus Regulation revamped the summary regime, focusing on both content and format.[310] In doing so, special attention was given to making the summary a more useful tool for retail investors[311] and avoiding overlaps with other retail documents, especially the key information document (KID) under the PRIIPS Regulation.[312] This is expected to support investors in making more informed decisions, while reducing administrative burden for issuers.[313]

b. Format and Content

In a significant departure from the tabular format of the previous regime, the Regulation mandates that the summary consist of four sections, presented in a standardised sequence: introduction and warnings, key information on the issuer, key information on the securities, and key information on the public offer and/or admission to trading.[314] The information under each specific section shall follow a predefined order to enhance comparability, with the last three sections further divided into sub-sections with specific headings using a Q&A format (eg, 'Who is the issuer of the security?', 'What are the main features of the security?', 'Why is this prospectus being produced?').[315] Moreover, to ensure that more investors will read the summary and to incentivise issuers to provide essential information,[316] the summary must be short and concise, not exceeding 7 A4-pages when printed.[317] However, this may be extended in case of more complex issuances, such as those with guarantees attached to the securities.[318] Additionally, to improve comprehensibility and accessibility, the summary must be written in clear, non-technical language and presented in an easy-to-read format using characters of readable size.[319] ESMA shall develop guidelines to ensure that the information included in the summary meets these conditions.[320] Charts, graphs or tables may also be contained in the summary provided that the maximum length

[308] ibid Annex 6, 44.
[309] ibid Annex 5, 19.
[310] Art 7 Prospectus Regulation.
[311] ibid recital 28.
[312] Regulation (EU) No 1286/2014 [2014] OJ L352/1.
[313] Recital 32 Prospectus Regulation.
[314] ibid Art 7(4) as amended by the Listing Act Regulation.
[315] ibid Art 7(6)–(8) as amended by the Listing Act Regulation.
[316] ibid recital 30.
[317] ibid Art 7(3) first subparagraph.
[318] In such cases, the summary may be extended by one additional page for each guarantor, Art 7(7) fifth subparagraph Prospectus Regulation as amended by the Listing Act Regulation.
[319] ibid Art 7(3)(a) and (b).
[320] Ibid Art 7(14) as inserted by the Listing Act Regulation.

is not exceeded.[321] Finally, to ensure consistency in the application of these provisions, the Commission is authorised to adopt implementing technical standards, based on advice from ESMA, specifying the template and layout of the summaries, including the font size and style requirements.[322]

In terms of content, the new prospectus summary offers greater flexibility compared to the previous regime. While the Regulation provides indicative contents for each section of this document, issuers have the discretion to choose the information they deem material and meaningful.[323] This information, however, should be accurate, clear, fair, and not misleading, ensuring the summary is a reliable introduction consistent with the rest of the prospectus.[324] Accordingly, the summary should not incorporate information by reference or contain cross-references to other parts of the prospectus[325] to prevent it from becoming a mere compilation of excerpts and hyperlinks. The freedom granted to issuers over the summary content is nevertheless restricted when it comes to key financial information, given its importance in enabling an informed assessment of the issuer's financial position. Hence, the Commission has adopted regulatory technical standards that specify the historical financial information to be included in the summary, depending on the type of issuer and the securities involved.[326] Moreover, to avoid an overlap between the summary and the KID for PRIIPs, where the securities offered or admitted to trading are also 'packaged products', issuers may substitute the content of the section regarding the securities with the information included in the KID.[327] Finally, to tackle information overload, the total number of risk factors to be included in the summary is limited to 15, selected by issuers based on their relevance for investors.[328]

ii. Revised Format of the Standard Prospectus

The standard prospectus for primary issuances is the most detailed type of prospectus. It can be prepared either as a single document or as separate documents, which shall include a registration document containing information about the issuer, a securities note containing information regarding the securities, and a summary.[329] In addition, it can be drawn up even when issuers or offerors have the option to use an alleviated prospectus.[330]

[321] ibid Art 7(3) second subparagraph as inserted by the Listing Act Regulation.
[322] ibid Art 7(15) as inserted by the Listing Act Regulation.
[323] ibid recital 31.
[324] ibid Art 7(2).
[325] ibid Art 7(11).
[326] Arts 1–8 and Annexes I-VI Delegated Regulation (EU) 2019/979.
[327] Art 7(7) second subparagraph Prospectus Regulation. In such cases, the length of the summary may be extended by three A4 pages for each additional security, ESMA, *Q&A on the Prospectus Regulation* (129) 61.
[328] Art 7(10) Prospectus Regulation.
[329] ibid Art 6(3).
[330] SWD (2022) 762 final (n 75) 161.

While the Prospectus Regulation introduced significant improvements to both the content and format of the standard prospectus, the targeted consultation on the Listing Act revealed that it did not achieve an appropriate balance between effectively protecting investors and reducing the administrative burden for issuers.[331] In particular, many stakeholders argued that this document remained too lengthy,[332] deterring several retail investors from consulting it.[333] At the same time, larger investors incurred higher investment costs due to the intense effort involved in studying hundreds of pages of disclosure.[334] Finally, divergences in format across the Union affected the comparability of prospectuses and hindered cross-border investing.[335]

In view of the above, the Listing Act Regulation has introduced targeted reforms aimed at further standardising and harmonising the format of the standard prospectus. Specifically, to improve the readability of prospectus documentation for all investors across the Union, the Regulation establishes a standardised format for both equity and non-equity prospectuses and mandates that the information contained therein be presented in a standardised sequence.[336] The standardised format and sequence of the information to be included in the prospectus are outlined in the amended Annexes I, II and III of the Prospectus Regulation, regardless of whether it is prepared as a single document or separate documents.[337] These Annexes also form the basis for the amendment of Delegated Regulation 2019/980 by the Commission, which further specifies the format and order of sections in the prospectus and the disclosure items within those sections.[338] Furthermore, to facilitate investors in analysing and navigating through the prospectus, a 300-page limit is introduced for IPO prospectuses.[339] However, this limit does not apply in the case of public offerings or admissions to trading on regulated markets of securities other than shares.[340] Moreover, the summary, information incorporated by reference, as well as additional information required for issuers with a complex financial history or significant financial commitments,[341] or in the case of significant gross changes,[342] are not counted towards the size-limit.[343] Finally, to ensure that the information included in the prospectus is presented in a concise, comprehensible and analysable form, ESMA shall adopt guidelines on clarity and the use

[331] ibid 86.
[332] As of March 2019, the median length of an IPO prospectus in the EU was 400 pages, with significant variations among Member States, ibid 164 (table 2).
[333] ibid 23.
[334] ibid.
[335] ibid 168.
[336] Art 6(2) first subparagraph Prospectus Regulation as amended by the Listing Act Regulation.
[337] Recital 17 Listing Act Regulation.
[338] Art 13(1) first subparagraph Prospectus Regulation and recital 17 Listing Act Regulation.
[339] Art 6(4) Prospectus Regulation as inserted by the Listing Act Regulation.
[340] Recital 16 Listing Act Regulation.
[341] Art 18 Delegated Regulation (EU) 2019/980.
[342] ibid Art 1(e).
[343] Art 6(5) Prospectus Regulation as inserted by the Listing Act Regulation.

of plain language.[344] Similarly, to achieve greater consistency in prospectus format among Member States, the Commission is authorised to adopt implementing technical standards specifying the template, layout, font size and style requirements for prospectuses.[345] It should be noted, however, that the revised rules on the prospectus format, including those on maximum length, do not apply to information included in a URD, nor to the prospectus relating to the admission to trading on a regulated market in the EU of securities which are simultaneously offered or privately placed with investors in a third country where an offering document is prepared under national law.[346]

iii. The Disclosure of Risk Factors

a. Need for Reform and its Aims

The 'size inflation' of prospectuses, largely driven by issuers' efforts to mitigate potential legal liability, has been identified as one of the main shortcomings of the previous regime.[347] The tendency to use prospectuses as liability shields was most evident in the 'risk factors' section, which outlined the main risks related to the issuer's ability to meet their payment obligations under the securities. Indeed, despite the specificity and materiality test governing their content,[348] market practice evolved in such a way that issuers included large quantities of generic and boilerplate risk factors. As a result, not only did the overall length of the prospectus increase, but many important or specific risks were also obscured, thus reducing its comprehensibility.[349]

In this regard, the introduction of more detailed requirements for the risk factors featured in the prospectus has been a principal concern of the Commission towards enhancing its relevance and effectiveness for potential investors. Under the new rules, risk factors should not only be limited to those that are material and relevant to the specific situation of the issuer and its securities but should also be corroborated by the content of the prospectus.[350] Moreover, issuers, offerors or persons asking for admission to trading on a regulated market are required to categorise risk factors based on their nature.[351] These rules aim to help investors identify and assess the most important risks associated with their investments, enabling them to make fully informed investment decisions.[352]

[344] ibid Art 6(7) as inserted by the Listing Act Regulation.
[345] ibid Art 6(8) as inserted by the Listing Act Regulation.
[346] ibid Art 6(2) second subparagraph and 6(6) as inserted by the Listing Act Regulation.
[347] SWD (2015) 255 final (n 7) 9.
[348] Art 2(3) Regulation (EC) No 809/2004.
[349] SWD (2015) 255 final (n 7) 17.
[350] Art 16(1) first subparagraph Prospectus Regulation as amended by the Listing Act Regulation.
[351] ibid Art 16(1) fifth subparagraph as inserted by the Listing Act Regulation.
[352] ibid recital 54.

b. Specificity, Materiality and Presentation of Risk Factors

While the Commission has the authority to specify criteria for assessing the specificity and materiality of risk factors, as well as categorising them based on their nature,[353] it has not yet done so. Therefore, guidance on this issue can only be found in the Prospectus Regulation and the guidelines developed by ESMA to assist NCAs in reviewing the specificity, materiality, and categorisation of risk factors.[354]

Based on these, for a risk factor to be considered specific, the person responsible for the prospectus must establish a clear and direct link between the potential risk and the issuer, guarantor,[355] or securities being offered or admitted to trading.[356] In this regard, risk factors that consist of generic disclosure or merely serve as disclaimers, without adequately describing how they affect the issuer, the guarantor, or the securities, shall not be considered specific and shall not be featured in the prospectus.[357] The assessment of whether a risk factor is specific to the issuer, guarantor or the securities should be made on an ad-hoc basis, taking into account the situation of the issuing entity (size, sector of activity, exposure to the risk) and the characteristics of the securities. However, it remains the responsibility of the issuer, the offeror, or the entity seeking admission to trading to ensure that the disclosure of a risk factor clearly reflects these conditions.[358]

The materiality of a risk factor, now, depends on the probability of its occurrence and the expected magnitude of its negative impact.[359] When assessing this criterion, the person tasked with drafting the prospectus can rely on either quantitative or, where unavailable, qualitative information.[360] In the latter scenario, the probability and expected impact of the risk may also be presented using a scaled ranking of low, medium, or high.[361] This ranking should align with the overall depiction of the issuer and the securities as portrayed in the prospectus.[362] Moreover, the materiality of the risk factor should be clearly evidenced from its description in the prospectus.[363] Therefore, while the use of mitigating language relative to a risk factor is not prohibited, it should not be excessive to avoid obscuring the reader's understanding of the true extent of the risk's negative impact or probability of occurrence. This is the case, for instance, when lengthy and detailed descriptions of risk management policies are provided.[364]

[353] ibid Art 16(5).

[354] ESMA, Guidelines on risk factors under the Prospectus Regulation (ESMA31-62-1293) 1 October 2019. These guidelines have been drafted pursuant to Art 16(4) of the Prospectus Regulation.

[355] See also Art 16(3) Prospectus Regulation.

[356] ESMA (n 354) 9.

[357] ibid 9–10 and Art 16(1) second and fourth subparagraphs Prospectus Regulation as amended by the Listing Act Regulation.

[358] ibid 9.

[359] Art 16(1) third subparagraph Prospectus Regulation as amended by the Listing Act Regulation.

[360] ESMA (n 354) 10–11.

[361] Art 16(1) fourth subparagraph Prospectus Regulation as amended by the Listing Act Regulation.

[362] ESMA (n 354) 12.

[363] ibid 10.

[364] ibid 11.

Finally, the presentation of risk factors across categories should help investors understand the source and nature of each disclosed risk. Accordingly, each risk factor should only appear once in the most appropriate category.[365] In addition, the prospectus should contain only a limited number of categories, typically not exceeding ten in total, unless necessary to support comprehensibility. These categories should be easily identifiable by using suitable headings that reflect the nature of the risk factors, while sub-categories should only be used if justified by the particular circumstances of the case.[366] Within each category, risk factors must be listed in a manner consistent with their materiality assessment.[367] However, after the Listing Act Regulation, the requirement to rank risk factors in strict order of materiality has been abolished, as it imposed undue burden and liability risk on issuers and their management.[368]

iv. Publication and Storage of EU Prospectuses

a. Shortcoming of the Previous Regime

Once approved, the prospectus must also be made available to the public, ensuring that the necessary information reaches its recipients in a timely manner.[369] Under the Prospectus Directive, issuers had the option to publish an approved prospectus either solely through electronic means or in combination with conventional distribution channels.[370] Furthermore, the home NCA was required to publish all prospectuses over a 12-month period, or at least a list thereof, on its website, along with a hyperlink to the prospectus published on the issuer's or the regulated market's website.[371] ESMA was required to publish a list of approved prospectuses, including a hyperlink to the website of the competent authority.[372]

Despite these provisions, investors still encountered difficulties in accessing and searching prospectuses, especially across the EU, hindering their ability to compare and assess different investment opportunities. More specifically, considering recent technological advancements and the benefits of accessing information through the internet, offering printed prospectuses seemed outdated and inefficient. Meanwhile, ESMA's website lacked centralised access to the full text of all approved prospectuses in an easily searchable form. Instead, it compiled a list of hyperlinks, which were often inoperative or led to invalid offers.[373] Given these shortcomings, it was deemed beneficial to introduce electronic publication as

[365] ibid 12.
[366] ibid 13.
[367] Art 16(1) fifth subparagraph Prospectus Regulation as amended by the Listing Act Regulation.
[368] SWD (2022) 762 final (n 75) 166 (fn 387).
[369] Grundmann (n 4) 500.
[370] Art 14(1) Prospectus Directive.
[371] ibid Art 14(4).
[372] ibid Art 14(4a).
[373] SWD (2015) 255 final (n 7) 41.

the only suitable distribution channel for all approved prospectuses and establish a centralised and free storage system operated by ESMA.[374] These measures are expected to provide a more efficient and reliable access to prospectuses and support cross-border investments.[375]

b. Electronic Publication and Online Database at ESMA

An approved prospectus must, in principle, be published by the beginning of the public offer or admission to trading of the securities involved, though in the case of an IPO this time limit is extended to at least three working days before the end of the offer.[376] To be considered publicly available, the prospectus must be published in a digitally searchable, downloadable and printable format on a dedicated and easily accessible section of one of the following: the website of the issuer, the offeror or the entity asking for admission to trading; the website of the financial intermediaries placing or selling the securities; or the website of the operator of the trading venue where the admission to trading is sought.[377] This section shall also include documents incorporating information by reference, any supplements and/or final terms related to the prospectus, and a separate copy of the summary.[378] However, if a prospectus comprises several documents and/or includes information incorporated by reference, they can be published and distributed separately.[379] Finally, access to the prospectus should not require registration, payment of a fee or acceptance of a disclaimer limiting legal liability;[380] rather, any potential investor should be able to request and receive an electronic copy for free.[381]

All approved prospectuses, or alternatively, a list of those prospectuses with hyperlinks to the websites where they can be found, should be published on the website of the NCA of the issuer's home Member State.[382] An electronic copy of the prospectus or of any supplement, along with the data necessary for their classification must also be transmitted to ESMA.[383] Using this data, ESMA should maintain an online register with appropriate search facilities, enabling investors to access all approved prospectuses across the Union free of charge.[384] Prospectuses should remain publicly available in the relevant websites for at least 10 years after their publication, and where hyperlinks are used they shall remain functional for

[374] ibid 46.
[375] Recitals 62 and 63 Prospectus Regulation.
[376] ibid Art 21(1) as amended by the Listing Act Regulation.
[377] ibid Art 21(2) and (3) first subparagraph.
[378] ibid Art 21(3) second subparagraph.
[379] ibid Art 21(9).
[380] ibid Art 21(4). However, warnings or statements specifying the jurisdiction(s) targeted by the offer or listing are not considered disclaimers that limit legal liability.
[381] ibid Art 21(11) as amended by the Listing Act Regulation.
[382] ibid Art 21(5) first subparagraph.
[383] ibid Art 21(5) second subparagraph in conjunction with Arts 11 and 12 Delegated Regulation (EU) 979/2019.
[384] ibid Art 21(6).

the same period.[385] This does not imply, however, that prospectuses should be kept updated even after their validity ends and each prospectus should include a clear warning to this effect.[386]

v. *Enhanced Convergence of Public Enforcement Mechanisms*

a. Divergent Sanctioning Practices under the Prospectus Directive

Before the Prospectus Directive came into force, supervisory and enforcement powers varied significantly among Member States and were often dispersed among various authorities.[387] The previous regime aimed to address this issue by establishing a central and independent administrative authority in each Member State, equipped with an extensive list of common supervisory and investigatory powers necessary to fulfil its functions.[388] These powers, which remain largely unaltered under the Prospectus Regulation,[389] are intended to ensure effective supervision and compliance with the imposed legal obligations.[390] Nevertheless, the previous regime did not result in significant convergence among the powers available to competent authorities to enforce the Directive and its implementing acts ex post. In fact, Member States were only required to ensure that competent authorities could impose suitable administrative measures or sanctions against those responsible for breaching the Directive.[391] This resulted in different types of administrative sanctions and measures being applied to the same infringements across Member States,[392] which had negative effects on investor protection and cross-border investment activity.[393] In this framework, the Regulation introduces a more comprehensive sanctioning system for infringements of the obligations stipulated therein. The envisaged approach aims to ensure greater convergence among national administrative liability regimes while increasing their deterrent effect.[394]

b. Revised Administrative Sanctioning System

The minimum sanctioning powers to be conferred on NCAs in accordance with national law, as well as some common procedures and arrangements for their

[385] ibid Art 21(7).
[386] ibid Art 21(8).
[387] Schammo (n 26) 225.
[388] Art 21(3) and (4) Prospectus Directive.
[389] Art 32(1) Prospectus Regulation.
[390] Recitals 37–38 Prospectus Directive and recitals 71–72 Prospectus Regulation.
[391] Art 25(1) Prospectus Directive.
[392] ESMA, 'Comparison of Liability Regimes in Member States in Relation to the Prospectus Directive', Report, ESMA/2013/619, 30 May 2013, 17 ff.
[393] Commission, 'Reinforcing Sanctioning Regimes in the Financial Services Sector', COM (2010) 716 final, 8 December 2010, 10.
[394] Recital 74 Prospectus Regulation.

application, are laid down in Articles 38 to 43 of the Prospectus Regulation. Administrative sanctions cover a wide range of violations of the Regulation, including offering securities to the public without prior publication of a prospectus, omitting or misstating material information in the prospectus, and failing to comply with inspection or investigation procedures aimed at detecting and proving an infringement.[395] However, if these offenses are already subject to criminal sanctions under national law, Member States are not obliged to establish rules for administrative sanctions.[396]

As with the previous regime, administrative sanctions must be effective, proportionate, and dissuasive,[397] while the decisions imposing them should be properly reasoned and subject to a right of appeal.[398] However, what is new is the specification of some minimum sanctions that NCAs should be able to impose.[399] These include, in particular: (a) a public statement, indicating the nature of the infringement and the identity of the persons responsible,[400] unless such publication is disproportionate or would jeopardise financial market stability or an ongoing investigation;[401] (b) an order compelling the responsible persons to cease the conduct constituting the infringement; and (c) administrative pecuniary sanctions, equivalent to at least twice the profits gained or losses avoided due to the infringement, provided this amount can be determined.[402] Information on the administrative and criminal sanctions imposed, as well as anonymised and aggregated data on all criminal investigations conducted, should be submitted to ESMA annually.[403]

Another significant novelty is the specification of certain circumstances that should guide NCAs in determining the type and level of administrative sanctions and measures. These considerations, aimed at reducing national discrepancies in decision-making, encompass the seriousness and duration of the offence, its impact on retail investors' interests, the degree of liability, financial strength and level of cooperation of the infringer, the significance of profits gained and/or

[395] ibid Art 38(1)(a) and (b) as amended by the Listing Act Regulation.

[396] ibid Art 38(1) second subparagraph. According to recital 76, however, such a choice should not affect the ability of NCAs to cooperate, access, and exchange information with NCAs in other Member States, including after the referral of relevant infringements to competent judicial authorities for criminal prosecution.

[397] ibid Art 38(1) first subparagraph.

[398] ibid Art 40 first subparagraph.

[399] ibid Art 38(2).

[400] This should remain available on the competent authority's website for at least five years after publication, ibid Art 42(4).

[401] In such cases, the competent authority may delay the publication of the sanction decision until the reasons for non-publication cease to exist, publish the decision anonymously, or not publish it at all, ibid Art 42(2).

[402] For legal persons, these pecuniary sanctions should be at least EUR 5 million or 3% of their annual turnover, while for natural persons, the minimum amount should be at least EUR 700,000, ibid Art 38(2)(d) and (e).

[403] ibid Art 43(1). ESMA shall also publish this information and data in an annual report.

losses avoided, as well as any previous violations and actions taken to prevent their recurrence in the future.[404]

Finally, special emphasis is placed on establishing effective mechanisms to encourage the reporting of information that could assist competent authorities in detecting potential infringements and imposing sanctions.[405] The role of the infringers' employees is particularly crucial in this regard, as they may possess valuable information but might not feel safe to disclose it. To that end, the Regulation provides for certain mechanisms which seek to ensure that whistleblowers can safely alert the authorities while at the same time being protected from potential retribution.[406]

IV. A Critical Assessment of the Prospectus Regulation

The reforms introduced by the Prospectus Regulation aim to achieve three main objectives: first, to enhance the prospectus as a more effective and comprehensible disclosure tool for potential investors, leading to better-informed investment decisions and increased investor confidence; second, to facilitate access to capital markets for companies by reducing the costs associated with preparing and publishing the prospectus; and, finally, to harmonise regulatory, supervisory, and enforcement practices in the EU, thereby reducing barriers to cross-border capital-raising and investment activities.[407] In this context, ensuring the effectiveness of these measures is seen as a crucial step towards further developing and integrating European primary markets and, thus, to the successful completion of the CMU. Therefore, it is important to assess the extent to which the revised prospectus regime has successfully served this purpose and determine which improvements or adaptations would be necessary or desirable, in accordance with the principles set out in chapter two.

A. Developing EU Primary Markets – Calibration and Differentiation

As already discussed, one of the biggest shortcomings of the Prospectus Directive was its inability to adequately address and accommodate the diverse characteristics and needs of market actors within its scope. Although the reforms introduced by the 2010 Amending Prospectus Directive partially alleviated the inefficiencies

[404] ibid Art 39(1).
[405] ibid Art 41(1).
[406] Ibid 41(2).
[407] See L Pospiech, 'Die neue EU-Prospektverordnung' (2019) 15 *Neue Juristische Wochenschrift-Spezial* 463.

resulting from the blanket application of the one-size-fits-all approach, they did not fully address the issue. The EU Prospectus Regulation seeks to tackle these shortcomings by introducing greater calibration and differentiation in the prospectus regime. This becomes even more apparent following the Listing Act Regulation which puts forward new provisions aimed at making prospectus disclosure more flexible and tailored to the diverse types of securities and issuers covered, particularly SMEs, while also increasing its relevance for investors, especially retail ones. Despite these commendable efforts, certain regulatory choices raise concerns regarding their potential impact on the development of stronger primary markets.

i. Removing Barriers to Capital Raising on Public Markets

a. The Revised Threshold for Small Public Offerings

Over the years, the scope of the EU prospectus regime has been defined by certain thresholds aimed at reducing regulatory burdens for small issues while ensuring investor protection and market confidence. However, new market developments and emerging empirical evidence have necessitated the recalibration of these thresholds. Most recently, the Listing Act Regulation increased the lower threshold triggering the obligation to publish a prospectus for public offerings to EUR 12 million, although Member States may opt to lower this threshold to EUR 5 million. Moreover, national regulators may impose other disclosure requirements for such offers, as long as the level of disclosure is equivalent to or lower than that included in the prospectus summary.

While the aforementioned discretion could theoretically promote regulatory solutions better tailored to local preferences and needs,[408] it appears to contradict the stated objective of equally supporting small issuers across the EU by failing to achieve the desired convergence in their disclosure obligations. For one thing, the possibility for each Member State to apply a lower exemption threshold and develop separate disclosure rules for exempted small offers could result in discrepancies in the cost of capital based on the country of establishment. Additionally, the purely national character of such exempted offers limits the cross-border capital-raising capacity of issuers, placing companies domiciled in countries with a limited investor base at a competitive disadvantage compared to their peers in Member States with more developed capital markets. Finally, and more indirectly, investors are left with less information to make informed investment decisions, which may further hamper businesses' ability to cover their financing needs.

Interestingly, regarding this last point, the Commission notes that even without mandatory prospectus requirements at the EU or national level, issuers would

[408] K Gatsios and P Holmes, 'Regulatory Competition' in P Newman (ed), *The New Palgrave Dictionary of Economics and the Law*, Vol. 1 (Palgrave Macmillan, 1998) 273–75.

still need to provide appropriate information to convince and attract investors.[409] This observation implicitly points to the role of trust as a 'functional equivalent' of mandatory disclosure,[410] potentially also explaining the local character of exempted small public offers. Indeed, unlike everyday transactions, where personal interaction may suffice to establish the necessary trust among market participants, in more complex settings like capital markets, the dynamics are different. In such cases, trust in the system itself becomes essential, which, in turn, requires institutional arrangements recognised and complied with by all participants.[411] This does not imply, however, that interpersonal trust is negligible in capital markets. In fact, the greater proximity characterising local markets could hinder opportunistic behaviour.[412] In this respect, even in the absence of mandatory and extensive information, strong local social networks could still sustain investors' confidence in the market mechanism and their propensity to invest.

In any case, the preceding analysis only offers an explanation of why no or less stringent disclosure requirements for small public offers might not be detrimental. It does not address the issues arising from potential discrepancies in disclosure practices and the inability of issuers opting for this exemption to offer securities cross-border. In that regard, the solution proposed here is that, instead of prescribing 27 divergent national regimes, a more effective approach for the EU legislator would be to set some minimum disclosure standards that are necessary for investor protection and allow issuers to freely passport the prospectus to other Member States. This strategy could harness the benefits of regulatory experimentation at the national level while fostering competition between national rules through mutual recognition, potentially resulting in improved regulatory solutions. Alternatively, an optional regime at the EU level could be introduced, which issuers could choose for both cross-border and domestic offers instead of relying on national laws.

b. SME Finance and the Prospectus Regulation

The Prospectus Regulation, especially following its amendment by the Listing Act, shows an increased awareness of the importance of addressing the financing needs of SMEs. This is mainly evidenced by the introduction of alleviated disclosure requirements for both public offerings of securities and admissions to trading. As with other legislative initiatives of the CMU era,[413] special attention is given to

[409] SWD (2015) 255 final (n 7) 20.

[410] See eg D-U Gilbert, 'Vertrauen als Gegenstand der Ökonomischen Theorie' (2007) 2 *Zeitschrift für Management* 60, 71; P Müllbert and A Sajnovits, 'The Element of Trust in Financial Markets Law' (2017) 18 *German Law Journal* 1, 6.

[411] On the role of trust in the system of EU capital markets law, see S Grundmann, 'Vertrauen und (EU-) Kapitalmarkt – Theorie und Fallstudien zu einer neuen Mesotes im Wirtschaftsrecht' in G Bachman et al (eds), *Festschrift für Christine Windbichler zum 70. Geburstag* (De Gruyter, 2020).

[412] See also M Granovetter, 'Economic Action and Social Structure: The Problem of Embeddedness' (1985) 91 *American Journal of Sociology* 481, 490.

[413] See eg Regulation (EU) 2019/2115.

promoting the use of SME growth markets as a promising tool for small, growing companies to raise capital.[414] On the upside, this choice allows for a meaningful distinction between regulated markets, which are subject to the highest level of regulation, and other trading venues. On the other hand, limited to SME growth markets, these measures might not reach a sufficient number of SMEs. Indeed, several imperfections in these markets, including low market capitalisation and trading time thresholds for SMEs that can be listed there,[415] inadequate differentiation between equity and debt issuers, insufficient liquidity, and lack of homogeneous admission requirements, have impeded their development.[416] As a result, out of the 9,882 companies whose shares were traded on EU exchanges in 2021, only 1,740 (17.6 per cent) were SMEs listed on growth markets, while activity in the issuance and trading of bonds was even more limited in these markets.[417]

In this context, two options could be considered. The first would be to enhance the appeal of this market segment to issuers. Recent initiatives, such as the introduction of the EU growth issuance prospectus, which can now be utilised by issuers beyond SMEs if listed on an SME growth market, or the creation of a Union framework enabling all issuers of financial instruments traded on such markets to conclude liquidity contracts with liquidity providers,[418] represent significant steps in this direction. However, further actions are needed. These could include, for instance, implementing additional alleviations for smaller issuers seeking access to capital markets via an SME growth market, improving SME visibility by generating more reliable financial data,[419] and reassessing provisions that contribute to the concentration of transactions on large caps.[420]

An alternative option would be to broaden the application of the new alleviated prospectus regimes to include regular MTFs. However, given the variety of issuers whose securities are traded in these markets, any relaxation should be meticulously calibrated to prevent the potential for arbitrage by large companies. US securities regulation could provide a model in this regard. For instance, Article 8 of SEC Regulation S-X gives small reporting companies[421] the possibility

[414] Recital 51 Prospectus Regulation and recital 2 Listing Act Regulation.

[415] Article 77 of Delegated Regulation (EU) 2017/565 defines an SME issuer, for the purposes of Art 33(3)(a) of MiFID II, as an issuer whose shares have been admitted to trading for less than three years with a market capitalisation below EUR 200 million.

[416] A Pietrancosta, 'Recent Initiatives in Favor of Listed and Non Listed Small and Medium-Sized Enterprises: A Legal Perspective' in F Allen et al (eds), *Capital Markets Union and Beyond* (MIT Press, 2019) 176.

[417] SWD(2022) 762 final (n 75) 108.

[418] Art 13(12) MAR as inserted by Regulation (EU) 2019/2115.

[419] See also P Schammo, 'Market Building and the Capital Markets Union: Addressing Information Barriers in the SME Funding Market' (2017) 14 *European Company and Financial Law Review* 271, 286 ff.

[420] Characteristic in this regard are the provisions of MiFID II concerning product governance and the remuneration of order execution and research services.

[421] These are defined as those companies with a public equity float under $250 million or annual revenues under $100 million, Item 10(f)(1) of SEC Regulation S-K.

to prepare prospectus disclosures using less burdensome reporting standards. In addition, the 2012 JOBS Act allows 'emerging growth companies' to offer their securities to the public without being subject to the registration requirements of the Securities Act, provided they make available an offering statement filed with the SEC.[422] Issuers may choose to conduct such exempted offerings under two different tiers: Tier 1, for offerings of up to $20 million, and Tier 2, for offerings of up to $50 million within a 12-month period. In the second case, the offering statement does not require approval by a state securities regulator, though certain limitations apply with regard to the participation of non-accredited investors. As previously mentioned, the revised proportionate prospectus regime for SMEs and other small-caps includes a provision similar to that for Tier 2 issuers. However, from a regulatory perspective, it would be sensible to consider aligning the EU regime more closely with the more advanced and finely-tuned US model.

c. Risk Factors and Shelf Registration

Another concern for issuers under the new Prospectus Regulation arises from the prescriptive requirements regarding the materiality and specificity of the risk factors that must be included in the prospectus. Under the new rules, NCAs must not allow issuers to include very general risk factors in the prospectus and must challenge their inclusion if they are not directly linked to the issuer and the securities or if they are not material for an informed investment decision. However, this could cause further delays in the approval of prospectuses due to potential protracted negotiations over the inclusion or omission of a risk factor. In addition, the obligation to list risk factors in a manner consistent with the assessment of their materiality not only imposes an additional burden on issuers but also raises liability concerns if such assessment is not precise. For example, it is unclear what claims investors might have if a risk factor, which was not considered highly probable or, even worse, was not listed at all, ends up causing them harm.[423] Despite ESMA's efforts to clarify such issues through the issuance of guidelines, legal uncertainty persists. Accordingly, the Commission should utilise the authorisation in Article 16(5) of the Prospectus Regulation to delineate criteria regarding the assessment of the specificity and materiality of risk factors.

But apart from the above, the new shelf-registration system, designed to facilitate repeat access by issuers to the market, also raises some concerns. Based on this system, for an issuer to qualify as a frequent issuer and thus benefit from a faster approval process, they must have a URD approved by the competent authority for at least one financial year. Nonetheless, this requirement might result in unwarranted delays for established companies whose securities are already actively

[422] Title 17 of the Code of Federal Regulations, chapter 2, part 230, also known as Regulation A.
[423] See also Lucantoni (n 103) 982.

traded on the secondary market. Hence, a more effective approach by the EU legislator would have been to implement an automatic shelf registration system, akin to the US regime for well-known seasoned issuers (WKSIs).[424] This system would enable such companies to promptly access the market, bypassing any review from the relevant authority. Furthermore, the URD serves as a multi-purpose shelf document that does not distinguish between equity and debt issuances, potentially increasing the burden for issuers to produce in certain cases. Finally, the discretion granted to NCAs to request amendments to the URD even after its publication raises legitimate reputational and liability concerns for issuers. Therefore, it is crucial for NCAs to be particularly vigilant when reviewing the completeness, consistency, and comprehensibility of the information provided in the URD.

ii. Broadening the Investor Base

a. Historical versus Forward-looking Information

The core aim of prospectus disclosure is to address the significant information asymmetry between the offeror and investors, thereby protecting the latter from making poor resource allocation decisions. However, the very nature of the information items that must be included in the prospectus could undermine this objective. Indeed, in contrast with the US approach, the various schedules that comprise the prospectus, as outlined in the Prospectus Regulation and its Delegated Acts, consist mainly of historical information (eg, about the issuer, its managers and shareholders, the development of the issuer's business, and its financial position up to the date of the application for admission). Conversely, although not entirely prohibited, the inclusion of forward-looking information is highly constrained. Hence, if an issuer decides to voluntarily include a profit forecast or estimate in a registration document, they must ensure that it is understandable, reliable, comparable and relevant.[425] Moreover, if assumptions are used, they should be reasonable, easily understandable by investors, specific and precise, and not relate to the general accuracy of the estimates underlying the forecast. Furthermore, there must be a clear distinction between assumptions regarding factors that the members of the administration can influence and those exclusively outside their influence. Finally, in the case of a forecast, the assumptions should highlight uncertain factors that could significantly alter the forecast outcome.[426]

These obligations are quite burdensome and raise liability concerns for issuers, potentially dissuading them from including forward-looking information in the prospectus. Of course, the regulator's choice is understandable. Forward-looking

[424] Rule 405 of the Securities Act. For an analysis, see S Choi and A Pritchard, *Securities Regulation: Cases and Analysis*, 4th edn (Foundation Press, 2015) 410.

[425] ESMA, 'Guidelines on disclosure requirements under the Prospectus Regulation' (ESMA 32-382-1138) 4 March 2021, 17 f (Guideline 11).

[426] See eg Delegated Regulation (EU) 2019/980, Annex I (Item 11.2).

information tends to be speculative and conjectural, while it can be presented in an optimistic way, thus misleading investors.[427] Historical data, on the other hand, are factual, making them easier to verify and compare, even across different companies. However, it is somewhat questionable whether and to what extent such information is truly useful for investors, given that the value of a security is primarily influenced by the future performance of the issuer. In this context, it is prudent for the EU legislator to reconsider its approach to the inclusion of forward-looking information, possibly by adopting a model similar to that of the US, which encourages such disclosure by relieving the issuer from civil liability under specific circumstances.[428]

b. The Prospectus Summary

Product disclosure holds significant appeal as a retail market tool. This stems largely from the almost self-evident assumption that consumers armed with more comprehensive information should be better equipped to make decisions than if their choices were based on limited knowledge about the product's attributes.[429] In this framework, the informed and empowered retail investor is a recurring theme in the EU prospectus regime. This is evident not only in the core requirement that information in the prospectus 'shall be written and presented in an easily analysable, concise, and comprehensible form',[430] but also in the obligation to provide a summary alongside the full prospectus. The effectiveness of disclosure in enhancing the decision-making capacity of the average investor has been investigated in a plethora of empirical and experimental studies, some of which were discussed in the previous chapter.[431] Suffice it to say here that, despite their cognitive limitations and bounded rationality, engaged retail investors have the capacity to learn, and disclosure plays a central role in encouraging them to make informed decisions.[432]

However, the usefulness of disclosure extends beyond its 'availability'; it also depends on its 'processability',[433] namely how easily investors can utilise the provided information to make informed decisions about whether and where to invest.[434] Hence, an effective disclosure regime for retail markets requires more

[427] Lucantoni (n 103) 989.

[428] This is mainly the case when a false forward-looking statement is immaterial, unintentional, or is accompanied by significant cautionary statements identifying important factors that could lead to actual results differing materially from those in the statement. For an analysis see C Schneider and J Dubow, 'Forward-Looking Information-Navigating in the Safe Harbor' (1996) 51 *The Business Lawyer* 1071.

[429] M Mazis et al, 'A Framework for Evaluating Consumer Information Regulation' (1981) 45 *Journal of Marketing* 11, 12.

[430] Art 6(2) Prospectus Regulation as amended by the Listing Act Regulation.

[431] Chapter 2, section III, para iii(a).

[432] Moloney (n 303) 300.

[433] J Cox and J Payne, 'Mutual Fund Expense Disclosure: A Behavioral Perspective' (2005) 83 *Washington University Law Review* 907, 931.

[434] J Kozup and J Hogarth, 'Financial Literacy, Public Policy, and Consumers' Self-Protection – More Questions, Fewer Answers' (2008) 42 *The Journal of Consumer Affairs* 127, 131.

than just refining the content of information provided to investors. It necessitates a dedicated effort to facilitating information processing, in light of their specific needs and weaknesses.[435] In this regard, while the revised prospectus summary marks a significant improvement over the previous regime, especially following the format reforms of the Listing Act Regulation, it still faces shortcomings regarding its processability. For one thing, despite the intensive efforts of the new reforms to standardise and simplify key information for investors, the summary largely remains an accumulation of core features of the issuer and securities already included in the prospectus, without significantly enhancing investors' knowledge. For another, unlike the KID for PRIIPs, the summary was not tested on retail investors,[436] it does not require generic warnings about investment risks, and does not calibrate disclosure based on the type of investors it is addressed to.

Of course, it is true that, unlike manufacturers of packaged products, corporate issuers do not market securities solely to retail investors. Therefore, creating a prospectus summary aimed solely at empowering the average investor is a near-impossible task, given especially the complexity of the investment. However, since the summary is now an integral part of the prospectus regime and retail investors do, albeit not in large numbers, make direct investments in corporate securities, further improvements are necessary.[437] At the very least, NCAs, supported by ESMA, should effectively enforce the content and format requirements of the new prospectus summary, ensuring the comprehensibility and processability of the information it contains. At the same time, regulators should become more responsive to new empirical and experimental findings. Yet, given the level of flexibility such an endeavour requires, it might also be advisable to grant Member States a margin of regulatory discretion. Harmonised EU rules are difficult to amend and could potentially impede constructive innovation at the national level.

c. Increasing Household Investments

As a critical component of the CMU initiative, the Prospectus Regulation is particularly focused on enhancing the engagement of EU households with capital markets. In this context, ensuring investor protection under the prospectus regime involves not only providing retail investors with clear and accessible information for efficient resource allocation but also ensuring their access to a wide variety of investment options that align with their needs and preferences.[438] In practice,

[435] Moloney (n 1) 828.

[436] London Economics and Ipsos, *Consumer Testing Study of the Possible New Format and Content for Retail Disclosures of Packaged Retail and Insurance-based Investment Products*, Final Report (European Union, 2015).

[437] This is in line with the Retail Investment Package proposed by the Commission in May 2023, Commission, 'Capital Markets Union: Commission proposes new rules to protect and empower retail investors in the EU', Press Release, 24 May 2023, ec.europa.eu/commission/presscorner/detail/en/ip_23_2868.

[438] SWD (2015) 255 final (n 7) 16.

however, and without disregarding the previous concerns about the prospectus summary, two features of the Regulation could hinder retail investors' access to primary markets. The first pertains to the favouritism shown to wholesale issuers of non-equity securities, achieved through calibrations and exemptions from prospectus obligations. Already under the previous regime, this preferential treatment incentivised issuers to issue bonds only in large denominations (above EUR 100,000), resulting in a notable contraction of retail bond markets.[439] Despite initial proposals to eliminate such incentives for issuers,[440] an effective lobbying effort not only resulted in retaining the dual disclosure standard but also expanded it to include all debt issuances, provided only qualified investors can access them. This could be harmful to retail investors, especially as an increasing number of them seek access to high-quality debt securities to invest their savings in preparation for retirement.[441]

The second concern relates to the restrictions imposed by certain Member States on the participation of non-qualified investors in exempted small public offerings.[442] For instance, Article 6 of the German Securities Prospectus Act (*Wertpapierprospektgesetz – WpPG*) mandates that such offerings take place exclusively through investment advice or brokerage by an authorised investment firm, which must ensure that non-qualified investors do not exceed specified thresholds based on their financial standing when acquiring securities.[443] While these obligations aim to protect retail investors, they also impose significant burdens on issuers and underwriters, who may prefer to offer securities solely to qualified investors. Consequently, non-qualified investors could miss out on important investment opportunities.

B. Integrating EU Primary Markets – Convergence and Diversity

The new Prospectus Regulation and its delegated acts aim to establish a comprehensive set of substantive disclosure rules that apply uniformly across the EU, providing Member States with only limited liberty in their implementation. As a result, the new rules on the content and format of the prospectus are more detailed

[439] The depth of European retail bond markets decreased from EUR 147.4 billion in 2003 to EUR 97.6 billion in 2007, see Centre for Strategy & Evaluation Services, 'Study on the Impact of the Prospectus Regime on EU Financial Markets', Final Report, 2008, 55–56.

[440] COM (2015) 583 final (n 35) 16–17.

[441] SWD (2015) 255 final (n 7) 29.

[442] These restrictions refer to exempted public offerings before the amendments introduced by the Listing Act Regulation, namely those up to EUR 8 million. However, it is reasonable to assume that these or similar rules will persist under the revised regime, as it does not include any prohibitions in this regard.

[443] See generally L Klöhn, 'Die neue Prospektfreiheit „kleiner" Wertpapieremissionen unter 8 Mio. €' (2018) 30 *Zeitschrift für Wirtschaftsrecht* 1713.

than ever before in EU primary market disclosure legislation.[444] A single European rulebook for prospectus disclosure aligns well with the overall CMU concept, as it could promote further integration of primary markets. Indeed, applying uniform disclosure rules and standards to every public offer or admission of securities to trading in the EU could enhance the comparability of competing investment opportunities. This can reduce national bias in investment decisions and unlock more savings for deserving projects across the entire EU market.[445] Admittedly, this approach sacrifices flexibility and innovation, as a uniform law disregards the diverse preferences and needs of Member States and precludes the potentially beneficial contributions of national initiatives to the development of effective disclosure rules. In this respect, given that an effective passport mechanism is already in place, allowing for a limited degree of regulatory competition could have been beneficial, promoting experimentation and knowledge sharing among regulators.

But despite the maximum harmonisation approach, the potential for regulatory arbitrage in the prospectus regime remains significant. This is mainly because certain substantive aspects of the Regulation are still left to Member States for implementation, with civil liability for incorrect or omitted disclosure being chief among them.[446] Furthermore, notwithstanding the active involvement of ESMA in the supervisory system of EU capital markets, operational supervision and enforcement largely remain the responsibility of Member States, led by their respective NCAs.[447] Finally, the persistence, until recently, of an outdated official listing regime[448] has created tension with the rigorous and sophisticated rules governing admission to trading on regulated markets, thus also leading to legal uncertainty and risks for issuers of securities targeting pan-European markets.

i. Civil Liability in the Prospectus Regime

Prospectus liability, the civil liability attached to the persons responsible for the prospectus concerning the accuracy and completeness of the information contained therein, serves two main functions.[449] First, to the extent that a prospective investor trusts the information in the prospectus and uses it 'as the basis for

[444] For a similar analysis under the Prospectus Directive, see Ferran (n 3) 138.

[445] See also J Coffee Jr., 'Racing Towards the Top: The Impact of Cross-Listing and Stock Market Competition on International Corporate Governance' (2002) 102 *Columbia Law Review* 1757, 1827–28.

[446] Enriques and Tröger (n 67) 526.

[447] See N Moloney, *The Age of ESMA: Governing EU Financial Markets* (Hart Publishing, 2018) 181, 184.

[448] Directive 2001/34/EC of the European Parliament and of the Council on the admission of securities to official stock exchange listing and on information to be published on those securities [2001] OJ L184/1 (Listing Directive).

[449] See generally H-D Assmann and C Kumpan, in H-D Assmann, R Schütze and P Buck-Heeb (eds), *Handbuch des Kapitalanlagerechts*, 5th edn (C.H. Beck, 2020) §5 (recital 2).

their investment decision',[450] it grants them a claim against the responsible parties in the event of a misstatement or omission, thus guaranteeing individual investor protection. Second, through its deterrence effect, liability ensures that the prospectus serves as a reliable information tool, contributing to the primary market's main function of efficiently allocating investable capital to investment opportunities. Accordingly, a system of civil liability rules for false or misleading information in the prospectus and for the omission of material information is an integral part of any prospectus regime.

However, like its predecessor,[451] the Prospectus Regulation does not include any detailed harmonised provisions on prospectus liability. Article 11(1) merely requires Member States to ensure that their legal and administrative rules on civil liability also apply to those responsible for the information given in the prospectus and any supplements, including at least the issuer, the offeror, the person seeking admission of the securities to trading, or the guarantor. Moreover, pursuant to Article 11(2), Member States must ensure that civil liability does not attach to any person solely based on the summary (including any translation), unless, when read together with the other parts of the prospectus, it is misleading, inaccurate, or incomplete, or it fails to provide key information needed by investors to decide whether to invest in the securities. Finally, concerning misstatements or omissions in the registration document or the URD, Article 11(3) specifies that no liability shall arise unless these documents are used as part of an approved prospectus. Consequently, prospectus liability remains largely governed by national law.[452]

In most Member States, prospectus liability arises from general civil law provisions on tort and contractual liability, though some countries have established specific liability regimes.[453] Besides the persons mentioned in Article 11(1) of the Prospectus Regulation, some Member States also extend liability to other parties under certain conditions, such as the auditing firm for the accuracy of the financial statements, or the investment broker who has an independent disclosure duty and relies on a defective prospectus to fulfil it.[454] Several discrepancies also arise regarding the general conditions that must be satisfied to substantiate a civil claim for damages resulting from a defective prospectus. In particular, apart from the inclusion of false or misleading statements or the omission of material information from prospectuses, civil liability in some countries may also emerge in case of a public offer without a duly approved prospectus. The degree of fault required is typically negligence, although in certain cases, strict liability may apply.[455]

[450] BGH, 31.05.2011 – II ZR 141/09: Übernahme des Prospekthaftungsrisikos als Einlagenrückgewähr – Dritter Börsengang (2011) 64 *Neue Juristische Wochenschrift* 2719, 2721.

[451] Art 6 Prospectus Directive.

[452] For an overview of the prospectus liability regimes in selected EU countries and the UK, see Busch, Ferrarini and Franx (eds) (n 255) 409 ff.

[453] For a comparative analysis in selected Member States, see P-H Conac and M Gelter (eds), *Global Securities Litigation and Enforcement* (CUP, 2019).

[454] ESMA (n 392) 12.

[455] ibid 13.

Furthermore, aside from material damages, some countries also permit compensation for loss of profit. The burden of proof usually falls on the plaintiff, although in some Member States, the fault of the defendant or the causal link between the infringement and the damage is presumed.[456] Finally, while class action suits are permitted in some EU countries, most national legislators either prohibit them altogether or authorise consumer associations to bring civil liability claims.[457]

The diversity in prospectus liability approaches across Member States poses a significant risk for cross-border offers, since a defective prospectus could potentially trigger parallel proceedings in multiple legal systems, increasing both reputational risks and potential litigation costs.[458] This was further highlighted in the *Kolassa* judgment,[459] where the CJEU determined, under the Rome II Regulation, that the law applicable in claims against an issuer of securities based on an allegedly false prospectus is determined by the investor's domicile, particularly when the bank managing the investor's account is located there.[460]

Based on the above, the question arises whether some form of harmonisation of national prospectus liability regimes should be pursued. Procedurally, this should not pose any significant challenge, given that Article 114 TFEU grants European legislative institutions broad competence to adopt measures for the approximation of national provisions directed towards the establishment and functioning of the internal market.[461] In terms of political feasibility, post-Brexit regulatory initiatives in EU capital markets law suggest that the EU is more willing to introduce substantive liability rules, albeit gradually. For instance, the newly enacted Market in Crypto-Assets Regulation (MiCAR)[462] provides more detailed provisions, compared to the Prospectus Regulation, regarding the circumstances under which purchasers of crypto-assets that do not qualify as securities can pursue a claim for damages against the offeror of such instruments.[463] In particular, the crypto-asset holder must prove that the white paper accompanying the offer infringes the Regulation by containing incomplete, unclear, or misleading information. They must also show that this infringement influenced their decision to buy, sell, or exchange the crypto-assets, and that they suffered damages as a result.[464] Hence,

[456] ibid 14.

[457] ibid 16.

[458] L Burn and B Wells, 'The Pan-European Retail Market – Are We There Yet?' (2007) 2 *Capital Markets Law Journal* 263, 275; E Ferran, 'Cross-border Offers of Securities in the EU: The Standard Life Flotation' (2007) 4 *European Company and Financial Law Review* 461, 482–84.

[459] Case C-375/13 *Harald Kolassa v Barclays Bank plc* ECLI:EU:C: 2015:37, [2016] 1 All ER (Comm) 733.

[460] For a critical analysis see M Lehmann, 'Prospectus Liability and Private International Law – Assessing the Landscape After the CJEU's Kolassa Ruling (Case C-375/13)' (2016) 12 *Journal of Private International Law* 318.

[461] See also D Busch and M Lehmann, 'Uniform Prospectus Liability Rules for Europe' (2023) 14 *Journal of European Tort Law* 113, 117–18.

[462] Regulation (EU) 2023/1114 of the European Parliament and of the Council on markets in crypto-assets [2023] OJ L150/40.

[463] ibid Arts 15, 26 and 52.

[464] For a more comprehensive analysis see Busch and Lehmann (n 461) 119 ff.

it is evident that agreeing on some uniform substantive rules on prospectus liability, such as regarding the burden of proof or causation, is not an impossible task. However, this does not inevitably imply that such an approach is the right way forward.

Recent evidence on the economic consequences of corporate disclosure and financial reporting regulation indicates that private enforcement harmonisation through standardised rules is unlikely to achieve the desired convergence without some accompanying institutional changes that affect enforcement mechanisms.[465] In fact, imposing uniform rules in countries with varying institutional conditions could unintentionally amplify national divergences instead of reducing them.[466] In this regard, considering the various institutional and cultural differences among Member States, it is unrealistic to believe that merely approximating substantive liability rules, without introducing some common procedural principles regarding the administration of justice, could result in a more level playing field for cross-border offers. This realisation is already apparent in EU competition law, where Directive 2014/104/EU establishes procedural rules to coordinate the enforcement of antitrust damages claims under national law, based on the principle of effectiveness.[467] This does not suggest, of course, that such a soft and piecemeal approach to harmonising Member States' procedural frameworks is likely to achieve the desired convergence.[468] Therefore, it does not necessarily need to be the approach taken regarding private enforcement of prospectus disclosure rules. However, it does suggest that alongside substantive rules, some level of harmonisation of procedural rules on prospectus liability is not only necessary but also achievable.

In any case, significant harmonisation is unlikely to occur, at least in the short term, despite some commendable efforts in this direction.[469] In the meantime, the EU legislator should intervene to alleviate the adverse effects of the absence of a common liability regime for cross-border issuances. Perhaps the most convincing solution suggested to date is the introduction of a new conflict of laws rule for financial torts, including prospectus liability, into the Rome II Regulation.[470] More specifically, it has been suggested that the applicable law in prospectus liability

[465] C Leuz and P Wysocki, 'The Economics of Disclosure and Financial Reporting Regulation: Evidence and Suggestions for Future Research' (2016) 54 *Journal of Accounting Research* 525, 594–95.

[466] H Christensen, L Hail and C Leuz, 'Capital-Market Effects of Securities Regulation: Prior Conditions, Implementation, and Enforcement' (2016) 29 *The Review of Financial Studies* 2885, 2915.

[467] See generally B Rodger, M Sousa Ferro and F Marcos, 'Promotion and Harmonization of Antitrust Damages Claims by Directive EU/2014/104' in B Rodger, M Sousa Ferro and F Marcos (eds), *The EU Antitrust Damages Directive Transposition in the Member States* (OUP, 2018).

[468] See also S Peyer, 'The Antitrust Damages Directive – Much Ado About Nothing?' in M Marquis and R Cisotta (eds), *Litigation and Arbitration in EU Competition Law* (Edward Elgar, 2015) 33–46.

[469] See eg the International Working Group on Prospectus Liability rules in Europe, led by Professor Danny Busch and Professor Matthias Lehmann.

[470] F Garcimartín, 'The Law Applicable to Prospectus Liability in the European Union' (2011) 5 *Law and Financial Markets Review* 449, 455; M Lehmann, 'Vorschlag für eine Reform der Rom II-Verordnung im Bereich der Finanzmarktdelikte' (2012) 32 *Praxis des Internationalen Privat- und Verfahrensrechts* 399.

cases should be the law of the country where the securities were admitted to trading or offered and acquired by investors. Applying the law of the relevant market would not only enhance predictability for issuers and investors but could also foster competition among national legislators.[471] This could trigger a regulatory race to the top, as issuers, aiming to attract more investors, would prefer to issue their securities in markets with robust private enforcement systems.[472] However, the benefits of competition remain uncertain, considering that, as will be explained below, the EU prospectus regime is anchored to home Member State control.

ii. Enhancing Convergence in Supervisory and Enforcement Practices

The Prospectus Regulation attains a high degree of harmonisation concerning substantive legal provisions. However, achieving convergence in the supervision and public enforcement of prospectus requirements has proven to be more challenging. This is because compliance with prospectus requirements is controlled by the issuer's home Member State. In particular, the review of public offerings and admissions to trading, except for debt issues with a denomination exceeding EUR 1,000, falls within the competence of the NCA where the issuer is registered.[473] Therefore, issuer choice and supervisory competition in the prospectus sphere are significantly limited. Given that company law arbitrage is not readily accessible, this elimination of issuer choice has been criticised for removing the potentially corrective effects of competition. More specifically, the concept of home Member State control was criticised for its inability to allow high-quality equity issuers in countries with less effective regulators to opt for a more competent supervisory authority in another country, thereby also weakening regulators' incentives to enhance their supervisory practices.[474] At the same time, there were concerns about whether the NCA of the home Member State would have sufficient incentives to oversee the prospectus requirements in cases where the issuance occurs entirely in another Member State.[475]

It is true, however, that the supervisory competition argument regarding equity issues might be overstated. Indeed, while the intensity of ex-ante supervision varies among Member States – with some NCAs taking a more proactive approach and regularly monitoring market participants, while others following a more risk-based approach[476] – fears of supervisory arbitrage at the expense of

[471] Garcimartín (n 470) 453.
[472] Lehmann (n 470) 400.
[473] Art 2(m) Prospectus Regulation.
[474] Enriques and Tröger (n 67) 538–39; Moloney (n 1) 139.
[475] Moloney (n 1) 139.
[476] For a general discussion on the different forms of supervision see E Pan, 'Understanding Financial Regulation' (2012) 4 *Utah Law Review* 1897, 1910–14.

market efficiency and investor protection have not been confirmed.[477] The tasks and powers conferred on ESMA to enhance cross-border supervisory coordination and convergence have been particularly important in this respect. Especially concerning the prospectus regime, ESMA's supervisory convergence activities exhibit both a coordinating (horizontal) and hierarchical (vertical) quality. These activities seek to establish a high-quality common supervisory culture, thus ensuring the consistent and effective application of prospectus rules.[478] They include, inter alia, developing draft regulatory and implementing technical standards;[479] issuing guidelines and recommendations to competent authorities under the 'comply or explain' principle;[480] issuing individual decisions to NCAs regarding breaches of the regime, inter-NCA mediation, and emergency situations;[481] organising and conducting peer reviews of NCAs' activities;[482] and providing opinions to the Union institutions.[483] All these powers, combined with ESMA's operational expertise and the strong political and market support it enjoys, have bolstered its capacity to exert technocratic influence over NCAs' supervisory functions, thereby promoting a more consistent application and implementation of EU prospectus rules.[484]

Yet, despite these positive developments, convergence in operational supervisory and enforcement practices across Member States has been rather weak, undermining the passport mechanism and posing a significant challenge to the integration of EU primary markets. The 2016 peer review on the prospectus approval process[485] is instructive in this regard, as it demonstrated that, although most NCAs complied with ESMA's good practices,[486] several weaknesses persisted. These included volatility in prospectus approval times; operational inefficiencies related to the number and expertise of the staff involved in the approval procedure; difficulties in addressing issues affecting prospectus comprehensibility; and variations in the approaches applied during the scrutiny of the prospectus. Despite the considerable efforts of both the EU legislator and ESMA to further promote convergence within the framework of the Prospectus Regulation, certain shortcomings are likely to persist. Indeed, prospectus approval and the imposition of sanctions for infringements of prospectus rules remain largely dependent on the home NCA's monitoring and investigatory activities. Consequently, their

[477] See eg ESMA, 'Annual Report 2018', 14 June 2019, 23 ff.
[478] Art 8(1) Regulation (EU) No 1095/2010 of 24 November 2010 establishing a European Supervisory Authority (European Securities and Markets Authority) [2010] OJ L331/84 (ESMA Regulation).
[479] ibid Arts 10 and 15.
[480] ibid Art 16.
[481] ibid Arts 17–19.
[482] ibid Art 30.
[483] ibid Art 34.
[484] Moloney (n 1) 148.
[485] ESMA (n 286).
[486] Article 1(3) of Directive 2014/51/EU [2014] OJ L153/1 (Omnibus II) empowered ESMA to propose RTS regarding the prospectus approval procedures and the conditions under which time limits may be adjusted.

effectiveness hinges on local politico-economic factors (eg, adequate budgets, qualified and motivated staff, institutional support),[487] which cannot realistically be controlled directly by the EU legislator or ESMA, regardless of the rigour of their actions.

In view of the above, it becomes pertinent to determine the direction in which supervision and public enforcement in the prospectus sphere should evolve. The 2017 Regulation proposal for the review of the European System of Financial Supervision (ESFS)[488] presented an opportunity to substantially bolster ESMA's role in supervising and enforcing the prospectus regime. This involved granting ESMA approval and oversight competencies over specific types of prospectuses,[489] along with administrative sanctioning authority for Regulation-related infringements concerning these prospectus types.[490] But while centralising prospectus supervisory and enforcement activities could create a more level playing field for issuers and reduce costs stemming from divergent NCA practices,[491] delegating executive powers to ESMA raises significant concerns regarding both its legitimacy and practical effectiveness.

More specifically, as an EU agency not mentioned in the Treaties, ESMA's authority to supervise and enforce the prospectus regime – or specific parts thereof – would be subject to the strict requirements of the fundamental Meroni doctrine, which, ever since the eponymous ruling,[492] has shaped the delegation of powers to EU agencies.[493] While the original doctrine has been reshaped over the years, especially following the ESMA Short Selling judgment,[494] two requirements seem to recur constantly. First, the delegating authority cannot entrust an agency with more powers than it itself enjoys under the Treaty (*nemo plus iuris ad alium transferre potest quam ipse habet*);[495] and second, only clearly defined executive

[487] J Armour et al, *Principles of Financial Regulation* (OUP, 2016) 590.

[488] COM (2017) 536 final, 20 September 2017.

[489] ibid Art 9(10) designated ESMA as the 'competent authority' for supervising four categories of prospectuses: wholesale non-equity prospectuses, prospectuses for complex securities like asset-backed securities, and prospectuses prepared by specialist or third-country issuers.

[490] ibid Art 9(15).

[491] ibid 8.

[492] Case 9-56 *Meroni & Co., Industrie Metallurgiche, SpA v High Authority of the European Coal and Steel Community* ECLI:EU:C:1958:7.

[493] See also D Curtin, 'Holding (Quasi-)Autonomous EU Administrative Actors to Public Account' (2007) 13 *European Law Journal* 523, 527; M Chamon, 'EU Agencies Between Meroni and Romano or the Devil and the Deep Blue Sea' (2011) 48 *Common Market Law Review* 1055, 1056–57.

[494] Case C-270/12 *United Kingdom of Great Britain and Northern Ireland v European Parliament and Council of the European Union* ECLI:EU:C:2014:18, [2014] 2 CMLR 44. For a comprehensive discussion of this case see M Scholten and M van Rijsbergen, 'The ESMA-Short Selling Case: Erecting a New Delegation Doctrine in the EU upon the Meroni-Romano Remnants' (2014) 41 *Legal Issues of European Integration* 389; CF Bergström, 'Shaping the New System for Delegation of Powers to EU Agencies: United Kingdom v. European Parliament and Council (Short Selling)' (2015) 52 *Common Market Law Review* 219.

[495] D Geradin, 'The Development of European Regulatory Agencies: What the EU Should Learn from American Experience' (2004) 11 *Columbia Journal of European Law* 1, 10.

powers, subject to strict review in light of objective criteria, may be delegated.[496] Regarding the first condition, given the legal and administrative inconsistencies among Member States with respect to prospectus approval and the imposition of sanctions, it could be argued that the measures in question aim to establish and ensure the functioning of the internal market under Article 114 TFEU. In this respect, they fall within the competence of the EU legislator, which, according to the Court's Short Selling ruling, has considerable discretion in selecting the most appropriate measures for the approximation of national provisions and practices, including through the delegation to 'a Union body, office or agency powers for the implementation of the harmonisation sought'.[497] Regarding the second condition, the post-crisis experience on the oversight of credit rating agencies,[498] trade repositories,[499] and short selling transactions[500] suggests that a potential transfer of the direct operational supervision and enforcement of prospectus rules to ESMA is feasible. Although this transfer would be subject to detailed and stringent requirements, it would not entirely preclude ESMA's ability to exercise some discretion in the application of these rules.[501]

But while satisfying the above requirements should not pose an insurmountable obstacle, any effort to allocate prospectus approval and sanctioning functions to ESMA, even to a limited extent, faces practical challenges. Indeed, unlike the supervision of relatively small and discrete sectors such as rating agencies and short sales, the sheer number of prospectuses approved every year would render it impossible for ESMA, under its current structure, to effectively fulfil its duties. At the same time, these functions are so deeply entrenched within NCAs, and the expertise developed within some of them is so robust that many Member States would be highly hesitant to relinquishing their competitive advantage.[502] In this regard, given the complexities and practical difficulties involved, it is unlikely that any significant centralisation of powers within ESMA for operational supervision and enforcement in the prospectus sphere will occur in the near future.

[496] H Hofmann and A Morini, 'Constitutional Aspects of the Pluralisation of the EU Executive through "Agencification"' (2012) 36 *European Law Review* 412, 423.

[497] Case C-270/12 (n 494) para 105.

[498] Regulation (EU) No 462/2013 of the European Parliament and of the Council amending Regulation (EC) No 1060/2009uon credit rating agencies [2013] OJ L146/1.

[499] Regulation (EU) No 648/2012 of the European Parliament and of the Council on OTC derivatives, central counterparties and trade repositories [2012] OJ L201/1.

[500] Regulation (EU) No 236/2012 of the European Parliament and of the Council on short selling and certain aspects of credit default swaps [2012] OJ L86/1.

[501] N Moloney, 'European Banking Union: Assessing its Risks and Resilience' (2014) 51 *Common Market Law Review* 1609, 1660. See also C Gortsos and K Lagaria, 'The European Supervisory Authorities (ESAs) as "direct" Supervisors in the EU Financial System' in D Chrysochoou et al (eds), *European Governance in Times of Uncertainty/ Gouvernance Européenne en Temps Incertains* (Nomiki Bibliothiki, 2020).

[502] This is why the provisions aimed at bolstering ESMA's role in the prospectus regime did not make it into the final text of the 2017 ESA Proposal.

iii. Official Listing and the Prospectus Regulation

The EU prospectus regime's reliance on the concept of 'admission of securities to trading on a regulated market' as a means of perimeter control for issuer disclosure stems from the pragmatic need to guarantee that primary issuances occur on well-established, organised, liquid, and transparent public trading platforms that adhere to the most stringent standards.[503] These standards are primarily intended to facilitate capital-raising by signalling that the issuer has fulfilled rigorous disclosure requirements.[504] Moreover, financial instruments admitted to trading in this market segment must meet some minimum conditions, which are consistently monitored by the market operator.[505] In this regard, the criteria for the admission of securities to 'official listing', which, despite the significant dismantling of the 2001 Listing Directive, have persisted in certain countries, appear not only outdated but also inconsistent with the recognition in EU securities law that admission (or listing) services can be offered by high-quality trading segments operating outside the 'official' stock exchange segment.[506]

More specifically, the existence of an 'official listing' concept alongside that of admission to trading on a regulated market might suggest that securities admitted to official listing are of superior quality compared to those solely admitted to trading on a regulated market.[507] However, this does not appear to be the case, since admission rules overlap in both instances. For one thing, the admission requirements for shares and debt securities under the 2001 Listing Directive[508] closely resemble those outlined in MiFID II,[509] both aiming to facilitate efficient capital allocation by ensuring fair, orderly, and liquid trading, and fostering accurate price formation. In fact, the limited harmonisation achieved by the Listing Directive implies that the official listing system is, in practice, less sophisticated and rigorous compared to the admission requirements applied by most regulated markets under MiFID II.[510] Moreover, the Listing Directive requires that the official listing be overseen by a competent authority but does not specify its legal form, allowing trading venues to carry out the relevant function, similar to the admission of securities to trading.[511] Finally, the initial and ongoing disclosure requirements for officially listed securities are the same as those for securities admitted to a regulated market, as prescribed by the Prospectus Regulation and the Transparency Directive.

[503] See also Moloney (n 1) 193.
[504] ibid 190.
[505] Art 51 MiFID II.
[506] P Mäntysaari, *The Law of Corporate Finance: General Principles and EU Law – Volume III: Funding, Exit, Takeovers* (Springer, 2010) 195.
[507] ESME, 'Report on MiFID and admission of securities to official stock exchange listing' (2007) 8.
[508] Arts 42–63 Listing Directive.
[509] Art 51 MiFID II in conjunction with Commission Delegated Regulation (EU) 2017/568.
[510] Moloney (n 1) 196.
[511] Recital 112 of MiFID II.

Based on the above, the official listing concept can be best characterised as an additional branding device for the regulated market, allowing Member States to compete on the quality of the admission processes available to issuers. As such, it is unclear whether its persistence adds significant value to the capital-raising process, considering its conceptual implications and limited practical application.[512] On the contrary, it could even undermine the objective of greater convergence in EU primary markets, given that Member States enjoy broad discretion to deviate from certain rules set out in the Listing Directive, such as the free float requirement or the required minimum market capitalisation.[513]

In this regard, it is not surprising that, as part of the Listing Act Package, the European Parliament and the Council adopted a new Directive repealing the Listing Directive and transferring certain relevant provisions to MiFID II.[514] Notably, the new rules reduce the minimum free float threshold to 10 per cent,[515] as the previous requirement of 25 per cent was considered excessive and unsuitable.[516] Furthermore, as under the previous regime, Member States are required to ensure that a company seeking admission of shares to trading has a foreseeable market capitalisation of at least EUR 1 million or, if this cannot be assessed, that its capital and reserves, including profit and loss, from the latest financial year, meet this threshold.[517] These rules are expected to foster a more uniform application of listing requirements across the Union, as MiFID II is a maximum harmonisation Directive.[518] At the same time, though, Member States will retain some discretion, albeit more limited, in framing their national laws. For instance, they may allow regulated markets to adopt alternative methods for assessing if a sufficient number of shares have been distributed to the public where the 10 per cent threshold is deemed excessive given the size and characteristics of local issuances.[519] Besides, the repeal of the Listing Directive will not prevent Member States from maintaining national regimes for admission to official listing on stock exchanges.[520] Therefore, it remains to be seen whether the new rules will reduce implementation disparities among Member States, to the advantage of issuers pursuing cross-border admissions of their securities.

[512] Except for a few Member States, including Ireland, Luxembourg, and previously the UK, the concept of official listing has become synonymous to admission to trading, Moloney (n 1) 196–97.

[513] SWD (2022) 762 final (n 75), Annex 7, 205 ff.

[514] Directive (EU) 2024/2811 of the European Parliament and of the Council amending Directive 2014/65/EU to make public capital markets in the Union more attractive for companies and to facilitate access to capital for small and medium-sized enterprises and repealing Directive 2001/34/EC OJ L, 2024/2811.

[515] Art 51a(4) MiFID II as inserted by Directive (EU) 2024/2811.

[516] Recital 12 Directive (EU) 2024/2811.

[517] Art 51a(1) MiFID II as inserted by Directive (EU) 2024/2811.

[518] SWD (2022) 762 final (n 75), Annex 7, 210.

[519] Art 51a(5) MiFID II as inserted by Directive (EU) 2024/2811.

[520] Recital 13 Directive (EU) 2024/2811.

4

The Regulation on European Crowdfunding Service Providers – A Systematic Analysis and Evaluation

I. Introduction

As explained in the previous chapter, within the framework of the CMU, EU policymakers have paid specific attention to reducing the administrative and compliance costs relating to the drawing up and dissemination of a securities prospectus for SMEs. Yet, despite their importance, it is questionable whether the recent reforms in the EU prospectus regime would have any significant impact on the ability of smaller companies, especially early-stage start-ups, to raise the capital they need to thrive through the primary market. Indeed, even in the absence of mandatory prospectus requirements, the costs associated with going public (eg, underwriting fees, legal and accounting adviser fees, listing fees etc.)[1] are prohibitive for nascent ventures in search of a profitable business model. At the same time, start-up firms, with their untested ideas and often inexperienced entrepreneurs, would still find it very challenging to access capital through a private placement of equity or debt.[2] Against this background and considering the critical role of such businesses in creating jobs[3] and driving economic growth,[4] broadening the range of non-bank financing options available to them was seen by the Commission as a prerequisite for a successful CMU.[5]

In the capital market domain, an attractive funding tool, investment-based crowdfunding, has recently become available to start-ups and other high-growth companies. As the name implies, it involves raising capital from a multitude of individual investors (the 'crowd'), each of whom typically contributes a small sum in exchange for an equity stake in the company, a share in its future profits or

[1] FESE, 'European IPO Report 2020', 6 March 2020, 12.

[2] A Schwartz, 'Crowdfunding Securities' (2013) 88 *Notre Dame Law Review* 1457, 1468.

[3] J Block, C Fisch and M van Praag, 'Quantity and Quality of Jobs by Entrepreneurial Firms' (2018) 34 *Oxford Review of Economic Policy* 565, 567.

[4] R Crudu, 'The Role of Innovative Entrepreneurship in the Economic Development of EU Member Countries' (2019) 15 *Journal of Entrepreneurship, Management and Innovation* 35.

[5] Commission, 'Action Plan on Building a Capital Markets Union', COM (2015) 468 final, 30 September 2015, 7.

revenues, or any other security, such as a bond or a preferred share.[6] The funds are channelled through the intermediation of a web-based platform, which collects business plans from fund-seekers and allows potential investors to navigate through the different projects and choose the solution best fitting their needs.[7] In this respect, investment-based crowdfunding resembles a public offering, the main novelty being that the whole process takes place by utilising the potential of the internet.

It is exactly due to this last feature that crowdfunding is expected to benefit both issuers and investors in the primary market. With respect to the former, the use of internet technologies not only significantly reduces the cost of raising capital from the public, but it also provides access to a network of international investors whom, in an offline context, it would be almost impossible to meet. As regards the latter, it can help 'democratise',[8] at least to some extent, their access to capital markets since it allows ordinary investors with modest means to participate in the financing of speculative start-up companies, an activity previously confined almost exclusively to wealthy and connected investors. But despite its unquestionable benefits, investment-based crowdfunding also poses some important risks, especially for retail investors. Indeed, the investee company is at an early stage, thus manifesting the three fundamental problems of start-up financing (ie, uncertainty, information asymmetry and agency costs) in an extreme form.[9] At the same time, the usual mechanisms which protect retail investors, with their cognitive limitations and biases, when investing in newly issued securities are unavailable in the crowdfunding context.[10] Absent a workable regulatory response these problems might lead to poor investment decisions, thus causing the misallocation of capital within the market.

Following a wait-and-see approach and after protracted trialogue negotiations, the European Parliament and the Council adopted Regulation (EU) 2020/1503 ('ECSPR')[11] establishing a common regulatory framework for the provision and reception of crowdfunding services in the internal market. The aim of this Regulation is to build an efficient single market for crowdfunding services, which shall improve access to cross-border alternative financing opportunities for European start-ups and other unlisted companies, while providing investors,

[6] ESMA, 'Opinion on Investment-based crowdfunding', ESMA/2014/1378, 18 December 2014, 6; F Pichler and I Tezza, 'Crowdfunding as a New Phenomenon: Origins, Features and Literature Review' in R Bottiglia and F Pichler (eds) *Crowdfunding for SMEs: A European Perspective* (Springer, 2016) 11–12.

[7] J Armour and L Enriques, 'Individual Investors' Access to Crowdinvesting: Two Regulatory Models' in D Cumming and L Hornuf (eds), *The Economics of Crowdfunding* (Springer, 2018) 255.

[8] E Mollick and A Robb, 'Democratizing Innovation and Capital Access: The Role of Crowdfunding' (2016) 58 *California Management Review* 72; Schwartz (n 2) 1459.

[9] RJ Gilson, 'Locating innovation: The Endogeneity of Technology, Organizational Structure, and Financial Contracting' (2010) 110 *Columbia Law Review* 885, 901.

[10] Armour and Enriques (n 7) 257.

[11] Regulation (EU) 2020/1503 of the European Parliament and of the Council on European crowdfunding service providers (ECSP) for business [2020] OJ L347/1.

especially retail ones, with additional opportunities to put their money to work. That way, it can be seen as an integral part of the overall strategy to support the CMU ambitions of strengthening and further integrating EU capital markets, especially in the primary markets domain.[12] This chapter seeks to provide an analysis of the ECSPR within the system of EU primary market law and to assess whether and to what extent the provisions contained therein can effectively contribute to the efforts to complete the CMU project.

II. Understanding Investment-based Crowdfunding and its Regulation

A. Concept, Characteristics and Definition

The exponential development of technology-enabled innovation in financial services (FinTech)[13] in recent years, has resulted in the advent of new business models, which have had a significant effect on the expansion of capital raising and investment opportunities through the market. Prominent among them is investment-based crowdfunding,[14] which seeks to provide a complement (if not an alternative) to unsecured bank lending, such as credit lines or overdrafts, which has consistently been the main source of external financing among European SMEs, including during the initial period of their activity.[15]

To understand the essence of this innovative funding mechanism it is critical to identify the main actors that are typically involved in the crowd-investing process. These include at least: (a) a project owner (normally a start-up company-seeking to raise a relatively modest amount of capital through the offer of financial instruments); (b) an investor who forms part of the 'crowd' that participates in the funding campaign, usually by placing small amounts; and (c) an internet platform which serves as an intermediary between the investor and the project owner.[16]

[12] Commission, 'Impact Assessment accompanying the Proposal for a Regulation on European Crowdfunding Service Providers (ECSP) for Business', SWD (2018) 56 final, 8 March 2018, 6 and 31.

[13] For a definition, see Commission, 'FinTech Action plan: For a more competitive and innovative European financial sector', COM (2018) 109 final, 8 March 2018, 2.

[14] This term is consistently used by EU institutions and bodies to describe crowdfunding transactions involving the sale of financial instruments, see ESMA (n 6); Commission, 'Crowdfunding in the EU Capital Markets Union', SWD (2016) 154 final, 3 May 2016. In German-speaking countries, the preferred term is 'crowdinvesting', see eg L Klöhn and L Hornuf, 'Crowdinvesting in Deutschland – Markt, Rechtslage und Regulierungsperspektive' (2012) 24 *Zeitschrift für Bankrecht und Bankwirtschaft* 237; S Baumann, *Crowdinvesting im Finanzmarktrecht* (Schulthess, 2014). Finally, in common law countries, the term used is 'equity' or 'securities' crowdfunding, see eg T Knight, H Leo and A Ohmer, 'A Very Quiet Revolution: A Primer on Securities Crowdfunding and Title III of the JOBS Act' (2012) 2 *Michigan Journal of Private Equity & Venture Capital Law* 135; G Ahlers et al, 'Signaling in Equity Crowdfunding' (2015) 39 *Entrepreneurship Theory and Practice* 955.

[15] Commission, 'Survey on the Access to Finance of Enterprises (SAFE)', Analytical Report 2021, 17–20.

[16] ESMA (n 6) 6.

While investment-based crowdfunding is an evolving and dynamic phenomenon thus making it practically impossible to identify all existing contractual features, in the archetypal model, the project owner will prepare a 'pitch', that is a short description of the venture, usually in the form of a text or film, displayed on the platform's website. This is accompanied by a standardised contract offered to the crowd and featuring comprehensive information about the funding procedure, including at least the target amount to be reached, normally within a predetermined time limit, the manner in which the funds for the specific project are to be used, as well as the type, properties, and price of the instruments to be issued.[17] In most crowdfunding campaigns, the project owner sets a minimum funding goal and does not keep any of the pledged funds unless the fixed amount is collected ('all-or-nothing' model).[18] Alternatively, the entrepreneurial firm can keep the whole amount obtained by the end of the campaign, irrespective of whether the stated funding goal is achieved ('keep-it-all' model).[19] Moreover, in the great majority of cases, the project owner undertakes to use any sums received exclusively for the purposes of financing the specific project as described in the pitch and will consequently be held liable in case any of the funds are dedicated to other uses.[20] Finally, as regards the issued instruments, these will normally take the form of securities,[21] but might also include other investments, mainly certain hybrid instruments which entitle their holders to participate in the future profits but not the management of the investee company.[22] The securities to which investors acquire rights might be transferable (eg, shares and bonds) or non-transferable (eg, minibonds[23]), although it is quite probable that even in the first case there will be a limited secondary market.[24] For debt instruments (including minibonds) the

[17] C Estevan de Quesada, 'Crowdfunding in Europe' in S Grundmann (ed), *European Contract Law in the Digital Age* (CUP, 2018) 110–11.

[18] D Cumming, G Leboeuf and A Schwienbacher, 'Crowdfunding Models: Keep-It-All vs. All-Or-Nothing' (2020) 49 *Financial Management* 331, 332. Under this model, founders will typically allocate the issued instruments on a first-come, first-served basis. This means that they will set an overall funding limit, which is usually larger than the funding goal, and stop selling securities to investors once this limit is reached, see L Hornuf and A Schwienbacher, 'The Emergence of Crowdinvesting in Europe', Munich Discussion Paper No. 2014-43, 4 epub.ub.uni-muenchen.de/21388/.

[19] This funding model is usually used by entrepreneurs with less promising projects as it allows them to raise smaller amounts, see Cumming, Leboeuf and Schwienbacher (n 18) 332.

[20] This implies that the promoter should return the contributions to the funders if they are not used as described in the call. To that end, each funder will have to recover the funds which have been improperly spent by bringing a civil action directly against the promoter, unless the platform has guaranteed that the invested capital will be used as promised, see also Estevan de Quesada (n 17) 111.

[21] ESMA (n 6) 6.

[22] This is the case, for example, with profit-participating loans, subordinated loans and similar investments which are brokered by crowdinvesting platforms in Germany, see §2a in combination with §1(2) no. 3, 4 and 7 of the German Investment Act (Gesetz über Vermögensanlagen or 'VermAnlG').

[23] These are a type of interest-bearing notes (*bons de caisse*), ie registered and non-negotiable securities which are issued by a privately held company or a stock corporation in exchange for a loan and bear the commitment by the issuer to effect payment on a specific maturity time.

[24] However, the recent years have seen the emergence of organised secondary markets for securities or loans in crowdfunding projects, which are operated either by the crowdfunding platform (usually in the form of a bulletin board) or a stock exchange, like the ExtraMOT PRO market in Borsa Italiana.

interest rate will be specified, while for equity investments the participation of each share to the firm's capital and the rights attached to them will be stated.

As a general rule, any person with access to the internet can invest in a project through a crowdfunding platform.[25] In fact, the application of internet technology – which powers social networking – in the field of business finance, as exemplified in the crowdfunding context,[26] makes this funding tool particularly attractive for retail investors, though in recent years institutional involvement (eg, venture capitals co-investing with the crowd) has also become a widespread practice.[27] In most instances, financial backers will invest directly in the project company, either by purchasing the issued instrument or by obtaining the beneficial rights in that instrument which is held by the platform in a nominee account. However, indirect investments are also possible through the acquisition of instruments issued by a special purpose vehicle (SPV) or a collective investment scheme (CIS) which in turn holds financial instruments or has some other interests in the project.[28] In all these cases, the instruments are offered by the project owner and/or the issuer – where the latter is not the project owner – to potential investors on a primary market[29] which, however, does not form part of a trading venue since most platforms do not operate an MTF, such as an SME growth market, or a regulated market.[30] Moreover, the fact that the instruments are, at least in principle, made available for sale to the 'crowd' rather than to a limited group of qualified investors[31] implies that crowdfunding offerings do not constitute private placements but rather public offers within the meaning of the Prospectus Regulation.

The offer and sale of financial instruments through crowdfunding was practically made possible since internet technology evolved to such a point that it allowed the penetration of internet platforms into virtually every aspect of economic activity.[32] In the context of the crowd-investing process, these platforms essentially act as two-sided transaction markets[33] which facilitate the conclusion

[25] In practice, potential investors must register with the platform and satisfy certain criteria before having access to the full 'pitch' information and investing.

[26] JM Heminway, 'Business Lawyering in the Crowdfunding Era' (2013) 3 *American University Business Law Review* 149, 155.

[27] This 'institutionalisation' of crowdfunding in terms of the participating investors has been facilitated, among other things, by the practice of many platforms to impose high minimum investment tickets, thus limiting the participation of retail investors, see L Hornuf and A Schwienbacher, 'Crowdinvesting – Angel Investing for the Masses?' in C Mason and H Landström (eds), *Handbook of Research on Business Angels* (Edward Elgar, 2016) 388.

[28] ESMA (n 6) 6 f.

[29] ibid 7. See also J Armour and L Enriques, 'The Promise and Perils of Crowdfunding: Between Corporate Finance and Consumer Contracts' (2018) 81 *The Modern Law Review* 51, 74.

[30] ESMA (n 6) 18.

[31] Nevertheless, there have been cases where project owners or issuers place the securities directly with a certain number of qualified investors, mainly to bypass the strict prospectus requirements.

[32] For a comprehensive analysis of this process, which is typically defined as 'platformisation', see T Poell, D Nieborg and J van Dijck, 'Platformisation' (2019) 8 *Internet Policy Review* 1.

[33] A two-sided market can be generally defined as a market in which the firm acts as a platform and somehow connects distinct but interdependent customer groups (or 'sides') in a way that generates value for at least one of them, see L Filistrucchi, D Geradin and E van Damme, 'Identifying Two-Sided

of an investment contract between the 'crowd' of investors and the project owner seeking funding.[34] More specifically, with respect to the latter, the main service provided by platforms is to give them access to a large pool of potential investors and collect commitments from those deciding to invest. Correspondingly, as regards investors, their key function is to provide information about available investment opportunities and communicate their decision or interest to invest to the issuer.[35] In many aspects, these constitute typical intermediation activities, though the utilisation of new online technologies has given rise to synergies which would be unattainable – both practically and economically – in an offline setting.[36] At the same time, platforms may also provide additional services to both market sides, such as legal compliance support during the preparation of the issue or due diligence investigation on the investee company, typically by charging an additional fee.[37] In any case, however, such variations in the way platforms function do not significantly alter the main business model.

Based on the above, investment-based crowdfunding could be defined as an offer of securities or other investment instruments by an issuer – typically an unlisted company – to the public, which, in principle, takes place in a primary market without admission on a trading venue and results in the acquisition of specific financial rights. This occurs either directly to the project company or indirectly through another intermediary entity. Under this definition, investment-based crowdfunding is therefore distinct from lending-based crowdfunding, where businesses seek to obtain funds in the form of loan agreements.

B. Rationale for Regulatory Intervention – The Perils of Crowdfunding

Having described the main features of investment-based crowdfunding, it becomes apparent that it holds great opportunities for both enterprises and investors. Besides providing an alternative, cost-efficient channel for bringing together companies seeking finance with a theoretically endless pool of potential financiers, thus offering both market sides additional opportunities to meet their respective needs,[38] crowdfunding is associated with numerous other benefits: it can validate a business idea, thus also help young firms to attract other funding sources if the

Markets' (2013) 36 *World Competition* 33, 37. On the distinction between two-sided transaction and non-transaction markets, see L Filistrucchi et al, 'Market Definition in Two-Sided Markets: Theory and Practice' (2014) 10 *Journal of Competition Law and Economics* 293, 298.

[34] See also L Hornuf, L Klöhn and T Schilling, 'Financial Contracting in Crowdinvesting: Lessons from the German Market' (2018) 19 *German Law Journal* 509, 522.

[35] ESMA (n 6) 8 f.

[36] ibid 7.

[37] The remuneration can also be a proportion of the amount raised or invested, ibid 9.

[38] P Chapman, 'Crowdfunding' in J Madir (ed), *Fintech – Law and Regulation* (Edward Elgar, 2019) 50.

campaign is successful; it can serve as a valuable marketing tool, giving borrowers access not only to financial backers but also to individuals providing insights and feedback;[39] and it can contribute to the 'democratisation of capital'[40] – with potentially broader societal benefits[41] – by making it possible for ordinary people to make investments in businesses and projects which were previously available solely to professional investors.[42] In this respect, investment-based crowdfunding can be viewed as part of a wider universe of technological innovations with potentially transformative implications for the financial system and its users.[43]

But despite its numerous advantages, as with most investment methods, crowdfunding raises three fundamental problems for investors: information asymmetry, uncertainty, and agency costs in the form of managerial opportunism.[44] Especially within the context of crowdfunding, however, this 'trio of problems' manifests itself in an extreme way[45] given that the beneficiary companies are usually start-ups in their infancy[46] which have, thus, not signalled their quality and intentions. This is particularly relevant for unsophisticated, retail investors who typically lack experience and knowledge in the field of project financing, while the standard mechanisms which support the protection of investors in primary markets are unavailable in the crowdfunding context. That said, in the absence of appropriate regulatory safeguards, the unusually high degree of risk associated with this form of fundraising could deter crowd-funders from allocating capital in this setting, possibly leading to a market failure also with negative results for social welfare.

i. Information Asymmetry

Information asymmetry applies forcefully to crowdfunding and hence, if left unaddressed, might lead to adverse selection.[47] Nevertheless, this problem does not arise from the fact that typically it will only be start-ups of low quality (so-called 'lemons') that will resort to investment-based crowdfunding in the first place, as

[39] EBRD and Clifford Chance, 'Regulating Investment- and Lending-based Crowdfunding: Best Practices', 23 August 2018, 5, www.ebrd.com/news/publications/guides/.

[40] Heminway (n 26) 151.

[41] For example, through crowdfunding retail investors can engage capital to finance local projects, female entrepreneurship, and sustainable growth, see eg J Greenberg and E Mollick, 'Activist Choice Homophily and the Crowdfunding of Female Founders' (2017) 2 *Administrative Science Quarterly* 341.

[42] Schwartz (n 2) 1459. See also C Catalini, C Fazio and F Murray, 'Can Equity Crowdfunding Democratize Access to Capital and Investment Opportunities?' MIT Lab for Innovation Science and Policy Report, May 2016, ssrn.com/abstract=2780551.

[43] SWD (2016) 154 final (n 14) 3–4.

[44] This tripartite analysis was first presented in this clear form by RJ Gilson, 'Engineering a Venture Capital Market: Lessons from the American Experience' (2003) 55 *Stanford Law Review* 1067, 1076.

[45] A Schwartz, 'The Digital Shareholder' (2015) 100 *Minnesota Law Review* 609, 630.

[46] S Oranburg, 'Bridgefunding: Crowdfunding and the Market for Entrepreneurial Finance' (2015) 25 *Cornell Journal of Law and Public Policy* 397, 401.

[47] G Tomboc, 'The Lemons Problem in Crowdfunding' (2013) 30 *John Marshall Journal of Information Technology & Privacy Law* 253, 267; DM Ibrahim, 'Equity Crowdfunding: A Market for Lemons?' (2015) 100 *Minnesota Law Review* 561, 587 et seq.

some commentators have suggested.[48] In fact, there are many reasons why project owners would choose crowdfunding over other forms of market finance.[49] On the contrary, it is mostly related to the specific features of this financing tool as well as to the identity and nature of potential beneficiaries and investors. Indeed, one of the biggest challenges when it comes to investing in young start-ups is to know in advance the exact price of the instruments offered, so that the investment decisions correspond with the real potentials of the issuer and do not exaggerate return projections.[50] In a traditional IPO, this issue is typically addressed through the process of 'book-building', during which the underwriter (typically an investment bank) will determine the price based on non-binding orders from institutional investors.[51] Retail investors can then free ride on the efforts of sophisticated investors and make informed decisions.

Yet, things look different in the case of investment-based crowdfunding. There, no price-setting mechanism usually operates since issuers will target retail investors directly. In addition, the issued instruments will rarely be traded on a secondary market and as a result their price does not respond to demand fluctuations which could serve as indicators of their value.[52] Accordingly, any inferences about the quality of the investment shall be drawn from the information which is voluntarily disclosed by the project owner as well as from the behaviour of other investors. However, these last features may prove inadequate to ensure the accurate pricing of the offered assets. For one thing, corporate disclosure entails externalities since it can confer benefits on competitors and other stakeholders which have opposing interests to those of the disclosing firm. Hence, from a private cost-benefit perspective, project owners would probably be very hesitant to disclose sensitive and detailed information, no matter how important it is for an informed judgement on the investment and its risks.[53] Furthermore, the observed demand for a crowdfunding campaign, rather than serving as a quality signal, is likely to generate herding.[54] This is because, given the lack of the necessary information or specialist knowledge and skills to assess the quality of the project, retail investors might instead base their decision on the 'collective wisdom' of the investing

[48] See eg M Dorff, 'The Siren Call of Equity Crowdfunding' (2014) 39 *Journal of Corporation Law* 493, 496–97; C Hurt, 'Pricing Disintermediation: Crowdfunding and Online Auction IPOs' (2015) 1 *University of Illinois Law Review* 217, 254.

[49] Armour and Enriques (n 7) 258–61.

[50] E Burkett, 'A Crowdfunding Exemption? Online Investment Crowdfunding and U.S. Securities Regulation' (2011) 13 *Tennessee Journal of Business Law* 63, 97.

[51] M Fleuriet, *Investment Banking Explained: An Insider's Guide to the Industry*, 2nd edn (McGraw-Hill Education, 2019) 56.

[52] Armour and Enriques (n 7) 262.

[53] This is especially true where project owners seek funding for path-breaking, innovative ideas, see A Ley and SK Weaven, 'Exploring Agency Dynamics of Crowdfunding in Start-Up Capital Financing' (2011) 17 *Academy of Entrepreneurship Journal* 85, 96–97.

[54] DA Hirshleifer, 'The Blind Leading the Blind: Social Influence, Fads, and Informational Cascades' in M Tommasi and K Ierulli (eds), *The New Economics of Human Behaviour* (CUP, 1995) 189, 191.

crowd.[55] The problem, though, is that other investors might equally be basing their decisions on the behaviour of others, including potentially several biased initial backers, like the family, friends, and personal acquaintances of the project owners,[56] ultimately creating a vicious cycle of poor investment decisions.[57] In view of these risks, a robust regulatory framework is needed to ensure the efficient allocation of resources.

ii. Uncertainty

Uncertainty is an inherent feature of every investment since it is virtually impossible to predict how the future will unfold.[58] However, this problem is at its peak for the type of ventures that will typically resort to investment-based crowdfunding, which include nascent businesses operating outside of established markets.[59] Indeed, the assets of most start-ups consist of intangible rights on an untested product or idea, thus being highly illiquid and very difficult to evaluate. In addition, nearly all of the important decisions that will determine the success of the business, such as the development and marketing of the product, are still to be taken and most importantly by managers whose intentions, but also quality, cannot be known in advance.[60] As a result, crowd-funders, who, unlike venture capitalists and other professional investors, lack specialised expertise and knowledge in market financing, would find it hard to assess the quality and prospects of the issuer.[61] At the same time, contrary to a traditional IPO, in the context of a crowdfunding offering it appears almost unattainable for fund seekers to ensure coverage by gatekeepers, notably investment analysts, trading venues, investment banks and lawyers,[62] who could pledge their own reputation to overcome this cognitive constraint.[63] Of course, given the strong reputational dynamics associated with their business, most crowdfunding platforms will struggle to maintain a

[55] Crowdfunding is deeply rooted in the idea of 'collective wisdom', that is the knowledge that emerges from the collaboration of many individuals, see J Surowiecki, *The Wisdom of Crowds: Why the Many are Smarter than the Few and How Collective Wisdom Shapes Business, Economies, Societies and Nations* (Random House Large Print, 2004). See also FA von Hayek, 'The Use of Knowledge in Society' (1945) 35 *The American Economic Review* 519, 521–22.

[56] AK Agrawal, C Catalini and A Goldfarb, 'The Geography of Crowdfunding' (2011) NBER Working Papers, No 16820, 3; E Mollick, 'The dynamics of crowdfunding: An exploratory study' (2014) 29 *Journal of Business Venturing* 1, 8.

[57] Armour and Enriques (n 29) 61.

[58] Therefore, in the way it is used here, uncertainty refers to contingencies that cannot be predicted by the investor nor the issuer, RJ Gilson and DM Schizer, 'Understanding Venture Capital Structure: A Tax Explanation for Convertible Preferred Stock' (2003) 116 *Harvard Law Review* 874, 879 (cit. 14).

[59] AJB Cable, 'Fending for Themselves: Why Securities Regulations Should Encourage Angel Groups' (2010) 13 *University of Pennsylvania Journal of Business Law* 107, 121.

[60] Gilson (n 44) 1076–77.

[61] Armour and Enriques (n 29) 58.

[62] N Moloney, *EU Securities and Financial Markets Regulation*, 4th edn (OUP, 2023) 637. On the evolution, responsibilities, and standards of the gatekeeping professions, see JC Coffee Jr., *Gatekeepers: The Role of the Professions and Corporate Governance* (OUP, 2006).

[63] Armour and Enriques (n 7) 262.

record of good-quality investments.[64] Nevertheless, the presence of unscrupulous intermediaries that will try to take advantage of unsuspecting investors cannot be excluded. In this respect, unless uncertainty is properly addressed, investors would be extremely hesitant to participate in crowdfunding which may in turn raise the cost of capital or even shut off companies from the crowdfunding market.[65]

iii. Agency Costs

While information asymmetry and uncertainty are ex-ante investment problems, agency costs appear in the post-investment phase.[66] The latter arise from the fact that, following the investment, the beneficiary ('agent') might not always act in the best interests of the investors ('principals') but rather advance his own interests instead.[67] Undoubtedly, agency costs, which can be both direct (ie, positive monitoring and bonding expenditures as well as residual losses) and indirect (ie, the damage incurred due to lost opportunities), emerge in various contexts and organisational structures, even if no evident principal-agent relationship exists (eg, universities, government authorities, unions etc).[68] However, this fundamental problem is even more prominent in companies with dispersed ownership, where control is left to the management, giving them a wide margin of discretion in determining the corporate policy.[69] This is a typical agency relationship where the interests of the principle (ie, the owner) and those of the agent (ie, the ultimate manager) may – and often do – diverge.[70] Assuming, therefore, that both parties seek to maximise their personal utility,[71] it is expected that, once they have obtained control, managers will misuse their position for their own interests.[72]

Due to its specific nature and characteristics, investment-based crowdfunding creates a fertile ground for the emergence of agent misbehaviour. Indeed, once a project goes public, each crowd-funder will contribute a relatively small amount of capital, thus assuming the role of principal. Meanwhile, considering that investors are unlikely to participate actively in the operation of the crowdfunded company,[73] day-to-day management will remain under the control of the project owner who

[64] Hornuf, Klöhn and Schilling (n 34) 520.
[65] Gilson (n 44) 1077.
[66] Ibrahim (n 47) 573.
[67] M Jensen and WH Meckling, 'Theory of the Firm: Managerial Behavior, Agency Costs and Ownership Structure' (1976) 3 *Journal of Financial Economics* 305, 308.
[68] ibid 309.
[69] This governance issue of publicly held businesses was initially identified in the famous book of AA Berle and GC Means, *The Modern Corporation and Private Property* (Macmillan, 1932). Later, it would find application even in private companies funded by VCs, see RP Bartlett III, 'Venture Capital, Agency Costs, and the False Dichotomy of the Corporation' (2006) 54 *UCLA Law Review* 37, 51.
[70] Berle and Means (n 69) 6.
[71] SG Marks, 'The Separation of Ownership and Control' in B Bouckaert and G De Geest (eds), *Encyclopaedia of Law and Economics: Vol. II* (Edward Elgar, 2000) 696.
[72] FH Easterbrook, 'Managers' Discretion and Investors' Welfare: Theories and Evidence' (1984) 9 *Delaware Journal of Corporate Law* 540, 543.
[73] Schwartz (n 45) 647.

would, thus, act as agent. This separation between ownership and control implies, therefore, that the latter would be just as prone to pursue their own interests as any other agent.[74] Nonetheless, addressing such agency costs is much more challenging in the case of crowdfunding, where the most important techniques employed in traditional forms of entrepreneurial finance seem ineffective.[75] For example, unlike venture capital and angel investments, mechanisms like geographic concentration or the granting of control rights would not be very helpful in the crowdfunding context, given the geographic dispersion and the insufficient technical background of investors. Moreover, compared to a typical IPO, there is no – liquid – secondary market which could discipline the management to increase shareholders' value, eg, through the threat of a takeover bid.[76] For crowdfunding to function, therefore, agency costs should be dealt with through legislative action.

C. Regulatory Challenges – Striking the Right Balance

In dealing with the 'trio of problems', regulatory practice in the field of public primary markets has come down firmly in favour of conduct regulation, a central plank of which is the imposition of mandatory and extensive disclosure obligations on issuers.[77] Nevertheless, the appropriateness of this approach is heavily contested within the domain of investment-based crowdfunding. More specifically, providing investors with full information would imply exorbitant costs for start-ups seeking to raise small amounts of capital from the dispersed crowd, thus rendering access to this financing tool unaffordable.[78] At the same time, empirical research in behavioural sciences has provided abundant evidence that all kinds of biases and heuristics result in retail investors not acting on the grounds of rational processing of available information and systematically making poor investment decisions.[79] These specificities raise the thorny policy question, therefore, of how to best devise the crowdfunding regulatory framework in order to strike an appropriate balance

[74] P Staikouras, 'The European Union Proposal for a Regulation on Cross-Border Crowdfunding Services: A Solemn or Pie-Crust Promise?' (2020) 31 *European Business Law Review* 1047, 1058.

[75] For a detailed analysis on why this is the case, see Schwartz (n 45) 636 ff.

[76] S Grundmann, *Bankvertragsrecht. Investment Banking II* (De Gruyter, 2016) 13 (para 8).

[77] For an analysis of the development of mandatory issuer disclosure in primary markets, see E Ferran, *Building an EU Securities Market* (CUP, 2004) 34 ff.

[78] E Härkönen, 'Crowdfunding and the Small Offering Exemption in European and US Prospectus Regulation: Striking a Balance Between Investor Protection and Access to Capital?' (2017) 14 *European Company and Financial Law Review* 121, 127.

[79] See, among others, HA Simon, 'Rational Choice and the Structure of the Environment' (1956) 63 *Psychological Review* 129; D Kahneman and A Tversky, 'Prospect Theory: An Analysis of Decision under Risk' (1979) 47 *Econometrica* 263; CR Sunstein, C Jolls and RH Thaler, 'A Behavioral Approach to Law and Economics' (1998) 50 *Stanford Law Review* 1471; RB Korobkin and TS Ulen, 'Law and Behavioral Science: Removing the Rationality Assumption from Law and Economics' (2000) 88 *California Law Review* 1051.

between the financing needs of young, innovative businesses on the one hand, and the protection of investors on the other. According to the view followed here, and in light of the principles set out in chapter two, such framework shall comprise two main strands: mandatory disclosure obligations tailored to the specificities and needs of the companies and investors participating in crowdfunding, as well as effective and proportionate measures specifically targeted at crowdfunding platforms and their activities.

i. Context-sensitive Mandatory Disclosure

The paradigm of 'more information is always better',[80] although a long-standing feature of primary market law and deeply rooted in legal scholarship as an effective means for protecting investors and supporting the efficient functioning of the market,[81] also entails significant transaction and compliance costs which weigh heavily on fund seekers. Especially as regards small-scale offerings, the costs of drawing up a standard prospectus can be disproportionately high in relation to the funds raised,[82] also with negative effects on SMEs' access to finance.[83] But still, despite these costs, mandating large amounts of information at this level has traditionally been considered a fundamental prerequisite for ensuring market efficiency since it allows sophisticated investors, who can and do process that information, to correctly determine the value of the offered securities.[84] Against this background, any effort to reduce the cost of capital raising on public markets has been weighed against institutional investors' interest in having access to as much information as possible.

However, as we saw earlier, within the framework of investment-based crowdfunding, where securities are offered directly to the public, there are usually no market mechanisms (eg, a book-building process) which could help retail investors identify the investment price on the basis of sophisticated investors' analysis of all publicly available information. Consequently, the strongest signal regarding the valuation of the fundraiser's business is the amount of capital collected by prior

[80] As better summarised by the Nestor of US capital markets law, Louis Loss: 'Disclosure, again disclosure, and still more disclosure', L Loss, *Securities Regulation Vol. 1*, 2nd edn (Wolters Kluwer, 1961) 21.

[81] See, among others, J Seligman, 'The Historical Need for a Mandatory Corporate Disclosure System' (1983) 9 *The Journal of Corporation Law* 1; JC Coffee Jr., 'Market Failure and the Economic Case for a Mandatory Disclosure System' (1984) 70 *Virginia Law Review*, 717; A Ferrell, 'The Case for Mandatory Disclosure in Securities Regulation Around the World' (2007) 2 *Brooklyn Journal of Corporate, Financial & Commercial Law* 81.

[82] Considering that the average cost for preparing a prospectus is EUR 700.000, see Commission, 'Impact assessment accompanying the Proposal for a Regulation on the prospectus to be published when securities are offered to the public or admitted to trading' SWD (2015) 255 final, 30 November 2015, 24.

[83] G Ferrarini and A Ottolia, 'Corporate Disclosure as a Transaction Cost: The Case of SMEs' (2013) 9 *European Review of Contract Law* 363, 365.

[84] See eg S Grundmann, *European Company Law*, 2nd edn (Intersentia, 2012) 484.

investors and their individual contributions. But again, these do not permit an accurate determination of the offering price, since they cannot reveal how many other investors found that the price does not correspond to the quality of the investment.[85] In this respect, for disclosure to be effective it must be designed with particular emphasis on the processing capacities of crowd-funders who, unlike professional investors, are beset by significant cognitive limitations and biases. From a policy-making perspective the following seem particularly relevant:[86] (a) they display a tendency towards inertia and procrastination, thus preferring ease and simplification to complexity; (b) their choices do not depend on the amount of the information provided but, crucially, on its content and presentation ('framing effect');[87] (c) they are influenced by the social environment and tend to copy the behaviour of their peers ('herd behaviour');[88] and (d) they focus on events that are readily available to them ('availability bias'),[89] thereby making inaccurate judgements. What these features suggest is that, in contrast to a typical public offering, the costs of requiring small-sized enterprises that are seeking to raise funds through crowdfunding to abide by extensive disclosure obligations would outweigh the potential benefits for investors. It follows, therefore, that behaviourally-driven disclosure rules are more appropriate in the crowdfunding context.

ii. Intervention Beyond Disclosure – The Focus on Platform Activity

Although indisputably desirable and useful within the crowdfunding context, a more structured disclosure approach, which puts greater emphasis on the cognitive and behavioural patterns of retail investors, is not sufficient on its own to ensure the integrity and development of this market. Indeed, as already explained, those who invest or seek finance through crowdfunding have no other choice than to do so via the intermediation of internet platforms. However, because of their indispensable role in the process and the excessive reliance placed on them by market participants, these platforms also pose significant risks, especially in terms of investor protection.[90] Such risks include, among others: the failure probability

[85] Armour and Enriques (n 29) 74.

[86] C Sunstein, 'Empirically Informed Regulation' (2011) 78 *University of Chicago Law Review* 1349, 1350–61; A Alemanno and AL Sibony, *Nudge and the law: A European perspective* (Hart Publishing, 2015) 3–5.

[87] A Tversky and D Kahneman, 'The Framing of Decisions and the Psychology of Choice' (1981) 211 *Science* 453.

[88] D Hirshleifer and SH Teoh, 'Herd Behaviour and Cascading in Capital Markets: a Review and Synthesis' (2003) 9 *European Financial Management* 25.

[89] A Tversky and D Kahneman, 'Availability: A Heuristic for Judging Frequency and Probability' (1973) 5 *Cognitive Psychology* 207, 221.

[90] See eg S Grundmann and W Kerber, 'Information Intermediaries and Party Autonomy – The Example of Securities and Insurance Markets' in S Grundmann, W Kerber and S Weatherhill (eds), *Party Autonomy and the Role of Information in the Internal Market* (De Gruyter, 2001) 277; V Colaert, 'Investor Protection in the Capital Markets Union' in D Busch, E Avgouleas and G Ferrarini (eds), *Capital Markets Union in Europe* (OUP, 2018) 352.

of the platform operator and its implications on the continuity of the services provided; the possible miscalculation from the side of investors of the level of due diligence conducted by the platform in respect of the reliability and prospects of project owners; or the potential misalignment of interests between the platform and investors, especially when the former participates in the investment or receives any remuneration from the project owner.[91]

Consequently, it becomes apparent that an effective regulatory regime on crowdfunding should appropriately address the issues that are related to the intermediation activity of platforms, without burdening them with disproportionate or unnecessary obligations. Such a scheme should comprise specific requirements and mechanisms which could at least: safeguard the operational continuity of the platform; ensure that investment opportunities will reach the appropriate investor group; protect the interests of crowd-funders both before and after the investment; and clarify the nature of the platform's responsibilities towards their clients, including their organisational and conduct-of-business requirements.[92]

D. Towards an EU Crowdfunding Regime – The Role of the CMU

Although the EU lags far behind other developed regions around the world in terms of both the number and volume of crowdfunding transactions,[93] this alternative financing method has been identified as being very important for the growth of start-ups, especially innovative ones,[94] and other SMEs at the beginning of the funding escalator. For such businesses, raising capital through more traditional funding channels can prove particularly challenging, considering, among other things, their relatively short track record and lack of collateral, their insufficient financial knowledge, and the prohibitively high costs associated with accessing public markets.[95] In this respect, by widening the range of financing options available to these companies, investment-based crowdfunding can contribute decisively to fill the funding gap at the early-stage of business growth.[96] It is no surprise, therefore, that enabling the development of this new source of funding across the EU while addressing key risks that may arise, notably for investors, has long been considered a necessary step towards a successful CMU.[97]

[91] ESMA (n 6) 11; SWD (2016) 154 final (n 14) 16.

[92] ESMA (n 6) 12.

[93] See T Ziegler, R Shneor and BZ Zhang, 'The Global Status of the Crowdfunding Industry' in R Shneor, L Zhao and BT Flåten (eds), *Advances in Crowdfunding* (Springer, 2020) 43–61.

[94] MA Stanko and DH Henard, 'Toward a Better Understanding of Crowdfunding, Openness and the Consequences for Innovation' (2017) 46 *Research Policy* 784, 785.

[95] Commission, 'Staff Working Document accompanying the Mid-Term Review of the Capital Markets Union Action Plan', SWD (2017) 224 final, 8 June 2017, 24–26.

[96] This stage is famously known as the 'valley of death', see DJ Cumming and S Johan, *Venture Capital and Private Equity Contracting: An International Perspective*, 2nd edn (Elsevier, 2014) 5.

[97] COM (2015) 468 final (n 5) 7; SWD (2016) 154 final (n 14) 4.

i. The Need for EU Action

As a basis for enabling crowdfunding to expand, while ensuring that risks are appropriately mitigated and investors are sufficiently protected, several EU countries introduced bespoke regulatory frameworks for crowdfunding activities over the last decade, with requirements for issuers, platform intermediaries, and investors. The start was made at the end of 2012, with Italy becoming the first Member State to establish a regulatory scheme specifically targeting investment-based crowdfunding.[98] Very soon, though, this initiative would find followers in other EU jurisdictions as well. For example, in October 2014, it was France's turn to put in place a special regulation which enabled companies to raise capital by offering financial securities (*titres financiers*) through crowdfunding (*financement participatif*).[99] In a similar vein, on 10 July 2015, the German Small Investor Protection Act (*Kleinanlegerschutzgesetz*) entered into force, laying down specific rules on business financing through the public offer of investments using dedicated internet platforms ('crowdinvesting').[100]

Overall, however, despite the regulatory actions taken at the Member State level, the EU market for investment-based crowdfunding has developed asymmetrically, with most transactions taking place in the Netherlands ($1,806 billion), Germany ($1,276 billion) and France ($935 million), which together accounted for more than 50 per cent of the total market volume in 2018 ($7,72 billion), followed by Italy ($532 million), Spain ($419 million) and Finland ($379 million).[101] At the same time, crowdfunding activity has remained heavily fragmented along national lines with only a small – albeit increasing – proportion of the actual volume being attributed to inward and outward funding flows.[102] There are two main reasons behind this. First, the diverging and usually conflicting regulatory standards imposed on investment-based platform operators under the respective national legislations created significant barriers to the cross-border scale-up of their activities.[103] Consequently, most crowdfunding platforms have remained concentrated in countries with larger and more established markets which can

[98] Legislative Decree no. 179 of 18 October 2012 (Decreto Sviluppo Bis), as implemented by CONSOB Regulation no. 18592 of 26 June 2013 (CONSOB Regulation).

[99] Ordinance 2014-559 of 30 May 2014 as specified by Decree no. 2014-1053 of 16 September 2014.

[100] For a comprehensive analysis of the German crowdfunding framework, see L Klöhn, L Hornuf and T Schilling, 'The Regulation of Crowdfunding in the German Small Investor Protection Act: Content, Consequences, Critique, Suggestions' (2016) 13 *European Company Law* 56.

[101] T Ziegler and R Shneor (eds), *The Global Alternative Finance Benchmarking Report* (Cambridge Centre for Alternative Finance, 2020). Note, however, that these figures also include other segments of alternative finance which are evolving rapidly in certain EU countries (eg balance sheet property lending in the Netherlands or invoice trading in Italy) but do not – at least directly – involve the offer of financial instruments to the public.

[102] T Ziegler et al, *Shifting Paradigms: The 4th European Alternative Finance Benchmarking Report* (Cambridge Centre for Alternative Finance, 2019) 50.

[103] For example, while crowdfunding platforms operating in Germany fall under the ambit of the Trade Regulation Act (GewO) and, hence, are only subject to some rudimentary organisational and conduct of business rules, if they choose to expand their business in the Italian market they would have to adhere to a set of onerous MiFID-mimicking conduct rules which create considerable compliance

better ensure their long-term sustainability.[104] Second, the dispersed nature of investor protection rules[105] generated unnecessary confusion for prospective investors which, if combined with the inherent uncertainty involved in investing in an unknown and risky market, has deterred them from channelling funds through crowdfunding, especially on a cross-border basis.[106] Considering these shortcomings, eliminating the major legal barriers obstructing cross-border crowdfunding development was considered an important step towards increasing the efficiency and diversification of EU capital markets and thereby completing the CMU.[107]

ii. Interinstitutional Negotiations

After a short waiting period, during which the focus was on the close monitoring of crowdfunding market developments[108] and the rise of SMEs' awareness of the potentials of this alternative source of finance,[109] the Commission proposed in March 2018, on the basis of Article 114 TFEU, a European crowdfunding legal framework[110] in an effort to react to the market fragmentation resulting from the divergent approaches taken by Member States. The proposed Regulation introduced the option for investment and lending-based crowdfunding platforms to apply for a single EU-wide authorisation. This empowered them to seamlessly passport their services across European borders in accordance with uniform and more proportionate, compared to MiFID II, regulatory requirements under ESMA's supervision.[111] This voluntary regime, which applied to crowdfunding offers not exceeding EUR 1 million per issuer each year, enabled those platforms opting for the EU label to scale up their operations throughout the Union, whilst leaving domestic legislations unchanged for those wishing to remain active at the national level only. As such, it also preserved some degree of regulatory competition to the benefit of local innovation and experimentation.[112]

costs, see E D'Ippolito, M Musitelli and A Sciarrone Alibrandi, 'Protecting Crowdfunders: Is a MiFID-Mimicking Approach Appropriate?' (2016) 13 *European Company Law* 27, 35.

[104] G Dushnitsky et al, 'Crowdfunding in Europe: Determinants of Platform Creation Across Countries' (2016) 58 *California Management Review* 44.

[105] Under the German Investment Act (VermAnlG), for example, the amount that retail investors may place with a single issuer is capped at EUR 25,000, whereas the corresponding threshold in Greece was set at EUR 10,000.

[106] European Crowdfunding Network and Osborne Clarke, *Identifying market and regulatory obstacles to cross-border development of crowdfunding in the EU*', Final Report (European Union, 2017) 33 ff.

[107] ibid 31.

[108] For the initiatives taken by the Commission services in this regard, see SWD (2016) 154 final (n 14) 6–7.

[109] Commission, 'Crowdfunding explained – A guide for small and medium enterprises on crowdfunding and how to use it', 27 April 2015.

[110] Commission, 'Proposal for a Regulation on European Crowdfunding Service Providers (ECSP) for Business', COM (2018) 113 final, 8 March 2018 (ECSPR Proposal).

[111] ibid recitals 14 and 25.

[112] SWD (2018) 56 final (n 12) 49.

Nevertheless, while the position adopted by the European Parliament at first reading maintained the optional character of the proposed regime,[113] the compromise text that was agreed between the Parliament and the Council provided for a single set of rules applying horizontally in EU crowdfunding services, for up to EUR 5 million. The authorisation and supervision of the service providers was also transferred from ESMA to the NCAs of the Member States.[114] On May 2020 and following some technical amendments, the European Parliament's Committee on Economic and Monetary Affairs (ECON) and the Permanent Representatives Committee approved this interinstitutional agreement, which would soon be reflected in the Council's position at first reading pursuant to Article 294 TFEU.[115]

iii. The Adoption of the ECSPR and its Objectives

With no leftovers or loose ends to tie up, the approval of the Council's position at first reading was only a matter of time. Thus, on 5 October 2020, the European Parliament adopted the final text of Regulation (EU) 2020/1503 on European Crowdfunding Service Providers for business (ECSPR),[116] along with some related amendments to MiFID II.[117] The ECSPR, which establishes uniform requirements for the authorisation, operation, organisation, and supervision of crowdfunding service providers (CSPs) as well as for the transparency and marketing communications in relation to the provision of crowdfunding services in the Union,[118] shall apply from 10 November 2021.[119] For reasons of legal certainty, however, a transitional period of one year (extendable once by one more year) is provided for, during which legal entities authorised under national law to provide crowdfunding services covered by the Regulation may continue to do so.[120] If, following the expiry of this period, the service provider has failed to adapt its business activities to the Regulation, it must cease all crowdfunding operations, except for those relating to the servicing of ongoing contracts.[121]

As an integral part of the Commission's strong commitment to completing the CMU,[122] the overarching objective of the ECSPR is to create a well-functioning single market for crowdfunding services which shall improve access to alternative

[113] European Parliament, 'Legislative resolution of 27 March 2019 on the proposal for a Regulation on European Crowdfunding Service Providers (ECSP) for Business', TA/2019/0301.

[114] European Parliament, 'EU rules to boost European crowdfunding platforms agreed' (19 December 2019), Press Release, www.europarl.europa.eu/news/en/press-room/.

[115] Council, 'Position at first reading with a view to the adoption of a Regulation on European crowdfunding service providers for business and amending Regulation (EU) 2017/1129 and Directive (EU) 2019/1937', 6800/1/20 REV 1, Brussels, 22 July 2020.

[116] OJ L347/1.

[117] Directive (EU) 2020/1504 of the European Parliament and of the Council amending Directive 2014/65/EU on markets in financial instruments [2020] OJL 347/50.

[118] Art 1(1) ECSPR.

[119] ibid Art 51.

[120] ibid Art 47 in conjunction with recital 76.

[121] ibid recital 77.

[122] COM (2018) 113 final (n 110) 2; SWD (2018) 56 final (n 12) 6.

finance for European SMEs, especially start-ups and other fast-growing companies, while increasing the possibility for efficient portfolio diversification for investors, especially retail ones.[123] In doing so, this regulatory initiative builds on two more specific objectives: first, enabling platforms to expand across national borders by laying down less burdensome requirements for the provision of crowdfunding services; and second, ensuring a high level of investor protection, by reducing operational risks at platform level while improving transparency as regards the project owner, the crowdfunding process and the investments offered.[124] In the following section, the measures put forward to achieve these goals will be further analysed.

III. Unfolding the EU Crowdfunding Regulation

If we were to break down the provisions of the ECSPR we would conclude that they can be divided into two main categories: the first one deals with the essential rules and conditions governing the provision of crowdfunding services within the internal market. These are mainly related to the applicable principles and procedures for the authorisation of crowdfunding platform operators as well as to the relevant actions for the effective supervision of their activities.[125] In addition, they comprise the organisational and operational requirements which CSPs must fulfil when carrying out their business, with a view to protecting the interests of their clients and securing the smooth functioning and growth of the market.[126] The second category addresses the complex and demanding issue of investor protection. It primarily consists of disclosure obligations which seek to ensure a high level of transparency while avoiding unnecessary costs for project owners. These are further complemented by certain 'Know Your Customer' rules which apply exclusively to non-sophisticated investors who, given their cognitive limitations and biases, are more likely to misjudge the risks associated with crowdfunding investments.[127] In the following text, these provisions will be discussed in further detail. But before that, the scope of application of this Regulation shall be defined.

A. Scope of Application

The establishment of a pan-European crowdfunding regime is beset with many challenges. These are associated not only with the diverging views and interests of the involved stakeholders, but also with the disruptive nature of this funding

[123] Recitals 6 and 7 ECSPR; SWD (2018) 56 final (n 12) 31.
[124] ibid.
[125] Chapters III, VI and VII ECSPR.
[126] ibid Chapter II.
[127] ibid Chapter IV.

tool which was developed in the shadow of the traditional financial legislation and largely in an effort to avoid the strict requirements imposed therein.[128] In this respect, the ECSPR builds on a more 'structural' approach,[129] whereby its scope of application is defined by reference to three determinative factors: (1) the activities performed; (2) the type and size of the investments offered; and (3) the services provided. On top of that, crowdfunding intermediaries falling under the scope of the Regulation are explicitly exempted from the application of the MiFID II regime.

i. The Crowdfunding Activities Covered

Under the ECSPR, crowdfunding is defined as a type of intermediation, whereby a legal entity, without taking on own risk, operates or manages a publicly accessible web-based information system (ie, a crowdfunding platform) which facilitates the matching of prospective investors or creditors with businesses seeking funding.[130] Such funding can be either in the form of an interest-bearing loan or another capital contribution in exchange for a transferable (equity or debt) financial instrument.[131] Accordingly, the scope of the Regulation encompasses both investment and lending-based crowdfunding, on the grounds that these models can be structured as comparable funding alternatives.[132] This is because they not only deal with the marketing of comparable – at least in economic terms – financial products, namely products embedding a future financial return,[133] but they also seem to pose similar risks, that are mainly associated with the highly dispersed nature of the fund providers which makes it rather challenging to exercise effective control over the project owner.[134]

It seems, therefore, that the EU crowdfunding regime's move towards a more cross-sectoral approach,[135] emphasises the core functions and processes performed

[128] E Macchiavello, 'Financial-return Crowdfunding and Regulatory Approaches in the Shadow Banking, FinTech and Collaborative Finance Era' (2017) 14 *European Company and Financial Law Review* 662, 667.

[129] On this approach, see J Armour et al, *Principles of Financial Regulation* (OUP, 2016) 505–29.

[130] Art 2(1)(a) and recital 1 ECSPR.

[131] As will be explained below, the transferability of the acquired instrument is an important safeguard for the protection of investors who participate in crowdfunding projects.

[132] Recital 1 ECSPR.

[133] G Ferrarini and E Macchiavello, 'Investment-based Crowdfunding: Is MiFID II Enough?' in D Busch and G Ferrarini (eds), *Regulation of the EU Financial System: MiFID II and MiFIR* (OUP, 2017) 659; G Ferrarini and E Macchiavello, 'Fintech and Alternative Finance in the CMU – The Regulation of Marketplace Investing' in Busch, Avgouleas and Ferrarini (n 90) 213; E Macchiavello, 'The European Crowdfunding Service Providers Regulation and the Future of Marketplace Lending and Investing in Europe: The "Crowdfunding Nature" Dilemma' (2021) 32 *European Business Law Review* 557.

[134] Besides, according to EU policy makers, the provision of a loan with a dispersed lending structure practically does not differ from investments in financial instruments, see SWD (2018) 56 (n 12) 45 and 47.

[135] For the role of cross-sectoral aspects in the regulation of Fintech more generally, see E Macchiavello, 'FinTech Regulation from a Cross-Sectoral Perspective' in V Colaert, D Busch and T Incalza (eds), *European Financial Regulation: Levelling the Cross-sectoral Playing Field* (Hart Publishing, 2019) 63–85.

by the platforms, which, even in the case of loan agreements, are thought to be closer to those of financial intermediaries in capital markets.[136] This choice to disregard the typical – at least among national regimes[137] – distinction between the investment and lending business models, albeit not immune to criticism,[138] does not imply, however, the uniform application of all provisions to both activities. In fact, as will become apparent, in certain cases, the Regulation provides for some degree of differentiation, with lending-based crowdfunding being subject to more detailed and stringent rules, especially when more complex services are involved.[139]

ii. Type and Size of Crowdfunding Offers

In any case, the effective scope of the ECSP Regulation and, by extension, its cross-sectoral and cross-border application, remains limited, especially when compared to the scope of national bespoke regimes, considering the restrictions in the type and size of the products which can be offered through pan-European crowdfunding platforms.

More specifically, in relation to lending-based crowdfunding, the Regulation applies exclusively to business loan agreements ('peer-to-peer business lending'),[140] whereby an investor makes available to the project owner a fixed amount of money for an agreed period of time in return for the unconditional repayment of that amount, together with the accrued interest, according to an instalment payment schedule.[141] On the contrary, consumer loans ('peer-to-peer consumer lending')[142] do not fall within the ambit of the Regulation,[143] given that they are reserved for natural persons in need of capital for the financing of personal, family or household expenditures. As such they are unfit for businesses seeking growth capital, while they are already partly covered by existing EU legislation, namely the Consumer Credit Directive (CCD)[144] and the Mortgage Credit

[136] Macchiavello (n 133) 581.

[137] For an overview, see European Crowdfunding Network, 'Review of Crowdfunding Regulation 2017: Interpretations of existing regulation concerning crowdfunding in Europe, North America and Israel' (2017).

[138] In fact, as will be discussed in further detail below, this choice raises important questions with regard to the coherence and effectiveness of the regime.

[139] While the focus of this chapter is on investment-based crowdfunding, some references to those provisions that particularly target activities related to lending dealings are deemed necessary not only for the sake of completeness but mainly in order to help understand whether the choice to encompass both business models under the same regime is appropriate.

[140] For this term, see R Shneor, 'Crowdfunding Models, Strategies, and Choices Between Them' in Shneor, Zhao and Flåten (n 93) 24; Y Pierrakis, 'Peer-to-peer Lending to Businesses: Investors' Characteristics, Investment Criteria and Motivation' (2019) 20 *The International Journal of Entrepreneurship and Innovation* 239.

[141] Art 2(1)(b) ECSPR.

[142] Shneor (n 140) 24 and 31.

[143] Art 1(2)(a) ECSPR.

[144] Directive 2008/48/EC of the European Parliament and of the Council on credit agreements for consumers and repealing Council Directive 87/102/EEC [2008] OJ L133/66. Note that the CCD will be repealed by Directive (EU) 2023/2225 as of 20 November 2026.

Directive (MCD).[145] Nonetheless, it should be kept in mind that these Directives and their protective provisions are principally confined to credit agreements between consumers and professional creditors.[146] Therefore, in order to apply in the context of peer-to-peer consumer lending, where the creditors are usually individuals acting outside the course of their business or profession, the platform shall either be a creditor itself or act as a credit intermediary as defined in Articles 3(f) and 4(5) of the CCD and MCD respectively.[147]

With regard to investment-based crowdfunding, the principal consideration for EU regulators was to limit the illiquidity risks inherent in investing in unlisted or poorly capitalised firms, like those typically seeking finance through crowdfunding.[148] This was all the more necessary given that the lack of exit opportunities is generally perceived as one of the most important risks for crowdfunding investors,[149] thereby negatively affecting the development of a deep and efficient crowdfunding market in the EU.[150] Against this background, and with a view to ensuring a potentially easy exit for investors, the Regulation covers and permits crowdfunding offers related mainly to transferable securities as defined in Article 4(1)(44) of MiFID II,[151] since the latter are freely negotiable and can be easily disposed on the capital markets.[152] Nonetheless, considering the significant differences among Member States in identifying transferable securities, such a limitation would imply that certain private limited liability companies whose shares do not, according to the applicable national law, constitute 'securities' within the meaning of MiFID II, would in fact be deprived of this important source of finance even when such instruments are not subject to any restrictions preventing them from being transferred.[153] In order to counteract this problem, the scope of the regime is further extended to include such 'admitted instruments'[154] though without affecting the national requirements governing their transferability, such as the authentication of the transfer by a notary.[155] On the contrary, other financial

[145] Directive 2014/17/EU of the European Parliament and of the Council on credit agreements for consumers relating to residential immovable property and amending Directives 2008/48/EC and 2013/36/EU and Regulation (EU) No 1093/2010 [2014] OJ L 60/34.

[146] Arts 2(1) and 3(c) CCD and Arts 3(1) and 4(2) MCD. Nevertheless, national regulators may extend the scope of these Directives to include credit agreements between consumers and non-professional creditors, thus also covering P2P consumer lending. This is the case, for example, with the Danish Credit Agreement Act, which permits such agreements provided that the loan is concluded or disseminated by a professional entity which acts on behalf of the lender, see T Jørgensen, 'Peer to Peer Lending in Denmark' (2016) 4 *Journal of European Consumer and Market Law* 185.

[147] SWD (2018) 56 final (n 12) 112–13; A Sciarrone Alibrandi et al, *Marketplace lending: Verso nuove forme di intermediazione finanziaria?* (CONSOB Quaderni FinTech, luglio, 2019) 144. See also recital 22 of Directive (EU) 2023/2225 of the European Parliament and of the Council on credit agreements for consumers and repealing Directive 2008/48/EC [2023] OJ L67/1.

[148] Chapman (n 38) 53.

[149] SWD (2016) 154 final (n 14) 16.

[150] SWD (2018) 56 final (n 12) 30.

[151] Art 2(1)(m) ECSPR.

[152] ibid recital 13.

[153] ibid.

[154] ibid Art 2(1)(n).

[155] ibid recital 14.

instruments within the meaning of Article 4(1)(15) of MiFID II – including security tokens that qualify as such[156] – or investments offered by corporations under national law, are not covered by this Regulation.

As regards, finally, the size of the crowdfunding offerings, the threshold is set at EUR 5 million per project owner. This shall be calculated over a period of 12 months as the sum total of the value of the financial instruments placed and loans granted through pan-European[157] crowdfunding platforms, and – where applicable – the total consideration of the public offers of securities made based on an exemption from the prospectus publication requirement under Articles 1(3) or 3(2) of the Prospectus Regulation.[158] This threshold, which constitutes a compromise between the initial proposal of the Commission[159] and the position of the Parliament,[160] is supposed to correspond to a monetary amount below which no prospectus is required under the national law of most Member States[161] and reflects an attempt to strike a right balance between the support of young businesses in need of finance and the adequate protection of investors.[162] At the same time, however, in view of the fact that in implementing the Prospectus Regulation some Member States still required a prospectus for offers below EUR 5 million[163] and in an effort to reduce the risk of regulatory arbitrage, while providing those countries with the necessary time to adjust their national law to the single threshold,[164] the ECSP Regulation provided for a temporary derogation

[156] Security tokens are types of crypto-assets, which are digital representations of value or rights, which may be transferred, stored or traded electronically, using distributed ledger or similar technology. They are generally issued by entities for purposes of: (a) capital raising (eg, through an Initial Coin Offering), (b) the tokenisation of ownership rights; or (c) profit sharing, see C Brown, T Dolan and K Butler, 'Cryptoassets and Initial Coin Offerings' in Madir (n 38) 77. However, as discussed below, security tokens may, under certain conditions, qualify as transferable securities, raising questions about their regulatory treatment under the ECSPR.

[157] For the purpose of calculating the EUR 5 million threshold under the ECSPR, therefore, project owners shall consider the total amount of crowdfunding offers to investors, regardless of whether they have taken place though investment- or lending-based crowdfunding platforms, see also M Hobza and A Vondráčková, 'The New Financial Crowdfunding Regulation and Its Implications for Investment Services under MiFID II', Prague Law Working Papers Series, No. 2020/III/2, ssrn.com/abstract=3725997.

[158] Art 1(2)(c)(i) and (ii) ECSPR.

[159] Under the Commission's proposal the threshold for each crowdfunding offer was limited to EUR 1 million per project owner, reflecting the threshold for the mandatory publication of a prospectus as initially set out in Art 1(3) of the Prospectus Regulation, Art 2(2)(d) and recital 12 ECSPR Proposal.

[160] The Parliament had instead proposed the rise of the maximum threshold to EUR 8 million per project owner, which was the maximum optional exemption under Art 3(2) of the Prospectus Regulation as applicable at that time, while explicitly excluding crowdfunding offers from its scope, European Parliament (n 113) Arts 2(2)(d) and 38(a).

[161] However, this threshold does not appear in line with the most recent data published by ESMA, according to which 14 Member States have set the prospectus publication threshold at EUR 8 million, see ESMA, 'National thresholds below which the obligation to publish a prospectus does not apply' 3 July 2023, www.esma.europa.eu/document/list-prospectus-thresholds.

[162] Recital 16 ECSPR. See also Macchiavello (n 133) 569.

[163] This is the case with 6 countries, namely Czech Republic, Hungary, Poland, Romania, Slovakia, and Sweden, ESMA, *National thresholds* (n 161) 2 ff.

[164] Recital 17 ECSPR.

of maximum 24 months following its application, during which Member States could maintain such lower thresholds even in the case of crowdfunding offers falling within its scope.[165]

iii. The Range of Permitted Services

a. Principal Services

As already described above, due to the fragmented regulatory environment, there have been significant discrepancies between Member States in terms of the specific services provided by crowdfunding platforms and, hence, the applicable legal rules.[166] Against this background, the ECSPR seeks to bring consistency and clarity to the issue, by limiting its application to certain services which are considered 'typical'[167] of the business models covered and which distinguish crowdfunding as a 'direct' funding activity.[168]

More specifically, with respect to lending-based crowdfunding, the principal service to be performed by the platform consists of the 'facilitation of granting of loans'.[169] Although the Regulation does not include an explicit definition of such service, recital 11 clearly stipulates that it should encompass various different functions which enable the conclusion of a loan agreement between investors and project owners without the platform at any point acting as a creditor, such as the presentation of projects to investors, the pricing of crowdfunding offers or the assessment of the credit risk of project owners.[170] In this respect, the role of the platform in the framework of lending-based crowdfunding is merely facilitative and shall be distinguished from the business of a credit institution, as defined in Article 4(1)(1) of the CRR,[171] which grants loans on its own account and takes deposits or other repayable funds from the public.[172] Consequently, Member States shall not require any authorisation as a credit institution for crowdfunding platforms – let alone for project owners or investors – which, in the framework of a loan agreement facilitated by the platform, accept funds or grant loans.[173]

[165] ibid Art 49.

[166] ESMA, 'Advice on investment-based crowdfunding, ESMA/2014/1560, 18 December 2014, 5; European Banking Authority (EBA), 'Opinion on lending-based crowdfunding', 26 February 2015, 10–11; SWD (2016) 154 final (n 14) Annex 2.

[167] ESMA, *Opinion on Investment-based crowdfunding* (n 6) 7–8; Hobza and Vondráčková (n 157) 11.

[168] Recital 22 ECSPR; Macchiavello (n 133) 572.

[169] Art 2(1)(a)(i) ECSPR.

[170] SN Hooghiemstra, 'The European Crowdfunding Regulation – Towards Harmonization of (Equity- and Lending-Based) Crowdfunding in Europe?', at 3, ssrn.com/abstract=3679142 Macchiavello (n 133) 570.

[171] Regulation (EU) No 575/2013 of the European Parliament and of the Council on prudential requirements for credit institutions and investment firms [2013] OJ L176/1 as amended by Regulation (EU) 2019/876 [2019] OJ L150/1 (CRR II).

[172] Recital 11 ECSPR.

[173] ibid Art 1(3) and recital 9. The explicit exemption of project owners and investors from the authorisation requirement pertaining to credit institutions was considered necessary in view of the fact that in implementing the CRD and particularly Art 9(1) thereof, some Member States require a stand-alone

With regard to investment-based crowdfunding, the main services offered by platform operators under the ECSPR involve the 'reception and transmission of client orders' in relation to transferable securities or admitted instruments for crowdfunding purposes and the 'placing without a firm commitment basis' of such instruments, as provided for in points 1 and 7 of Section A of Annex I to MiFID II respectively.[174] In this sense, the reception and transmission of client orders covers the reception of a purchase order from an investor and the immediate transmission of this order to the project owner or – where applicable – another third-party intermediary for execution.[175] Whereas the placing without a firm commitment basis comprises the act of finding investors on behalf of the project owner without any commitment to take up some or all of the financial instruments which were not placed.[176] However, the role of crowdfunding platforms as two-sided markets[177] which bring together the supply and demand sides of risk capital[178] implies that, contrary to typical financial intermediaries, they act as agents not only to prospective investors but for project owners as well. For this reason, the Regulation clarifies that in the framework of investment-based crowdfunding, the two services which form the basis of the platform's activity shall be offered jointly.[179]

b. Ancillary Services

In view of the variety of business models which could be observed under the national crowdfunding regimes, one of the key issues that arose during the intense inter-institutional negotiations following the Commission's initial proposal was the expansion of the range of permissible services. Indeed, while the Parliament was more open to the demands of the industry, the Council insisted that the EU regime should be restricted to mainstream business models, even at the expense of flexibility.[180] In this context, the final text of the Regulation largely reflects a compromise between these diverging views, since it enables platforms to provide some ancillary crowdfunding services, though it explicitly differentiates them from regulated activities reserved – principally under MiFID II – for other market operators.

banking licence for market players which grant loans and accept repayable funds from the public, see Hooghiemstra (n 170) 9.

[174] Art 2(1)(a)(ii) ECSPR.

[175] ESMA (n 6) 16; SWD (2018) 56 final (n 12) 102.

[176] See FCA, 'Perimeter Guidance Manual, 'Section 13.3: Investment Services and Activities, Q22', (1 January 2021) www.handbook.fca.org.uk/handbook; SWD (2018) 56 final (n 12) 102.

[177] J Viotto Da Cruz, 'Competition and Regulation of Crowdfunding Platforms: A Two-sided Market Approach' (2015) 99 *Communications and Strategies* 33, 38.

[178] D Zetzsche and C Preiner, 'Cross-Border Crowdfunding: Towards a Single Crowdlending and Crowdinvesting Market for Europe' (2018) 19 *European Business Organization Law Review* 217, 237.

[179] Recital 10 ECSPR.

[180] Macchiavello (n 133) 573.

More specifically, CSPs are permitted to suggest to individual investors specific projects on the basis of one or more parameters or risk indicators (filters) which have been communicated by their clients in advance.[181] The provision of such filtering tools shall, nonetheless, be distinguished from the service of investment advice under Art 4(1)(4) MiFID II, provided they present investment offers in a neutral manner which does not constitute a personal recommendation.[182] This would be the case especially when those tools display results based on criteria relating to purely objective product features, such as pre-defined project features, including the type or sector of business activity, the instrument used, the interest rate, or the risk category, as well as key financial figures calculated without any scope of discretion.[183] Therefore, in deciding whether an investment proposal based on filtering tools constitutes an investment advice, a case-by-case assessment is necessary.[184] In any event, where investors wish to make an investment in one of the suggested crowdfunding projects, they shall review and expressly take an investment decision in relation to each individual crowdfunding offering.[185] In that regard, crowdfunding platforms providing this service on transferable securities or other admitted instruments do not exercise discretion on behalf of their investors and, hence, the authorisation obtained under the ECSPR does not grant them the right to provide portfolio management services, as defined in Article 4(1)(8) MiFID II.[186] Especially within the context of lending-based crowdfunding, however, CSPs may also offer the service of 'individual portfolio management of loans'. In this case they may exercise discretion on behalf of investors by allocating (also through automated processes or 'auto-bids') a predetermined amount of funds to one or multiple loans advertised on their platforms that correspond to previously agreed parameters, without requiring clients to review and take an investment decision in relation to each individual crowdfunding offer.[187]

Moreover, given the often illiquid or indivisible nature of the assets which are offered through crowdfunding, platforms are allowed to utilise a special purpose vehicle (SPV) which legally interposes itself between the counterparties, by acquiring the illiquid or indivisible asset from the project owner, which is then securitised and sold to investors.[188] To avoid creating regulatory arbitrage opportunities for

[181] Art 3(4) and recital 19 ECSPR.
[182] FCA (n 176) Q18.
[183] Recital 21 ECSPR.
[184] Such assessment shall focus on the recommendation's format, see Case C-604/11 *Genil 48 SL, Comercial Hostelera de Grandes Vinos SL v Bankinter SA, Banco Bilbao Vizcaya Argentaria SA* ECLI:EU:C:2013:344, para 53.
[185] Art 3(4) and recital 19 ECSPR.
[186] ibid recital 19.
[187] ibid Art 3(4) and (5) in conjunction with recital 20.
[188] Art 2(1)(q) ECSPR in conjunction with Article 1(2) Regulation (EU) 1075/2013 of the European Parliament and of the Council concerning statistics on the assets and liabilities of financial vehicle corporations engaged in securitisation transactions [2013] OJ L297/107.

asset managers, the Regulation poses strict limitations on the use of SPVs for the provision of crowdfunding services. In this respect, only one asset may be offered through an SPV, including the financial or legal structures which are partially or fully owned or controlled by it, and strictly on a non-discretionary basis, with the ultimate decision to take exposure to that asset lying exclusively with investors.[189]

Finally, CSPs can set up and operate a 'bulletin board', that is an electronic communication system which merely allows clients who have made investments through their platforms to advertise their interest in buying or selling products which have been originally offered through them.[190] However, the Regulation makes it explicit that a board should not bring together multiple third-party buying and selling interests in a way that results in a contract in relation to the advertised products.[191] Consequently, crowdfunding platforms operating a bulletin board shall not provide an internal matching system that executes client orders,[192] unless, as will be explained below, they have been granted a relevant authorisation under MiFID II.

c. Other Non-reserved Services

Such a strict delineation of crowdfunding services, as the one described above, would imply that platforms wishing to provide a broader – and possibly more complex – range of services to their clients, would be left outside the scope of the Regulation, to the detriment of the intended development of a pan-European crowdfunding market. Against this background, crowdfunding service providers are explicitly allowed to engage in activities which are not covered by this Regulation, as long as they comply with the relevant requirements applicable under EU or national law.[193] In this regard, a crowdfunding platform may, within the framework of its core business, provide parallel services which are typically reserved to other financial service providers, namely credit institutions, investment firms, payment institutions and electronic money institutions, provided that it is authorised in accordance with CRD,[194] MiFID II, PSD II[195] or EMD[196]

[189] Art 3(6) ECSPR.

[190] ibid Art 25(1) and recital 55.

[191] ibid Art 25(2) and recital 55.

[192] Bulletin boards under this Regulation should, therefore, be 'passive' in the sense that they should not allow clients to contact each other by means of the platform's protocols or internal operating procedures, Committee of European Securities Regulators (CESR), 'Standards for Alternative Trading Systems', July 2002, 5.

[193] Art 12(13) and recital 38 ECSPR.

[194] Directive 2013/36/EU of the European Parliament and of the Council on access to the activity of credit institutions and the prudential supervision of credit institutions and investment firms [2013] OJ L176/338 as amended and in force.

[195] Directive (EU) 2015/2366 of 25 November 2015 on payment services in the internal market [2015] OJ L337/35.

[196] Directive 2009/110/EC of the European Parliament and of the Council on the taking up, pursuit and prudential supervision of the business of electronic money institutions [2009] OJ L67/7.

respectively. Provided that these conditions are fulfilled, a crowdfunding platform may, therefore, accept deposits or other repayable funds from the public,[197] perform safekeeping and payment services,[198] operate a trading facility[199] and in general provide its clients with all the services that fall within the scope of any of the aforementioned Directives.

d. The Exemption of CSPs from the Scope of MiFID II

At a general level and considering the range of products and services covered by the ECSPR, it appears that the intermediation activities of crowdfunding platforms are comparable – at least in the investment model – with those provided by investment firms under MiFID II.[200] Therefore, following the principle of 'same activity creating the same risks should be regulated by the same rules', which characterises the EU approach on the FinTech regulation with a view to ensuring a level playing field between incumbents and new market entrants,[201] it could be argued that CSPs should not be treated any differently than traditional investment intermediaries. However, despite some obvious similarities, there are also substantial reasons justifying the application of a differentiated regulatory framework.

More specifically, with regard to authorisation procedures, although a MiFID II-licensed platform would be able to passport its services across the EU, Member States would still be able to impose additional requirements for investor protection, thus negatively affecting cross-border market activity.[202] Moreover, in light of the original concept of crowdfunding as an alternative financing method which seeks to fill the funding gap of early-stage start-ups by providing them access to a large pool of – typically – retail investors, it naturally follows that burdening crowdfunding platforms with the organisational, operational and disclosure requirements that govern the activities of large incumbents would impose a disproportionate burden, thereby stifling the development of the market.[203] Besides, the small amounts of money involved in each project combined with the fact that, despite showing a rising trend, EU crowdfunding volumes have been relatively modest,[204] implies that the risks that this activity poses to investors and the financial system

[197] Recital 9 ECSPR.
[198] ibid Art 10.
[199] ibid recital 55.
[200] Ferrarini and Macchiavello (n 133) 668 ff.
[201] See Expert Group on Regulatory Obstacles to Financial Innovation (ROFIEG), '30 Recommendations on Regulation, Innovation and Finance' Final Report to the European Commission, December 2019, p. 67 ff.
[202] SWD (2018) 56 final (n 12) 44–45.
[203] ibid 45; see also Commission, Proposal for a Directive amending Directive 2014/65/EU on markets in financial instruments, COM (2018) 99 final, 8 March 2018, 3.
[204] In 2018, the amount raised at the EU level (excluding UK) using equity crowdfunding was only USD 278 million, source: Statista, 'Equity-based crowdfunding transaction value in Europe (excluding the UK) from 2013 to 2018 (in USD)' (9 November 2020) www.statista.com/statistics/.

more generally are not comparable to those of financial institutions that manage huge investments.[205]

In view of the above and with the aim of enhancing legal certainty, while ensuring that the same activity is not subject to multiple authorisations within the Union,[206] CSPs are expressly excluded from the scope of MiFID II.[207] In other words, legal persons wishing to provide crowdfunding services covered by the ECSPR shall not adhere to the requirements set out in MiFID II or any of the national bespoke regimes, except when the total consideration of the crowdfunding offer exceeds the threshold value for the application of the Regulation, which, as already mentioned, is set at EUR 5 million.[208]

B. Rules and Conditions for the Provision of Crowdfunding Services

Developing a Union-wide crowdfunding market of sufficient scale requires a comprehensive strategy for removing obstacles to the smooth functioning of the internal market in crowdfunding services.[209] In this respect, one of the main concerns of the ECSPR has been the establishment of a uniform, proportionate and effective framework for the authorisation, organisation, operation and supervision of CSPs, in an effort to foster cross-border activity, reduce operational risks, and ensure a high degree of transparency and investor protection.

i. The ECSPR Authorisation System

a. Getting Authorised – Requirements and Procedure

The provision of crowdfunding services under the ECSPR is reserved solely to legal persons that are established in the Union,[210] subject to prior authorisation in accordance with the standards and procedures laid down in Article 12 therein,[211]

[205] E Kirby and S Worner, 'Crowd-funding: An Infant Industry Growing Fast' IOSCO Staff Working Paper No 3/2014, 32 ff., noting, however, the possibility of future systemic challenges arising from the increasing interconnectedness of crowdfunding with the broader financial sector.

[206] Recital 3 Directive (EU) 2020/1504.

[207] Art 2(1)(q) MiFID II as inserted by Art 1 of Directive (EU) 2020/1504.

[208] Hobza and Vondráčková (n 157) 10–11; Hooghiemstra (n 170) 10.

[209] Recital 7 ECSPR.

[210] For the time being, the Regulation does not allow access to the ECSP regime to platform operators established in third countries, including the UK, though according to Art 45(2)(g) of the Regulation this will be further assessed in the future. For these entities to be able to provide their services in the EU, therefore, they must obtain the relevant authorisation through the establishment of a subsidiary company or any other stable and effective organisation with legal personality in one of the Member States, see Macchiavello (n 133) 579–80.

[211] Art 3(1) ECSPR.

as well as in Delegated Regulation (EU) 2022/2112.[212] In particular, pursuant to these provisions, the authorisation process begins with the submission of a standard application form[213] by the prospective crowdfunding service provider to the designated contact point of the competent authority of the Member State where it is established.[214] The application shall contain all the information and documentation necessary to enable the competent authority to assess compliance with the organisational, conduct of business and prudential requirements set out in the Regulation.[215] This also includes the good repute and the sufficient competence and expertise of the management, taking into consideration the nature, scale, and complexity of the planned crowdfunding services.[216]

Once the application has been received, the competent authority has a maximum of 10 working days to notify in writing the prospective CSP thereof and communicate the contact details of the persons who will handle the authorisation request.[217] During that period and no later than 25 working days following receipt of the application, the NCA shall also assess the completeness of the information that has been presented and, if necessary, set a specific deadline for the submission of any missing documents.[218] Where the competent authority concludes that, even after expiry of the said deadline, the application is incomplete, it may refuse to review the application and return the submitted documents to the applicant.[219] In all other cases, the competent authority shall, at the latest within three months from the date of receipt of the complete application,[220] conclude its assessment

[212] Commission Delegated Regulation (EU) 2022/2112 of the European Parliament and of the Council supplementing Regulation (EU) 1503/2020 with regard to regulatory technical standards specifying requirements and arrangements for the application for authorisation as a crowdfunding service provider [2022] OJ L287/5.

[213] This is set out in the Annex to Delegated Regulation (EU) 2022/2112.

[214] Art 12(1) ECSPR and Art 1 Delegated Regulation (EU) 2022/2112. Although the notion of 'establishment' is not defined in the legislative text, recital 31 clarifies that it essentially implies the effective and real exercise of activities through stable arrangements. It seems, therefore, that the ECSPR marks a shift of emphasis away from a formalistic approach, whereby a crowdfunding provider is considered to be 'established' solely in the place where it is registered, towards a more flexible approach which takes account of the specific nature of the services concerned, particularly the fact that they are offered exclusively through the internet. In this respect, and in light of the objectives pursued by the Regulation, it could be argued that even the presence of a subsidiary with a legal personality could suffice to create an establishment in the Union, as long as this entity operates with a sufficient degree of stability through the presence of the equipment which is necessary for the provision of the specific services concerned in the Member State, see also Case C-131/12 *Google Spain SL and Google Inc. v Agencia Española de Protección de Datos (AEPD) and Mario Costeja González* ECLI:EU:C:2014:317 and Case C-230/14 *Weltimmo s.r.o. v Nemzeti Adatvédelmi és Információszabadság Hatóság* ECLI:EU:C:2015:639.

[215] Art 12(2) and recital 34 ECSPR.

[216] Ibid Art 12 (3) and (8) and recital 32.

[217] Art 3 Delegated Regulation (EU) 2022/2112.

[218] Art 12(4) ECSPR. In case that the NCA requires the prospective crowdfunding provider to provide missing information, the time limit for the assessment of the completeness of the application shall be suspended until the date such information is received, Art 4 Delegated Regulation (EU) 2022/2112.

[219] Art 12(5) ECSPR.

[220] Where prospective CSPs notify the competent authority of any changes to the information provided in the application for authorisation which may affect the procedure of authorisation, the 3-month time

as to whether the requirements prescribed in the Regulation are fulfilled and adopt, where applicable after consulting the competent authority of another Member State,[221] a fully reasoned decision whether or not to grant the requested authorisation.[222] The relevant decision shall be notified to the prospective CSP within three working days from the date it was taken,[223] while all granted authorisations shall be reported to ESMA which shall keep an updated register to that effect.[224]

The authorisation duty of the competent authorities is ongoing, in the sense that they should ensure that a CSP authorised in their territory meets at all times the conditions for its initial authorisation.[225] At the same time, though, in order to avoid disproportionate administrative burdens, where the applicant is already authorised as a credit institution, an investment firm, a payment institution or an electronic money institution, or it already operates a crowdfunding platform under national law, competent authorities should not require the submission of documents or proof that are already at their disposal.[226] For the same reason, where a prospective crowdfunding service provider also intends, within the framework of its activity, to provide payment services, the information which is common to both applications shall only be submitted to the NCA once.[227] Finally, it should be noted that, with a view to facilitating cross-border provision of crowdfunding services and thereby allowing EU start-ups to reach a broader investor base across the Union, Member States should not be allowed to impose additional requirements on those CSPs that are seeking authorisation under this Regulation.[228]

b. Scope of Authorisation and the 'EU Passport'

Granting an authorisation in accordance with the rules and conditions described above, affords crowdfunding service providers the opportunity to benefit from a single passport, valid throughout the EU, allowing them to offer their services in any of the Member States, without further constraints or formalities, such as the

limit shall start to run from the date on which the competent authority receives that updated information, Art 5 Delegated Regulation (EU) 2022/2112.

[221] According to Art 12(7) ECSPR, this should be the case when the prospective crowdfunding service provider is a subsidiary of a crowdfunding service provider authorised in that other Member State or they are both controlled by the same natural or legal persons.

[222] Art 12(8) provides that a competent authority may, for example, refuse authorisation if there are objective and verifiable reasons to believe that the governing body of the prospective crowdfunding service provider could pose a threat to its effective, sound, and prudent management and business continuity, and to the adequate consideration of the interest of its clients and the integrity of the market.

[223] Art 12(10) ECSPR.

[224] ibid Arts 12(9) and 14. ESMA may also request information in order to ensure that NCAs grant authorisations in a consistent manner.

[225] ibid Art 12(11).

[226] ibid Art 12(14) and recital 35.

[227] ibid Art 12(15).

[228] ibid recital 33.

obligation to have a physical presence in their territory.[229] As a matter of fact, a crowdfunding platform operator that intends to expand its activity across national borders simply needs to inform the competent authority that granted the initial authorisation, accordingly, stating the countries in which the crowdfunding services are planned to be performed; the identity of the responsible natural or legal persons; the expected starting date of the activity; and – if applicable – any other provided activities which are not covered by the Regulation.[230] Within a period of 10 working days following the receipt of that information, the authorising authority shall communicate it to the competent authorities of the host Member States and ESMA, notifying the crowdfunding service provider thereof without delay.[231] The latter may start to provide its services in the selected Member States immediately after this communication, and in any case no later than 15 calendar days after the initial submission of the relevant information to the home NCA.[232] The passport is available only in respect of the crowdfunding services which the platform is allowed to provide and which shall be clearly specified in the authorisation.[233] As a result, a crowdfunding service provider seeking to extend the scope of its cross-border operations, shall first submit a request for extension of its authorisation by complementing and updating the information provided in the initial application.[234]

c. Withdrawal of Authorisation

The ECSPR authorisation system extends beyond establishing the common rules and procedures for the award of an authorisation to also including the terms for its withdrawal. Therefore, according to the relevant provisions, an authorisation under this Regulation should be withdrawn where the crowdfunding service provider in question has not made use of the authorisation within 18 months, has expressly denounced the authorisation, or has not provided any services for nine consecutive months, provided that it is no longer involved in the administration of any existing contracts which took place through the use of the platform.[235] Withdrawal is further possible where the authorisation has been obtained by irregular means, including making false statements, where the conditions under which the authorisation was granted are no longer met and, of course, as a disciplinary measure, where the CSP has seriously infringed the Regulation.[236] Finally, home NCAs are also entitled to withdraw an authorisation whenever a crowdfunding service

[229] According to Art 12(12) ECSPR, CSPs that provide their services on a cross-border basis should only have an effective and stable establishment in the country of their authorisation.
[230] ibid Art 18(1).
[231] ibid Art 18(2) and (3).
[232] ibid Art 18(4).
[233] ibid Art 13(1).
[234] ibid Art 13(2).
[235] ibid Art 17(1)(a), (b) and (c).
[236] ibid Art 17(1)(d), (e) and (f).

provider, or a third party acting on its behalf, has lost its authorisation allowing for the provision of payment or investment services under PSD II or MiFID II, or whenever a platform operator that is also a payment service provider, or its managers, employees or a third party acting on its behalf, has infringed national law implementing Directive (EU) 2015/849 in respect of money laundering or terrorist financing.[237] Where the competent authority which granted the authorisation ultimately decides – following, where applicable, consultation with the competent authority of another Member State[238] – to proceed with the withdrawal, it shall notify that decision to the competent authorities of the host Member States, as well as ESMA which shall update the relevant register accordingly.[239]

ii. Conduct of Business Obligations

The provision of crowdfunding services under the ECSPR is firmly anchored on the overarching principle, which is generally applicable to all financial intermediaries,[240] that platform operators shall act 'honestly, fairly and professionally in accordance with the best interests of their clients'.[241] In general, this core fiduciary duty (or duty of care) could be considered, by itself, an effective, catch-all mechanism for controlling the behaviour of CSPs, for preventing the risks posed by their activities, and for proactively rebalancing the asymmetry of bargaining power between them and their counterparties.[242] For reasons of legal clarity and efficiency, however, and reflecting the approach taken under MiFID II,[243] it is further utilised as an umbrella concept that encompasses a range of more detailed conduct of business obligations, that are owed to the transacting parties in a crowdfunding offer.[244]

a. Information Obligations

A large part of the more specific conduct obligations of CSPs are disclosure related.[245] Indeed, one of the core functions of platform operators under the EU

[237] ibid Art 17(1) second subparagraph and recital 37.
[238] ibid Art 17(3).
[239] ibid Art 17(2).
[240] See eg Art 12(1) AIFMD; and Art 24(1) MiFID II.
[241] Art 3(2) ECSPR.
[242] Moloney (n 62) 787.
[243] For a comprehensive analysis of the conduct of business rules under MiFID II, see, among others, D Busch, 'MiFID II: Stricter Conduct of Business Rules for Investment Firms' (2017) 12 *Capital Markets Law Journal* 340; L Enriques and M Gargantini, 'The Overarching Duty to Act in the Best Interest of the Client in MiFID II', in Busch and Ferrarini (n 133) 85–122; C Gortsos, *Stricto Investor Protection under MiFID II: A Systematic Overview of Articles 24–30* (CUP, 2018); Colaert (n 90) 353–54.
[244] The regulation refers to the 'clients' of crowdfunding service providers in general, without distinguishing between investors and project owners. This implies, therefore, that platform operators shall serve two masters, even though their interests may often diverge or even conflict with one another, see Staikouras (n 74) 1087.
[245] Disclosure obligations from the side of project owners will be discussed under section C, where the rules for the protection of investors will be reviewed.

crowdfunding regime consists in the provision of precontractual information that will enable prospective investors to gain a better understanding of their business; the costs, financial risks and charges related to crowdfunding services or investments; the criteria for the selection of crowdfunding projects; and the nature and risks associated with the specific services provided by them.[246] In this framework, particular attention is given to the quality and accessibility of that information, which should thus comply with the standards of fairness, clarity and correctness and be made available to all investors in a non-discriminatory manner and on a clearly identified and easily accessible section of the platform.[247]

In addition to the above, there are some further information obligations by which all CSPs are bound. In particular, they shall warn prospective investors that their services are not covered by the deposit guarantee scheme established in accordance with Directive 2014/49/EU, and that transferable securities or admitted instruments for crowdfunding purposes acquired through their platform are not covered by the investor compensation scheme established in accordance with Directive 97/9/EC.[248] At the same time, they shall also ensure that non-sophisticated investors are aware of the existence and conditions of a precontractual reflection period, providing the relevant information in a prominent place of the medium, including on every mobile application and webpage, where a crowdfunding offer is made.[249]

Finally, in order to reduce the asymmetry of information between CSPs and their clients, the Regulation introduces specific disclosure duties which are triggered in particular when the crowdfunding services provided consist in the facilitation of granting of loans.[250] In such cases, CSPs shall, above all, disclose annually the default rates of the loans offered through their platforms over at least the preceding 36 months,[251] based on the methodology provided for under Article 2 of the Commission Delegated Regulation (EU) 2022/2115.[252] In parallel, they shall publish, within four months from the end of each financial year, an outcome statement indicating: the actual and expected default rate of all loans they facilitated by risk category;[253] the assumptions used in determining expected default rates; and, where the target rate in relation to individual portfolio management of loans was offered, the actual return achieved.[254] Now, especially in those

[246] Art 19(1) and (4) in combination with recital 39 ECSPR.
[247] ibid Art 19(1) and (5).
[248] ibid Art 19(2).
[249] ibid Art 19(3).
[250] ibid recital 40.
[251] ibid Art 20(1)(a). It is obvious that where the platform operates for less than 36 months, then the default rates shall cover this shorter period.
[252] Commission Delegated Regulation (EU) 2022/2115 supplementing Regulation (EU) 2020/1503 with regard to regulatory technical standards specifying the methodology for calculating default rates of loans offered on a crowdfunding platform [2022] OJ L287/33.
[253] The methodology for the calculation of the actual and expected default rate of such loans is laid down in Arts 3 and 4 of Delegated Regulation (EU) 2022/2115 respectively.
[254] Art 20(1)(b) ECSPR.

cases where CSPs apply credit scores to crowdfunding projects or suggest the pricing of crowdfunding offers in their platforms, they should also disclose the key elements of their methodology to calculate such credit scores or prices.[255] In a similar vein, when offering the service of individual portfolio management of loans, CSPs shall further provide, both on an ongoing basis and upon an investor's request, all relevant information about each portfolio that they administer. This includes, among others, its composition, mainly the projects where the funds are invested, the features of the loans financing those projects, the risk mitigation measures taken for every loan and any default on credit agreements by the project owner over the past five years.[256] Besides, if for the provision of this service, a contingency fund has been established, CSPs shall also inform investors about the policies governing its operation and the risk of not receiving any pay-out in the case of loss, while they should also make public – on a quarterly basis – the size of the fund and the ratio between the payments made out of it and the total amount outstanding on loans.[257]

b. Conflict-of-interest Rules

As already explained, due to their vital role in the crowdfunding process and the trust put in them by their clients, crowdfunding intermediaries can also generate significant risks to the smooth functioning and integrity of the market. In fact, the simultaneous provision of crowdfunding services to many different natural and legal persons from both sides of the market can be expected to give rise to doubts concerning the neutrality of platform operators who – as any other financial agent[258] – might be prone to benefit certain clients at the expense of others, or even leverage their strong market position in an effort to pursue their own interests instead.[259] Against this background and with the aim of ensuring their impartiality,

[255] ibid Art 19(6) and recital 41. The elements to be included in the description of the method to calculate credit scoring and to suggest loan pricing are laid down in Commission Delegated Regulation (EU) 2024/358 supplementing Regulation (EU) 2020/1503 with regard to regulatory technical standards specifying requirements on credit scoring of crowdfunding projects, pricing of crowdfunding offers, and risk management policies and procedures [2024] OJ L, 2024/358.

[256] Art 6(4) ECSPR in conjunction with Arts 8–14 Commission Delegated Regulation (EU) 2022/2118 supplementing Regulation (EU) 2020/1503 with regard to regulatory technical standards on individual portfolio management of loans by crowdfunding service providers, specifying the elements of the method to assess credit risk, the information on each individual portfolio to be disclosed to investors, and the policies and procedures required in relation to contingency funds [2022] OJ L287/50.

[257] Art 6(5) and (6) ECSPR. The policies, procedures and organisational arrangements that CSPs must have in place as regards any contingency funds they have established and operated are laid down in Arts 15–21 Commission Delegated Regulation (EU) 2022/2118.

[258] S Grundmann and P Hacker, 'Conflicts of Interests' in Busch and Ferrarini (n 133) 166–67; L Enriques, 'Conflicts of Interest in Investment Services: The Price and Uncertain Impact of MiFID's Regulatory Framework' in G Ferrarini and E Wymeersch (eds), *Investor Protection in Europe: Corporate Law Making, The MiFID and Beyond* (OUP, 2006) 524.

[259] Very often, such conduct might even go unnoticed since clients will typically not be in a position to monitor the activities of the platform operators and their coherence with their best interests,

the Regulation provides that CSPs take all necessary steps to ensure the prevention, identification, management and disclosure of conflicts of interests between themselves, their shareholders, managers, employees, or persons indirectly linked to them by control and their clients, or between one client and another client.[260]

In particular, CSPs shall not participate in any of the crowdfunding offers marketed through their platform,[261] nor shall they grant or accept any remuneration, discount, or non-monetary benefit for routing the investors' orders to a particular crowdfunding offer made either on their own or on a third-party platform.[262] In addition, they shall establish in writing, implement and maintain effective internal rules to prevent conflicts of interest from adversely affecting the interests of their clients, which should be appropriate to their size and organisation as well as to the nature, scale and complexity of their business.[263] In this framework, particular attention should be given to ensuring that their major shareholders,[264] managers or employees, as well as any natural or legal person linked to them by way of control,[265] do not act as project owners in relation to the services provided under the Regulation.[266] At the same time, where CSPs accept these persons as investors in the projects offered on their platform, they shall further disclose this fact on their website, and ensure that the relevant investments are made under the same conditions as those of other investors and that no preferential treatment or privileged access to information is granted.[267] Finally, when the organisational or administrative arrangements made by a CSP are not sufficient to ensure, with reasonable confidence, that risks of damage to clients' interests will be prevented, it shall publish and keep updated, in a prominent and easily accessible place of its website, specific and clear information regarding the general nature and sources of conflicts of interests, as well as the measures taken to mitigate them.[268] Such disclosure shall be made on a durable medium and should be appropriate to the nature of the clients to whom it is addressed, in particular their qualification as sophisticated or non-sophisticated investors, so as to enable them to take an

considering especially their limited resources but also – in the case of retail investors – their limited knowledge and bargaining power.

[260] Art 8(4) and recital 26 ECSPR.

[261] ibid Art 8(1).

[262] ibid Art 3(3). This provision follows the wording of Art 27(2) MiFID II regarding the ban of inducements, though it appears stricter and narrower, see also Macchiavello (n 133) 583.

[263] Art 8(3) ECSPR in conjunction with Art 1(1) and recital 2 Commission Delegated Regulation (EU) 2022/2111 supplementing Regulation (EU) 2020/1503 with regard to regulatory technical standards specifying conflicts of interest requirements for crowdfunding service providers [2022] OJ L287/1.

[264] According to Art 8(2)(a), these are shareholders holding 20%, or more, of share capital or voting rights.

[265] According to Art 4(1)(35)(b) MiFID II, this control link exists between a parent undertaking and a subsidiary (including any of its subsidiaries), or between any natural or legal person and an undertaking.

[266] Art 8(2) ECSPR in conjunction with Art 1(3)(a) Commission Delegated Regulation (EU) 2022/2111.

[267] Art 8(2) ECSPR.

[268] Art 8(5) ECSPR in conjunction with Art 3(1) Commission Delegated Regulation (EU) 2022/2111.

informed decision with regard to the acceptance of the service in the context of which the conflict arises.[269]

c. Requirements on Marketing Communications

The final set of overarching, conduct-shaping obligations on the part of CSPs are related to marketing communications about their services. Indeed, such communications typically represent the first step towards luring potential clients into the capital market and, thus, might have a significant impact on their decision to participate in the relevant services.[270] This is even more the case in crowdfunding, where participants from both sides of the market are generally ill-equipped to decode the complexity and risks of the transaction and, thus, might place greater trust in communications made by the platform.[271] Consequently, marketing rules could have a great impact on the development of the EU crowdfunding market, considering especially the tendency of cross-border investors – especially retail ones – to rely on marketing material.[272] In this regard, the ECSPR pays particular attention to addressing marketing risks, whilst ensuring the fair and non-discriminatory treatment of clients.[273]

More specifically, it is, first, provided that all marketing communications addressed by CSPs with regard to their services shall be clearly identifiable as such, and contain information that is fair, clear, not misleading and consistent with the key investment information sheet.[274] At the same time, in the interest of maintaining the neutrality of crowdfunding platforms, marketing communications shall not target, in a disproportionate manner, individual crowdfunding projects (whether planned, pending or ongoing) prior to the offer closure.[275] Moreover, specific rules apply with respect to the language of the communications, which shall either correspond to the official language(s) of the Member State where the marketing takes place, or to a language accepted by the relevant competent authority.[276] Finally, with a view to ensuring that clients' interests are adequately protected, the Regulation entrusts NCAs with the task of monitoring and enforcing compliance with the national laws, regulations and administrative provisions that govern marketing communications, though it explicitly prohibits them from

[269] Art 8(6) ECSPR in conjunction with Art 3(2) Commission Delegated Regulation (EU) 2022/2111.

[270] Moloney (n 62) 788.

[271] For the role of trust in crowdfunding platforms as an important factor for the participation of contributors in a crowdfunding transaction, see K Moysidou and P Hausberg, 'In Crowdfunding We Trust: A Trust-building Model in Lending Crowdfunding' (2020) 58 *Journal of Small Business Management* 511.

[272] European Parliament Committee of Inquiry into the Crisis of the Equitable Life Assurance Society, 'Report on the crisis of the Equitable Life Assurance Society', 4 June 2007, 197 and 254.

[273] Recital 57 ECSPR.

[274] ibid Art 27(1) and (2).

[275] ibid Art 27(2).

[276] ibid Art 27(3) and recital 60.

requiring ex-ante notification and approval of such communications.[277] In order to enhance legal certainty for CSPs operating across the Union and to reduce barriers to cross border market entry, competent authorities shall further publish those national rules, including a summary thereof in a language customary in the sphere of international finance, and any subsequent changes on their website and notify ESMA accordingly,[278] using the standard templates and procedures laid down in Commission Delegated Regulation (EU) 2022/2123.[279] ESMA shall, in turn, publish and maintain on its website an up-to-date list of the notified summaries along with hyperlinks to the webpages of the competent authorities.[280]

iii. Organisational and Operational Requirements

As is the case with investment intermediaries more generally,[281] one of the main challenges with respect to the regulation of crowdfunding platforms is setting up the right measures in order to eliminate or at least adequately mitigate potential operational and business risks, without unduly restricting productive intermediation and innovation.[282] To achieve this, the ECSPR subjects crowdfunding intermediaries to a series of ex-ante organisational and operational requirements which, although closely based on the related regime which applies with regard to the provision of investment services and activities,[283] are still more tailored to the size, nature, and complexity of their business. These risk management requirements address, in particular, governance arrangements, internal control mechanisms, as well as the prevention of illicit activities and the protection of clients' data.

a. Governance Arrangements

As already explained, there are many risks relating to the role of crowdfunding platforms as intermediaries, including the prospect of serving as vehicles for the financing of fraudulent or nonviable projects; the danger of professional misconduct from the side of their representatives; and the potential disruption of their activities due to insolvency or technical reasons.[284] In many ways, these risks are

[277] ibid Art 27(4) and (5).

[278] Ibid Art 28(1), (2) and (3) and recital 58.

[279] Arts 1, 2 and 3 Commission Delegated Regulation (EU) 2022/2123 laying down implementing technical standards for the application of Regulation (EU) 2020/1503 with regard to the standard forms, templates and procedures for the notifications of national marketing requirements applicable to crowdfunding service providers by competent authorities to ESMA [2022] OJ L287/120.

[280] Art 28(6) ECSPR. However, ESMA shall not be held liable for the information presented in the summaries provided by the NCAs.

[281] See, generally, J-H Binder, 'Corporate Governance of Financial Institutions: In Need of Cross-Sectoral Regulation? A comparative analysis of banks, investment firms, asset managers, and pension funds' in D Busch, G Ferrarini and G van Solinge (eds), *Governance of Financial Institutions* (OUP, 2019).

[282] In the framework of MiFID II, see Moloney (n 62) 348.

[283] ibid 383 ff, providing a thorough analysis of organisational requirements under Art 16 MiFID II.

[284] ESMA (n 6) 11; SWD (2016) 154 final (n 14) 16.

associated with weaknesses in governance structures, especially in areas such as risk management or the prevention of misalignment of interests.[285] In this respect, ensuring a robust system of governance was considered essential for enhancing the credibility of CSPs and, thereby, the growth potential of the EU crowdfunding industry.[286]

At the basis of the governance regime applicable to platform operators that are authorised under the ECSPR, lies the fundamental duty of their management body to establish, maintain, and oversee the implementation of policies and procedures that ensure effective and prudent management, including the segregation of duties, business continuity and the prevention of conflicts of interests, in a manner that promotes market integrity, but also the interests of their clients.[287] In particular, the natural persons responsible for the management and operation of the crowdfunding platform shall, as already mentioned, be of good repute and possess sufficient knowledge, skills and experience in order to perform the duties assigned to them.[288] Moreover, they shall develop a detailed business continuity plan to address the risks associated with its failure,[289] that is the initiation of insolvency or pre-insolvency proceedings under national law or any significant interruption of their business.[290] This plan shall be adapted to the business model of the CSP and contain specific measures and procedures which can ensure the uninterrupted provision of critical services related to existing investments, the smooth administration of outstanding agreements and transactions between the crowdfunding platform and its clients, as well as the sound management of critical business data.[291] Finally, they must ensure that the crowdfunding platform meets, at all times, certain minimum prudential capital requirements[292] in the

[285] SWD (2018) 56 final (n 12) 19. It should be noted, however, that the introduction of governance requirements in the field of investment services is a relatively novel approach and, therefore, their role in supporting better risk management is still uncertain.

[286] Recital 23 ECSPR.

[287] ibid Art 4(1).

[288] ibid recital 23 in combination with Art 12(2)(k) and (l). However, the Regulation leaves it to the discretion of Member States to choose the most appropriate form and methods for implementing these principles in their national legal system since, contrary to the detailed MiFID II governance regime, it does not specify the capacity-related conditions that apply. This might in turn lead to discrepancies among Member States as regards the competence requirements of platform managements, probably with negative effects to the functioning of the internal market for crowdfunding services. For a general assessment of the consistency of the governance requirements with the Regulation's objective of creating a single market for crowdfunding services, see the discussion below, under section IV.

[289] ibid Art 12(2)(j) in combination with Art 2(1) Commission Delegated Regulation (EU) 2022/2116 of the European Parliament and of the Council supplementing Regulation (EU) 2020/1503 with regard to regulatory technical standards specifying the measures and procedures for crowdfunding service providers' business continuity plan [2022] OJ L287/38.

[290] Art 1(b) and (c) Commission Delegated Regulation (EU) 2022/2116.

[291] Art 12(2)(j) ECSPR in combination with Art 2(2) Commission Delegated Regulation (EU) 2022/2116. The minimum content of the measures and procedures to be included in the business continuity plan are laid down in Arts 3 to 5 of Commission Delegated Regulation (EU) 2022/2116.

[292] This should be equal to an amount of at least EUR 25,000 plus a quarter of the overhead fixed costs of the previous year, which shall also include the costs for servicing loans for three months where the platform operator facilitates the granting of loans. Where a crowdfunding platform operates for less

form of own funds,[293] a professional liability insurance policy, or a combination of both,[294] unless the latter is already subject to such requirements as a credit institution, investment firm, payment institution or electronic money institution.[295] At least once every two years, the management body shall review the prudential safeguards and the business continuity plan, in view of the nature, scale and complexity of the services provided.[296]

In addition to the preceding general requirements, the Regulation lays down some special rules applicable to CSPs when they facilitate the conclusion of loan agreements between investors and project owners. More specifically, their management body shall define and oversee the implementation of effective systems and controls to assess the risks associated with the loans which are intermediated on the crowdfunding platform.[297] Moreover, where such CSPs offer individual portfolio management of loans they shall, apart from ensuring an adequate risk management framework, also have in place robust internal processes and methodologies, and shall use appropriate data in order to allow investors to specify the parameters for the provision of that service, based on specific predetermined criteria that every loan in the portfolio must comply with.[298] At the same time, they shall assess, on the basis of sound and well-defined methods which should be disclosed to the clients, the credit risk of the individual projects chosen for the investor's portfolio, the credit exposure at the portfolio level and the default prospects of the selected project owners.[299] Lastly, a series of prudentially orientated measures shall be additionally taken if crowdfunding intermediaries suggest the pricing of an offer, including: undertaking a prior credit risk assessment of the crowdfunding project or the project owner, based on sufficient information and in accordance with appropriate policies and procedures;[300] ensuring the fair and orderly pricing of the offer, accompanied, in certain cases, by a valuation of the loan;[301] and maintaining a record of each facilitated loan agreement, including sufficient information to prove compliance with the previous requirements, in line with an effective risk-management framework.[302]

than a year, it may instead use forward-looking business estimates in calculating the fixed overheads, provided that it starts using historical data as soon as it becomes available, Art 11(1) and (5) ECSPR.

[293] These shall consist of Common Equity Tier 1 as defined in Arts 26–30 of the CRR II, after the deduction of the items mentioned in Art 36, without the application of threshold exemptions pursuant to Arts 46 and 48 thereof.

[294] Art 11(2) ECSPR.

[295] ibid Art 11(3) and (4).

[296] ibid Art 4(3).

[297] ibid Art 4(2).

[298] ibid Art 4(2) in combination with Art 6(1) and (2). In addition, according to Art 6(3), crowdfunding service providers are required to keep records of all mandates received and of every loan in an individual portfolio for at least three years following its maturity.

[299] ibid Art 6(2)(a), (b) and (c).

[300] ibid Art 4(4)(a), (b) and (c).

[301] ibid Art 4(4)(d) and (e).

[302] ibid Art 4(4)(f) and (g).

b. Internal Control Mechanisms

Over and above governance arrangements, regulatory responses to the risks faced by the clients of financial intermediaries typically also comprise adequate internal processes (including sound administrative and accounting procedures)[303] which aim at ensuring adherence to applicable regulatory requirements and standards, safeguarding client assets, while also preventing, detecting and handling errors and misconduct of the responsible managers or staff. Provisions of this type seem particularly important in retail markets where monitoring costs are high, thereby creating opportunities for performance irregularities.[304] In this context, therefore, the EU regime governing the provision of crowdfunding services is further supported by specific requirements related to internal control mechanisms.

To begin with, CSPs must establish 'effective and transparent' procedures to receive and handle clients' complaints in a 'prompt, fair and consistent' manner and publish an up-to-date, clear and easily accessible description of those procedures on their website.[305] In particular, they shall ensure that clients are able to file complaints against them by electronic means free of charge, based on a standard template which shall be publicly and readily available;[306] investigate all complaints impartially, diligently and in a timely fashion, gathering and examining all relevant information and evidence and providing complainants with complete, coherent and properly justified decisions within a reasonable and predefined period of time;[307] and maintain a record of all complaints received and the measures taken in this regard.[308] Moreover, with a view to ensuring the efficient and smooth provision of crowdfunding services, while adequately addressing outsourcing risks, crowdfunding intermediaries are, in principle, allowed to rely, either wholly or partly, on a third party for the performance of operational functions. Nevertheless, such outsourcing must not impair their internal controls or the ability of NCAs to perform their supervisory duties.[309] In any case, CSPs shall remain fully and unconditionally responsible for compliance with the Regulation in relation to the outsourced activities.[310] Finally, additional conditions, which are designed to protect client assets against the risks of insolvency and fraud on the side of platform operators, apply where asset safekeeping and payment services are

[303] See eg Art 16(5) MiFID II; Art 74(1) CRD; and Regulation (EU) 648/2012 of the European Parliament and of the Council on OTC derivatives, central counterparties and trade repositories [2012] OJ L201/1, Art 78(1).

[304] Moloney (n 62) 348–49.

[305] Art 7(1) ECSPR in combination with Art 1 Commission Delegated Regulation (EU) 2022/2117 supplementing Regulation (EU) 2020/1503 with regard to regulatory technical standards specifying the requirements, standard formats and procedures for complaint handling [2022] OJ L287/42.

[306] ibid Art 7(2) and (3) in combination with Art 2 Commission Delegated Regulation (EU) 2022/2117.

[307] ibid Art 7(4) in combination with Arts 4 and 5 and Commission Delegated Regulation (EU) 2022/2117.

[308] ibid Art 7(2).

[309] ibid Art 9(1) and (2).

[310] ibid Art 9(3).

provided.[311] In such cases, CSPs shall, first of all, inform their clients of the nature and terms of those services and whether they are provided by them – given that the relevant authorisation has been granted – or through qualified third parties.[312] With respect to safekeeping services, the relevant assets shall, depending on their type, either be held in custody, as is the case with transferable securities or privately held shares which can be registered in a financial instruments account or be physically delivered, or subject to ownership verification and record-keeping.[313] With regards to payment services, now, where a platform carries out payment transactions in relation to transferable securities or admitted instruments, the funds shall be deposited either in a central bank or a credit institution.[314]

c. Due Diligence and Data Protection Requirements

From a market integrity perspective, CSPs remain vulnerable to problems related to the security of client data and the use of crowdfunding for money laundering, terrorist financing and, in general, illicit activities.[315] Leaving these challenges unaddressed would have a direct negative impact on the integrity and credibility of platform operators, thus also leading to mistrust towards the crowdfunding sector as a whole.[316] Against this background and with a view to mitigating the risks of adverse cross-border spill-over effects, the ECSPR lays down specific due diligence and data protection rules pertaining to the provision of crowdfunding services.

As regards the first issue, before allowing a venture to be funded from the wider public through the digital platforms operated or managed by them, CSPs are obliged to conduct a background check on the project owner by obtaining evidence on its criminal status.[317] In particular, they must take all necessary measures to ensure that the project owner has no criminal record for violating national rules in certain legal fields (ie, commercial law, insolvency law, financial services law, anti-money laundering law, fraud law or professional liability obligations), and that it is not established in a non-cooperative jurisdiction for tax purposes[318]

[311] Even where crowdfunding service providers – or a delegated third party – do not provide payment services in relation to crowdfunding services, they are still required to ensure that project owners only accept funding or any other payment through a properly authorised payment service provider, ibid Art 10(5).

[312] ibid Art 10(1), (3) and (4) in combination with recitals 28 and 29.

[313] ibid Art 10(3).

[314] ibid Art 10(2).

[315] SWD (2016) 154 final (n 14) 16; SWD (2018) 56 (n 12) 19.

[316] For example, the 2015 scandal of Trustbuddy, a Scandinavian peer-to-peer crowdfunding platform which was forced to shut down its activities, and therefore file for bankruptcy, after a discrepancy of EUR 4.6 million was discovered in its books, had negative effects at the Scandinavian crowdfunding market as a whole.

[317] Art 5 ECSPR.

[318] European Council, Taxation: EU list of non-cooperative jurisdictions, www.consilium.europa.eu/en/policies/.

or a high-risk third country with strategic deficiencies.[319] With respect to the issue of data protection, crowdfunding intermediaries shall maintain records related to all of the services provided, the agreements concluded, and the transactions made through their platform on a durable medium[320] for a period of at least five years.[321] Therefore, to the extent that this activity requires the processing of clients' personal data, CSPs must comply with the relevant requirements of Regulation (EU) 2016/679 (GDPR), while they should, at all times, ensure that their clients have immediate access to such records.[322]

iv. Supervision and Enforcement

a. Competent Authorities and the Role of ESMA

In its original proposal, and in line with the post-Brexit aspiration towards the greater centralisation of capital market supervision,[323] the Commission designated ESMA as the competent authority for ensuring compliance by CSPs with applicable statutory requirements. It also entrusted ESMA with the necessary supervisory and enforcement powers to carry out the functions associated with this role, in particular the request for information, the conduct of investigations and on-site inspections, the imposition of sanctions and the withdrawal of a platform's authorisation.[324] However, during the preliminary discussions in the relevant parliamentary committees, it became clear that Member States were not ready to confer the direct supervisory and enforcement competence over CSPS on ESMA.[325] Rather, it was suggested, either implicitly[326] or explicitly,[327] that NCAs should be more actively involved in the relevant procedures, based on the assumption that they can identify and punish any breaches of the Regulation more promptly and effectively, while they can also show greater sensitivity to local circumstances and

[319] Commission Delegated Regulation (EU) 2016/1675 supplementing Directive (EU) 2015/849 by identifying high-risk third countries with strategic deficiencies [2016] OJ L254/1, as amended by Commission Delegated Regulation (EU) 2020/855 [2020] OJ L195/1.

[320] As defined in Art 2(1)(p) ECSPR.

[321] ibid Art 26(a) and (c).

[322] ibid Art 26(b). See also Art 36 on the data protection obligations of NCAs and ESMA.

[323] SWD (2017) 224 final (n 95) 14, 19–20. The concept of supervision must be understood in its broad sense, comprising four different phases: authorisation or licensing; supervision *stricto sensu*; sanctioning; and management of crises, see R Lastra, 'Defining Forward Looking, Judgement-based Supervision' (2013) 14 *Journal of Banking Regulation* 221, 221–22.

[324] Arts 22–25 and 27–29 ECSPR Proposal.

[325] This reflects the general political reluctance of Member States to give up control of national markets in favour of European financial supervision, see N De Arriba-Sellier, 'The Brexit Reform of European Financial Supervision: Lost in Transition?' (2019) 30 *European Business Law Review* 695, 717–18.

[326] European Economic and Social Committee, 'Opinion on the Proposal for a Regulation of the European Parliament and of the Council on European Crowdfunding Service Providers (ECSP) for Business', OJ C367/65, para 3.15.

[327] Committee on Economic and Monetary Affairs, 'Draft Report on the Proposal for a Regulation on European Crowdfunding Service Providers (ECSP) for Business', 2018/0048 (COD), 10 August 2018, 79.

needs. In this context, the Parliament, in its position at first reading, substantially reduced the tasks originally assigned to ESMA, thereby essentially eliminating the possibility to play any active role in the day-to-day supervision of the European crowdfunding market.[328]

Ultimately, the adopted text, following the compromise proposal presented by the Council,[329] resolved the issue in favour of decentralisation and local governance, by requiring that CSPs be subject to the on-going supervision of the competent authority designated for this purpose by their Member State of establishment.[330] Contrastingly, the authority of ESMA in the supervision and enforcement of the EU crowdfunding regime was seriously weakened, currently being confined to coordinating and supporting the work carried out by NCAs, through the provision of certain auxiliary services. As will be further explained below, these comprise, mainly, the settlement of disagreements among competent authorities when a request for cooperation has been rejected or not duly answered;[331] the coordination of on-site inspections or investigations with cross-border effect;[332] the publication of an annual report containing information on enforcement actions taken across the Union;[333] the management of a central database of penalties and administrative measures communicated by NCAs;[334] and the development of draft regulatory and implementing technical standards as well as guidelines, recommendations and Q&As to ensure the consistent application of the Regulation.[335]

b. NCA Supervisory and Investigatory Powers

In order to ensure the compliance of CSPs with the obligations laid down in the Regulation, Member States shall take all necessary measures to enable competent authorities to carry out their supervision functions and duties in an effective, independent and uniform manner, following a careful assessment of the specific circumstances of each individual case.[336] In this direction, the ECSPR also provides for some minimum supervisory and investigative powers to be entrusted to NCAs in accordance with national law.[337] These powers shall be exercised directly, in collaboration with other authorities, by delegation to such authorities, but under their responsibility, or by application to the competent judicial authorities.[338] They

[328] See also Macchiavello (n 133) 577–78.
[329] Council, 'Compromise proposal for a Regulation on European Crowdfunding Service Providers (ECSP) for Business and amending Regulation (EU) No 2017/1129', 24 June 2019.
[330] Art 15(1) in combination with Arts 12(1) and 29(1) ECSPR.
[331] ibid Art 31(5).
[332] ibid Art 32(2).
[333] Art 43(1).
[334] Art 43(3).
[335] ibid recitals 70–72.
[336] ibid Arts 15(2) and 30(6).
[337] ibid recital 62.
[338] ibid Art 30(5).

should include, in particular, the right to: require from platform operators, their managers, auditors, as well as from third parties appointed to perform certain functions related to the provision of crowdfunding services to provide information and documents;[339] carry out on-site inspections or investigations at premises, other than the private residences of natural persons, in order to access documents and other data, where there are reasons to suspect that the latter may be relevant to prove an infringement of the Regulation;[340] suspend, for a maximum of 10 consecutive working days, a crowdfunding offer, marketing communications or the provision of crowdfunding services, in every case where there are reasonable grounds for believing that the Regulation has been infringed;[341] prohibit a crowdfunding offer or the provision of crowdfunding services where it is proved that the Regulation has been infringed;[342] publicly disclose all information which may affect the provision of crowdfunding services, including the failure of a platform operator or a designated third party to comply with the obligations under the Regulation;[343] require the temporary suspension of crowdfunding services where their continuation would be at the detriment of investors' interests and the smooth functioning of the market;[344] and transfer the ongoing contracts of a CSP whose authorisation has been withdrawn to another legal entity authorised in the same country.[345]

In exercising their monitoring and investigating powers under the Regulation, NCAs are supported on the one hand by CSPs themselves and, on the other, by clients and other interested parties, including consumer associations. More specifically, with regards to the former, not only are they required to report, without undue delay, any material changes to the conditions for their authorisation to the relevant competent authority, but must also provide, upon request, any information relevant to the fulfilment of its obligations.[346] In relation to the latter, now, competent authorities shall set up and make available on their websites, procedures allowing them to communicate, either in writing or by electronic means, alleged breaches of this Regulation from platform operators.[347] On top of these measures, the material scope of the whistle-blowing regime is further extended to protect

[339] ibid Art 30(1)(a) and (b).

[340] ibid Art 30(1)(c). Recital 63 clarifies that access to such premises is further justified where a natural or legal person has failed to comply with a request for information, or where there are reasonable grounds for believing that, if such request were made, it would not be complied with or – even more – the related documents or information would be removed, tampered with, or destroyed.

[341] ibid Art 30(2)(a), (b) and (d).

[342] ibid Art 30(2)(c) and (e).

[343] ibid Art 30(2)(f) and (g).

[344] ibid Art 30(2)(h).

[345] ibid Art 30(2)(i) and (4).

[346] ibid Art 15(3). Moreover, according to Art 16, CSPs shall, on an annual and confidential basis, disclose detailed information on all projects funded through their platforms. This information should be forwarded by home NCAs to ESMA within one month upon their receipt, thus allowing the latter to analyse and observe the development of the crowdfunding market in the Union.

[347] ibid Art 38.

natural or legal persons that bring information to the attention of a competent authority which could expose actual or potential breaches of the Regulation.[348] As a result, whistle-blowers are brought into the ECSP supervisory framework as gatekeepers, protected from contractual, regulatory, or administrative liability related to the notifications made to NCAs.[349]

c. Supervisory Cooperation

With the aim of supporting an efficient and consistent supervision procedure across the EU, the ECSPR lays down provisions on the cross-border administrative cooperation between competent national authorities, as well as between them and ESMA or other authorities.[350] More specifically, for the purposes of carrying out their duties under the Regulation, NCAs shall, save in exceptional cases, exchange information without undue delay and collaborate in on-site inspections and investigatory activities.[351] Moreover, they shall coordinate their supervisory functions in order to prevent and remedy any infringements of the Regulation, create and promote best practices, support collaboration, foster coherence of interpretation, and provide cross-jurisdictional assessments in the event of disagreements.[352] In that context, competent authorities shall also be alert to breaches of the Regulation by passporting entities. This implies that, where the host NCA discovers or has clear reasons to believe that a CSP or a designated third party have committed irregularities or have violated their obligations, it shall inform the home NCA of its findings in a detailed manner and, if the infringement persists, take all appropriate action for the protection of investors, informing the Commission and ESMA accordingly.[353] In a similar vein, NCAs shall cooperate closely with ESMA for the purposes of the Regulation and shall provide it with all information necessary to perform the tasks and powers assigned to it.[354] All information exchanged under this Regulation between ESMA, NCAs and other authorities shall, provided that it concerns business or operational conditions, and other economic or personal affairs, be considered confidential and subject to the requirements of professional secrecy. Consequently, it may not be disclosed to any other natural or legal persons or authority except where such communication is permitted by the competent authority or is necessary for legal proceedings.[355]

[348] Part I.B(xxi) of the Annex to Directive (EU) 2019/1937, as inserted by Art 47 ECSPR.
[349] Art 30(7) and recital 68 ECSPR.
[350] In this framework, each Member State shall designate one competent authority as a single point of contact responsible for managing communications with ESMA and competent authorities across the Union, ibid Art 29(2).
[351] ibid Art 31(1)–(4).
[352] ibid Art 30(6).
[353] ibid Arts 31(7) and 37(1) and (2).
[354] ibid Art 32(1) and (3).
[355] ibid Art 35.

d. Enforcement and Sanctions

The ECSPR supervisory framework is complemented by a public enforcement mechanism which aims at ensuring that any infringements of the requirements set out in the Regulation are subject to appropriate administrative sanctions.[356] On the contrary, private enforcement does not form part of the ESCPR which, in line with the general approach taken in EU capital markets regulation, does not address in substance the question of how Member States should approach civil liability.

More specifically, according to Article 39(1), Member States shall ensure, under their national rules, that competent authorities have the power to impose administrative penalties and take suitable other administrative measures where it is shown that a natural or legal person has been in breach of their duties under the Regulation. These penalties and measures must be of an effective, deterrent and proportionate nature and are without prejudice to the national provisions on criminal sanctions as well as the supervisory and investigatory powers of NCAs. Competent authorities shall also be empowered to immediately publish and keep updated on their official websites any decision imposing an administrative sanction, along with information about the type of the infringement and the identity of the responsible person, save in cases where such disclosure is considered disproportionate to the gravity of the violation committed or would jeopardise an ongoing investigation.[357] The relevant decisions should be properly reasoned and subject to the right of appeal before a tribunal,[358] while all penalties and measures imposed by NCAs – even if not disclosed to the public – shall be reported to ESMA which is responsible for setting up and keeping updated a non-publicly accessible central database, with the sole purpose of facilitating competent national and EU authorities to exchange information that is necessary to carry out their duties under this Regulation.[359]

Finally, in an effort to create a more level playing field for platform operators established in different Member States, the Regulation also focuses on supporting stronger convergence in enforcement powers, standards and practices of NCAs. To that effect, it sets out the particular breaches which should, at least, be susceptible to enforcement proceedings in accordance with national law[360] and lays down the

[356] ibid recital 64. For a comprehensive analysis of the ECSPR enforcement system, see K Serdaris, 'Ex Post Enforcement of the EU Crowdfunding Regime: Administrative Sanctions and Measures (Arts 39–43)' in E Macchiavello (ed), *Regulation on European Crowdfunding Service Providers for Business: A Commentary* (Edward Elgar, 2022).

[357] Art 42(2) ECSPR provides that, in these cases, NCAs may instead: (i) decide to defer the publication of the relevant decision until the moment where the reasons for non-disclosure cease to exist; (ii) publish the decision on an anonymous basis; or (iii) not publish the decision at all, where the two previous options are considered to be disproportionate in relation to the nature of the sanctions imposed.

[358] ibid Art 41. This Article also clarifies that the right of appeal to the judicial authorities shall also apply where, in relation to an application for authorisation which provides all required information, no decision is taken within six months of its submission.

[359] ibid Art 43(2) and (3).

[360] ibid Art 39(1)(a) and (b).

minimum suite of administrative penalties and measures which shall be available to competent authorities.[361] At the same time, it provides for some common guidelines regarding how the appropriate level and type of administrative sanctions shall be determined,[362] and attaches greater importance to fostering coordination of NCAs in cross-border cases in order to avoid duplication and overlaps when exercising their tasks.[363]

C. Investor Protection Rules

As already explained at the beginning of this chapter, notwithstanding the important benefits that it offers, crowdfunding can also pose some serious threats to investors. More specifically, the specific characteristics of the companies which would typically rely on this funding tool, combined with the retail nature of most clients, imply that problems of uncertainty and information asymmetry would be exacerbated in the crowdfunding context. Indeed, fund-seekers mainly include young, innovative start-ups with no or very short track record and investors will most probably lack the necessary expertise to be able to evaluate the relevant risks. This situation becomes even more acute considering that crowdfunding offers take place via internet platforms which, as stipulated in the ECSPR, do not act as investment advisers. As a result, there are hardly any market mechanisms which could address the information deficit of retail investors.[364] Against this background and in order to avoid a vicious cycle of suboptimal decisions which could arise due to phenomena of 'herding',[365] the Regulation introduces specific obligations on CSPs aimed at protecting investors by ensuring they are well aware of the main characteristics and risks associated with each crowdfunding offer. These include, in particular, the disclosure of some key information about the investments offered through their platform, as well as compliance with certain 'know your customer' procedures.

i. Disclosure Requirements – The Key Investment Information Sheet

As discussed in the previous section, before allowing their potential clients to enter into a crowdfunding transaction, platform operators shall ensure that

[361] These range from a public statement indicating the nature of the infringement and the responsible person ('naming and shaming'), to prohibitions in the exercise of management functions in CSPs applicable to persons responsible for breaching the Regulation, to the imposition of administrative fines, see Art 39(2). Member States are, nonetheless, free to provide for additional sanctions and for higher levels of administrative fines, Art 39(3) ECSPR.

[362] ibid Art 40(1) and (2).

[363] ibid Art 40(3).

[364] Armour and Enriques (n 29) 74.

[365] ibid. Empirical evidence, however, suggests that in certain instances, instead of merely mimicking their peers ('irrational herding'), investors also engage in active observational learning ('rational herding'), see J Zhang and P Liu, 'Rational Herding in Microloan Markets' (2012) 58 *Management Science* 892.

they have sufficient and clear information on the economic features and risks of crowdfunding services and investments.[366] But in order to be able to make investment decisions on an informed basis, it is equally important that prospective investors have the ability to assess the quality and prospects of the project for which funding is sought. In the public markets sphere, the dominant regulatory tool for avoiding adverse investment outcomes has typically included mandatory issuer-disclosure obligations, mainly in the form of extensive prospectus requirements.[367] However, within the crowdfunding context, the effectiveness of such a mechanism is highly questionable, given both the heavy compliance costs that it carries for the fund-seeking companies and the – often widespread – cognitive limitations and biases of investors that participate in the relevant market.

Against this background, the ECSPR adopts a more behaviourally oriented approach to initial disclosure requirements,[368] which seeks to balance the businesses' need to optimise funding costs[369] on the one hand, and retail investors' need for comprehensible, meaningful and accurate information on the other.[370] This implies, in particular, replacing the detailed and costly prospectus with a less burdensome and more economic Key Investment Information Sheet (KIIS), which shall be drawn up by the project owners[371] and communicated by CSPs to prospective investors for each crowdfunding offer, without the need for prior approval by a competent authority.[372] This document should reflect the specific nature of crowdfunding as an alternative to traditional financing and be tailored to meet the information needs of investors.[373] In this respect, in contrast with the paradigm of full disclosure, special attention is paid to the content, quality and format of the KIIS as an alternative way to enable informed and, thus, allocatively efficient investment decisions.

[366] Art 19 ECSPR.

[367] Moloney (n 62) 73–74.

[368] For a detailed analysis see K Serdaris, 'Behavioural Economic Influences on Primary Market Disclosure – The Case of the EU Regulation on European Crowdfunding Service Providers' (2021) 18 *European Company and Financial Law Review* 428.

[369] This is in line with the broader effort to alleviate the administrative burden on SMEs and other small-caps when accessing capital markets, especially as reflected in the new EU Growth Prospectus introduced by Art 15 of the Prospectus Regulation.

[370] This is in line with the consistent focus of EU securities regulators on retail market disclosures as can be clearly observed in the Key Information Document ('KID') under the PRIIPs Regulation, the new prospectus summary, which is modelled after the KID, and more recently the PEPPs KID which should replace and adapt the PRIIPs KID in the case of portable pan-European Personal Pension Products (PEPP) as introduced by Regulation (EU) 2019/1238 [2019] OJ L198/1.

[371] Art 23(2) ECSPR. The project owner is believed to be in the best position to provide the information related to the offer, see recital 51.

[372] ibid Art 23(2) and (14). According to recital 54, the rationale of this provision is to ensure cheap, expedient and seamless access to the market for project owners, while avoiding costs and delays for CSPs.

[373] ibid recitals 51 and 67.

a. Content

In terms of content, the KIIS should be as complete and comprehensive as possible, taking into account however the particular characteristics and needs of participants within the crowdfunding market.[374] Accordingly, it is designed in such a way as to focus on information which is specific to the project owner and the investments offered and which is material and relevant for investors when assessing whether and how much to invest in a given crowdfunding project.[375] This information, which shall be made available once the relevant crowdfunding offer is published on the CSP's platform,[376] shall contain for both investment and lending-based crowdfunding: (a) details regarding the identity, legal composition, management, principal activities and financial position of the project owner; (b) a description of the crowdfunding project, including its purpose and main features; (c) the names and functions or, in the case of legal persons, the registered offices of those responsible for the information given in the KIIS; (d) a statement indicating the responsibility of the project owner for the preparation of the KIIS, along with an attestation that, to the best of their knowledge, no information has been omitted or is materially misleading or inaccurate; (e) the main features of the crowdfunding process and, as appropriate, the conditions for the capital raising or funds borrowing (eg, the minimum target amount and the period of the offer, the consequences of not reaching the target within the designated period, the amount of own funds committed to the project etc.); (f) a description of the risks that are inherent to the project and the specific sector, as well as the main risks associated with the project owner and the financial instruments or loans offered;[377] and (g) an analysis of the fees charged to investors, the procedure for obtaining free additional information, as well as the process for filing complaints and the persons responsible for handling them.[378]

Moreover, depending on the crowdfunding model, certain additional information shall be provided. More specifically, where the crowdfunding intermediation is related to the placing of transferable securities and other admitted instruments, the KIIS shall further encompass the basic aspects of the offer (eg, the total amount and type of financial instruments offered, the subscription price, the terms of subscription and payment, the nominal interest rate for non-equity securities etc), the principal rights of investors (eg, voting rights, distribution of capital, transferring and exit rights etc), and a reference to whether an SPV is used and its

[374] ibid recital 51.

[375] ibid.

[376] Art 1(2) Commission Delegated Regulation (EU) 2022/2119 supplementing Regulation (EU) 2020/1503 with regard to regulatory technical standards for the key investment information sheet [2022] OJ L 287/63.

[377] These risks shall be relevant to each specific offer and shall be prepared solely for the benefit of prospective investors. This implies that the KIIS shall not include general statements on investment risks or limit the liability of the project owner or any persons acting on their behalf, ibid Art 6(2).

[378] This information is set out in Parts A, B, C and H of Annex 1 to the ECSPR and is described in further detail in the relevant parts of the Annex to Commission Delegated Regulation (EU) 2022/2119.

contact details.[379] Where, on the other hand, the role of the platform consists of the facilitation of granting of loans, the KIIS shall contain information related to the specific credit agreement (eg, its nature, duration and terms, the applicable interest rates, the risk mitigation measures, the repayment schedule etc).[380]

Finally, by way of derogation from the foregoing provisions, in those cases where CSPs perform the function of individual portfolio management of loans, the Regulation provides for the publication of a different type of KIIS, which shall be drawn up at the platform level and contain information necessary for a proper evaluation of the benefits and risks associated with this activity. This includes the elements mentioned above under points (c) and (g), a responsibility statement similar to the one prepared by the project owners (see point (d) above), as well as the key aspects of the service, such as the minimum and maximum interest rate and maturity date of loans that may be available to the individual portfolios of investors, the internal methodology for the credit risk assessment of each crowdfunding project, the criteria and procedures for the selection of the projects to the individual portfolio, the coverage and conditions of any applicable capital guarantees, and the risk diversification strategies.[381]

b. Format

As far as the format of the KIIS is concerned, the ECSPR puts particular emphasis on the amount of information provided to investors as well as its framing. Indeed, to avoid situations where investors become overwhelmed with an overload of information, at the risk of missing out on essential facts and statements concerning the issuer and the investments, EU regulators have sought to ensure that the KIIS is written in a concise, coherent and easy-to-read manner. In this respect, following the example of other retail documents – mainly the PRIIPs KID[382] – the KIIS shall be produced as a separate document, which is clearly distinguishable from marketing communications, and shall consist of a maximum of six sides of A4-sized paper format, if printed.[383] Other than that, however, the Regulation does not contain any other specifications, concerning for example, the size of the characters used in this document.[384] Moreover, the KIIS shall be presented on a

[379] Parts D, E and F of the Annex to Commission Delegated Regulation (EU) 2022/2119.

[380] ibid Part G.

[381] Art 24(1) in combination with Annex I, Parts H and I ECSPR.

[382] In fact, where the underlying assets of a packaged retail investment product consist of transferable securities, other admitted instruments or loans offered through a crowdfunding platform, the KIIS may substitute the KID, see Arts 23(15) and 24(8) ECSPR. For a critical analysis of the PRIIPs KID as a tool for protecting retail investors, based on the insights of behavioural law and economics, see V Colaert, 'The Regulation of PRIIPs: Great Ambitions, Insurmountable Challenges?' (2016) 2 *Journal of Financial Regulation* 203.

[383] Arts 23(7) and 24(3) ECSPR. Especially in the case of admitted instruments for crowdfunding purposes, where the information required under Part F of Annex I regarding investor rights exceeds one side of A4-sized paper format if printed, the remainder shall be produced in an annex attached to the KIIS.

[384] On the contrary, according to Art 6(4)(a) of the PRIIPs Regulation, the KID shall be presented in a way that is easy to read, using characters of readable size.

durable medium and may not contain any footnotes, other than those with references, including quotations where relevant, to the applicable law.[385] In certain cases, project owners are nonetheless allowed to include hyperlinks within the KIIS, as long as this does not affect the comprehensiveness of the information given to investors.[386]

Now, in order to improve the comparability of the various crowdfunding offers and help project owners comply with their disclosure duties, great importance is also attached to the development of a standardised model for the presentation of the KIIS.[387] This shall ensure that all the items included in this disclosure document are displayed in the same order and fall under the same headings, whilst maintaining the flexibility needed to take account of the specificities of each offer.[388] Finally, in an effort to mitigate the cognitive biases of investors, particularly those affecting decision-making (eg, the availability and optimism biases), a disclaimer shall appear directly underneath the title of the KIIS, making it explicitly clear that the offer has not been approved or verified by any supervisory authority and that their experience and knowledge have not necessarily been assessed ex-ante.[389] This shall also be accompanied by a warning describing the main risks associated with crowdfunding investments (eg, the risk of losses, market liquidity risk etc),[390] thus nudging investors towards more prudent investment choices which should be proportionate to their financial capacity.

c. Quality

With regard to the quality of disclosure, the Regulation and its implementing rules provide that the information included in the KIIS shall be fair, clear and not misleading,[391] while it shall be communicated in a succinct and simple manner that can be easily understood by prospective investors, especially retail ones, considering also the potential comprehension difficulties arising from the nature, scale and complexity of the crowdfunding offer.[392] In this framework, technical jargon which is difficult to grasp should be avoided where common, everyday terms can be used instead.[393] At the same time, where the KIIS contains hyperlinks these shall be consistent with the rest of the information given there, and the external sources to which they redirect shall be freely and readily accessible.[394]

[385] Arts 23(7) and 24(3) ECSPR. Especially in the case of admitted instruments for crowdfunding purposes, where the information required under Part F of Annex I regarding investor rights exceeds one side of A4-sized paper format if printed, the remainder shall be produced in an annex attached to the KIIS.
[386] Art 5(1) in combination with recital 3 Commission Delegated Regulation (EU) 2022/2119.
[387] ibid Annex.
[388] ibid recital 1.
[389] Art 23(6)(b) ECSPR.
[390] ibid Art 23(6)(c).
[391] ibid Art 23(7).
[392] Art 2(1) and (2) Commission Delegated Regulation (EU) 2022/2119.
[393] ibid Art 2(2).
[394] ibid Art 5(3).

In addition to the above, special consideration is given to the drafting language of the KIIS which shall, as a general rule, correspond either to the official language of the home NCA, or to another language accepted by that authority.[395] Where, however, a CSP promotes a crowdfunding offer through marketing communications in another Member State, the KIIS shall also be made available in the official language of the country or in a language accepted by its competent authority.[396] In any case, CSPs are free to arrange – either on their own initiative or upon an investor's request – for the translation of the KIIS in any other language provided that it accurately and faithfully reflects its original content.[397]

But CSPs also play an important role in safeguarding the quality of the KIIS by ensuring that it is properly updated throughout the whole validity period of the crowdfunding offer,[398] and by setting up adequate procedures for verifying the completeness, correctness and clarity of the information contained therein.[399] Moreover, in the event that an inaccuracy, mistake or omission which could have a material impact on the expected return of the investment is detected, they shall ask the project owner to promptly complement or correct that information,[400] or, where the KIIS is produced at the platform level, rectify all identified irregularities by themselves.[401] Finally, CSPs are even allowed to provide investors with additional information, but only insofar as it is complementary and consistent with that included in the KIIS.[402]

ii. Know Your Customer Procedures

The disclosure requirements described above aim to provide more transparency to investors regarding the project owner and the crowdfunding project, the instruments being intermediated as well as the criteria and processes followed by platforms when providing individual portfolio management of loans. Yet, despite their importance, these measures cannot guarantee the full protection of the different types of investors participating in crowdfunding offerings. In fact, given the uncertainty and complexity surrounding such transactions, the average

[395] Art 23(2) ECSPR.

[396] ibid Art 23(3). For reasons of convenience, Art 23(5) requires NCAs to notify the drafting languages that they accept to ESMA, which shall in turn make that information available on its website.

[397] ibid Art 23(4) and (13).

[398] ibid Arts 23(8) and 24(2).

[399] ibid Arts 23(11) and 24(6). Nevertheless, according to ESMA, it is the project owners that should be held ultimately responsible for any inaccurate or misleading information provided in the KIIS, as well as any omissions. Rather, the liability of CSPs is limited to those cases where an omission can be directly attributed to the lack of adequate procedures from their side in the collection of that information, see ESMA, 'Questions and Answers on the European crowdfunding service providers for business regulation' ESMA35-42-1088 (last updated 23 September 2022), Question 5.2.

[400] ibid Art 23(12). Where such completion or correction is not made promptly, CSPs must follow an escalation procedure that starts from the suspension of the offer and might even lead to its revocation.

[401] ibid Art 24(7).

[402] ibid recital 52.

retail client may, even after reading the information included in the KIIS, still find it challenging to understand or properly assess the quality and prospects of the relevant crowdfunding projects. This could, in turn, lead to a spiral of suboptimal investment decisions with negative effects on the development prospects of the EU crowdfunding market. Therefore, in order to counteract this adverse development while also facilitating investment flows, the ECSPR distinguishes between two categories of investors, namely sophisticated and non-sophisticated ones,[403] and provides for certain safeguards that are tailored to the specific conditions and needs of the second group.[404]

a. Entry Knowledge Test and Simulation of the Ability to Bear Loss

It should be apparent by now that financial products marketed through crowdfunding platforms have certain features that differentiate them from traditional investment and savings products. Moreover, as already explained above, CSPs are exempted from the scope of MiFID II and, consequently, from its provisions pertaining to investor protection, in particular those relating to the application of the suitability and appropriateness tests.[405] Therefore, in view of their insufficient prior knowledge and skills, prospective non-sophisticated investors may misjudge or even disregard the level of risk associated with crowdfunding investments.[406] Against this background, before providing these investors full access to the projects marketed on their platform, CSPs shall run an entry knowledge test in order to assess whether and which crowdfunding services offered are appropriate for them.[407] In doing so, they shall request specific information about their experience, financial standing, investment objectives and basic understanding of the risks involved in investing both in general and in relation to the types of investments presented on the platform in particular.[408] If such information is not provided, or where CSPs conclude, based on the answers received, that a prospective investor lacks the necessary knowledge or experience to proceed with

[403] This distinction mainly builds on that between professional and retail clients under Section I of Annex II to MiFID II, though it clearly differs from it as regards both the criteria and the procedure for the relevant characterisation, see Art 2(1)(j) and (k) in combination with Annex II ECSPR. For an analysis and critique of this distinction see J de Smet and V Colaert, 'Between Investor Protection and Access to Crowdfunding: The Entry Knowledge Test and the Simulation of the Ability to Bear Loss (Art 21 and Annex II)' in Macchiavello (n 356) 282–86.

[404] Recital 42 ECSPR.

[405] Art 25 MiFID II.

[406] Recital 43 ECSPR.

[407] ibid Art 21(1).

[408] ibid Art 21(2). The exact pieces of information that CSPs shall collect for the purposes of the entry knowledge test as well as the steps that need to be followed in order to ensure that such information is accurate and reliable are fleshed out in Arts 2 and 3 of Commission Delegated Regulation (EU) 2022/2114 supplementing Regulation (EU) 2020/1503 with regard to regulatory technical standards specifying the entry knowledge test and the simulation of the ability to bear loss for prospective non-sophisticated investors in crowdfunding projects [2022] OJ L287/26.

the investment, they shall notify them accordingly and issue a risk warning which should explicitly state the risk of losing the entirety of the money invested.[409] Besides, in order to prevent impulsive investment decisions, CSPs shall not accept or execute any orders from non-sophisticated investors until the latter have expressly acknowledged that they have received and understood the risk warning,[410] which should, for that reason, remain visible in a prominent place on the platform's website.[411]

However, given the tendency of human beings to underestimate the likelihood of negative events, also known as optimism bias,[412] CSPs shall, in addition to the entry knowledge test, make available an online calculation tool that enables prospective non-sophisticated investors to simulate their loss bearing capacity.[413] That way, the financial risk to which they are exposed when participating in crowdfunding offers becomes more apparent, which in turn should lead to more prudent investment decisions. For the purposes of the simulation, the ability to bear loss is calculated as 10 per cent of the investors' net worth, on the basis of their net annual income, total of liquid assets and annual financial commitments.[414] It should be noted though that the outcome of the loss simulation is not binding[415] and, thus, does not deprive non-sophisticated investors of the possibility to enter into crowdfunding transactions.[416]

b. Pre-contractual Reflection Period and Investment Limits

The legal interventions described so far reflect a more liberal approach to conduct regulation which seeks to improve the economic welfare of investors by steering their decisions in a direction that will make them better-off, without, however, limiting the choices available to them and, thus, their autonomy.[417] Yet, despite these safeguards, different types of bias could still weigh negatively on the decision-making ability of non-sophisticated investors who, due to their limited bargaining power, might find themselves in a situation where, by accepting a crowdfunding offer, they also enter into a legally binding contract without any possibility of withdrawal within a reasonable period of time.[418] Therefore, in

[409] Art 21(4) ECSPR in combination with Art 4(1) and (2) Commission Delegated Regulation (EU) 2022/2114.

[410] Art 21(4) and recital 45 ECSPR.

[411] Art 4(3) and (4) Commission Delegated Regulation (EU) 2022/2114.

[412] T Sharot, 'The Optimism Bias' (2011) 21 *Current Biology* R941.

[413] Art 21(5) ECSPR in combination with Art 5(1) Commission Delegated Regulation (EU) 2022/2114.

[414] Art 21(5) ECSPR in combination with Arts 5(2) and 7 Commission Delegated Regulation (EU) 2022/2114. The exact components used to determine the net worth as well as their valuation date are laid down in Arts 8–11 of the latter.

[415] This outcome shall, nevertheless, be communicated to the CSP and taken into account when assessing the financial situation of prospective investors, Art 3(3) and 12 Commission Delegated Regulation (EU) 2022/2114.

[416] Art 21(6) ECSPR. Investors shall, nonetheless, acknowledge receipt of the simulation's result.

[417] R Thaler and C Sunstein, 'Libertarian Paternalism' (2003) 93 *American Economic Review* 175.

[418] Recital 47 ECSPR.

order to avoid such erroneous developments and further strengthen the position of financial contributors in crowdfunding projects, the Regulation introduces a pre-contractual reflection period of four calendar days,[419] during which prospective non-sophisticated investors can revoke an offer to invest or an expression of interest in a particular crowdfunding offer without giving a reason and without incurring a penalty.[420] Platform operators play an important role in this context: not only should they provide their retail clients with accurate, clear and timely information about the existence of the reflection period, its duration and the modalities to revoke an offer or an expression of interest, but they should also ensure that no money is collected from them or transferred to the project owners before this period has expired.[421]

Finally, given the high investment risk associated with crowdfunding projects, the ECSPR sets out certain safeguards which aim to prevent the overexposure of non-sophisticated investors to them.[422] In this respect, where the amount invested in an individual crowdfunding offer exceeds either EUR 1,000 or 5 per cent of an investor's net worth income as calculated under the simulation test, CSPs shall refuse execution of the relevant order unless such investor receives a risk warning, provides explicit consent about the investment, and proves to have sufficient understanding of the investment and its risks.[423]

IV. A Critical Evaluation of the ECSPR

The measures put forward in the ECSPR, as analysed in the previous section, form the result of the EU's attempt to develop a deep and efficient single market for crowdfunding services which shall improve access to market-based financing for SMEs, especially start-ups and other early-stage firms, and provide investors, mainly retail ones, with more opportunities to diversify their portfolio.[424] As such, they are considered an essential part of the overall endeavour to complete the CMU project,[425] most notably in the area of primary capital markets. In light of this, it is important to evaluate the extent to which the new crowdfunding regime can effectively contribute to this effort and to identify ways for improving it.

[419] This should start upon receipt by the CSP of the investor's offer or expression of interest, ibid Art 22(3).

[420] ibid Art 22(2) and recital 47.

[421] ibid Art 22(6) and recital 47. For a more detailed analysis of the obligations of CSPs as well as the modalities for the exercise of the right of withdrawal, see K Serdaris, 'Withdrawal Rights in Crowdfunding Transactions: The Precontractual Reflection Period (Art 22)' in Macchiavello (n 356) 305–07.

[422] Recital 46 ECSPR.

[423] ibid Art 21(7). Where investors have taken the entry knowledge test of Art 21(1), this can be used as proof of their knowledge of the investment and its risks.

[424] SWD (2018) 56 final (n 12) 31.

[425] Recital 3 ECSPR.

A. Deepening Europe's Crowdfunding Market

The regulation of crowdfunding presented the EU decision-makers with the challenge of achieving an appropriate balance between the aim of easing the regulatory burden on smaller issuers on the one hand and the need to maintain an adequate level of investor protection on the other. In accomplishing this demanding task, the ECSPR follows a twofold strategy which involves: first, the tailoring of disclosure requirements to the specific needs, potentials and characteristics of both project owners and potential funders; and second the bigger emphasis on the conduct and organisational obligations of platform operators. While this approach is, overall, a move in the right direction, certain shortcomings could still endanger market participants' recourse to crowdfunding.

i. Improving Access to Crowdfunding for EU Businesses

Despite its imperfections, crowdfunding has the merit of playing an economically and socially valuable role in Europe. Indeed, the imposition of strict collateral requirements, which renders access to bank financing unfeasible for businesses without hard assets, the high costs associated with capital raising on public primary markets, as well as the fragmentation of the European venture capital market suggest that, without this alternative funding solution, many potentially worthy start-ups would probably not get funded.[426] Consequently, it is crucial to ensure that crowdfunding will grow into an attractive and reliable source of financing for project owners across the EU. This implies, however, dealing with certain shortcomings in the current regulatory framework, namely with regard to the types of financial instruments covered, the current capital-raising limits and the role of platforms as 'gatekeepers'.

a. The Types of Financial Instruments Covered

Under the original Commission's proposal, the scope of the ECSPR in relation to investment-based crowdfunding was confined to the placing of transferable securities as defined in Article 4(1)(44) MiFID II,[427] that is securities which are freely negotiable on the capital market. Nevertheless, this left open the question of whether offers of shares in a private limited liability company would be covered as well, since in some Member States these instruments are not considered securities[428] or their transferability is subject to certain formal

[426] Armour and Enriques (n 29) 77.
[427] Art 3(1)(i) and recital 11 ECSPR proposal.
[428] In Germany, for example, shares in private limited liability companies (*GmbH-Anteile*) are considered investment products, see K Wenzlaff and A Odorović, 'The Crowdfunding Regulation in Germany – on the Path to Self-Isolation?' in Macchiavello (n 356) 674, 680.

requirements.[429] Given, therefore, that this last corporate form is quite popular among European SMEs, the adopted text extends the Regulation's ambit to also include these assets, provided that they are not subject to any restrictions that would 'effectively prevent them from being transferred'.[430] But while this is surely a welcome development, the problem remains that the decision as to whether this requirement is met lies with the home NCA.[431] This in turn constitutes a source of legal uncertainty for project owners, considering the lack of some standardised criteria in this regard.[432] It is thus essential to clarify in greater detail the transferability restrictions that may exclude the admission of shares in private limited companies to the EU crowdfunding market.

Uncertainty as to the exact range of investments covered by the ECSPR is expected to become even more pronounced in cases where project owners wish to offer hybrid instruments, which combine both equity and debt features (eg, profit-participating rights, subordinated loans, silent partnerships etc).[433] These products are used extensively in crowdfunding offers, especially in countries like Germany and Austria.[434] This is because they provide issuers with the opportunity to raise much-needed capital at the critical start-up phase, while avoiding a widely dispersed ownership structure which could dissuade growth or late-stage professional investors from participating in future funding rounds.[435] However, it is highly doubtful whether the Regulation can be interpreted in such a way as to encompass such contractual arrangements, given the absence of any reference to asset classes which are not transferable securities or otherwise qualify as admitted instruments for crowdfunding purposes. Therefore, unless the scope of the EU crowdfunding regime is adjusted to account for hybrid investments, it is likely that many promising project owners will be deterred from resorting to this financing solution.

On a final note, it should be stressed that whilst the Regulation explicitly excludes from its scope Initial Coin Offerings (ICOs),[436] it is questionable whether security tokens, commonly used in such transactions, are also covered

[429] The Dutch Civil Code (BW), for example, requires a notarial deed for the transfer to take effect, see Art 2:196.

[430] Art 2(1)(n) ECSPR.

[431] ibid Art 2(2).

[432] For example, while shares in Dutch private limited companies (B.V.) are subject to the ECSPR, the same does not apply for shares in GmbHs as the German regulator considered the notary requirement to be a restriction to their transferability, Wenzlaff and Odorović (n 428) 681.

[433] ESMA (n 6) 14.

[434] SWD (2018) 56 final (n 12), Annex 4, 76.

[435] See, among others, RS Weinstein, 'Crowdfunding in the U.S. and Abroad: What to Expect When You're Expecting' (2013) 46 *Cornell International Law Journal* 427, 452–53; JS Wroldsen, 'The Crowdfund Act's Strange Bedfellows: Democracy and Start-up Company Investing' (2013) 62 *University of Kansas Law Review* 357, 368. Others, however, suggest that a further expansion of the crowdfunding model could positively affect the provision of post-seed investments, see M D' Ambrosio and G Gianfrate, 'Crowdfunding and Venture Capital: Substitutes or Complements?' (2016) 20 *The Journal of Private Equity* 7, 10.

[436] Recital 15 ECSPR.

by this exemption.[437] The rationale behind excluding ICOs is that their characteristics differ considerably from crowdfunding services regulated under the Regulation, thus warranting different regulatory treatment.[438] According to both the Commission and ESMA, however, security tokens are investment-like crypto-assets that could, depending on their form and the rights they grant to holders, qualify as transferable securities or other financial instruments under MiFID II, thereby falling under financial services law.[439] It is therefore imperative for EU legislators or ESMA to clarify whether these types of crypto assets fall within the Regulation's ambit, considering especially their potential to enhance funding opportunities for start-ups and other scale-ups.[440]

b. The Crowdfunding Offering Threshold

In view of the high risks associated with investments in crowdfunding projects, the ECSPR introduces a EUR 5million cap on the amount that each project owner may raise through crowdfunding offers over a 12-month period.[441] In so doing, it seeks to increase investors' confidence in this new innovative market segment,[442] albeit at the expense of fund seekers who might not be able to raise all the capital required to finance their future growth.[443] Yet, while such limitations appear justifiable and feature in most legislative actions taken in this field,[444] it is disputable whether the threshold set by EU regulators is proportionate to the aim pursued.

Indeed, one might rightly wonder why the investor protection safeguards described above combined with the extensive conduct of business requirements imposed on platform operators are considered sufficient enough to ensure that investment decisions are taken with an informed appreciation of the relevant risks in a crowdfunding offer of EUR 5 million, but not in an offer of EUR 8 million, for instance. This paradox becomes even more evident when considering that the main argument put forward for the support of the adopted threshold was its consistency with the threshold used by most Member States to exempt public offers of securities from the obligation to publish a prospectus.[445] However, this observation is not accurate, bearing in mind that, at that time, most national legislators had made use of the option given in Article 3(2)(b) of the Prospectus Regulation to raise

[437] On this issue see F Annunziata and T de Arruda, 'Crowdfunding and DLTs: The Imperative Need for More Clarity' in Macchiavello (n 356).
[438] ibid.
[439] COM (2020) 593 final (n 156) 139.
[440] See also J Rohr and A Wright, 'Blockchain-Based Token Sales, Initial Coin Offerings, and the Democratization of Public Capital Markets' (2019) 70 *Hastings Law Journal* 463, 510.
[441] Art 1(2)(c) ECSPR.
[442] EBA (n 166) 2 and 6.
[443] According to some authors, however, this offering threshold corresponds to the financing needs of EU start-ups and even seems overambitious considering the current development of the EU crowdfunding market, see Staikouras (n 74) 1076.
[444] European Crowdfunding Network (n 137).
[445] Recital 16 ECSPR.

the small offering exemption threshold to EUR 8 million. Hence, the approach followed by the ECSPR is not only substantively flawed in terms of its assumptions and reasoning, but it also fails to create a level playing field among EU issuers, who are required to abide by different thresholds, depending on whether they decide to market their securities through crowdfunding or through a typical public offering.[446] It is therefore important that the maximum threshold for crowdfunding offers be further reviewed, having also regard to the dynamic development of the industry and the growing interest of institutional investors in alternative finance,[447] which could lead to an increase in funding volumes.

c. The Role of Crowdfunding Platforms as Gatekeepers

Despite the disclosure duties provided for by the ECSPR, project owners might still face great difficulties in signalling their credibility to investors: on the one hand, they have in principle a clear incentive to omit or misstate important information in order to inflate the value of their company or to avoid conferring any advantage on their competitors; on the other hand, their short track record and the absence of an underwriting process, makes it challenging to reliably prove that the offer price reflects a true and fair valuation of the underlying investments. Therefore, in the absence of independent market actors ('gatekeepers') who could vouch for the quality of crowdfunding offers, potential investors would probably discount the price which they are willing to pay, ultimately driving high-quality companies with growth potential out of the market and exacerbating adverse selection.[448]

In this context, the participation of crowdfunding platforms in the capital raising process appears decisive in reducing information asymmetry and promoting trust between market participants.[449] Indeed, like most financial intermediaries, CSPs are repeat players in the market and are exposed to the risk of suffering reputational loss if they let project owners exaggerate or misrepresent their business prospects. As such, they are expected to act more impartially, considering that the possible gains from colluding with fund seekers should be insignificant compared to the value of the reputational capital at risk.[450] Hence, it is no surprise that the Regulation entrusts them with the task of verifying the completeness, accuracy

[446] This problem is further exacerbated by the recent amendment to the Prospectus Regulation, which raises the exemption threshold to EUR 12 million, see Art 3(2)(b) Prospectus Regulation as amended by Regulation (EU) 2024/2809 of the European Parliament and the Council amending Regulations (EU) 2017/1129, (EU) No 596/2014 and (EU) No 600/2014 to make public capital markets in the Union more attractive for companies and to facilitate access to capital for small and medium-sized enterprises OJ L, 2024/2809.

[447] Ziegler et al (n 102) 41–42.

[448] B Black, 'The Legal and Institutional Preconditions for Strong Securities Markets' (2001) 48 *UCLA Law Review* 781, 786–87.

[449] In fact, their business model is only viable to the extent that investors trust that the fundraisers using them are reliable, see Armour and Enriques (n 29) 74.

[450] JC Coffee Jr., 'Gatekeeper Failure and Reform: The Challenge of Fashioning Relevant Reforms' (2004) 84 *Boston University Law Review* 301, 308.

and clarity of the information contained in the KIIS.[451] But other than this, their role as gatekeepers is quite limited, considering especially that the liability for any mistakes or omissions in this disclosure document lies primarily with the project owner.[452] It therefore becomes necessary to further expand and clarify the range of gatekeeping functions that platforms can perform, including with regard to the services of risk valuation and pricing of crowdfunding offers which are currently confined to lending-based crowdfunding.[453] This should enable investors to identify support-worthy projects, thus increasing the attractiveness of crowdfunding as an alternative financing solution for promising start-ups in the EU.

ii. Strengthening Investors' Confidence in Crowdfunding

Mandatory disclosure forms the linchpin of EU financial market regulation, inasmuch as it protects investors from fraudulent or otherwise unsound issuers, thus increasing their confidence in the market.[454] The ECSPR is no exception in this respect, though special emphasis is also placed on the content, framing and quality of disclosure as a means for dealing with the cognitive limitations and biases of non-sophisticated investors. According to policy makers, this will allow for better informed investment decisions and, thereby, increase the overall efficiency of capital allocation through crowdfunding.[455] But while this behaviourally-informed approach to disclosure requirements could have a positive debiasing effect,[456] especially when combined with the KYC rules imposed on platform operators, some additional, targeted interventions are needed in order to enhance investors' trust towards crowdfunding. These should be concentrated primarily on reducing investor exposure to agency costs, mitigating the operational risk of crowdfunding platforms and facilitating the development of a liquid and efficient secondary crowdfunding market.

a. Reducing Agency Costs

As already explained, crowdfunding investors face significant agency costs, given that, unlike in other forms of start-up financing, they are unable to bargain for protection or get more actively involved in the governance of the investee

[451] Arts 23(11) and 24(6) ECSPR.

[452] ESMA, *Q&As on the European crowdfunding service providers for business regulation* (n 399).

[453] Art 4(2) and (4) in combination with recital 11 ECSPR.

[454] L Enriques and S Gilotta, 'Disclosure and Financial Market Regulation' in E Ferran, N Moloney and J Payne (eds), *Oxford Handbook on Financial Regulation* (OUP, 2014) 514–16.

[455] SWD (2018) 56 final (n 12) 55.

[456] Experimental studies, however, have questioned the effectiveness of similar interventions in yielding large changes in investors' behaviour, see J Beshears et al, 'How Does Simplified Disclosure Affect Individuals' Mutual Fund Choices?', in DA Wise (ed), *Explorations in the Economics of Aging* (De Gruyter, 2010); London Economics and Ipsos, 'Consumer testing study of the possible new format and content of for retail disclosures of packaged retail and insurance-based investment products', Final Report, November 2015.

company so as to effectively monitor the compliance of corporate decisions with their interests.[457] The ECSPR seeks to address this problem mainly by requiring crowdfunding platforms to undertake a systematic pre-screening of project owners[458] and to ensure that the information included in the KIIS is accurate and allows for the objective assessment of the potential benefits and risks pertaining to the offer.[459] But despite their obvious importance, the ability of these due diligence requirements to improve the monitoring capacity of investors and thereby reduce post-investment managerial opportunism seems rather limited. Therefore, it appears necessary to lay down some more effective methods for reducing agency costs in crowdfunded companies.

One solution might be to build on the contractual mechanisms used by angel investors and VCs, who normally reserve control, participation and preferential rights for themselves.[460] However, the amounts at stake would typically be too low for crowd-funders to even consider bearing the coordination costs associated with such mechanisms. In this respect, it would be more effective to further review and strengthen the intermediary role of CSPs so that they can act as the representatives of investors in negotiating contractual rights and exercising them on their behalf.[461] Alternatively, EU legislators could consider the possibility of facilitating the use of corporate structures, such as special purpose entities or collective investment schemes, which could hold and manage the securities, admitted instruments or loans on behalf of the investors who would retain the beneficial ownership of the assets.[462]

A more innovative regulatory solution which is, in fact, better adapted to the institutional context of crowdfunding, though, would be to further leverage the huge potentials of modern internet technologies. Indeed, in the digital world, business monitoring is rather inexpensive: all relevant corporate information, such as client, invoice or staff data, can be shared in real time, managers can arrange regular teleconferences to provide updates on the company's strategy and development, while investors may establish online communication systems where they can exchange information and work collectively towards achieving their common goals.[463] Therefore, if properly applied, digital methods could help reduce agency costs and thus increase investors' confidence in the crowdfunding market.

[457] Armour and Enriques (n 29) 79–80.

[458] With the aim of verifying their identity and the absence of criminal record, Art 5(2) ECSPR.

[459] ibid Arts 23(11) and 24(6).

[460] See, among others, SN Kaplan and P Strömberg, 'Financial Contracting Theory Meets the Real World: An Empirical Analysis of Venture Capital Contracts' (2003) 70 *Review of Economic Studies* 281, 286 ff.

[461] In fact, some platforms wittingly market themselves as protecting investors by acting as their proxies in the relationship with the issuers, see Armour and Enriques (n 29) 80.

[462] Indirect investment structures are popular among EU national crowdfunding regimes, see ESMA, 'Investment-based Crowdfunding: Insights from Regulators in the EU', 13 May 2015, 5.

[463] Schwartz (n 45) 683–84.

b. Operational Continuity Safeguards for Crowdfunding Platforms

The potential collapse of platform operators due to malpractice is perceived as being a principal factor deterring investors from participating in crowdfunding.[464] It comes as no surprise, therefore that the ECSPR pays particular attention to ensuring the operational continuity of CSPs, mainly by requiring them to comply with some minimum prudential requirements,[465] segregate their own funds from those of their clients[466] and develop detailed business continuity plans.[467] Yet, while these provisions hold the potential to contribute to the future growth of the industry, more needs to be done to mitigate the operational risk of crowdfunding platforms.

First, concerning the prudential safeguards imposed on CSPs, these shall be equal to at least EUR 25,000 or one quarter of the annual fixed overhead costs, whichever is higher.[468] Nevertheless, the first amount appears really low, especially when considering that the own funds requirement for 'small' investment firms that provide similar services under MiFID II and do not hold client money is set at EUR 75,000.[469] It therefore appears necessary to further increase the minimum capital adequacy requirements for platform operators, since it would not only create a more level-playing field, but it would also decrease the risks for investors without erecting excessively high market entry barriers. Second, while the Regulation defines some strict standards for the competence of the managers of CSPs,[470] the same does not apply with regard to the capabilities of their personnel. Considering, however, that crowdfunding is built on very complex technologies requiring extensive knowledge and experience to operate properly, it is equally important to adopt some minimum requirements regarding the qualifications and skills of the staff, especially in the area of IT services. Finally, although crowdfunding platforms are generally too small to be systemically important,[471] it is true that the volume of transactions processed is often too big to ignore. In such cases, therefore, NCAs should be empowered to appoint an interim board to run the platform in so far as it is deemed necessary for safeguarding its operational continuity.[472]

[464] B Zhang et al, 'Sustaining Momentum – The 2nd European Alternative Finance Industry Report', September 2016, 47; Ziegler et al (n 102) 53.

[465] Art 11 ECSPR. For a detailed analysis of these requirements, see M Louisse, 'Prudential Requirements for Crowdfunding Service Providers (Art 11)' in Macchiavello (n 356).

[466] ibid Art 10(2).

[467] Art 12(2)(j) ECSPR and Commission Delegated Regulation (EU) 2022/2116.

[468] Art 11(1) ECSPR.

[469] Art 9(2) Directive (EU) 2019/2034 of the European Parliament and of the Council on the prudential supervision of investment firms and amending Directives 2002/87/EC, 2009/65/EC, 2011/61/EU, 2013/36/EU, 2014/59/EU and 2014/65/EU [2019] OJL 314/64.

[470] Recital 25 ECSPR.

[471] Zetzsche and Preiner (n 178) 225.

[472] ibid 245.

c. The Need for a Robust Secondary Crowdfunding Market

According to the Regulation, CSPs shall operate in the primary market only. Indeed, even though they are allowed to administer bulletin boards, that is online information exchange systems where clients can advertise buying and selling interests in assets that were originally offered on their platforms,[473] such facilities shall, in principle, not consist of internal matching systems that execute client orders on a multilateral basis.[474] This implies that there can be no interaction between the potential counterparties within bulletin boards, namely through the protocols or internal operating procedures of CSPs, and the conclusion of any agreement shall only take place bilaterally, outside the platform.[475] Consequently, investors have a very limited secondary market to dispose of or realise their initial crowdfunding investments, a situation which could adversely affect their readiness to enter the market, with far-reaching effects on the development of crowdfunding in the EU and, thus, the funding opportunities of businesses.

In theory, of course, CSPs could obtain an authorisation to operate a trading venue in accordance with MiFID II, thus enabling multiple third parties to negotiate and conclude buying or selling contracts in relation to crowdfunded securities admitted for trading there. Considering, however, the heavy compliance costs associated with running a regulated market, an MTF or an OTF,[476] it is rather improbable that CSPs would opt for that option. Besides, this solution would not only create additional burdens for project owners,[477] but it would leave the problem partly unaddressed, given that loans and other admitted instruments for crowdfunding purposes which do not qualify as transferable securities cannot be listed on such venues.[478] Therefore, it appears necessary to put measures in place aimed at facilitating the development of a liquid and efficient secondary market for crowdfunding investments. For example, CSPs should enjoy greater latitude in deciding which market participants can access bulletin boards, since this right currently seems to be confined only to clients who have already invested in crowdfunding offers facilitated by them.[479] In addition, platform operators could engage more actively in the external negotiation process, perhaps by providing their clients with appropriate contract templates which can ensure the orderly

[473] Art 25(1) ECSPR.

[474] ibid Art 25(2) and recital 55.

[475] A Hakvoort, 'Secondary Trading of Crowdfunding Investments' in P Ortolani and M Louisse (eds), *The EU Crowdfunding Regulation* (OUP, 2021) 274; M Gargantini, 'Secondary Markets for Crowdfunding: Bulletin Boards (Art 25)' in Macchiavello (356) 360. See also ESMA, 'MiFID II Review Report on the Functioning of Organised Trading Facilities (OTF)' ESMA 70-156-4225, 23 March 2021, 27–28.

[476] These arise mainly due to the organisational and operational requirements imposed by MiFID II, but also due to internal rules and policies.

[477] These are associated primarily with the ongoing and ad-hoc disclosure requirements provided for in the Transparency Directive and the Market Abuse Regulation (MAR) respectively.

[478] Hakvoort (n 475) 280–81; Gargantini (n 475) 362.

[479] Recital 55 ECSPR; Gargantini (n 475) 355–56.

and sound execution of the transaction.[480] Finally, EU regulators could consider allowing CSPs to perform certain functions which have the potential to improve secondary market activity, without requiring an authorisation as trading venue. For instance, crowdfunding platforms could support pre-arranged transactions between their clients, provided that these transactions are ultimately formalised on an authorised trading venue on the basis of an outsourcing agreement.[481]

B. Building a Single Market for Crowdfunding Services

As discussed earlier in this chapter, the Commission's initial proposal aspired to create a stand-alone optional EU crowdfunding regime, which would allow platforms to expand their operations across national borders whilst leaving national regulatory frameworks unaffected. Nevertheless, the adopted Regulation employs a maximum harmonisation model, expressly prohibiting Member States from imposing additional or more stringent requirements with regard to the provision of crowdfunding services that fall within its scope.[482] The rationale behind this change in strategy was that the co-existence of multiple legal regimes would run the risk of generating uncertainty among market actors, thereby inhibiting rather than encouraging cross-border market activity.[483] This, however, is a rebuttable presumption, given that in a dynamic and innovative environment like that of crowdfunding, it is extremely important that regulators have the capacity to keep pace with changing market developments and respond promptly to new business models. In this respect, the approach advocated by the Commission, although admittedly imperfect, might have proven more effective at this stage, since it would help reduce cross-border market entry costs, while leveraging the convergence dynamics of regulatory competition, mainly through the discovery and sharing of best practices.[484] Be that as it may, it is still doubtful whether the current regime is capable of achieving the objective of building a truly integrated crowdfunding market in the EU. This is attributable partly to the problematic scope of the ECSPR, but also to the lack of convergence in key areas, namely private enforcement and operational supervisory practices.

i. *Refining the Scope of the ECSPR*

a. One Size does not Fit All

As has already been explained, the EU crowdfunding regime focuses primarily on the nature of the transactions enabled by the platforms, rather than the features of

[480] Hakvoort (n 475) 284.
[481] ESMA (n 475) 26. See also Hakvoort (n 475) 285.
[482] Recital 33 ECSPR.
[483] ibid recitals 5 and 6. See also Macchiavello (n 133) 564.
[484] On the merits of regulatory competition, see in detail ch 2, III B.ii.

the offered contracts.[485] Accordingly, the scope of its application expands to all business models which involve the intermediation of products embedding a financial return, irrespective of whether they are classified as loans, transferable securities or other admitted instruments for crowdfunding purposes. However, placing both investment and lending-based crowdfunding under a single framework could prove problematic from a legal certainty point of view,[486] if not accompanied by specific rules that take sufficient account of the different challenges that these activities pose to the smooth functioning of the market. Indeed, the essential functions and risks associated with business loans are distinctive from those related to investments in financial instruments, thus also justifying their separate regulatory treatment. Considering, therefore, that the provisions laid down in the Regulation are, for the most part, modelled on those of EU securities regulation,[487] market participants might be reluctant to engage in cross-border lending activity through crowdfunding. In this regard, it would be advisable to establish a separate regime for lending-based crowdfunding.

b. Expanding the Range of Crowdfunding Services

Another aspect of the Regulation's scope which appears to contradict the desired objective of creating a single EU crowdfunding market is related to the strict delineation of the services that platforms can provide. More specifically, as mentioned above, before the entry into force of the ECSPR, several EU countries had set up bespoke national regimes, specifically catered to the needs of local markets. In certain instances, the services covered by national law even escape the reach of the Regulation, as is the case, for example, with Germany,[488] which is also home to some of the leading crowdfunding platforms in Europe.[489] However, these disparities are likely to have an impact on the function of the internal market, given that the Regulation does not deprive Member States of the right to impose national rules regarding the provision of crowdfunding services which relate to those reserved for platform operators holding a CSP licence.[490] Indeed, although the wording of the relevant provision does not allow for unambiguous conclusions on the exact types of services that correspond to these criteria, the discretion granted to national platforms to operate outside the EU regulatory perimeter might decrease their incentives to scale up their operations across the single market to

[485] SWD (2018) 56 final (n 11) 7.

[486] ibid 42.

[487] In fact, not only is MiFID II the main reference point for the most part of the Regulation's provisions (eg, platform authorisation, organisational and operational requirements, investor protection rules etc), but also the KIIS is based on the prospectus to be published when securities are offered to the public.

[488] Wenzlaff and Odorović (n 428) 686.

[489] Some of the most renowned European crowdfunding platforms, like Companisto, Seedmatch and Startnext are located in Germany.

[490] Art 1(2)(b) ECSPR.

the detriment of investors and project owners. Against this background, EU legislators should reconsider the scope of the services covered by the ECSPR in order to reduce the incentives of platform operators to resort to national regimes.

c. Increasing the Size of Crowdfunding Offers

Considerations similar to those raised in the previous paragraph also apply with regard to the size of the offers that fall within the ambit of the EU regime. In particular, it could be argued that the EUR 5 million cap on the maximum amount that a single issuer may raise via crowdfunding on an annual basis, combined with the restrictive criteria which shall be cumulatively applied when calculating this amount,[491] might prompt some project owners – especially in countries with developed crowdfunding markets – to opt for the national law of their place of establishment. This risk becomes particularly evident when considering that the Regulation does not seem to prohibit the application of national regimes in relation to crowdfunding offers exceeding the threshold of EUR 5 million,[492] while certain Member States already have rules in place that allow them to move in this direction.[493] Therefore, it would appear more appropriate to increase the size of the offers that are covered by the ECSPR so as to increase its attractiveness and incentivise more platforms to obtain a relevant authorisation.

ii. Improving Convergence of Supervisory and Enforcement Systems

a. Operational Supervision and the Role of ESMA

As has been rightly pointed out, 'regulation does not operate in a vacuum'.[494] As a matter of fact, the crisis era has led to the realisation that rule-making is only part of a bundle of measures which are needed to tackle the risks and challenges posed by the dynamic development of financial markets.[495] Another important part is the operationalisation of the legal provisions which, in turn, requires the establishment of an effective supervisory system that guarantees full and rigorous compliance with the relevant regulatory requirements and standards.[496] There are several compelling reasons for this. First, in contrast to policymakers,

[491] As already explained, the maximum offer threshold is calculated by adding up not only the considerations of investment and lending-based crowdfunding offers, but also the total consideration of certain types of exempted public offers.

[492] In fact, Art 1(2)(c) ECSPR explicitly states that the Regulation does not apply to offers with a consideration of more than EUR 5 million, thus implying that offers above this threshold may be covered by national law.

[493] This is the case, especially, with Germany, see §2a (1) VermAnlG.

[494] N Moloney, *EU Securities and Financial Markets*, 3rd edn (OUP, 2014) 944.

[495] See eg AW Lo, 'Regulatory Reform in the Wake of the Financial Crisis of 2007–2008' (2009) 1 *Journal of Financial Economic Policy* 4.

[496] See eg HM Treasury, 'A New Approach to Financial Regulation: Judgement, Focus and Stability', July 2010, 28.

supervisory authorities are better insulated from the influence of industry lobbying, thus offering the prospect of being less prone to risks of regulatory capture and corruption.[497] Second, given the increasing complexity of the legal framework for securities markets, supervisors hold a crucial role in ensuring its consistent application, identifying possible deficiencies and, consequently, increasing legal certainty.[498] Besides, proactive supervision can act as the first line of defence against potential market failures and malpractices, thereby helping to build public confidence in the financial system.[499]

However, the factors that influence the effectiveness of financial market supervision are multi-layered, while the choice of an optimal organisational structure can be difficult and complex.[500] This is particularly true in the EU where the supervisory framework must also be configured in such a way that it responds to the specific challenges posed by cross-border activity. In this context, a great deal of attention has been given to increasing the ability of ESMA to support supervisory convergence and co-ordination, that is to promote sound, efficient and consistent supervisory practices across the EU.[501] But despite the enhanced role of ESMA in building a common supervisory culture among Member States, operational supervision remains primarily a local function.[502] Such is the case with the ECSPR which anchors the *lato sensu* supervision[503] of crowdfunding activities to the home NCA.

From the perspective of market integration, though, the problem with a decentralised system is that it might give rise to risks of supervisory arbitrage, especially when taking into account the disparities between NCAs in terms of technical expertise, resource availability and political support.[504] On the other hand, of course, this should not lead to the conclusion that a 'single supervisor' model would be the correct way forward.[505] Indeed, even leaving aside the legal conundrums posed by the possible delegation of supervisory powers to ESMA – associated mainly

[497] DC Langevoort, 'The SEC as a Lawmaker: Choices About Investor Protection in the Face of Uncertainty' (2006) 84 *Washington University Law Review* 1591, 1598.

[498] N Moloney, 'The European Supervisory Authorities and Discretion: Can the Functional and Constitutional Circles be Squared?' in J Mendes (ed), *EU Executive Discretion and the Limits of Law* (OUP, 2019) 100.

[499] E Wymeersch, 'The Structure of Financial Supervision in Europe' (2007) 8 *European Business Organization Law Review* 237, 243. See, also, The High-Level Group in Financial Supervision in the EU, Final Report, 25 September 2009, 38–39 (The de Larosière Report).

[500] See, generally, N Moloney, 'Supervision in the Wake of the Financial Crisis: Achieving Effective Law in Action – A Challenge for the EU' in E Wymeersch, K Hopt and G Ferrarini (eds), *Financial Regulation and Supervision: A Post Crisis Analysis* (OUP, 2012) 80 et seq.

[501] Regulation (EU) No 1095/2010) [2010] OJ L331/84 ('ESMA Regulation'), Art 29.

[502] ibid recital 9, describing the ESFS as 'an integrated network of national and Union supervisory authorities, leaving day-to-day supervision at the national level'.

[503] This includes, in particular, the authorisation of crowdfunding platforms, their ongoing supervision and the initiation of public enforcement actions.

[504] Moloney (n 494) 1004.

[505] In favour of a centralised supervisory authority in the EU, see eg DC Langevoort, 'Structuring Securities Regulation in the European Union: Lessons from the U.S. Experience' in Ferrarini and Wymeersch (n 258) 501–02.

with its compatibility with the *Meroni* doctrine[506] – it should be borne in mind that operational supervision is essentially the only device through which Member States can exercise actual control over national markets.[507] Consequently, the more ESMA engages in direct supervision, the higher the possibility of resistance from NCAs and the relevant threats to its effectiveness. Besides, despite its shortcomings, reliance on NCAs permits greater geographic proximity to the supervised entities and thus more efficient functioning of the public intervention scheme.[508] In view of the above, it can be concluded that the optimal solution for the supervision of the EU crowdfunding market would consist of a judicious combination of local autonomy, supranational governance and intensified cooperation aimed at sufficiently accommodating national preferences and interests, without jeopardising the smooth functioning of the internal market in this field.

b. Private Enforcement Mechanisms in the EU Crowdfunding Framework

Although private enforcement mechanisms carry the potential to complement supervisory actions,[509] they have long been the Achilles heel of EU capital markets regulation. Indeed, while the regulatory reforms in the post-crisis era have led to a significantly more harmonised approach to administrative infringements and sanctions, the approximation of Member States' civil liability regimes has, with very few exceptions,[510] been met with scepticism, resistance and even hostility. This is not only the result of the diverging approaches taken by national legislators in terms of, for example, the degree of fault, or the design of causes of action and the nature of remedies. It also reflects the varying views on the role of private litigation in the enforcement of EU securities laws more generally.[511] Against this background, it is scarcely surprising that the ECSPR does not lay down a common framework with regard to damages actions for breach of the rules contained therein. Rather, it merely requires Member States to ensure that responsibility for the information given in the KIIS attaches, at least, to the project owner or its administrative, management or supervisory bodies.[512] Moreover it establishes that

[506] Difficulties arise mainly with regard to how much discretion can be granted to ESMA and whether the margin of discretion can be considered overly wide where policy choices are, to some extent, engaged.

[507] Moloney (494) 1004.

[508] E Ferran, 'Understanding the New Institutional Architecture of EU Financial Market Supervision' in Wymeersch, Hopt and Ferrarini (eds) (n 500) 142.

[509] On the role of private enforcement in increasing financial market discipline, see HE Jackson and M Roe, 'Public and Private Enforcement of Securities Laws: Resource-Based Evidence' (2009) 93 *Journal of Financial Economics* 207.

[510] Regulation (EU) No 462/2013 of the European Parliament and of the Council amending Regulation (EC) No 1060/2009 on credit rating agencies [2013] OJ L146/1 provides, for the first time, for a harmonised civil liability regime, the key determinants of which, though, depend almost entirely on national interpretation.

[511] Moloney (n 494) 968.

[512] Art 23(9) ECSPR. These persons must be clearly identified in the KIIS by their names and functions (or in the case of legal persons their registered offices), while they must provide written declarations

those persons responsible for the information provided in the KIIS – including any translations thereof – shall, according to national laws, regulations and administrative provisions, be held liable at least for misleading or inaccurate statements, or for the omission of key information which is important for investors when deciding on whether to finance a specific project.[513]

Nonetheless, the absence of a comprehensive system of private enforcement in the EU crowdfunding regime can be regarded as problematic from an integration point of view.[514] Admittedly, the creation of a Union-wide civil liability scheme for CSPs and project owners would not only limit regulatory arbitrage risks, but it would also increase legal certainty, with positive effects on cross-border activity.[515] At the same time, though, it is clear that the considerable differences in the substantive and procedural laws and practices of the Member States regarding civil liability (both contractual and tortious), make harmonisation a complex, costly and, ultimately, inefficient proposition – at least in the short run. Consequently, it is necessary to think of some less intrusive solutions to help drive forward the regulatory convergence process in this field. One step towards that direction would be the introduction of an online database, comprising decisions issued by national courts and extrajudicial settlement bodies across the EU on civil liability cases under the ECSPR.[516] This would provide greater legal predictability while it could also contribute to market integration by inspiring imitation and fruitful cooperation. In addition to this, EU policymakers should consider expanding the scope of the Collective Redress Directive[517] to also include infringements of the Regulation. This initiative seeks to approximate certain aspects of the laws, regulations and administrative practices of Member States concerning representative actions – both for injunctive and for redress measures[518] – brought by qualified entities representing consumers' interests[519] and could thus help to create a level playing field for the entities that operate in the EU crowdfunding market, while also stimulating investor confidence to engage in cross-border

that, to the best of their knowledge, the information contained is in accordance with the facts and that the KIIS does not make any omission likely to affect its import.

[513] ibid Art 23(10).

[514] On this issue see K Wenzlaff et al, 'On the merits of the Key Investment Information Sheet in the ECSPR (Arts 23–24 and Annex 1)' in Macchiavello (n 356) 333–35.

[515] On the role of harmonised private enforcement mechanism in capital market integration see Moloney (n 494) 968.

[516] This could be part of the European e-Justice Portal which is administered by the Commission and collates with the court rulings from across the Union on the interpretation of national and EU law.

[517] Directive (EU) 2020/1828 of 25 November 2020 on representative actions for the protection of the collective interests of consumers and repealing Directive 2009/22/EC [2020] OJ L409/1.

[518] ibid Art 2(1) and recital 6.

[519] The Directive provides a broad definition of the concept of 'consumer' who can be represented by a qualified entity in a redress action, comprising any natural person that acts for purposes outside of their trade, business, craft or profession, irrespective of how this person is referred to in the legal act allegedly infringed (eg, retails investor, data subject, traveller, user etc.), Art 3(1) in conjunction with recital 14.

transactions.[520] Finally, the application of uniform rules of private international law to determine the national liability regime applicable in cases with a foreign element is also of great importance. This is because, apart from its obvious ability to reduce legal uncertainty for market participants, it could provide evidence on how harmonisation in this area should proceed to the extent that clear evidence of market support for the regulatory choices of certain Member States emerges.[521]

[520] On the potential application of the EU's collective redress strategy to the financial markets see N Moloney, *How to Protect Investors – Lessons from the EC and the UK* (CUP, 2010) 458–63.

[521] For example, a possible indicator of such support could be the relocation of CSPs to certain Member States and the choice of investors to fund projects which are offered through their platform. On the potential of regulatory competition to serve as a pointer for harmonisation, see Ferran (n 77) 54.

Conclusion

I. Balancing Unity and Differentiation in EU Primary Markets

The significant vulnerabilities of a bank-based and poorly integrated EU financial system, exposed by the global financial crisis, prompted the Commission to intensify its efforts in creating a truly single market for capital across Member States through the establishment of a Capital Markets Union (CMU). Within this framework, this policy initiative rests upon two main pillars: fostering a more diversified financial ecosystem to support the development of capital markets in all EU countries, and promoting a more sustainable financial integration process by removing any barriers to cross-border interconnectedness among market actors. Consequently, its successful completion is considered pivotal for achieving the key economic objectives set by the EU.[1] More specifically, by seeking to enhance the size, depth, and efficiency of national capital markets and foster closer links among these markets and their participants, the CMU can facilitate broader access to funding for EU businesses and offer investors a wider range of investment opportunities. This would enable these parties to better fulfil their respective objectives and needs. At the same time, well-functioning and integrated capital markets are crucial for stimulating economic activity, smoothing fluctuations in the business cycle, and enabling more efficient cross-border risk sharing. From a macroeconomic standpoint, the CMU can thus enhance growth and financial stability in the EU, particularly during economic downturns.

Unlike the Banking Union, however, which represents the other major post-crisis reform toward a more integrated financial system, the CMU is a multifaceted and long-term project. This means that its successful completion requires persistent efforts and substantial reforms. Consequently, one of the most notable aspects of the CMU project is the wide range and diversity of actions put forward for implementation. Among these actions, this study focused on two regulatory initiatives introduced in the primary market domain: the 2017 Prospectus Regulation, including its amendments by the EU Listing Act, and the Regulation on European crowdfunding service providers for businesses (ECSPR). As explained, these legislative measures collectively constitute a regulatory system aimed at enhancing market efficiency and fostering the internal market for capital. Hence, they

[1] Commission, 'A Capital Markets Union for People and Businesses-New Action Plan', COM (2020) 590 final, 24 September 2020, 3–4.

represent two significant milestones toward realising the CMU's goal of establishing a deep and well-functioning single market for capital in the EU. In this context, the question arose regarding the extent to which these measures have effectively advanced the completion of the CMU.

In addressing this question, specific attention was given to the interplay between unity and differentiation that transcends the CMU project. In particular, the analysis demonstrated that creating a regulatory framework which can support the attractiveness of primary markets for EU businesses and investors, while removing barriers to cross-border funding and investment activities, requires a careful consideration of both the design and scope of legal interventions. Regarding the design, it was stressed that any legislative action should ensure a fair balance between the divergent interests and needs of the targeted market participants, who range from small startups to large multinationals and from individual savers to professional institutions. This implies that regulatory policies should be tailored to align more closely with the specific characteristics and demands of end users within the EU capital markets. In terms of the range of interventions, it was argued that while imposing a single set of rules 'from the top-down' can theoretically facilitate primary market integration, within the EU's financial law-making process, Member States are inclined to protect their entrenched institutional economic models and associated comparative advantages. Therefore, in certain cases, they should be afforded some discretion in selecting regulatory tools and strategies to better accommodate national economic preferences and local market needs.

With this in mind, the study sought to develop a normative framework to assess the effectiveness of the introduced measures in achieving the CMU's objectives. Drawing on insights from welfare economics and the economics of federalism, it was concluded that such a framework should be based on the following four key elements: (i) a well-balanced issuer disclosure regime; (ii) sound supervisory and private enforcement mechanisms; (iii) effective intermediation channels; and (iv) a mixed integration model that leaves some room for both harmonisation and regulatory competition.

More specifically, the regulation of primary markets in the EU focuses on the disclosure requirements for issuers when selling securities to the public. Its main objective is to provide investors with the essential information needed to make informed and efficient investment decisions. Hence, designing an effective mandatory disclosure regime that meets investors' needs is crucial for the development of robust primary markets. Particular emphasis in this effort should be placed on defining the investor base. Specifically, considering the cognitive limitations and biases affecting investors' decisions, regulators should distinguish between situations where concise, well-framed information is beneficial and those where the price mechanism is already influenced by a sufficient number of rational, well-informed investors. But apart from meeting investors' needs, preserving market efficiency requires that disclosure requirements do not unduly burden issuers, potentially deterring promising projects from entering the market. Therefore, when determining disclosure duties, it is essential to consider the specific circumstances of businesses, ensuring that the marginal costs of disclosure do not outweigh the benefits of seeking market funding.

Nevertheless, the effectiveness of disclosure rules in driving market development would be compromised without a robust supervisory and enforcement mechanism to ensure compliance by market actors. Consequently, ensuring prompt and efficient recovery of any losses incurred by investors due to false or misleading statements is crucial. This requires implementing a carefully calibrated civil liability regime that adequately protects investors while avoiding a formalistic approach to disclosure by issuers. Furthermore, given the pivotal role of financial intermediaries in primary market transactions, a comprehensive regulatory system should also include provisions safeguarding the quality and independence of these intermediation channels. These provisions should encompass at least some organisational and conduct-of-business rules, along with authorisation requirements, to prevent market access by fraudulent or unsound firms.

Finally, to deepen primary market integration, and considering the diverging preferences, priorities, and views of Member States, the optimal regulatory approach should combine top-down harmonisation with the judicious use of regulatory competition, consistent with the principle of subsidiarity.[2] Following this approach, harmonisation should be the preferred regulatory tool when economic and legal distortions create obstacles to the cross-border movement of capital, thereby affecting overall welfare, and cannot be effectively resolved through national legislation. In contrast, when legislation requires flexibility to accommodate market innovations and local needs, the solution of competition appears preferable. The same holds true in historical status quo situations, where the quality of national rules is high and the experience accumulated through their application is substantial, thus rendering the costs of harmonisation significantly high compared to the potential benefits. Even in these cases, however, a certain level of harmonisation is considered necessary to prevent regulatory competition from resulting in a 'race to the bottom'. This could involve either the imposition of minimum EU standards applied directly to Member States, or the establishment of a two-tier system under which a common set of optional rules enacted at the EU level would coexist with national rules, allowing market participants to freely choose the applicable law.

II. Key Findings and Recommendations

Expanding upon this framework, this study proceeded to evaluate the Prospectus Regulation, which lays down uniform requirements for the preparation, approval,

[2] See also R van den Bergh, 'Regulatory Competition or Harmonization of Laws? Guidelines for the European Regulator' in A Marciano and J-M Josselin (eds), *The Economics of Harmonizing European Law* (Edward Elgar, 2002) 28.

and dissemination of the prospectus which must be published when securities are publicly offered or admitted to trading on a regulated market of a Member State. It also examined the recently adopted EU crowdfunding regime, which introduces harmonised rules for the authorisation, operation, organisation, and supervision of crowdfunding operators. These two initiatives are intricately linked and reinforce each other, as they regulate capital raising activities across various stages of a company's development. At the same time, though, they exhibit differences in the regulatory approach followed, primarily driven by the distinct characteristics of participants in the respective market. Accordingly, their joint evaluation and comparison was considered crucial in comprehending the regulation of primary markets within the CMU and drawing conclusions for future guidance. Based on this analysis, it was concluded that while these reforms are generally moving in the right direction, several shortcomings persist, which are at odds with the CMU's strategic objective of constructing a strong, efficient, and genuinely integrated EU capital market. Consequently, specific recommendations for future regulatory actions and reforms were proposed.

A. The EU Prospectus Regulation

The adoption of the EU Prospectus Regulation in 2017 marked the long-awaited reform of the 2003 Prospectus Directive which, despite its positive impact in enhancing a more efficient single primary market, had faced significant criticism from stakeholders. This was primarily attributed to the inadequate differentiation of disclosure rules among specific situations and issuers, but also to its failure to attain the desired clarity and convergence in certain practices and approaches among Member States. In this regard, the Prospectus Regulation, particularly after its recent reform through the EU Listing Act, deserves commendation for addressing many of these shortcomings. More specifically, the broadening of exceptions from prospectus obligations, the refinement and alleviation of disclosure requirements for certain issuer types (ie, SMEs, secondary issuers, frequent issuers, and issuers of wholesale debt securities), as well as the introduction of harmonised rules on prospectus scrutiny and approval processes, have the potential to improve access to primary markets for EU companies, including across borders. At the same time, the overhaul of the content and format of the prospectus summary, the implementation of stricter criteria regarding the inclusion of risk factors in the prospectus, the establishment of a centralised system for electronic access to EU-approved prospectuses, along with the creation of a more robust regime for administrative sanctions in case of infringements of the Regulation collectively increase the level of investor protection, thus holding the potential of promoting their participation in primary markets.

Despite these positive developments, however, the revised prospectus regime has only partially met its goals of advancing the development and integration of EU primary markets. Indeed, the analysis revealed that some of the shortcomings besetting issuers and investors, especially smaller ones, are likely to persist in primary markets because the Regulation has not sufficiently addressed them. These include mainly the absence of some common minimum disclosure standards for exempted small public offers (ie, below EUR 12 or 5 million, as the case may be), the still relatively low incentives to encourage SMEs' access to public markets, liability concerns for issuers due to the omission or false categorisation of risk factors, the unbalanced emphasis on historical information, persistent obstacles to the processability of the prospectus summary, and the favourable treatment of high-denomination debt securities. Furthermore, the lack of a procedural EU legal framework on prospectus liability, inadequate harmonisation of operational supervisory and enforcement practices among NCAs, and the discretion granted to Member States in defining certain aspects governing the admission of securities to trading on regulated markets may continue to pose significant challenges to cross-border activity, thereby undermining the efforts to complete the CMU.

In light of these shortcomings, four sets of improvements were suggested to promote the development and integration of EU primary markets. First, to facilitate access to primary markets for EU issuers, the new exception thresholds for small offers should be reassessed to ensure greater consistency across the EU. Moreover, additional measures should be taken to alleviate barriers for SMEs and other small caps seeking access to the capital market through SME growth markets or MTFs more broadly. Second, the EU legislator should consider clarifying the criteria for assessing the specificity and materiality of risk factors and introducing an automatic shelf registration system, similar to the US regime for WKSIs. Third, to promote household investments, it is advisable to facilitate the inclusion of forward-looking information in the prospectus, enhance the processability of the prospectus summary for retail investors, and reduce incentives for issuers and underwriters to place securities exclusively with qualified investors. Finally, to ensure the proper functioning of the internal market, centralising certain supervisory and enforcement activities and harmonising national prospectus liability regimes could help create a level playing field for market participants across the EU. Meanwhile, more consistency is needed regarding the conditions for the admission of securities to trading, especially following the repeal of the Listing Directive.

B. The Regulation on European Crowdfunding Service Providers

The decision to introduce the ECSP Regulation, while possibly immature, is, in principle, a welcome step. Indeed, by establishing a harmonised, proportionate, and sound framework for the authorisation, organisation, and supervision of crowdfunding service providers, it can facilitate the cross-border expansion of platform operators, thereby increasing the level of risk capital available to EU start-ups and other fast-growing businesses. At the same time, by ensuring adherence to a common set of market conduct and disclosure rules, designed to make investors, particularly retail investors, aware of the risks associated with their activities, it can enhance confidence in the market's integrity and help establish crowdfunding as a reliable tool for risk diversification in the long term.

Nevertheless, the assessment of the ECSPR identified several shortcomings that may adversely affect its ability to support the development of a well-functioning single market for crowdfunding in the EU. These relate mainly to the limited scope of the Regulation, both in terms of the services covered and the type and size of crowdfunding offers; the reliance on a decentralised supervisory model; and the absence of a uniform private enforcement system for infringements of its provisions. Moreover, the lack of effective control mechanisms for ensuring the quality of marketed projects; the inadequate safeguards against post-investment managerial opportunism; the insufficient measures taken to secure the operational continuity of platforms; the absence of a liquid secondary crowdfunding market; and the limitations of disclosure – even behaviourally informed – as an investor protection tool, raise serious concerns about the adequacy of the regulatory framework to foster the participation of a critical number of issuers and investors in the market.

Against this background, several improvements were suggested to address weaknesses in the crowdfunding regime, prioritising three key policy interventions: enhancing the attractiveness of crowdfunding to project owners, especially in Member States with less developed capital markets; fostering transparency and trust among investors; and addressing regulatory barriers currently hindering cross-border market activity. Regarding the first issue, it is essential to clarify and expand the range of products available through crowdfunding, increase the maximum offering threshold, and promote the gatekeeping functions of platform operators. To address the second issue, additional measures are needed to safeguard the operational continuity of CSPs and enhance monitoring of their management. Finally, expanding the scope of transactions covered by the ECSPR and improving convergence in supervisory and enforcement practices can contribute to the integration of the crowdfunding market.

III. Suggestions for Future Research

Perhaps the most important conclusion that can be drawn from this study is that creating a diversified financial system in the EU, where more integrated and robust primary markets can boost investment flows and provide companies with greater funding opportunities, is a complex task. This complexity is further highlighted by the wide range of interests and the diverse priorities and views among Member States and market participants. In this context, the importance of more tailored and flexible regulatory solutions, as opposed to a 'one-size-fits-all' approach, becomes particularly apparent. It goes without saying that achieving the optimal balance between unity and differentiation is a challenging task for policymakers, which necessitates flexibility in thinking and action, as well as responsiveness to future developments and needs. Legal scholars have a key role to play in this process, leveraging their expert knowledge and potentially more objective perspectives, which are less influenced by personal interests. Consequently, it is essential for them to keep the dialogue open and engage with as many stakeholders as possible.[3]

Another important issue that surfaced from the analysis and warrants further examination over time is the extent to which disclosure can mitigate the behavioural weaknesses experienced by retail investors. Indeed, while behaviourally oriented disclosure has gained popularity during the CMU era, especially in the context of financial-return crowdfunding, the success of private ordering in certain liberal economies challenges the supremacy of this model in enhancing the decision-making ability of retail investors. Characteristic in this regard are the examples of New Zealand and the United Kingdom. Despite having essentially abandoned mandatory disclosure for investment-based crowdfunding offers,[4] both countries have witnessed exponential growth in their crowdfunding markets.[5] In light of this, it becomes crucial to further test the possibilities and limitations of the new disclosure approach and to identify additional or alternative types of regulatory and government interventions aimed at mitigating the risks posed by cognitive limitations and biases in EU retail markets, such as financial literacy and education initiatives.[6]

Furthermore, despite some commendable efforts in this area,[7] more research is required to assess the effectiveness of private enforcement practices across Member States and suggest initiatives in the direction of fostering greater convergence in the implementation of EU primary market law. In this context, special attention should be paid to reducing legal uncertainty and minimising regulatory arbitrage risks stemming from the coexistence of different national civil liability regimes, though without disregarding the diverse procedural and cultural approaches to private litigation across the EU. One potential solution in this direction could be the creation of an optional European code on prospectus liability.[8] This code would establish both substantive and procedural rules, allowing market participants to voluntarily opt in to address potential disputes arising from their transactions.

[3] For a remarkable attempt in this direction see T van den Brink and V Passalacqua (eds), *Balancing Unity and Diversity in EU Legislation* (Edward Elgar, 2024).

[4] See generally A Schwartz, *Investment Crowdfunding* (OUP, 2023) 159 ff.

[5] ibid 35 (Table 2.2).

[6] For instance, the Commission's recent Proposal for an Omnibus Directive as regards the Union retail protection rules, COM (2023) 279 final, places particular emphasis on increasing the level of financial literacy of retail investors, including through the promotion of financial education measures at national level to ensure more responsible investments.

[7] D Busch and M Lehmann (eds), *Towards Uniform Prospectus Liability Rules in Europe and Beyond* (OUP, forthcoming).

[8] This idea draws from the proposal for codifying European private law, see eg H Collins, *The European Civil Code – The Way Forward* (CUP, 2010).

An area which also guarantees deeper investigation pertains to how regulation can leverage the potential of primary markets to finance the digital transformation of the EU economy. Several legislative initiatives aim to ensure that financial services are fit for the digital age. For example, the recently adopted Market in Crypto-Assets Regulation (MiCAR) establishes uniform requirements for the public offering or admission to trading on a trading platform of certain types of crypto-assets, along with requirements for the provision of crypto-asset related services.[9] This framework seeks to facilitate capital-raising activities for companies, while upholding a high level of protection for holders of crypto-assets and maintaining the integrity of the relevant market.[10] To achieve this, MiCAR adopts several legislative practices from traditional capital markets law. These include mandatory disclosure obligations for offerors of crypto-assets in the form of a white paper, requirements for the authorisation and supervision of crypto-asset service providers, and measures to prevent insider dealing, unlawful disclosure of inside information, and market manipulation related to crypto-assets.[11] However, MiCAR excludes crypto-assets that qualify as securities from its scope.[12] This implies that offers of such crypto-assets will fall under the Union rules governing traditional securities offerings,[13] including the Prospectus Regulation and the ECSPR. Accordingly, it is crucial to explore the interaction between different regulatory regimes and consider how the specificities of security-like crypto-assets may affect traditional primary market legislation.

Finally, attention should be given to the interplay between prospectus requirements and the promotion of green financing. The European Green Bonds Regulation,[14] which applies from December 2024, sets forth uniform requirements for issuers seeking to designate their environmentally sustainable bonds as 'European green bonds' ('EuGB') within the Union. In parallel, it introduces voluntary disclosure requirements for other environmentally sustainable bonds and sustainability-linked bonds issued in the EU.[15] Moreover, the recent amendment of the Prospectus Regulation by the Listing Act Regulation aims to combat greenwashing by stipulating the inclusion of relevant ESG-related information in the prospectus for equity or non-equity securities offered to the public or admitted to trading on a regulated market.[16] However, no measures have yet been taken

[9] Art 1(1) MiCAR. See generally F Annunziata, 'An Overview of the Markets in Crypto-Assets Regulation (MiCAR)', European Banking Institute Working Paper Series No 158, 11 December 2023.

[10] Recital 6 MiCAR.

[11] ibid Art 1(2).

[12] ibid Art 4(2)(a).

[13] ibid recital 3.

[14] Regulation (EU) 2023/2631 of the European Parliament and of the Council on European Green Bonds and optional disclosures for bonds marketed as environmentally sustainable and for sustainability-linked bonds [2023] OJ L68/1.

[15] ibid Art 1.

[16] Recital 26 Regulation (EU) 2024/2809 of the European Parliament and of the Council amending Regulations (EU) 2017/1129, (EU) No 596/2014 and (EU) No 600/2014 to make public capital markets in the Union more attractive for companies and to facilitate access to capital for small and medium-sized enterprises OJ L, 2024/2809.

toward alleviating prospectus obligations for issuers of securities seeking to fund environmentally sustainable projects. This choice seems rather unfortunate given the urgent need to fund Europe's transition to a more sustainable economy. In this regard, it should be considered whether a new type of simplified prospectus could be introduced, allowing issuers of green bonds and similar securities to reduce the cost of raising capital through the markets. If this is the case, the conditions and standards for issuing such a 'green' prospectus should also be established to ensure a high level of investor protection and mitigate the risk of greenwashing.

BIBLIOGRAPHY

Achleitner, A-K, *Handbuch Investment Banking*, 3rd edn (Gabler, 2002).

Aghion, P, Akcigit, U and Howitt, P, 'What Do We Learn from Schumpeterian Growth Theory?' NBER Working Paper No. 18824, 2013.

Agrawal, AK, Catalini, C and Goldfarb, A, 'Some Simple Economics of Crowdfunding' (2014) 14 *Innovation Policy and the Economy* 63.

Ahlers, G et al, 'Signaling in Equity Crowdfunding' (2015) 39 *Entrepreneurship Theory and Practice* 955.

Akerlof, GA, 'The Market for "Lemons": Quality Uncertainty and the Market Mechanism' (1970) 84 *The Quarterly Journal of Economics* 488.

Alemanno, A and Sibony, A-L, *Nudge and the law: A European perspective* (Hart, 2015).

Allard, J and Blavy, R, 'Market Phoenixes and Banking Ducks, Are Recoveries Faster in Market-Based Financial Systems?' IMF Working Paper No. 2011/213.

Allen, F, 'Stock Markets and Resource Allocation' in C Mayer and X Vives (eds), *Capital Markets and Financial Intermediation* (Cambridge University Press, 1993).

Allen, F et al, 'Financial Intermediation, Markets, and Alternative Financial Sectors' in G Constantinides, M Harris and RM Stulz (eds), *Handbook of the Economics of Finance*, Vol. 2A (North Holland, 2012) 759–98.

Allen, F and Gale, D, 'A Welfare Comparison of Intermediaries and Financial Markets in Germany and the US' (1995) 39 *European Economic Review* 179.

Allen, F and Gale, D, 'Financial Markets, Intermediaries, and Intertemporal Smoothing' (1997) 105 *Journal of Political Economy* 523.

Allen, F and Gale, D, *Comparing Financial Systems* (MIT Press, 2000).

Allen, F and Pástor, L, 'The Capital Markets Union: Key Challenges' in Allen, F et al (eds), *Capital Markets Union and Beyond* (MIT, Press 2019) 3–24.

Andreadakis, S, 'Regulatory Competition or Harmonization: The Dilemma, the Alternatives and the Prospect of Reflexive Harmonization' in M Andenas and C Baasch Andersen (eds), *Theory and Practice of Harmonization* (Edward Elgar, 2012) 52–64.

Annunziata, F and Arruda, T de, 'Crowdfunding and DLTs' in E Macchiavello (ed), *Regulation on European Crowdfunding Service Providers for Business – A Commentary* (Edward Elgar, 2022) 565–76.

Arcand, JL, Berkes, E and Panizza, U, 'Too much Finance?' (2015) *20 Journal of Economic Growth* 106.

Armour, J and Enriques, L, 'Individual Investors' Access to Crowdinvesting: Two Regulatory Models' in DJ Cumming and L Hornuf (eds), *The Economics of Crowdfunding* (Springer, 2018) 255–78.

Armour, J and Enriques, L, 'The Promise and Perils of Crowdfunding: Between Corporate Finance and Consumer Contracts' (2018) 81 *The Modern Law Review* 51.

Armour, J et al, *Principles of Financial Regulation* (OUP, 2016).

Arriba-Sellier, N de, 'The Brexit Reform of European Financial Supervision: Lost in Transition?' (2019) 30 *European Business Law Review* 695.

Arrow, KJ and Debreu, G, 'The Existence of an Equilibrium for a Competitive Economy' (1954) 22 *Econometrica* 265.

Arye Bebchuk, L, 'Federalism and the Corporation: The Desirable Limits on State Competition in Corporate Law' (1992) 105 *Harvard Law Review* 1435.

Asdrubali, P, Sørensen, B and Yosha, O, 'Channels of interstate risk sharing: United States 1963–1990' (1996) 111 *The Quarterly Journal of Economics* 1081.

Assmann, H-D and Kumpan, C, 'Prospekthaftung' in H-D Assmann, RA Schütze and P Buck-Heeb, *Handbuch des Kapitalanlagerechts*, 5th edn (CH Beck, 2020) 258–398.

Avgouleas, E, 'The Harmonisation of Rules of Conduct in EU Financial Markets: Economic Analysis, Subsidiarity and Investor Protection' (2000) 6 *European Law Journal* 72.
Avgouleas, E, 'Reforming Investor Protection Regulation: The Impact of Cognitive Biases' in M Faure and F Stephen (eds), *Essays in the Law and Economics of Regulation: In Honour of Anthony Ogus* (Intersentia, 2008) 143–66.
Avgouleas, E, 'The Global Financial Crisis and the Disclosure Paradigm in European Financial Regulation: The Case for Reform' (2009) 6 *European Company and Financial Law Review* 440.
Avgouleas, E, *Governance of Global Financial Markets: the Law, the Economics, the Politics* (CUP, 2012).
Avgouleas, E and Ferrarini, G, 'A Single Listing Authority and Securities Regulator for the CMU and the Future of ESMA' in D Busch, E Avgouleas and G Ferrarini (eds), *Capital Markets Union in Europe* (OUP, 2018) 55–78.
Baddeley, A, 'Working Memory: Theories, Models, and Controversies' (2012) 63 *Annual Review of Psychology* 1.
Barnard, C and Deakin, S, 'Market Access and Regulatory Competition' in C Barnard and J Scott (eds), *The Law of the Single Market: Unpacking the Premises* (Hart Publishing, 2002) 197–224.
Barr, MS, Mullainathan, S and Shafir, E, 'Behaviourally Informed Regulation' in E Shafir (ed), *Behavioural Foundations of Public Policy* (Princeton University Press, 2012) 44–464.
Bartlett, RP III, 'Venture Capital, Agency Costs, and the False Dichotomy of the Corporation' (2006) 54 *UCLA Law Review* 37.
Beaud, O, 'The Allocation of Competences in a Federation – A General Introduction' in L Azoulai (ed), *The Question of Competence in the European Union* (OUP, 2014) 19–38.
Becht, M, 'European Disclosure for the New Millennium' in K Hopt and E Wymeersch (eds), *Capital Markets and Company Law* (OUP, 2003) 87–91.
Beck, T, 'Does Europe Need a Capital Market Union? And How Would We Get There?' in F Allen, E Carletti and J Gray (eds), *The New Financial Architecture in the Eurozone* (European University Institute, 2015) 115–22.
Beck, T and Levine, R, 'Industry Growth and Capital Accumulation: Does having a Market- or Bank-Based System Matter?' (2002) 64 *Journal of Financial Economics* 147.
Beck, T, Demirgüg-Kunt, A and Maksimovic, V, 'Financing Patterns Around the World: Are Small Firms Different?' (2008) 89 *Journal of Financial Economics* 467.
Becker, GS, *The Economic Approach to Human Behavior* (University of Chicago Press, 1976).
Bencivenga, VR and Smith, BD, 'Financial Intermediation and Endogenous Growth' (1991) 58 *The Review of Economic Studies* 195.
Ben-Shahar, O and Schneider, CE, 'The Failure of Mandated Disclosure' (2011) 159 *University of Pennsylvania Law Review* 647.
Benston, GJ, 'Regulation of Stock Trading: Private Exchanges vs. Government Agencies – Commentary' (1997) 83 *Virginia Law Review* 1501.
Bergh, R van den, 'Regulatory Competition or Harmonization of Laws? Guidelines for the European Regulator' in A Marciano and J-M Josselin (eds), *The Economics of Harmonizing European Law* (Edward Elgar, 2002) 27–49.
Bergström, CF, 'Shaping the New System for Delegation of Powers to EU Agencies: United Kingdom v. European Parliament and Council (Short Selling)' (2015) 52 *Common Market Law Review* 219.
Berle, A and Means, GC, *The Modern Corporation and Private Property* (Macmillan, 1932).
Beshears, J et al, 'How Does Simplified Disclosure Affect Individuals' Mutual Fund Choices?' in DA Wise (ed), *Explorations in the Economics of Aging* (University of Chicago Press, 2011) 75–96.
Bhide, A, 'The hidden costs of stock market liquidity' (1993) 34 *Journal of Financial Economics* 1.
Biglaiser, G, 'Middlemen as Experts' (1993) 24 *RAND Journal of Economics* 212.
Binder, J-H and Gortsos, C, *The European Banking Union: A Compendium* (Beck/Hart Publishing, 2016).
Binder, J-H, 'Corporate Governance of Financial Institutions: In Need of Cross-Sectoral Regulation? A comparative analysis of banks, investment firms, asset managers, and pension funds' in D Busch, G Ferrarini and G van Solinge (eds), *Governance of Financial Institutions* (OU,P 2019) 18–42.

Black, BS, 'The Legal and Institutional Preconditions for Strong Securities Markets' (2001) 48 *UCLA Law Review* 781.

Black, J, 'Reconceiving Financial Markets – From the Economic to the Social' (2013) 13 *Journal of Corporate Law Studies* 401.

Block, JH, Fisch, CO and Praag, M van, 'Quantity and quality of jobs by entrepreneurial firms' (2018) 34 *Oxford Review of Economic Policy* 567.

Böhm, F, 'Rule of Law in a Market Economy' in A Peacock and H Willgerodt (eds), *Germany's Social Market Economy: Origins and Evolution* (Springer, 1989) 46–67.

Bolton, P et al, 'Relationship and Transaction Lending in a Crisis' (2016) 29 *Review of Financial Studies* 2643.

Bonfiglioli, A, 'Financial Integration, Productivity and Capital Accumulation' (2008) 76 *Journal of International Economics* 337.

Boodman, M, 'The Myth of Harmonization of Laws' (1991) 39 *The American Journal of Comparative Law* 699.

Boot, A and Thakor, A, 'Financial System Architecture' (1997) 10 *The Review of Financial Studies* 693.

Boot, A, Greenbaum, SI and Thakor, A, 'Reputation and Discretion in Financial Contracting' (1993) 83 *The American Economic Review* 1165.

Booth, JR and Smith, RL II, 'Capital Raising, Underwriting and the Certification Hypothesis' (1986) 15 *Journal of Financial Economics* 261.

Boyd, JH and Smith, BD, 'The Evolution of Debt and Equity Markets in Economic development' (1998) 12 *Economic Theory* 519.

Brinckmann, H, 'Foundations' in R Veil (ed), *European Capital Markets Law*, 2nd edn (Hart Publishing, 2017).

Brown, C, Dolan, T and Butler, K, 'Cryptoassets and Initial Coin Offerings' in J Madir (ed), *Fintech – Law and Regulation* (Edward Elgar, 2019) 74–101.

Buckley, J and Howarth, D, 'Regulating the So-Called "Vultures of Capitalism"' (2011) 49 (s1) *Journal of Common Market Studies* 123.

Búrca, G de, 'The Principle of Subsidiarity and the Court of Justice as an Institutional Actor' (1998) 36 *Journal of Common Market Studies* 217.

Burkett, E, 'A Crowdfunding Exemption? Online Investment Crowdfunding and U.S. Securities Regulation' (2011) 13 *Tennessee Journal of Business Law* 63.

Burn, L and Wells, B, 'The Pan-European Retail Market – Are we There Yet?' (2007) 2 *Capital Markets Law Journal* 263.

Burn, L, 'KISS, But Tell All: Short-form Disclosure for Retail Investors' (2010) 5 *Capital Markets Law Journal* 141.

Busch, D, 'A Capital Markets Union for a Divided Europe' (2017) 3 *Journal of Financial Regulation* 262.

Busch, D, 'A Stronger Role for the European Supervisory Authorities in the EU27' in D Busch, E Avgouleas and G Ferrarini (eds), *Capital Markets Union in Europe* (OUP, 2018) 28–54.

Busch, D, 'Capital Markets Union' in F Fabbrini and M Ventoruzzo (eds), *Research Handbook on EU Economic Law* (Edward Elgar, 2019) 434–76.

Busch, D, Avgouleas, E and Ferrarini, G, 'Capital Markets Union after Brexit' in D Busch, E Avgouleas and G Ferrarini (eds), *Capital Markets Union in Europe* (OUP, 2018) 3–8.

Busch, D and Ferrarini, G (eds), *European Banking Union* (OUP, 2015).

Busch, D and Lehmann, M, 'Uniform Prospectus Liability Rules for Europe' (2023) 14 *Journal of European Tort Law*.

Cable, A, 'Fending for Themselves: Why Securities Regulations Should Encourage Angel Groups' (2010) 13 *University of Pennsylvania Journal of Business Law* 107.

Cappelletti, M, Seccombe, M and Weiler, J, 'Integration Through Law: Europe and the American Federal Experience' in M Cappelletti, M Seccombe and J Weiler (eds), *Integration Through Law: Methods, Tools and Institutions, Book 1: A Political, Legal and Economic Overview* (De Gruyter, 1986) 3–68.

Chamon, M, 'EU Agencies between Meroni and Romano or the Devil and the Deep Blue Sea' (2011) 48 *Common Market Law Review* 1055.
Chapman, P, 'Crowdfunding' in J Madir (ed), *Fintech – Law and Regulation*, 2nd edn (Edward Elgar, 2021) 64–89.
Chen, J and Watson, S, 'Investor Psychology Matters: Is a Prescribed Product Disclosure Statement a Supplement for Healthy Investment Decisions?' (2011) 17 *New Zealand Business Law Quarterly* 412.
Chiti, E, 'An Important Part of the EU's institutional machinery: Features, Problems and Perspectives of European Agencies' (2009) 46 *Common Market Law Review* 1395.
Chiu, I, *Regulatory Convergence in EU Securities Regulation* (Kluwer Law International, 2008).
Choi, SJ, 'A Framework for the Regulation of Investment Intermediaries' (2004) 1 *Berkley Business Law Journal* 45.
Choi, SJ and Guzman, AT, 'Portable Reciprocity: Rethinking the International Reach of Securities Regulation' (1998) 71 *Southern California Law Review* 903.
Christensen, HB, Hail, L and Leuz, C, 'Capital-Market Effects of Securities Regulation: Prior Conditions, Implementation, and Enforcement' (2016) 29 *The Review of Financial Studies* 2885.
Cimadomo, J et al, 'Private and public risk sharing in the euro area' (2020) 121 *European Economic Review* 1.
Coase, RH, 'The Problem of Social Cost' (1960) 3 *The Journal of Law & Economics* 1.
Coffee, JC, 'Market Failure and the Economic Case for a Mandatory Disclosure System' (1984) 70 *Virginia Law Review* 717.
Coffee, JC, 'Competition Versus Consolidation: The Significance of Organizational Structure in Financial and Securities Regulation' (1995) 50 *The Business Lawyer* 447.
Coffee, JC, 'Law and Regulatory Competition: Can They Co-exist?' (2002) 80 *Texas Law Review* 1729.
Coffee, JC, 'Racing towards the Top: The Impact of Cross-Listing and Stock Market Competition on International Corporate Governance' (2002) 102 *Columbia Law Review* 1757.
Coffee, JC, 'Gatekeeper Failure and Reform: The Challenge of Fashioning Relevant Reforms' (2004) *Boston University Law Review* 301.
Coffee, JC, *Gatekeepers: The Role of the Professions and Corporate Governance* (OUP, 2006).
Colaert, V, 'The Regulation of PRIIPs: Great Ambitions, Insurmountable Challenges?' (2016) 2 *Journal of Financial Regulation* 203.
Colaert, V, 'Investor Protection in the Capital Markets Union' in D Busch, E Avgouleas and G Ferrarini (eds), *Capital Markets Union in Europe* (OUP, 2018) 341–71.
Colaert, V, 'Product Information for Banking, Investment and Insurance Products' in V Colaert, D Busch and T Incalza (eds), *European Financial Regulation: Levelling the Cross-sectoral Playing Field* (Hart Publishing, 2019) 303–16.
Collins, PS, *Regulation of Securities, Markets and Transactions: A Guide to the New Environment* (Wiley, 2011).
Colombatto, E, 'The Crisis of Europe's Centralized Federalism Ambiguities of a Harmonized Currency Union' (2000) 1 4 *The Independent Review* 533.
Conac, P-H and Gelter, M (eds), *Global Securities Litigation and Enforcement* (CUP, 2019).
Cowan, N, 'The Magical Number 4 in Short-term Memory: A Reconsideration of Mental Storage Capacity' (2001) 24 *Behavioural and Brain Sciences* 87.
Cox, JD, 'Rethinking US Securities Regulation in the Shadow of International Regulatory Competition' (1992) 55 *Law and Contemporary Problems* 157.
Cox, JD, 'Regulatory Competition in Securities Markets: An Approach for Reconciling Japanese and United States Disclosure Philosophies' (1993) 16 *Hastings International and Comparative Law Review* 149.
Cox, JD, 'Regulatory Duopoly in US Securities Markets' (1999) 99 *Columbia Law Review* 1200.
Cox, JD and Payne, JW, 'Mutual Fund Expense Disclosure: A Behavioral Perspective' (2005) 83 *Washington University Law Review* 907.
Cumming, DJ and Johan, SA, *Venture Capital and Private Equity Contracting: An International Perspective*, 2nd edn (Elsevier, 2014).

Cumming, DJ, Leboeuf, G and Schwienbacher, A, 'Crowdfunding models: Keep-It-All vs. All-Or-Nothing' (2020) 49 *Financial Management* 331.
Curtin, D, 'Holding (Quasi-)Autonomous EU Administrative Actors to Public Account' (2007) 13 *European Law Journal* 523.
D'Ambrosio, M and Gianfrate, G, 'Crowdfunding and Venture Capital: Substitutes or Complements?' (2016) 20 *The Journal of Private Equity* 7.
D'Ippolito, E, Musitelli, M and Sciarrone Alibrandi, A, 'Protecting Crowdfunders: Is a MiFID-Mimicking Approach Appropriate?' (2016) 13 *European Company Law* 27.
Dannreuther, C, 'A Zeal for a Zeal? SME Policy and the Political Economy of the EU' (2007) 5 *Comparative European Politics* 377.
Davies, P, 'Damages Actions by Investors on the Back of Market Disclosure Requirements' in D Busch, E Avgouleas and G Ferrarini (eds), *Capital Markets Union in Europe* (OUP, 2018) 318–37.
Deakin, S, 'Two Types of Regulatory Competition: Competitive Federalism Versus Reflexive Harmonisation. A Law and Economics Perspective on Centros' (1999) 2 *Cambridge Yearbook of European Legal Studies* 231.
Deakin, S, 'Is regulatory competition the future for European integration?' (2006) 13 *Swedish Economic Policy Review* 71.
Deakin, S, 'Legal Diversity and Regulatory Competition: Which Model for Europe?' (2006) 12 *European Law Journal* 440.
Dell' Ariccia, G, 'A Capital Markets Union: A Few Thoughts' in F Allen, E Carletti and J Gray (eds), *The New Financial Architecture in the Eurozone* (European University Institute, 2015) 107–13.
Demirgüg-Kunt, A and Maksimovic, V, 'Law, Finance, and Firm Growth' (1998) 53 *Journal of Finance* 2107.
Demirgüç-Kunt, A and Levine, R, *Financial Structures and Economic Growth: A Cross-Country Comparison of Banks, Markets, and Development* (MIT Press, 2001).
Demirguc-Kunt, A, Feyen, E and Levin,e R, 'The Evolving Importance of Banks and Securities Markets' (2013) 27 *The World Bank Economic Review* 476.
Demmo, NG, 'U.S. Securities Regulation: The Need for Modification to Keep Pace with Globalization' (1996) 17 *University of Pennsylvania Journal of International Law* 691.
Demyanyk, Y and Hemert, OV, 'Understanding the Subprime Mortgage Crisis' (2011) 24 *Review of Financial Studies* 1848.
Diamond, DW and Verrecchia, RE, 'Optimal Managerial Contracts and Equilibrium Security Prices' (1982) 37 *The Journal of Finance* 275.
Diamond, DW, 'Financial Intermediation and Delegated Monitoring' (1984) 51 *The Review of Economic Studies* 393.
Diamond, PA, 'The Role of a Stock Market in a General Equilibrium Model with Technological Uncertainty' (1967) 57 *The American Economic Review* 759.
Dorff, MB, 'The Siren Call of Equity Crowdfunding' (2014) 39 *Journal of Corporation Law* 493.
Einsele, D, 'Kapitalmarktrecht und Privatrecht' (2014) 69 *JuristenZeitung* 703.
Drahos, P (ed), *Regulatory Theory: Foundations and Applications* (ANU Press, 2017).
Dushnitsky, G et al, 'Crowdfunding in Europe: Determinants of Platform Creation Across Countries' (2016) 58 *California Management Review* 44.
Easterbrook, FH, 'Managers' Discretion and Investors' Welfare: Theories and Evidence' (1984) 9 *Delaware Journal of Corporate Law* 540.
Easterbrook, FH and Fischel, RD, 'Mandatory Disclosure and the Protection of Investors' (1984) 70 *Virginia Law Review* 669.
Easterly, W, Islam, R and Stiglitz, JE, 'Shaken and Stirred: Explaining Growth Volatility' in B Pleskovic and N Stern (eds), *Annual World Bank Conference on Development Economics 2000* (World Bank, 2001) 191–211.
Enriques, L, 'Conflicts of Interest in Investment Services: The Price and Uncertain Impact of MiFID's Regulatory Framework' in G Ferrarini and E Wymeersch (eds), *Investor Protection in Europe: Corporate Law Making, The MiFID and Beyond* (OUP, 2006) 321–38.

Enriques, L and Gargantini, M, 'The Overarching Duty to Act in the Best Interest of the Client in MiFID II' in D Busch and G Ferarrini (eds), *Regulation of the EU Financial System: MiFID II and MiFIR* (OUP, 2017) 85–122.

Enriques, L and Gatti, M, 'The Uneasy Case for Top-Down Corporate Law Harmonization in the European Union' (2006) 27 *University of Pennsylvania Journal of International Law* 939.

Enriques, L and Gatti, M, 'Is There a Uniform EU Securities Law After the Financial Services Action Plan?' (2008) 14 *Stanford Journal of Law, Business & Finance* 43.

Enriques, L and Gilotta, S, 'Disclosure and Financial Market Regulation' in E Ferran, N Moloney and J Payne (eds), *Oxford Handbook on Financial Regulation* (OUP, 2014) 512–42.

Enriques, L and Tröger, TH, 'Issuer Choice in Europe' (2008) 67 *The Cambridge Law Journal* 521.

Enriques, L et al, 'Corporate Law and Securities Markets' in R Kraakman et al (eds), *The Anatomy of Corporate Law: A Comparative and Functional Approach* (OUP, 2017) 243–66.

Estevan de Quesada, C, 'Crowdfunding in Europe' in S Grundmann (ed), *European Contract Law in the Digital Age* (Intersentia, 2018) 103–34.

Fabozzi, FJ and Peterson Drake, P, *Finance: Capital Markets, Financial Management, and Investment Management* (Wiley, 2009).

Fama, EF, 'Efficient Capital Markets: A Review of Theory and Empirical Work' (1970) 25 *The Journal of Finance* 383.

Ferran, E, *Building an EU Securities Market* (CUP, 2004).

Ferran, E, 'Cross-border Offers of Securities in the EU: The Standard Life Flotation' (2007) 4 *European Company and Financial Law Review* 461.

Ferran, E, 'Understanding the New Institutional Architecture of EU Financial Market Supervision' in E Wymeersch, K Hopt and G Ferrarini (eds), *Financial Regulation and Supervision: A Post Crisis Analysis* (OUP, 2012) 111–58.

Ferran, E, 'Crisis-driven Regulatory Reform: Where in the World is the EU Going?' in E Ferran et al (eds), *The Regulatory Aftermath of the Global Financial Crisis* (CUP, 2012) 1–110.

Ferran, E and Chan, Ho L, *Principles of Corporate Finance Law* (OUP, 2008).

Ferrarini, G, 'Pan-European Securities Markets: Policy Issues and Regulatory Responses' (2002) 3 *European Business Organization Law Review* 249.

Ferrarini, G and Ottolia, A, 'Corporate Disclosure as a Transaction Cost: The Case of SMEs' (2013) 9 *European Review of Contract Law* 363.

Ferrarini, G and Guidici, P, 'Liability for Misstatements to the Market: The Post-Parmalat Years' in RH Huang and NC Howson (eds), *Enforcement of Corporate and Securities Law: China and the World* (CUP, 2017).

Ferrarini, G and Macchiavello, E, 'Investment-based Crowdfunding: Is MiFID II Enough?' in D Busch and G Ferarrini (eds), *Regulation of the EU Financial System: MiFID II and MiFIR* (OUP, 2017) 659–92.

Ferrarini, G and Macchiavello, E, 'Fintech and Alternative Finance in the CMU – The Regulation of Marketplace Investing' in D Busch, E Avgouleas and G Ferrarini (eds), *Capital Markets Union in Europe* (OUP, 2018) 208–33.

Ferrell, A, 'The Case for Mandatory Disclosure in Securities Regulation Around the World' (2007) 2 *Brooklyn Journal of Corporate, Financial & Commercial Law* 81.

Filistrucchi, L et al, 'Market Definition in Two-Sided Markets: Theory and Practice' (2014) 10 *Journal of Competition Law and Economics* 293.

Filistrucchi, L, Geradin, D and Damme, E van, 'Identifying Two-Sided Markets' (2013) 36 *World Competition* 33.

Fisch, C, 'Initial coin offerings (ICOs) to finance new ventures' (2019) 34 *Journal of Business Venturing* 1.

Fishburn, PC and Kochenberger, GA, 'Two-Piece Von Neumann-Morgenstern Utility Functions' (1979) 10 *Decision Sciences* 503.

Fleuriet, M, *Investment Banking Explained: An Insider's Guide to the Industry*, 2nd edn (McGraw-Hill Education, 2019).

Fox, MB, 'Securities Disclosure in a Globalizing Market: Who Should Regulate Whom' (1997) 95 *Michigan Law Review* 2498.
Fox, MB, 'Mandatory Securities Disclosure: Why Issuer Choice Is Not Investor Empowerment' (1999) 85 *Virginia Law Review* 1335.
Fox, MB, 'Regulating Public Offerings of Truly New Securities: First Principles' (2016) 66 *Duke Law Journal* 673.
Fox, MB, 'Initial Public Offering in the CMU A US Perspective' in D Busch, E Avgouleas and G Ferrarini (eds), *Capital Markets Union in Europe* (OUP, 2018) 268–99.
Friedman, M and Savage, LJ, 'The Utility Analysis of Choices Involving Risk' (1948) 56 *Journal of Political Economy* 279.
Furubotn, EG and Richte,r R, *Institutions and Economic Theory: The Contribution of the New Institutional Economics*, 2nd edn (University of Michigan Press, 2005).
Garcimartín, F, 'The Law Applicable to Prospectus Liability in the European Union' (2011) 5 *Law and Financial Markets Review* 449.
Gargantini, M, 'Secondary Markets for Crowdfunding: Bulletin Boards (Art 25)' in E Macchiavello (ed), *Regulation on European Crowdfunding Service Providers for Business – A Commentary* (Edward Elgar, 2022) 349–65.
Gatsios, K and Holmes, P, 'Regulatory Competition' in P Newman (ed), *The New Palgrave Dictionary of Economics and the Law, Vol. 1* (Palgrave Macmilla,n 1998) 1671–75.
Geiger, U, 'The Case for the Harmonization of Securities Disclosure Rules in the Global Market' (1997) 2&3 *Columbia Business Law Review* 241.
Genschel, P and Jachtenfuchs, M, 'Beyond Market Regulation: Analysing the European Integration of Core State Powers' in P Genschel and M Jachtenfuchs (eds), *Beyond the Regulatory Polity(?): The European Integration of Core State Powers* (OUP, 2014) 1–23.
Geradin, D, 'The Development of European Regulatory Agencies: What the EU Should Learn from American Experience' (2004) 11 *Columbia Journal of European Law*.
Gerner-Beuerle, C, 'United in Diversity: Maximum versus Minimum Harmonization in EU Securities Regulation' (2012) 7 *Capital Markets Law Journal* 317.
Gerven, D van, 'General Provisions of Community Law Relating to the Prospectus to be Published when Securities are Offered to the Public or Admitted to Trading' in D van Gerven (ed), *Prospectus for the Public Offering of Securities in Europe: European and National Legislation in the Member States of the European Economic Area*, Vol. I (CUP, 2008) 3–68.
Gilson, RJ, 'Engineering a Venture Capital Market: Lessons from the American Experience' (2003) 55 *Stanford Law Review* 1067.
Gilson, RJ, 'Locating innovation: The endogeneity of technology, organizational structure, and financial contracting' (2010) 110 *Columbia Law Review* 885.
Gilson, RJ and Kraakman, RH, 'The Mechanisms of Market Efficiency' (1984) 70 *Virginia Law Review* 549.
Gilson, RJ and Kraakman, RH, 'The Mechanisms of Market Efficiency Twenty Years Later: The Hindsight Bias' (2003) 28 *The Journal of Corporation Law* 715.
Gilson, RJ and Schizer, DM, 'Understanding Venture Capital Structure: A Tax Explanation for Convertible Preferred Stock' (2003) 116 *Harvard Law Review* 874.
Glavina, S, 'European IPO Market: Global and Regional Stock Exchanges' (2013) 18 *Economics and Management* 634.
Gortsos, C, *Stricto Sensu Investor Protection under MiFID II: A Systematic Overview of Articles 24–30* (CUP, 2018).
Granovetter, M, 'Economic Action and Social Structure: The Problem of Embeddedness' (1985) 91 *American Journal of Sociology* 481.
Green, DP and Shapiro, I, *Pathologies of Rational Choice Theory: A Critique of Applications in Political Science* (Yale University Press, 1994).
Greenberg, J and Mollick, E, 'Activist Choice Homophily and the Crowdfunding of Female Founders' (2017) 2 *Administrative Science Quarterly* 341.

Greenwald, BC and Stiglitz, JE, 'Externalities in Economies with Imperfect Information and Incomplete Markets' (1986) 101 *The Quarterly Journal of Economics* 229.
Griller, S and Orator, A, 'Everything Under Control? The "Way Forward" for European Agencies in the Footsteps of the Meroni Doctrine' (2010) 35 *European Law Review* 3.
Grjebine, T, Szczerbowicz, U and Tripier, F, 'Corporate Debt Structure and Economic Recoveries' (2018) 101 *European Economic Review* 77.
Grossman, SJ, 'Further Results on the Informational Efficiency of Competitive Stock Markets' (1978) 18 *Journal of Economic Theory* 81.
Grossman, SJ and Hart, O, 'Disclosure Laws and Takeover Bids' (1980) 35 *The Journal of Finance* 323.
Grossman, SJ and Stiglitz, JE, 'On the Impossibility of Informationally Efficient Markets' (1980) 70 *The American Economic Review* 393.
Grundfest, JA, 'Internationalization of the World's Securities Markets: Economic Causes and Regulatory Consequences' (1990) 4 *Journal of Financial Services Research* 349.
Grundmann, S, 'Europäisches Kapitalmarktrecht' (1996) 115 *Zeitschrift für Schweizerisches Recht* 103.
Grundmann, S, *European Company Law*, 2nd edn (Intersentia, 2012).
Grundmann, S, 'Costs and Benefits of an Optional European Sales Law' (2013) 50 *Common Market Law Review* 225.
Grundmann, S, *Bankvertragsrecht. 'Organisation und Kreditwesen Bank-Kunden-Verhältnis* (De Gruyter, 2016).
Grundmann, S, *Bankvertragsrecht. Investment Banking II* (De Gruyter, 2016).
Grundmann, S, 'Targeted Consumer Protection' in D Leczykiewicz and S Weatherhill (eds), *The images of the consumer in EU law legislation, free movement and competition law* (Hart Publishing, 2016).
Grundmann, S, 'Vertrauen und (EU-) Kapitalmarkt – Theorie und Fallstudien zu einer neuen Mesotes im Wirtschaftsrecht' in G Bachman et al (eds), *Festschrift für Christine Windbichler zum 70. Geburstag* (De Gruyter, 2020) 67–96.
Grundmann, S, 'Knowledge and Information' in S Grundmann, H-W Micklitz and M Renner (eds), *New Private Law Theory: A Pluralist Approach* (CUP, 2021) 230–47.
Grundmann, S and Hacker, P, 'Conflicts of Interests' in D Busch and G Ferarrini (eds), *Regulation of the EU Financial System: MiFID II and MiFIR* (OUP, 2017) 165–204.
Grundmann, S and Kerber, W, 'Information Intermediaries and Party Autonomy – The Example of Securities and Insurance Markets' in S Grundmann, W Kerber and S Weatherhill (eds), *Party Autonomy and the Role of Information in the Internal Market* (De Gruyter, 2001) 264–310.
Grundmann, S and Kerber, W, 'European System of Contract Law – A Map for Combining the Advantages of Centralized and Decentralized Rule-making' in S Grundmann and J Stuyck (eds) *An Academic Greenpaper on European Contract Law* (Kluwer Law International, 2002) 295–342.
Grunewald, B and Schlitt, M, *Einführung in das Kapitalmarktrecht*, 3rd edn (C.H. Beck, 2014).
Guiso, L, Sapienza, P and Zingales, L, 'Does Culture Affect Economic Outcomes?' (2006) 20 *Journal of Economic Perspectives* 23.
Gullifer, L and Payne, J, *Corporate Finance Law: Principles and Policy*, 1st edn (Hart Publishing, 2011).
Hadfield, GK, Howse, R and Trebilcock, MJ, 'Information-Based Principles for Rethinking Consumer Protection Policy' (1998) 21 *Journal of Consumer Policy* 131.
Hal, S, 'Internationalization of Primary Public Securities Markets' (2000) 63 *Law and Contemporary Problems* 71.
Hall, PA and Soskice, D (eds), *Varieties of Capitalism. The Institutional Foundations of Comparative Advantage* (OUP, 2001).
Härkönen, E, 'Crowdfunding and the Small Offering Exemption in European and US Prospectus Regulation: Striking a Balance Between Investor Protection and Access to Capital?' (2017) 14 *European Company and Financial Law Review* 121.
Hartmann, P, Maddaloni, A and Manganelli, S, 'The Euro-Area Financial System: Structure, Integration and Policy Initiatives' (2003) 19 *Oxford Review of Economic Policy* 180.
Hauser, H and Hosli, M, 'Harmonization or Regulatory Competition in the EC (and the EEA)?' (1991) 4 *Aussenwirtschaft* 265.

Hayek, FA, 'The Use of Knowledge in Society' (1945) 35 *The American Economic Review* 519.
Heine, K and Kerber, W, 'European Corporate Laws, Regulatory Competition and Path Dependence' (2002) 13 *European Journal of Law and Economics* 47.
Heinze, S, *Europäisches Kapitalmarktrecht: Recht des Primärmarktes* (C.H. Beck, 1999).
Hellwig, M, 'Banking, Financial Intermediation and Corporate Finance' in A Giovannini and C Mayer (eds), *European Financial Integration* (Cambridge University Press, 1991) 35–63.
Hirschman, AO, *Exit, Voice and Loyalty: Responses to Decline in Firms, Organizations and States* (Harvard University Press, 1970).
Hirshleifer, DA, 'The Blind Leading the Blind: Social Influence, Fads, and Informational Cascades' in M Tommasi and K Lerulli (eds), *The New Economics of Human Behaviour* (CUP, 1995) 188–215.
Hirshleifer, DA, and Hong Teoh, S, 'Herd Behaviour and Cascading in Capital Markets: a Review and Synthesis' (2003) 9 *European Financial Management* 25.
Hirshleifer J, 'The Private and Social Value of Information and the Reward to Inventive Activity' (1971) 61 *The American Economic Review* 561.
Hoffmann, S, *The European Sisyphus: Essays on Europe, 1964–1994* (Westview Press, 1995).
Hofmann, H and Morini, A, 'Constitutional Aspects of the Pluralisation of the EU Executive through "Agencification"' (2012) 36 *European Law Review* 412.
Hooghiemstra, SN, 'The Provision of Crowdfunding Services under the ECSPR (Art) in E Macchiavello (ed), *Regulation on European Crowdfunding Service Providers for Business – A Commentary* (Edward Elgar, 2022) 68–85.
Hopt, K, *Der Kapitalanlegerschutz im Recht der Banken* (Beck, 1975).
Hopt, K, *Die Verantwortlichkeit der Banken bei Emissionen: Recht und Praxis in der EG, in Deutschland und in der Schweiz* (C.H. Beck, 1991).
Hopt, K, 'Die Schaffung einer Kapitalmarktunion in Europa – langwierig und schwierig, aber notwendig' (2015) 26 *Europäische Zeitschrift für Wirtschaftsrecht* 289.
Hornuf, L and Schwienbacher, A, 'Crowdinvesting – Angel Investing for the Masses?' in C Mason and H Landström (eds), *Handbook of Research on Business Angels* (Edward Elgar, 2016) 381–98.
Hornuf, L, Klöhn, L and Schilling, T, 'The Regulation of Crowdfunding in the German Small Investor Protection Act: Content, Consequences, Critique, Suggestions' (2016) 13 *European Company Law* 56.
Hornuf, L, Klöhn, L and Schilling, T, 'Financial contracting in crowdinvesting: Lessons from the German market' (2018) 19 *German Law Journal* 509.
Howarth, D and Quagli,a L, 'Brexit and the Single European Financial Market' (2017) 55 (s1) *Journal of Common Market Studies* 149.
Howell, E, 'An Analysis of the Prospectus Regime: The EU Reforms and the "Brexit" Factor' (2018) 15 *European Company and Financial Law Review* 69.
Howells, G, 'The Potential and Limits of Consumer Empowerment by Information' (2005) 32 *Journal of Law and Society* 349.
Hurt, CA, 'Pricing Disintermediation: Crowdfunding and Online Auction IPOs' (2015) 1 *University of Illinois Law Review* 217.
Ibrahim, DM, 'Equity Crowdfunding: A Market for Lemons?' (2015) 100 *Minnesota Law Review* 561.
Inman, RP and Rubinfield, DL, 'The Economics of Federalism' in F Parisi (ed), *The Oxford Handbook of Law and Economics: Volume 3: Public Law and Legal Institutions* (OUP, 2017) 84–105.
Jackson, HE, 'Centralization, Competition, and Privatization in Financial Regulation' (2001) 2 *Theoretical Inquiries in Law* 649.
Jackson, HE and Pan, EJ, 'Regulatory Competition in International Securities Markets: Evidence from Europe in 1999 – Part I' (2001) 56 *Business Lawyer* 653.
Jackson, HE and Roe, M, 'Public and private enforcement of securities laws: Resource-based evidence' (2009) 93 *Journal of Financial Economics* 207.
Jackson, HE and Zhang, JY, 'Private and Public Enforcement of Securities Regulation' in JN Gordon and W-G Ringe (eds), *The Oxford Handbook of Corporate Law and Governance* (OUP, 2018) 928–45.

Jayaratne, J and Strahan, PA, 'The Finance-Growth Nexus: Evidence from Bank Branch Deregulation' (1996) 111(4) *Quarterly Journal of Economics* 639.

Jensen, MC and Meckling, WH, 'Theory of the Firm: Managerial Behavior, Agency Costs and Ownership Structure' (1976) 3 *Journal of Financial Economics* 305.

Jensen, MC and Murphy, KJ, 'Performance Pay and Top-Management Incentives' (1990) 98 *Journal of Political Economy* 225.

Jørgensen, T, 'Peer to Peer lending in Denmark' (2016) 4 *Journal of European Consumer and Market Law* 185.

Kahan, M, 'Securities Laws and the Social Costs of "Inaccurate" Stock Prices' (1992) 41 *Duke Law Journal* 979.

Kahneman, D and Tversky, A, 'Prospect Theory: An Analysis of Decision under Risk' (1979) 47 *Econometrica* 263.

Kalss, S, Oppitz, M and Zollner, J, *Kapitalmarktrecht*, 2nd edn (Linde Verlag, 2015).

Kamba, WJ, 'Comparative Law: A Theoretical Framework' (1974) 23 *The International and Comparative Law Quarterly* 485.

Kaplan, SN and Strömberg, P, 'Financial Contracting Theory Meets the Real World: An Empirical Analysis of Venture Capital Contracts' (2003) 70 *Review of Economic Studies* 281.

Karmis, D and Norman, W, 'The Revival of Federalism in Normative Political Theory' in D Karmis and W Norman (eds), *Theories of Federalism: A Reader* (Palgrave Macmillan, 2005) 3–21.

Kerber, W and Grundmann, S, 'An optional European contract law code: Advantages and disadvantages' (2006) 21 *European Journal of Law and Economics* 215.

Klöhn, L, 'Private Versus Public Enforcement of Laws – A Law and Economics Perspective' in R Schulze (ed), *Compensation of Private Losses: The Evolution of Torts in European Business Law* (De Gruyter, 2011) 179–98.

Klöhn, L, 'Die neue Prospektfreiheit „kleiner" Wertpapieremissionen unter 8 Mio. €' (2018) 30 *Zeitschrift für Wirtschaftsrecht* 1713.

Klöhn, L, and Hornuf, L, 'Crowdinvesting in Deutschland – Markt, Rechtslage und Regulierungsperspektive' (2012) 24 *Zeitschrift für Bankrecht und Bankwirtschaft*.

Knight, TB, Leo, H and Ohmer, A, 'A Very Quiet Revolution: A Primer on Securities Crowdfunding and Title III of the JOBS Act' (2012) 2 *Michigan Journal of Private Equity & Venture Capital Law* 135.

Korobkin, RB and Ulen, TS, 'Law and Behavioral Science: Removing the Rationality Assumption from Law and Economics' (2000) 88 *California Law Review* 1051.

Kozup, J and Hogarth, JM, 'Financial Literacy, Public Policy, and Consumers' Self-Protection – More Questions, Fewer Answers' (2008) 42 *The Journal of Consumer Affairs* 127.

Kraakman, RH, 'Gatekeepers: The Anatomy of a Third-Party Enforcement Strategy' (1986) 2 *Journal of Law, Economics & Organization* 53.

Kraakman, RH, 'Regulation of Corporate Governance, in Particular Disclosure' in G Ferrarini et al (eds), *Reforming Company and Takeover Law in Europe* (OUP, 2004) 95–144.

Kukovec, D, 'Law and the Periphery' (2015) 21 *European Law Journal* 406.

Kumpan, C, 'Die Europäische Kapitalmarktunion und ihr Fokus auf kleinere und mittlere Unternehmen' (2016) 45 *Zeitschrift für Unternehmens- und Gesellschaftsrecht* 2.

La Porta, R et al, 'Legal Determinants of External Finance' (1997) 52 *Journal of Finance* 1131.

La Porta, R et al, 'Law and Finance' (1998) 106 *Journal of Political Economy* 1113.

La Porta, R, Lopez-de-Silanes, F and Shleifer, A, 'What Works in Securities Laws' (2006) 61 *The Journal of Finance* 1.

Langevoort, DC, 'Structuring Securities Regulation in the European Union: Lessons from the U.S. Experience' in G Ferrarini and E Wymeersch (eds), *Investor Protection in Europe: Corporate Law Making, The MiFID and Beyond* (OUP, 2006) 485–506.

Langevoort, DC, 'The SEC as a Lawmaker: Choices about Investor Protection in the Face of Uncertainty' (2006) 84 *Washington University Law Review* 1591.

Lannoo, K, 'EU Financial Market Access after Brexit' (2016) 51 *Intereconomics* 255.

Lastra, R, 'Defining forward looking, judgement-based supervision' (2013) 14 *Journal of Banking Regulation* 221.

Lehmann, M, 'Vorschlag für eine Reform der Rom II-Verordnung im Bereich der Finanzmarktdelikte' (2012) 32 *Praxis des Internationalen Privat- und Verfahrensrechts* 399.

Lehmann, M, 'Prospectus Liability and Private International Law – Assessing the Landscape after the CJEU's Kolassa Ruling (Case C-375/13)' (2016) 12 *Journal of Private International Law* 318.

Lenaerts, K, 'The Principle of Subsidiarity and the Environment in the European Union: Keeping the Balance of Federalism' (1993) 17 *Fordham International Law Journal* 846.

Lenenbach, M, *Kapitalmarktrecht*, 3rd edn (RWS, 2017).

Leuz, C and Wysocki, PD, 'The Economics of Disclosure and Financial Reporting Regulation: Evidence and Suggestions for Future Research' (2016) 54 *Journal of Accounting Research* 525.

Levin, IP, Schneider, SL and Gaeth, GJ, 'All Frames Are Not Created Equal: A Typology and Critical Analysis of Framing Effects' (1998) 76 *Organizational Behavior & Human Decision Processes* 149.

Levine, R, 'Stock Markets, Growth and Tax Policy' (1991) 46 *Journal of Finance* 1445.

Levine, R, 'Financial development and economic growth: Views and agenda' (1997) 35 *Journal of Economic Literature* 688.

Levine, R, 'Bank-based or market-based financial systems: which is better?' (2002) 11 *Journal of Financial Intermediation* 398.

Levine, R and Zervos, S, 'Stock Markets, Banks, and Economic Growth' (1998) 88 *American Economic Review* 537.

Liang, X, Hu, X and Jiang, J, 'Research on the Effects of Information Description on Crowdfunding Success within a Sustainable Economy – The Perspective of Information Communication' (2020) 12 *Sustainability* 650.

Liu, C and Wang, H, 'Initial Coin Offerings: What Do We Know and What Are the Success Factors?' in S Goutte, K Guesmi and S Saadi (eds), *Cryptofinance and Mechanisms of Exchange* (Springer, 2019) 145–64.

Lo, AW, 'Regulatory reform in the wake of the financial crisis of 2007–2008' (2009) 1 *Journal of Financial Economic Policy* 4.

Lohse, E, 'The Meaning of Harmonisation in the Context of EU Law – A Process in Need of Definition' in M Andenas and C Baasch Andersen (eds), *Theory and Practice of Harmonization* (Edward Elgar, 2012) 282–313.

Loss, L, *Securities Regulation*, 2nd edn, Vol. 1 (Wolters Kluwer, 1961).

Loss, L Seligman, J and Paredes, TA, *Fundamentals of Securities Regulation*, 7th edn (Wolters Kluwer, 2019).

Lucantoni, P, 'Prospectus Directive' in M Lehmann and C Kumpan (eds), *European Financial Services Law – Article-by-Article Commentary* (Nomos/Beck/Hart Publishing, 2019) 941–1032.

Macchiavello, E, 'Financial-return Crowdfunding and Regulatory Approaches in the Shadow Banking, FinTech and Collaborative Finance Era' (2017) 14 *European Company and Financial Law Review* 662.

Macchiavello, E, 'FinTech Regulation from a Cross-Sectoral Perspective' in V Colaert, D Busch and T Incalza (eds), *European financial regulation: levelling the cross-sectoral playing field* (Hart Publishing, 2019) 63–85.

Macchiavello, E, 'The European Crowdfunding Service Providers Regulation and the Future of Marketplace Lending and Investing in Europe: The "Crowdfunding Nature" Dilemma' (2021) 32 *European Business Law Review* 557.

Macchiavello, E, 'The scope of the ECSPR: the difficult compromise between harmonization, client protection and the "level playing field" (Arts 1–2, 46, 48–9, 51)' in E Macchiavello (ed), *Regulation on European Crowdfunding Service Providers for Business – A Commentary* (Edward Elgar, 2022) 44–67.

Macey, JR, 'A Pox on Both Your Houses: Enron, Sarbanes-Oxley and the Debate Concerning the Relative Efficacy of Mandatory Versus Enabling Rules' (2003) 81 *Washington University Law Review* 329.

MacLeod Heminway, J, 'Business Lawyering in the Crowdfunding Era' (2013) 3 *American University Business Law Review* 149.

Madura, J, *Financial Markets and Institutions*, 11th edn (Cengage Learning, 2015).

Mahoney, PG, 'The Exchange as Regulator' (1997) 83 *Virginia Law Review* 1453.

Mahoney, PG, 'Manager-Investor Conflicts in Mutual Funds' (2004) 18 *Journal of Economic Perspectives* 161.

Mäntysaari, P, *The Law of Corporate Finance: General Principles and EU Law, Volume III: Funding, Exit, Takeovers* (Springer, 2010).

Markham, JW, *A Financial History of Modern U.S. Corporate Scandals: From Enron to Reform* (Routledge, 2005).

Marks, SG, 'The Separation of Ownership and Control' in B Bouckaert and G De Geest (eds), *Encyclopaedia of Law and Economics: Vol. II* (Edward Elgar, 2000) 692–724.

Mathis, K and Steffen, AD, 'From Rational Choice to Behavioural Economics' in K Mathis (ed), *European Perspectives in Behavioural Law and Economics* (Springer, 2015) 31–48.

Mazis, MB et al, 'A Framework for Evaluating Consumer Information Regulation' (1981) 45 *Journal of Marketing* 11.

McKenzie, LW, 'On the Existence of General Equilibrium for a Competitive Economy' (1959) 27 *Econometrica* 54.

McNeil, IG, *An Introduction to the Law on Financial Investment*, 2nd edn (Hart Publishing, 2005).

McNeil, IG, 'Enforcement and Sanctioning' in E Ferran, N Moloney and J Payne (eds), *Oxford Handbook on Financial Regulation* (OUP, 2014) 280–306.

Merton, RC and Bodie, Z, 'A Conceptual Framework for Analyzing the Financial Environment', in DB Crane et al (eds), *The Global Financial System: A Functional Approach* (Harvard Business Law Press, 1995) 3–31.

Mikroule,a A, '"Collective Redress" in European Competition Law' (2016) 14 *Zeitschrift für Wettbewerbsrecht* 388.

Milesi-Ferretti, G-M et al, 'The Great Retrenchment: International Capital Flows During the Global Financial Crisis' (2011) 26 *Economic Policy* 287.

Möllers, T, 'Efficiency as a Standard in Capital Market Law – The Application of Empirical and Economic Arguments for the Justification of Civil Law' (2009) 20 *European Business Law Review* 243.

Mollick, E, 'The dynamics of crowdfunding: An exploratory study' (2014) 29 *Journal of Business Venturing* 1.

Mollick, E, and Robb, A, 'Democratizing Innovation and Capital Access: The Role of Crowdfunding' (2016) 58 *California Management Review* 72.

Moloney, N, *How to Protect Investors: Lessons from the EC and the UK* (CUP, 2010).

Moloney, N, 'Supervision in the Wake of the Financial Crisis: Achieving Effective Law in Action – A Challenge for the EU' in E Wymeersch, K Hopt and G Ferrarini (eds), *Financial Regulation and Supervision. A Post Crisis Analysis* (OUP, 2012) 71–110.

Moloney, N, *EU Securities and Financial Markets Regulation*, 3rd edn (OUP, 2014).

Moloney, N, 'European Banking Union: Assessing its Risks and Resilience' (2014) 51 *Common Market Law Review* 1609.

Moloney, N, 'Capital Markets Union: "Ever Closer Union" for the EU Financial System?' (2016) 41 *European Law Review* 307.

Moloney, N, 'Institutional Governance and Capital Markets Union: Incrementalism or a "Big Bang"?' (2016) 13 *European Company and Financial Law Review* 376.

Moloney, N, *The Age of ESMA: Governing EU Financial Markets* (Hart Publishing, 2018).

Moloney, N, 'The European Supervisory Authorities and Discretion: Can the Functional and Constitutional Circles be Squared?' in J Mendes (ed), *EU Executive Discretion and the Limits of Law* (OUP, 2019) 85–117.

Moloney, N, *EU Securities and Financial Markets Regulation*, 4th edn (OUP, 2023).

Mork, R and Nakkamura, M, 'Banks and Corporate Control in Japan' (1999) 54 *Journal of Finance* 319.

Moysidou, K and Hausberg, P, 'In Crowdfunding We Trust: A Trust-building Model in Lending Crowdfunding' (2020) 58 *Journal of Small Business Management* 511.
Müllbert, PO and Sajnovits, A, 'The Element of Trust in Financial Markets Law' (2017) 18 *German Law Journal* 1.
Myers, SC and Majluf, NS, 'Corporate Financing and Investment Decisions When Firms Have Information that Investors Do Not Have' (1984) 13 *Journal of Financial Economics* 187.
Neumann, J von and Morgenstern, O, *Theory of Games and Economic Behavior*, 60th Anniversary edn (Princeton University Press, 2004).
Nicolini, G, *Financial Literacy in Europe – Assessment Methodologies and Evidence from European Countries* (Routledge, 2019).
O'Sullivan, A and Sheffrin, SM, *Economics: Principles in Action* (Prentice Hall, 2003).
Oates, W, 'An Essay on Fiscal Federalism' (1999) 37 *Journal of Economic Literature* 1120.
Obstfeld, M and Taylor, A, *Globalization and Capital Markets: Integration, Crisis and Growth* (Cambridge University Press, 2004).
Obstfeld, M, 'Risk-taking, Global Diversification and Growth' (1994) 84 *American Economic Review* 1310.
OECD, *Financing SMEs and Entrepreneurs 2015 – An OECD Scoreboard* (OECD Publishing, 2015).
Ogus, A, 'Legal Culture as (Natural?) Monopoly' in A Marciano and J-M Josselin (eds), *The Economics of Harmonizing European Law* (Edward Elgar, 2002) 71–86.
Oranburg, SC, 'Bridgefunding: Crowdfunding and the Market for Entrepreneurial Finance' (2015) 25 *Cornell Journal of Law and Public Policy* 397.
Pagano, M and Röell, A, 'Auction and Dealership Markets: What is the difference?' (1992) 36 *European Economic Review* 613.
Page. AC and Ferguson, RB, *Investor Protection* (Weidenfeld and Nicolson, 1992).
Pan, EJ, 'Harmonization of U.S.-EU Securities Regulation: The Case for a Single European Securities Regulator' (2003) 34 *Law and Policy in International Business* 499.
Pan, EJ, 'Understanding Financial Regulation' (2012) 4 *Utah Law Review* 1897.
Paredes, TA, 'Blinded by the Light: Information Overload and Its Consequences for Securities Regulation' (2003) 81 *Washington University Law Quarterly* 417.
Pareto, V, *Manuale di Economia Politica con una Introduzione alla Scienza Sociale* (Università Bocconi Editore, 2006).
Payne, J, 'The Role of Gatekeepers' in N Moloney, E Ferran and J Payne (eds), *Oxford Handbook on Financial Regulation* (OUP, 2014) 254–79.
Pelkmans, J, 'The New Approach to Technical Harmonization and Standardization' (1987) 25 *Journal of Common Market Studies* 249.
Pellegrini, M, 'Critical Analysis of the Prospectus Directive' (2006) 17 *European Business Law Review* 1679.
Perry, MB, 'A Challenge Postponed: Market 2000 Complacency in Response to Regulatory Competition for International Equity Market' (1994) 34 *Virginia Journal of International Law* 701.
Peter, DU, 'Vertrauen als Gegenstand der Ökonomischen Theorie' (2007) 2 *Zeitschrift für Management* 60.
Peyer, S, 'The Antitrust Damages Directive – Much ado About Nothing?' in M Marquis and R Cisotta (eds), *Litigation and Arbitration in EU Competition Law* (Edward Elgar, 2015) 33–46.
Pichler, F and Tezza, I, 'Crowdfunding as a New Phenomenon: Origins, Features and Literature Review' in R Bottiglia and F Pichler (eds), *Crowdfunding for SMEs: A European Perspective* (Springer, 2016) 5–43.
Pierrakis, Y, 'Peer-to-peer lending to businesses: Investors' characteristics, investment criteria and motivation' (2019) 20 *The International Journal of Entrepreneurship and Innovation* 239.
Pietrancosta, A, 'Public Disclosure of Inside Information and Market Abuse' in M Ventoruzzo and S Mock (eds), *Market Abuse Regulation: Commentary and Annotated Guide* (OUP, 2017) 47–62.
Pietrancosta, A, 'Recent Initiatives in Favor of Listed and Non listed Small and Medium-Sized Enterprises: A Legal Perspective' in F Allen et al (eds), *Capital Markets Union and Beyond* (MIT Press, 2019) 173–86.

Pietrancosta, A and Marraud des Grottes, A, 'La Notion de «Placement Privé» Abolie par le Règlement Prospectus du 14 juin 2017?' (2018) 1 *Bulletin Joly Bourse* 60.

Pilbeam, K, *Finance and Financial Markets*, 2nd edn (Palgrave Macmillan, 2005).

Poell, T, Nieborg, D and Dijck, J van, 'Platformisation' (2019) 8 *Internet Policy Review* 1.

Porter M E, *Competitive strategy: Techniques for Analyzing Industries and Competitors* (Free Press 1980).

Portes, R and Rey, H, 'The Determinants of Cross-border Equity Flows' (2005) 65 *Journal of International Economics* 269.

Posner, RA, *Economic Analysis of Law*, 7th edn (Aspen Publishers, 2007).

Pospiech, L, 'Die neue EU-Prospektverordnung' (2019) 15 *Neue Juristische Wochenschrift-Spezial* 463.

Quaglia, L, 'Completing the Single Market in Financial Services: The Politics of Competing Advocacy Coalitions' (2010) 17 *Journal of European Public Policy* 1007.

Quaglia, L, and Howarth, D, 'The Policy Narratives of European Capital Markets Union' (2018) 25 *Journal of European Public Policy* 990.

Quaglia, L, Howarth, D and Liebe, M, 'The Political Economy of European Capital Markets Union' (2016) 54 (s1) *Journal of Common Market Studies* 185.

Rajan, RG, 'Insiders and Outsiders: The Choice Between Informed and Arm's-Length Debt' (1992) 47 *Journal of Finance* 1367.

Rajan, RG and Zingales, L, 'Which Capitalism? Lessons from the East Asian Crisis' (1998) 11 *Journal of Applied Corporate Finance* 40.

Ramakrishnan, R and Thakor, A, 'Information Reliability and a Theory of Financial Intermediation' (1984) 51 *The Review of Economic Studies* 415.

Ramana, N and Rhodes-Kropf, M, 'Financing Risk and Innovation' (2017) 63 *Management Science* 901.

Revell, S and Cole, E, 'Practical issues arising from the implementation of the Prospectus Directive – what are the equity capital markets worrying about?' (2006) 1 *Capital Markets Law Journal* 77.

Ringe, W-G, 'Capital Markets Union for Europe: A Commitment to the Single Market of 28' (2015) 9 *Law and Financial Markets Review* 5.

Ringe, W-G, 'The Politics of Capital Markets Union: From Brexit to Eurozone' in F Allen et al (eds), *Capital Markets Union and Beyond* (MIT Press, 2019) 341–54.

Rock, EB, 'Securities Regulation as a Lobster Trap: A Credible Commitment Theory of Mandatory Disclosure' (2002) 23 *Cardozo Law Review* 675.

Rodger, B, Sousa Ferro, M and Marcos, F, 'Promotion and Harmonization of Antitrust Damages Claims by Directive EU/2014/104' in B Rodger, M Sousa Ferro and F Marcos (eds), *The EU Antitrust Damages Directive Transposition in the Member States* (OUP, 2018) 24–57.

Rohr, J and Wright, A, 'Blockchain-Based Token Sales, Initial Coin Offerings, and the Democratization of Public Capital Markets' (2019) 70 *Hastings Law Journal* 463.

Romano, R, 'Empowering Investors: A Market Approach to Securities Regulation' (1998) 107 *The Yale Law Journal* 2359.

Romano, R, 'The Need for Competition in International Securities Regulation' (2001) 2 *Theoretical Inquiries in Law* 387.

Romer, PM, 'Endogenous Technological Change' (1990) 98 *The Journal of Political Economy* S71.

Ross, SA and Kripke, H, 'Disclosure Regulation in Financial Markets: Implications of Modern Finance Theory and Signaling Theory' in FR Edwards (ed), *Issues in Financial Regulation* (McGraw-Hill, 1979) 177–202.

Rousseau, PL and Wachtel, P, 'What Is Happening to the Impact of Financial Deepening on Economic Growth?' (2011) 49 *Economic Inquiry* 276.

Rubinstein, A and Wolinsky, A, 'Middlemen' (1987) 102 *Quarterly Journal of Economics* 581.

Ryan, E, 'Secession and Federalism' (2017) 96 *Oregon Law Review* 126.

Ryan, E, 'Federalism as Legal Pluralism' in P Schiff-Berman (ed), *The Oxford Handbook of Global Legal Pluralism* (OUP, 2020) 491–527.

Saint-Paul, G, 'Fiscal Policy in an Endogenous Growth Model' (1992) 107 *The Quarterly Journal of Economics* 1242.

Schackmann-Fallis, K-P and Scheffler, S, 'Aligning Financial Systems to Meet the Needs of Citizens and Enterprises' (2017) 86 *Vierteljahrshefte zur Wirtschaftsforschung*.

Schaeken Willemaers, G, *The EU Issuer – Disclosure Regime: Objectives and Proposals for Reform* (Kluwer Law International, 2001).
Schäfer, FA, 'Emission und Vertrieb von Wertpapieren nach dem Wertpapierverkaufsprospektgesetz' (1991) 23–24 *Zeitschrift für Wirtschaftsrecht* 1557.
Schammo, P, 'The Prospectus Approval System' (2006) 7 *European Business Organization Law Review* 501.
Schammo, P, *EU Prospectus Law: New Perspectives on Regulatory Competition in Securities Markets* (CUP, 2011).
Schammo, P, 'EU Day-to-Day Supervision or Intervention-based Supervision: Which Way Forward for the European System of Financial Supervision?' (2012) 32 *Oxford Journal of Legal Studies* 771.
Schammo, P, 'Capital Markets Union and Small and Medium-Sized Enterprises (SMEs): A Preliminary Assessment' in F Allen, E Carletti and J Gray (eds), *The New Financial Architecture in the Eurozone* (European University Institute, 2015) 137–76.
Schammo, P, 'Market Building and the Capital Markets Union: Addressing Information Barriers in the SME Funding Market' (2017) 14 *European Company and Financial Law Review* 271.
Schneider, CW and Dubow, JA, 'Forward-Looking Information-Navigating in the Safe Harbor' (1996) 51 *The Business Lawyer* 1071.
Schön, W, 'Corporate Disclosure in a Competitive Environment – the Quest for a European Framework on Mandatory Disclosure' (2006) 6 *Journal of Corporate Law Studies* 259.
Schulz, S, 'Neue Schwellenwerte für Wertpapierprospekte' (2018) 21 *Neue Zeitschrift für Gesellschaftsrecht* 921.
Schwartz, A, 'Crowdfunding Securities' (2013) 88 *Notre Dame Law Review* 1457.
Schwartz, A, 'The Digital Shareholder' (2015) 100 *Minnesota Law Review* 609.
Schwartz, A, *Investment Crowdfunding* (OUP, 2023).
Schwienbacher, A and Larralde, B, 'Alternative Types of Entrepreneurial Finance' in D Cumming (ed), *The Oxford Handbook of Entrepreneurial Finance* (OUP, 2012) 369–91.
Scott, HS, 'Internationalization of Primary Public Securities Markets' (2000) 63 *Law and Contemporary Problems* 71.
Seligman, J, 'The Historical Need for a Mandatory Corporate Disclosure System' (1983) 9 *The Journal of Corporation Law* 1.
Serdaris, K, 'Behavioural Economic Influences on Primary Market Disclosure – The Case of the EU Regulation on European Crowdfunding Service Providers' (2021) 18 *European Company and Financial Law Review* 428.
Serdaris, K, 'Ex Post Enforcement of the EU Crowdfunding Regime: Administrative Sanctions and Measures' in E Macchiavello (ed), *Regulation on European Crowdfunding Service Providers for Business – A Commentary* (Edward Elgar, 2022) 455–73.
Sharot, T, *The Optimism Bias: A Tour of the Irrationally Positive Brain* (Vintage, 2012).
Shavell, S, *Foundations of Economic Analysis of Law* (Belknap Press, 2004).
Shleifer, A, 'Understanding regulation' (2005) 11 *European Financial Management* 439.
Shneor, R, 'Crowdfunding Models, Strategies, and Choices Between Them' in R Shneor, L Zhao and B-T Flåten (eds), *Advances in Crowdfunding* (Springer, 2020) 21–42.
Siebert, H and Koop, MJ, 'Institutional Competition versus Centralization: Quo vadis Europe?' (1993) 9 *Oxford Review of Economic Policy* 15.
Simon, HA, 'Rational Choice and the Structure of the Environment' (1956) 63 *Psychological Review* 129.
Sirri, ER and Tufano, P, 'The Economics of Pooling' in DB Crane et al (eds), *The Global Financial System: A Functional Approach* (Harvard Business Law Press, 1995) 81–127.
Slovic, P, *The Perception of Risk* (Routledge, 2000).
Snell, J, 'Varieties of Capitalism and the Limits of European Economic Integration' (2011) 13 *Cambridge Yearbook of European Legal Studies* 415.
Spence, M, 'Job Market Signaling' (1973) 87 *The Quarterly Journal of Economics* 355.

Spulber, DF, 'Market Microstructure and Intermediation' (1996) 10 *Journal of Economic Perspectives* 135.
Staikouras, P, 'The European Union Proposal for a Regulation on Cross-Border Crowdfunding Services: A Solemn or Pie-Crust Promise?' (2020) 31 *European Business Law Review* 1047.
Stanko, MA and Henard, DH, 'Toward a Better Understanding of Crowdfunding, Openness and the Consequences for Innovation' (2017) 46 *Research Policy* 784.
Steil, B, *Competition, Integration and Regulation in EC Capital Markets* (Royal Institute of International Affairs, 1993).
Stigler, GJ, *The Organization of Industry* (University of Chicago Press, 1968).
Stiglitz, JE, 'Credit Markets and the Control of Capital' (1985) 17 *Journal of Money, Credit and Banking* 133.
Stout, LA, 'The Mechanisms of Market Inefficiency: An introduction to the new Finance' (2003) 28 *Journal of Corporation Law* 636.
Suckow, S, 'The European Prospectus' (1975) 23 *The American Journal of Comparative Law* 50.
Sun, J-M and Pelkmans, J, 'Regulatory Competition in the Single Market' (1995) 33 *Journal of Common Market Studies* 67.
Sunstein, CR, Jolls, C and Thaler, RH, 'A Behavioral Approach to Law and Economics' (1998) 50 *Stanford Law Review* 1451.
Sunstein, C, 'Empirically Informed Regulation' (2011) 78 *University of Chicago Law Review* 1349.
Surowiecki, J, *The Wisdom of Crowds: Why the Many are Smarter than the Few and How Collective Wisdom Shapes Business, Economies, Societies and Nations* (Random House Large Print, 2004).
Tadesse, S, 'The Allocation and Monitoring Role of Capital Markets: Theory and International Evidence' (2004) 39 *Journal of Financial and Quantitative Analysis* 701.
Thaler, RH and Sunstein, CR, 'Libertarian Paternalism' (2003) 93 *The American Economic Review* 175.
Tiebout, CM, 'A pure theory of local expenditure' (1956) 64 *Journal of Political Economy* 416.
Tomboc, GF, 'The Lemons Problem in Crowdfunding' (2013) 30 *John Marshall Journal of Information Technology & Privacy Law* 253.
Tountopoulos, V, 'Manipulation in Illiquid Markets-A Tale of Inefficiency?' (2017) 14 *European Company and Financial Law Review* 458.
Trachtman, JP, 'L'Etat, C'est Nous: Sovereignty, Economic Integration and Subsidiarity' (1992) 33 *Harvard International Law Journal* 459.
Trachtman, JP, 'International Regulatory Competition, Externalization, and Jurisdiction' (1993) 34 *Harvard International Law Journal* 47.
Trachtman, JP, 'Regulatory Competition and Regulatory Jurisdiction' (2000) 3 *Journal of International Economic Law* 331.
Tversky, A and Kahneman, D, 'Availability: A Heuristic for Judging Frequency and Probability' (1973) 5 *Cognitive Psychology* 207.
Tversky, A and Kahneman, D, 'Judgment under Uncertainty: Heuristics and Biases' (1974) 185 *Science* 1124.
Tversky, A and Kahneman, D, 'The framing of decisions and the psychology of choice' (1981) 211 *Science* 453.
Ulen, TS, 'Information and the Market Economy – Cognitive Errors and Legal Correctives' in S Grundmann, W Kerber and S Weatherhill (eds), *Party Autonomy and the Role of Information in the Internal Market* (De Gruyter, 2001) 98–129.
Valiante, D, *Europe's Untapped Capital Market: Rethinking financial integration after the crisis* (Centre for European Policy Studies, 2016).
Valiante, D, 'CMU and the Deepening of Financial Integration' in D Busch, E Avgouleas and G Ferrarini (eds), *Capital Markets Union in Europe* (OUP, 2018) 9–27.
Vandendriessche, E, *Investor Losses: A Comparative Legal Analysis of Causation and Assessment of Damages in Investor Litigation* (Intersentia, 2015).
Veil, R, 'Concept and Aims of Capital Markets Regulation' in R Veil (ed), *European Capital Markets Law*, 2nd edn (Hart Publishing, 2017) 23–29.

Véron, N and Wolff, G, 'Capital Markets Union: A Vision for the Long Term' (2016) 2 *Journal of Financial Regulation* 130.
Viotto Da Cruz, J, 'Competition and Regulation of Crowdfunding Platforms: A Two-sided Market Approach' (2015) 99 *Communications and Strategies* 33.
Vokuhl, N, *Kapitalmarktrechtlicher Anlegerschutz und Kapitalerhaltung in der Aktiengesellschaft* (Nomos, 2007).
Walker, N, 'Constitutional Pluralism Revisited' (2016) 22 *European Law Journal* 333.
Warren, MG III, 'Global Harmonization of Securities Laws: The Achievements of the European Communities' (1990) 31 *Harvard International Law Journal* 185.
Warren, MG III, 'The Harmonization of European Securities Law' (2003) 37 *The International Lawyer* 211.
Weaven, SK, 'Exploring Agency Dynamics of Crowdfunding in Start-Up Capital Financing' (2011) 17 *Academy of Entrepreneurship Journal* 85.
Weber, S, 'Kapitalmarkt- Börsen- und Investmentrecht' in M Dauses (ed), *Handbuch des EU-Wirtschaftsrechts* (C.H. Beck, 1994) 1–34.
Weber, S, *Kapitalmarktrecht – Eine Untersuchung des Österreichischen Rechts und des Europäischen Gemeinschaftsrechts* (Springer, 1999).
Weinstein, DE and Yafeh, Y, 'On the Costs of a Bank-centered Financial System: Evidence from the Changing Main Bank Relations in Japan' (1998) 53 *Journal of Finance* 635.
Weinstein, RS, 'Crowdfunding in the U.S. and Abroad: What to Expect When You're Expecting' (2013) 46 *Cornell International Law Journal* 427.
Weizsacker, CC von, 'A Welfare Analysis of Barriers to Entry' (1980) 11 *Bell Journal of Economics* 399.
White, LJ, 'International Regulation of Securities Markets: Competition or Harmonization?' in AW Lo, *The Industrial Organization and Regulation of the Securities Industry* (University of Chicago Press, 1996) 207–42.
Woolcock, S, *The Single European Market – Centralization or Competition among National Rules?* (Royal Institute of International Affairs, 1994).
Woolcock, S, 'Competition Among Rules in the Single European Market' in W Bratton et al (eds), *International Regulatory Competition and Coordination: Perspectives on Economic Regulation in Europe and the United States* (OUP, 1996) 289–321.
Wroldsen, JS, 'The crowdfund act's strange bedfellows: Democracy and start-up company investing' (2013) 62 *University of Kansas Law Review* 357.
Wroldsen, JS, 'Crowdfunding Investment Contracts' (2017) 11 *Virginia Law and Business Review* 543.
Wymeersch, E, 'The Structure of Financial Supervision in Europe' (2007) 8 *European Business Organization Law Review* 237.
Yavas, A, 'Marketmakers versus Matchmakers' (1992) 1 *Journal of Financial Intermediation* 33.
Zahid, A and McGee, A, 'A Defective Proposal in Need of a Rethink' (2002) 23 *The Company Lawyer* 250.
Zeller, B, *CISG and the Unification of International Trade Law* (Routledge/Cavendish, 2007).
Zetzsche, D, *Aktionärsinformation in der Börsennotierten Aktiengesellschaft* (Carl Heymanns, 2006).
Zetzsche, D and Preiner, C, 'Cross-Border Crowdfunding: Towards a Single Crowdlending and Crowdinvesting Market for Europe' (2018) 19 *European Business Organization Law Review* 217.
Zhang, J and Liu, P, 'Rational Herding in Microloan Markets' (2012) 58 *Management Science* 892.
Ziegler, T et al, *Shifting Paradigms: The 4th European Alternative Finance Benchmarking Report* (Cambridge Centre for Alternative Finance, 2019).
Ziegler, T and Shneor, R (eds), *The Global Alternative Finance Benchmarking Report* (Cambridge Centre for Alternative Finance, 2020).
Ziegler T, Shneor, R and Zhang, BZ, 'The Global Status of the Crowdfunding Industry' in R Shneor, L Zhao and B-T Flåten (eds), *Advances in Crowdfunding* (Springer, 2020) 43–61.
Zimmerman, H, 'Varieties of Global Financial Governance? British and German Approaches to Financial Market Regulation' in E Helleiner, S Pagliari and H Zimmerman (eds), *Global Finance in Crisis* (Routledge, 2010) 135–50.
Zingales, L, 'The Future of Securities Regulation' (2009) 47 *Journal of Accounting Research* 391.

INDEX

www.ingramcontent.com/pod-product-compliance
Ingram Content Group UK Ltd.
Pitfield, Milton Keynes, MK11 3LW, UK
UKHW020243290926
15470UKWH00002B/712

9 781509 974986